EDENSZERO

1 INTO THE SKY WHERE CHERRY BLOSSOMS FLUTTER

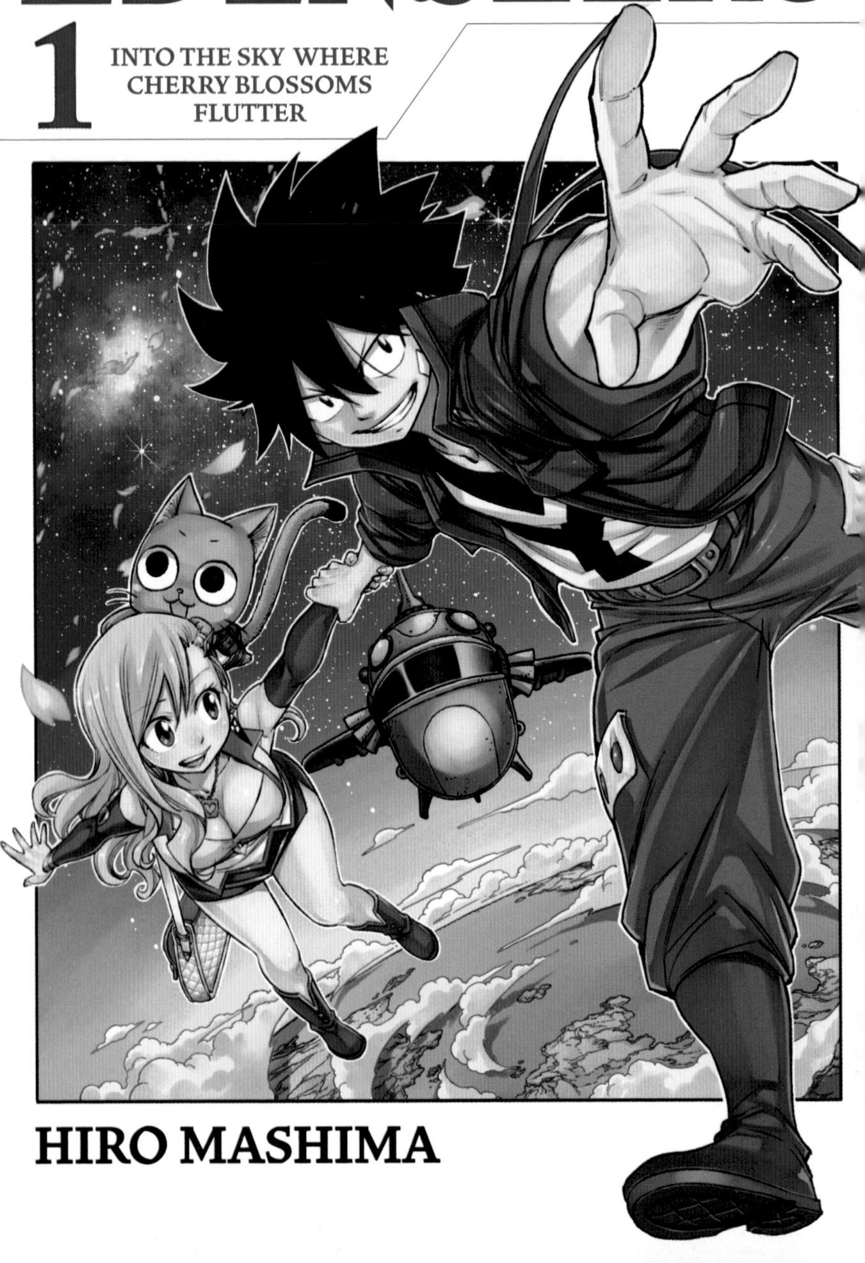

HIRO MASHIMA

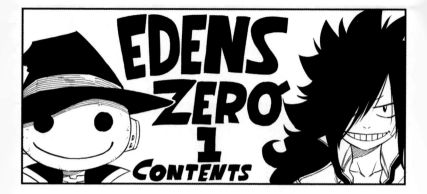

EDENS ZERO 1
CONTENTS

CHAPTER 1 ▶ Into the Sky Where Cherry Blossoms Flutter — 3

CHAPTER 2 ▶ A Girl and Her Blue Cat ———————— 85

CHAPTER 3 ▶ Adventurers ———————— 137

CHAPTER 4 ▶ Norma ———————— 167

EDENSZERO

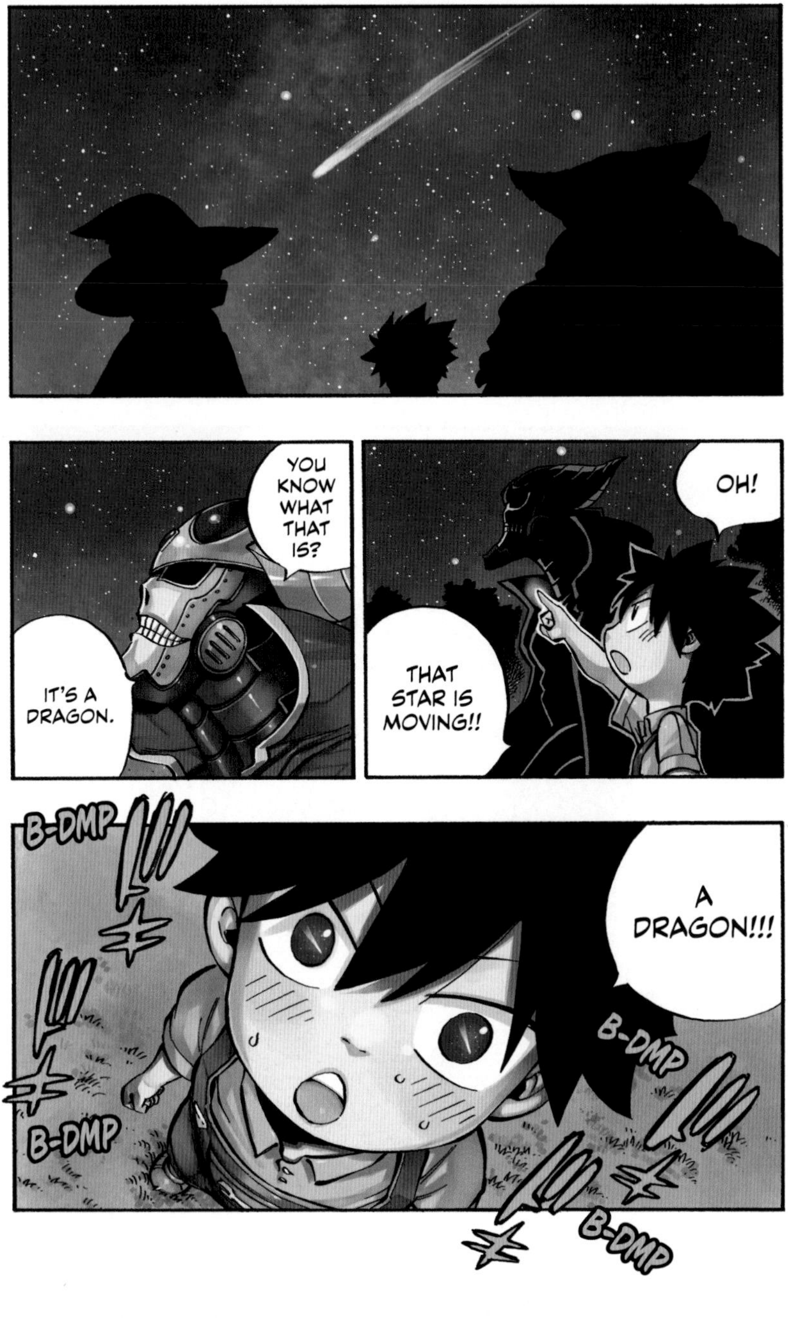
OH!
THAT STAR IS MOVING!!
YOU KNOW WHAT THAT IS?
IT'S A DRAGON.
A DRAGON!!!
B-DMP
B-DMP
B-DMP
B-DMP

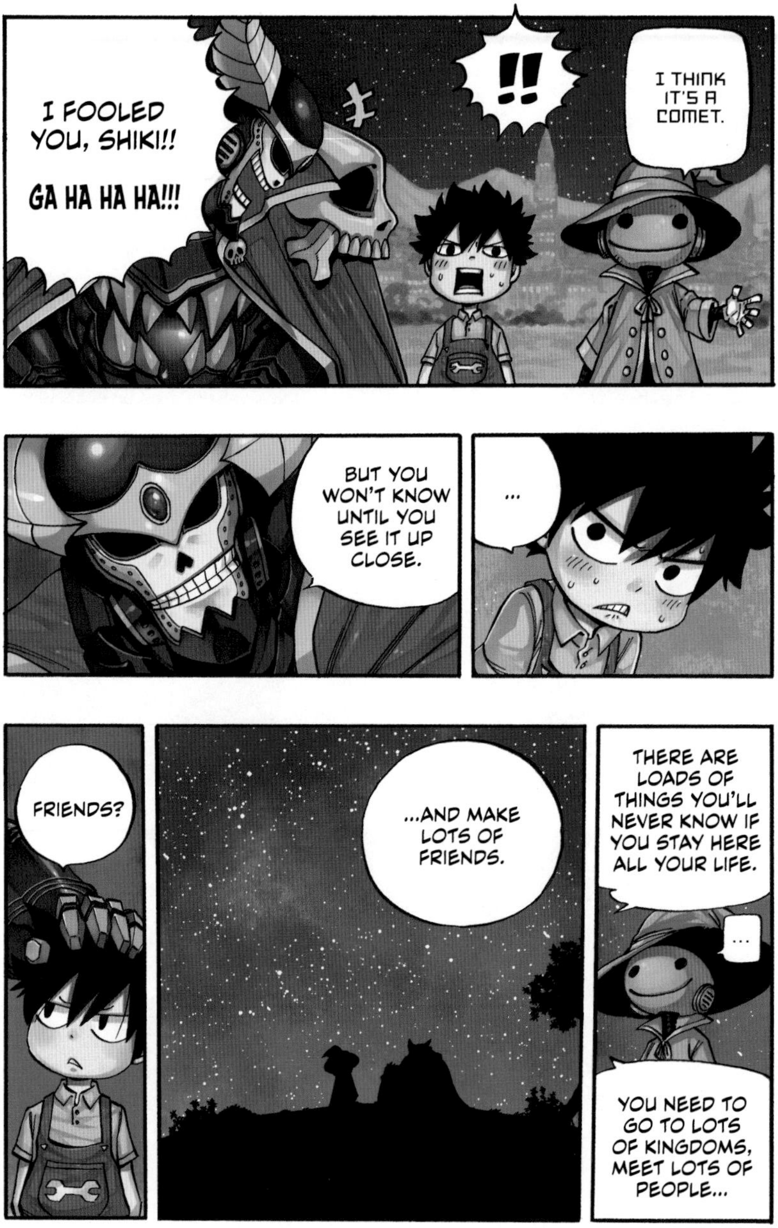
I THINK IT'S A COMET.
!!
I FOOLED YOU, SHIKI!!
GA HA HA HA!!!
...
BUT YOU WON'T KNOW UNTIL YOU SEE IT UP CLOSE.
THERE ARE LOADS OF THINGS YOU'LL NEVER KNOW IF YOU STAY HERE ALL YOUR LIFE.
...
YOU NEED TO GO TO LOTS OF KINGDOMS, MEET LOTS OF PEOPLE...
...AND MAKE LOTS OF FRIENDS.
FRIENDS?

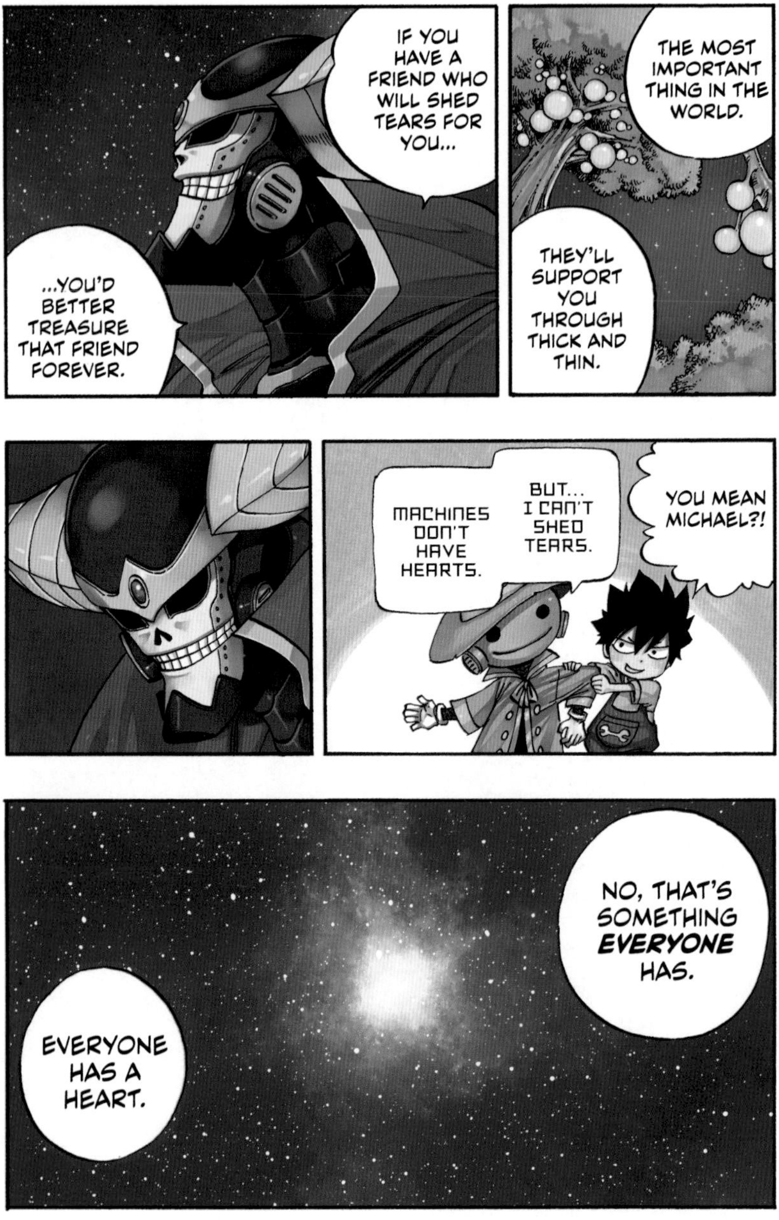
THE MOST IMPORTANT THING IN THE WORLD.
THEY'LL SUPPORT YOU THROUGH THICK AND THIN.
IF YOU HAVE A FRIEND WHO WILL SHED TEARS FOR YOU...
...YOU'D BETTER TREASURE THAT FRIEND FOREVER.
YOU MEAN MICHAEL?!
BUT... I CAN'T SHED TEARS.
MACHINES DON'T HAVE HEARTS.
NO, THAT'S SOMETHING ***EVERYONE*** HAS.
EVERYONE HAS A HEART.

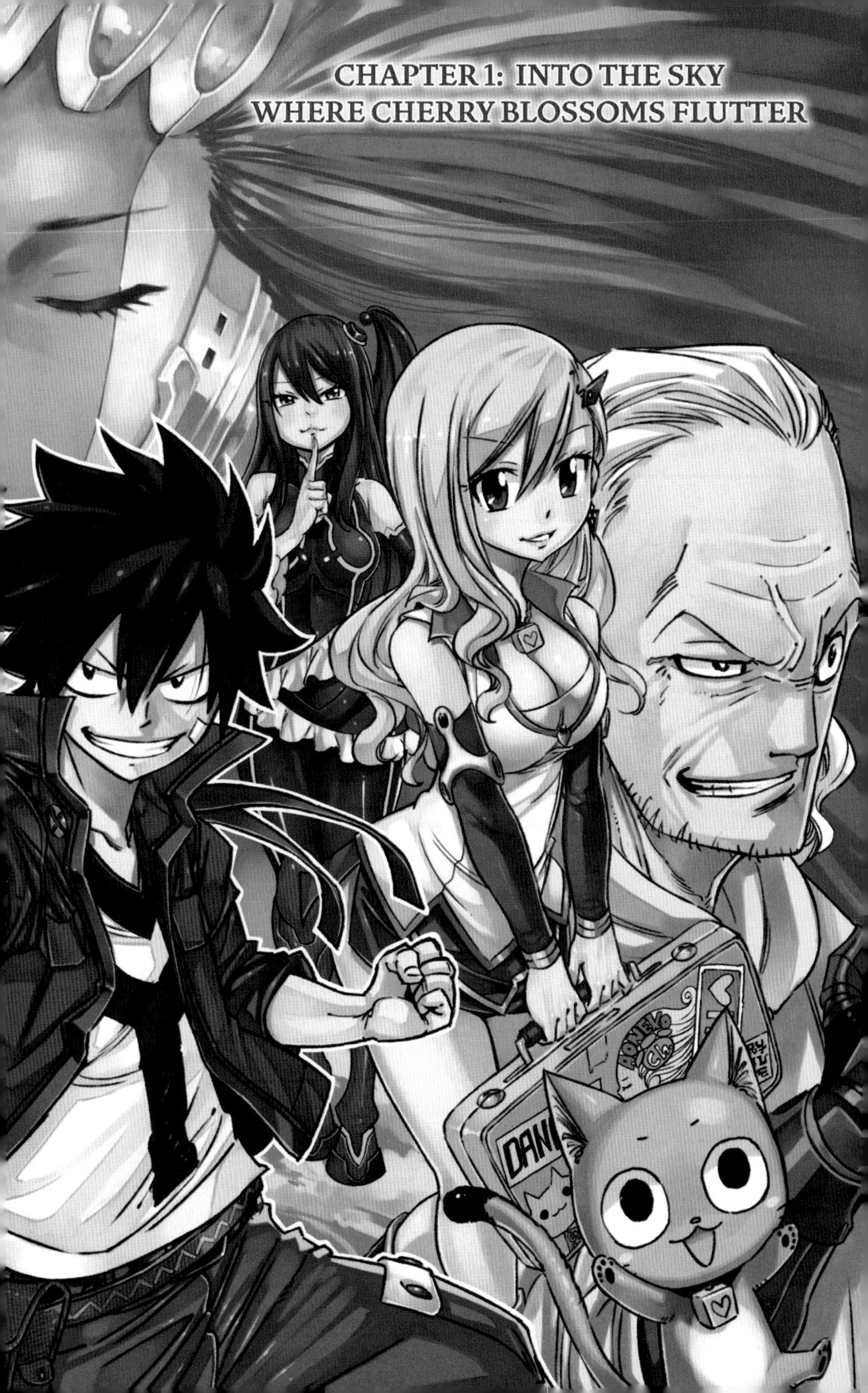
CHAPTER 1: INTO THE SKY
WHERE CHERRY BLOSSOMS FLUTTER

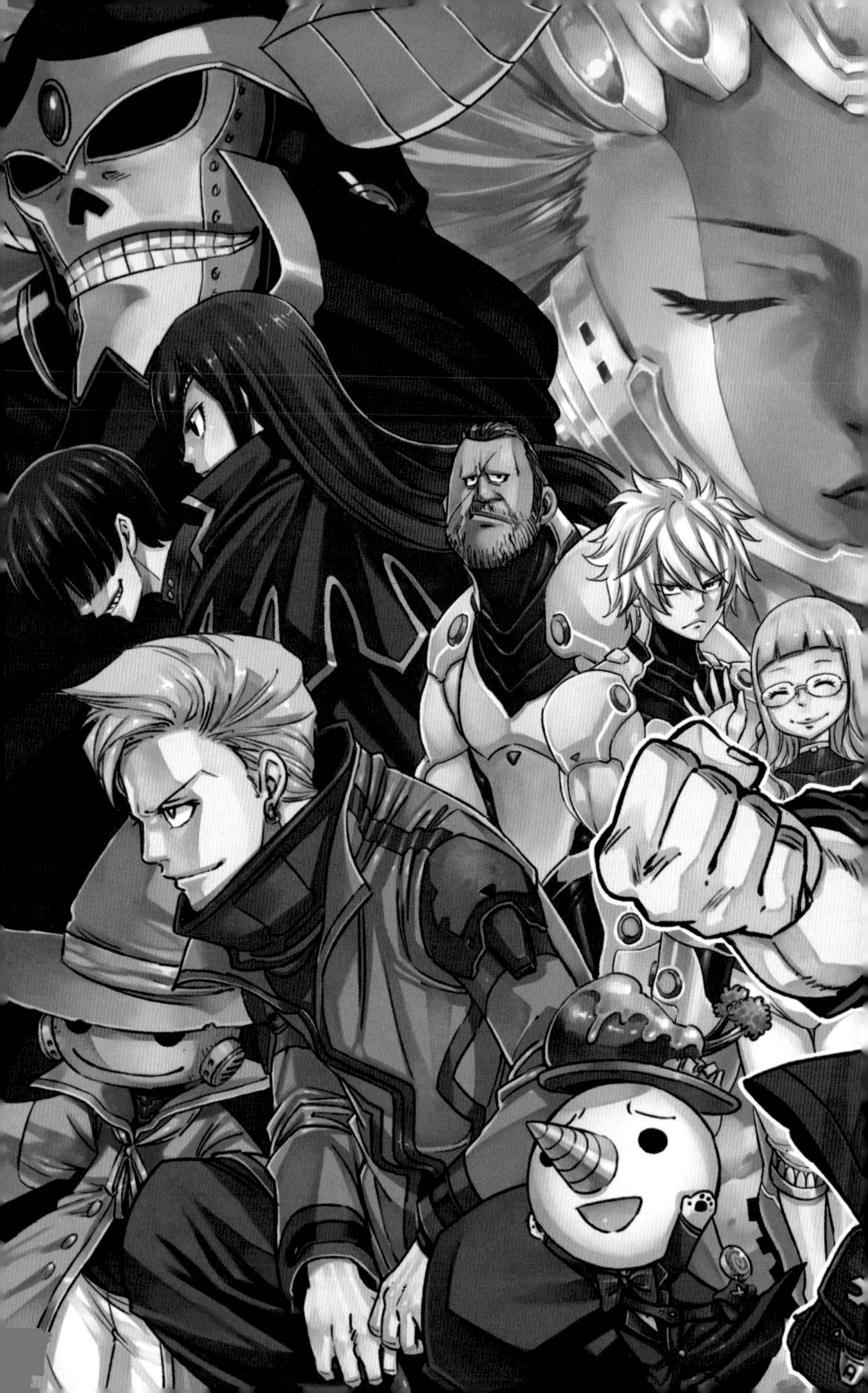

EDENSZERO

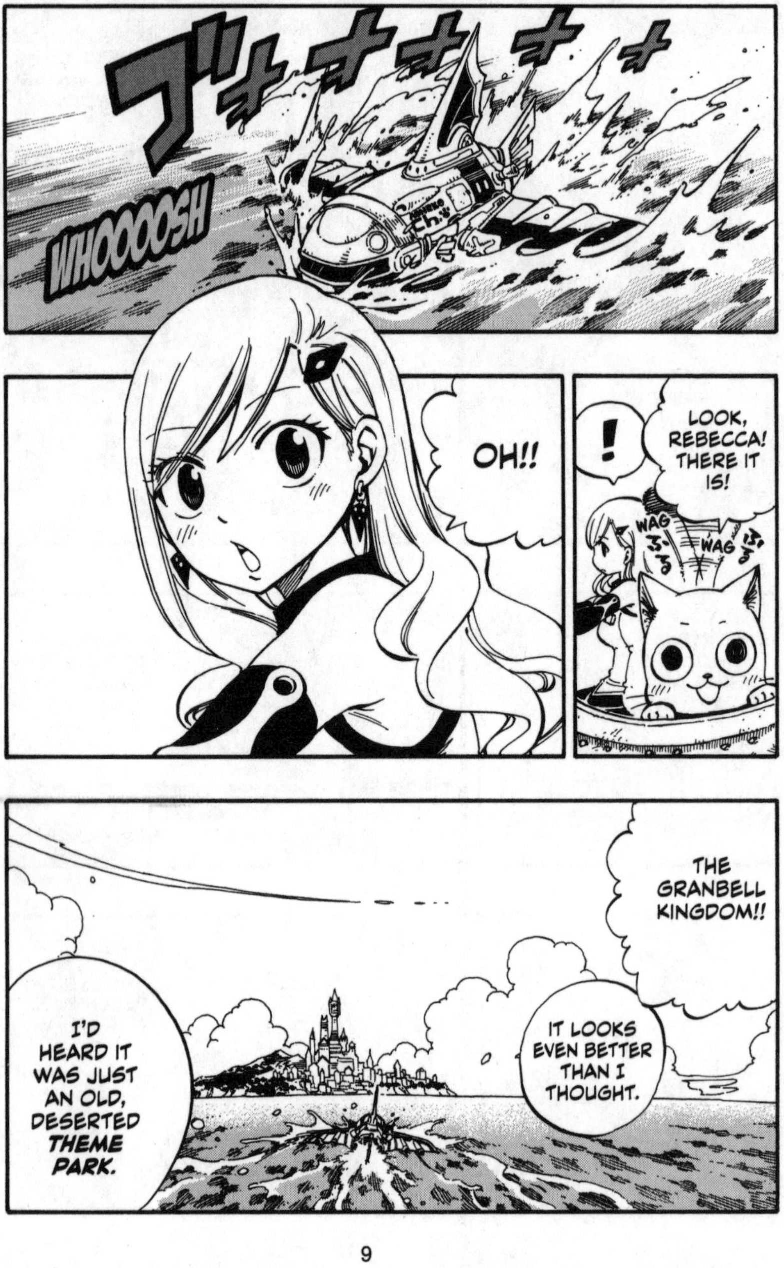
ブォォォォォ
WHOOOOSH
!
LOOK, REBECCA! THERE IT IS!
WAG
ふる
WAG
ふる
OH!!
THE GRANBELL KINGDOM!!
IT LOOKS EVEN BETTER THAN I THOUGHT.
I'D HEARD IT WAS JUST AN OLD, DESERTED *THEME PARK.*

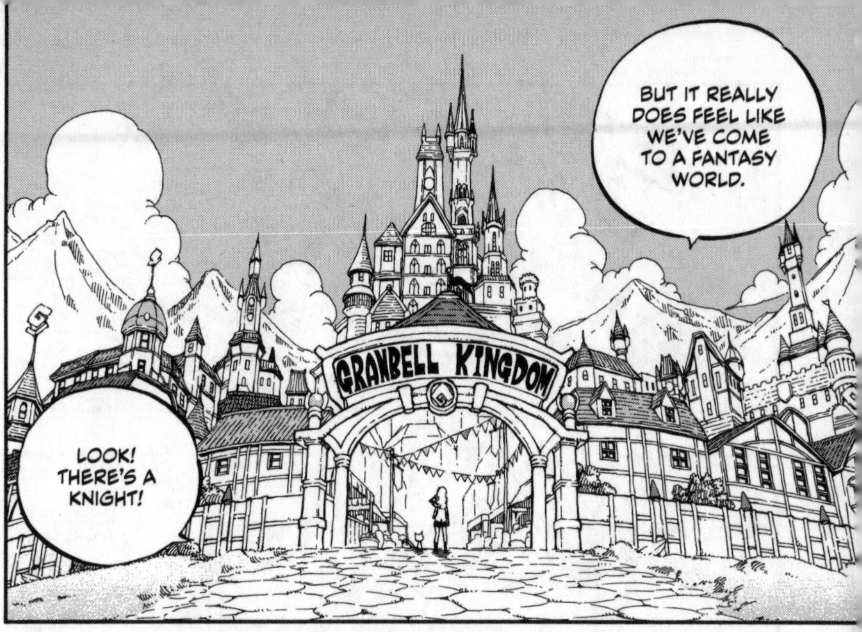
BUT IT REALLY DOES FEEL LIKE WE'VE COME TO A FANTASY WORLD.
GRANBELL KINGDOM
LOOK! THERE'S A KNIGHT!

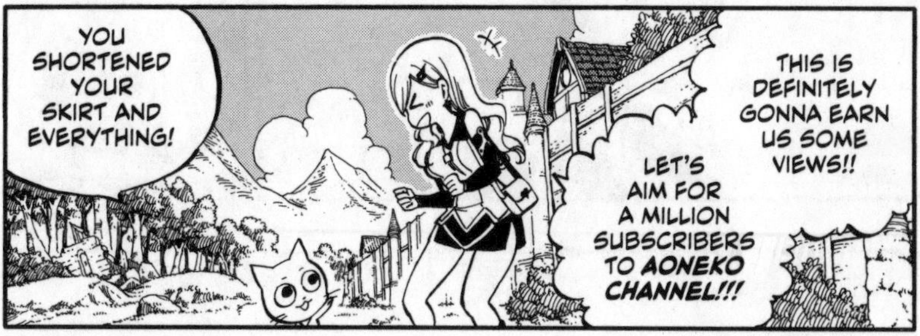
THIS IS DEFINITELY GONNA EARN US SOME VIEWS!!
LET'S AIM FOR A MILLION SUBSCRIBERS TO AONEKO CHANNEL!!!
YOU SHORTENED YOUR SKIRT AND EVERYTHING!

Aoneko is "Blue Cat" in Japanese.

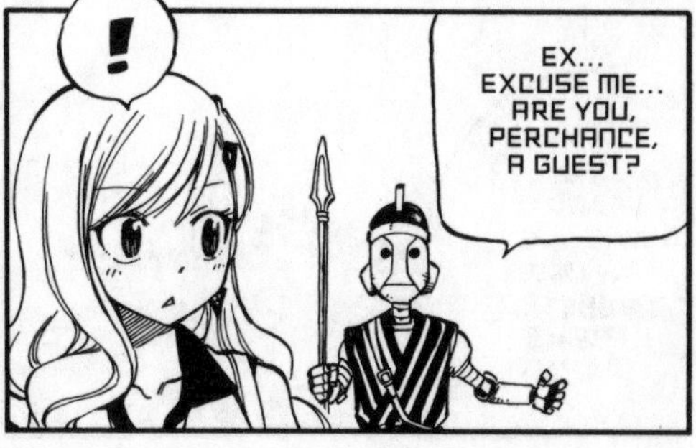
!
EX... EXCUSE ME... ARE YOU, PERCHANCE, A GUEST?

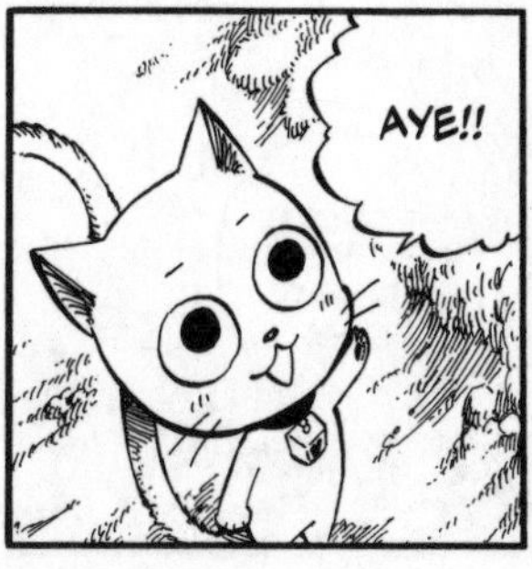
AYE!!

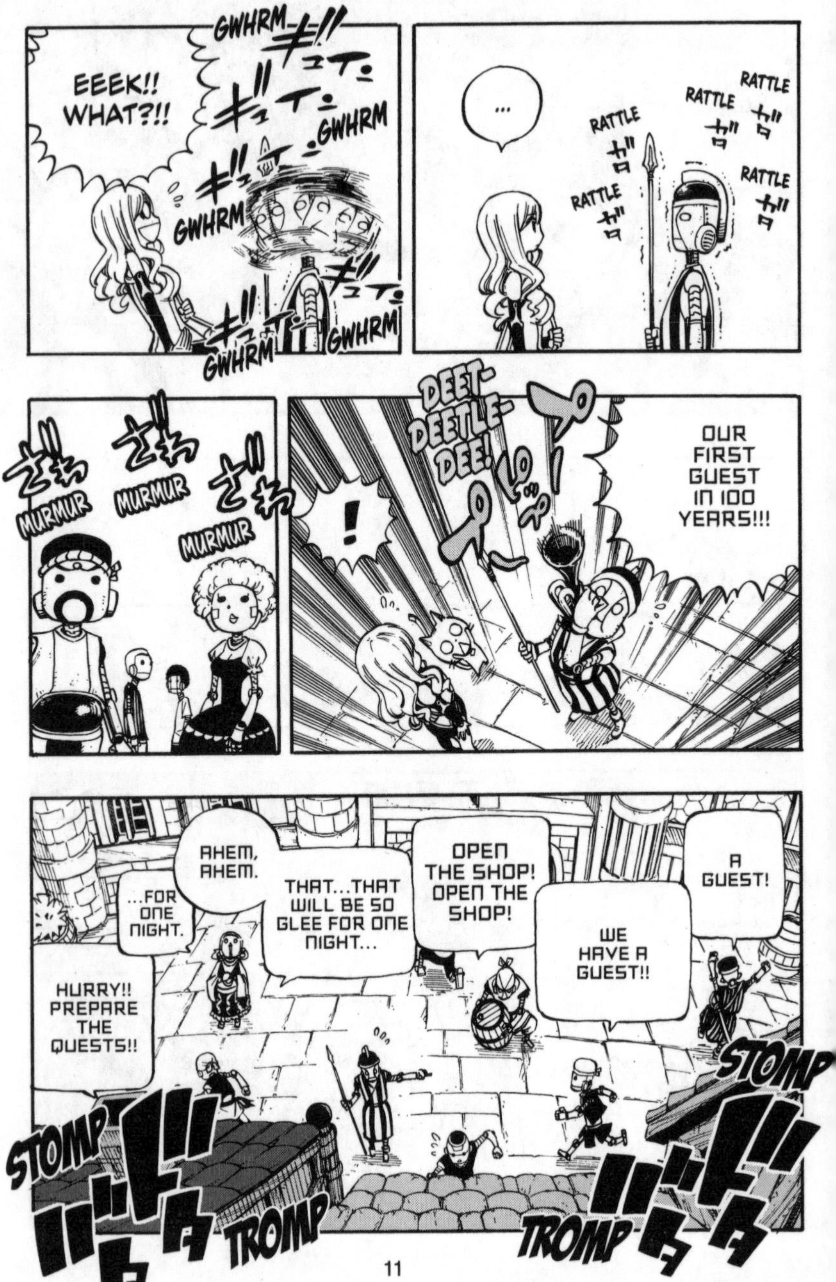
...
RATTLE
RATTLE
RATTLE
RATTLE
EEEK!! WHAT?!!
GWHRM
GWHRM
GWHRM
GWHRM
GWHRM
GWHRM
OUR FIRST GUEST IN 100 YEARS!!!
DEET-DEETLE-DEE!
!
MURMUR
MURMUR
MURMUR
A GUEST!
WE HAVE A GUEST!!
OPEN THE SHOP! OPEN THE SHOP!
STOMP
TROMP
THAT...THAT WILL BE SO GLEE FOR ONE NIGHT...
AHEM, AHEM.
...FOR ONE NIGHT.
HURRY!! PREPARE THE QUESTS!!
STOMP
TROMP

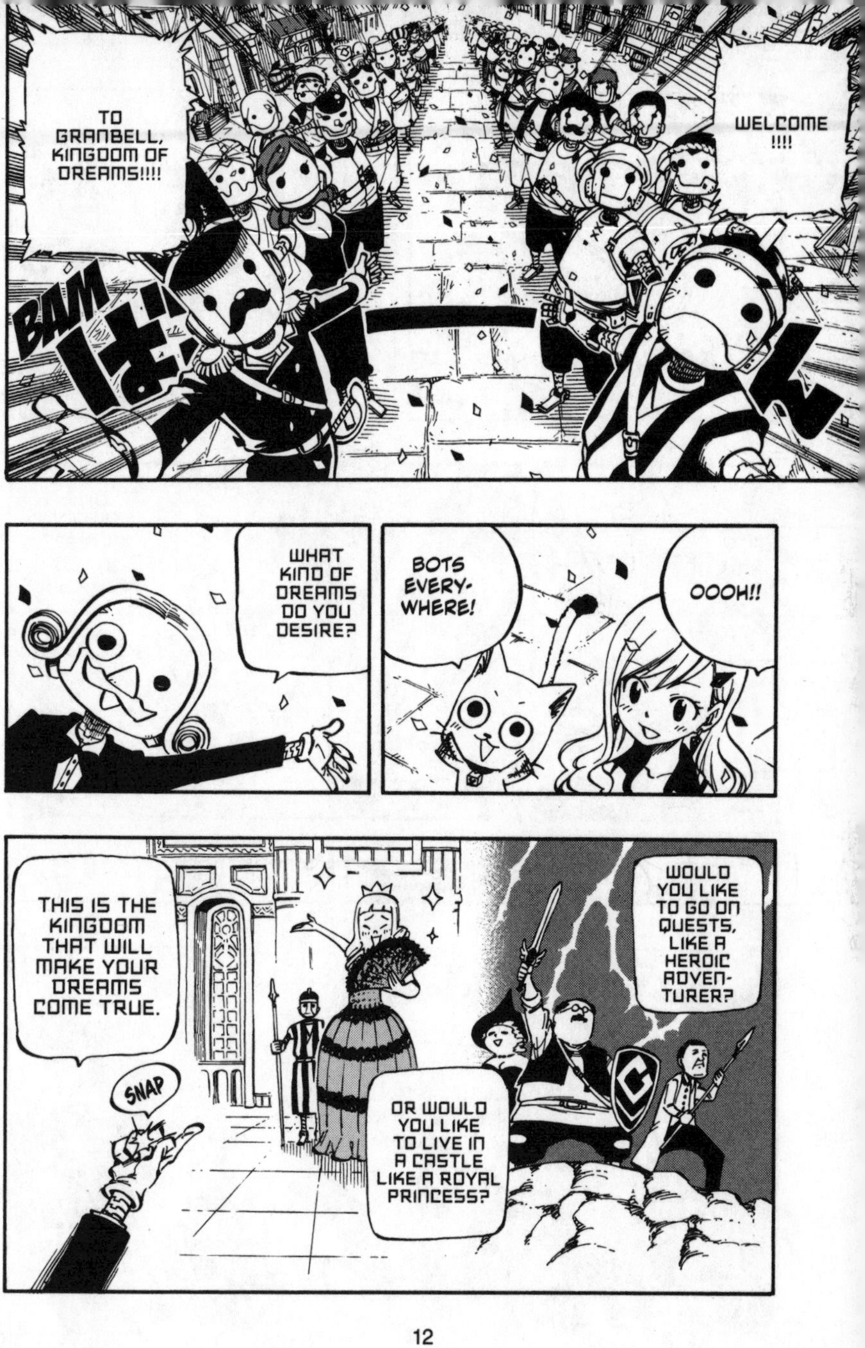
WELCOME !!!!
TO GRANBELL, KINGDOM OF DREAMS!!!!
BAM
OOOH!!
BOTS EVERY-WHERE!
WHAT KIND OF DREAMS DO YOU DESIRE?
WOULD YOU LIKE TO GO ON QUESTS, LIKE A HEROIC ADVEN-TURER?
OR WOULD YOU LIKE TO LIVE IN A CASTLE LIKE A ROYAL PRINCESS?
THIS IS THE KINGDOM THAT WILL MAKE YOUR DREAMS COME TRUE.
SNAP

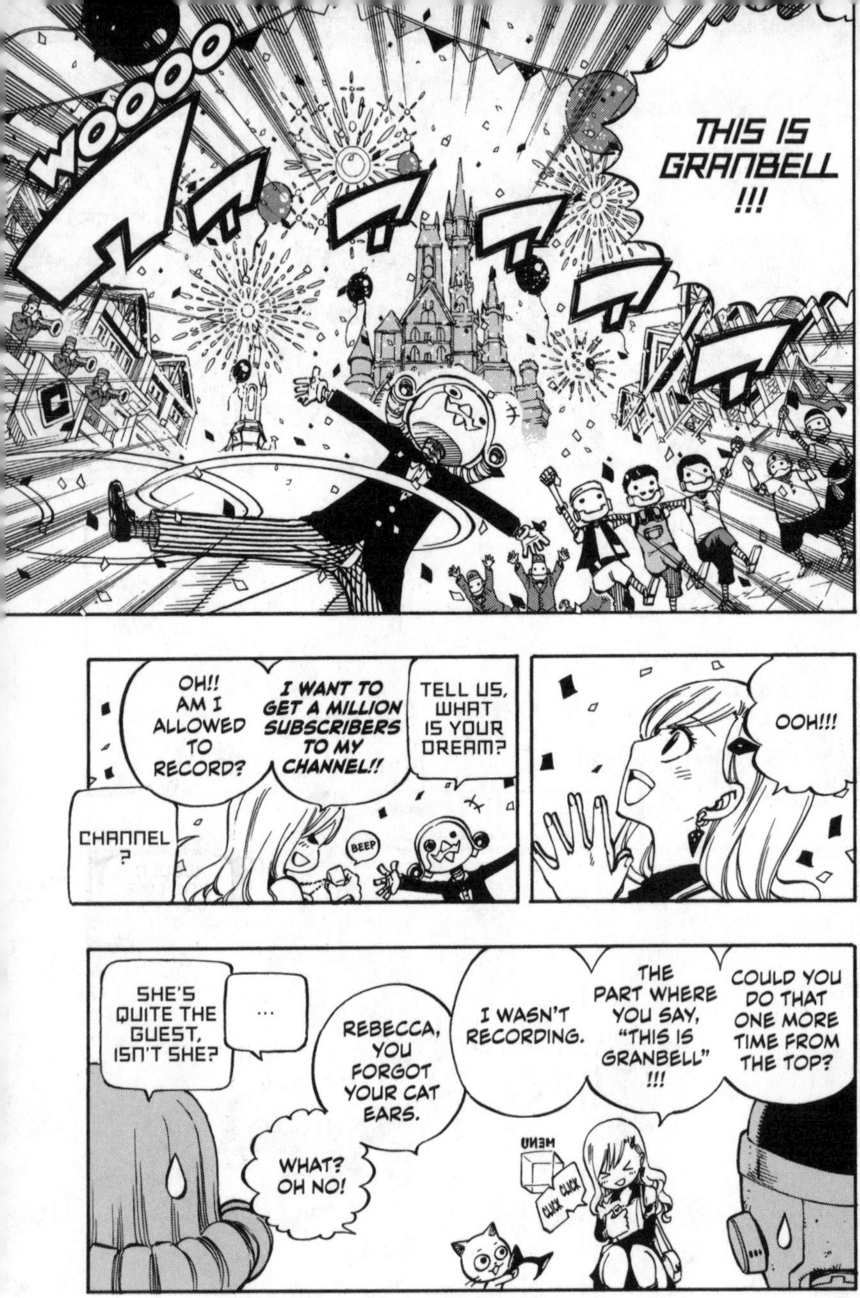
THIS IS GRANBELL !!!
WOOOO
OOH!!!
TELL US, WHAT IS YOUR DREAM?
I WANT TO GET A MILLION SUBSCRIBERS TO MY CHANNEL!!
OH!! AM I ALLOWED TO RECORD?
BEEP
CHANNEL?
COULD YOU DO THAT ONE MORE TIME FROM THE TOP?
THE PART WHERE YOU SAY, "THIS IS GRANBELL" !!!
I WASN'T RECORDING.
REBECCA, YOU FORGOT YOUR CAT EARS.
...
SHE'S QUITE THE GUEST, ISN'T SHE?
CLICK CLICK
WHAT? OH NO!

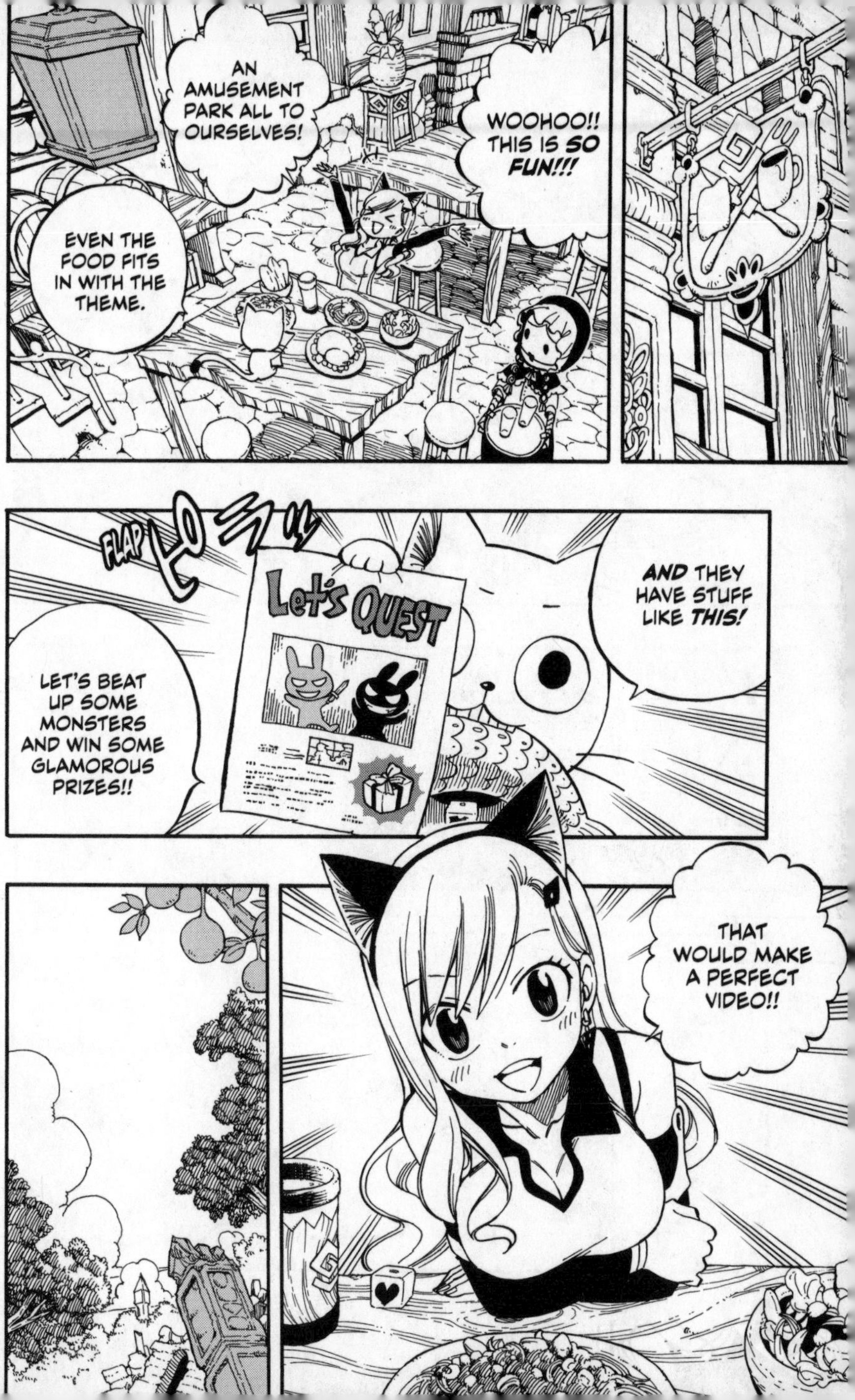
WOOHOO!! THIS IS SO FUN!!!
AN AMUSEMENT PARK ALL TO OURSELVES!
EVEN THE FOOD FITS IN WITH THE THEME.
AND THEY HAVE STUFF LIKE THIS!
FLAP
Let's QUEST
LET'S BEAT UP SOME MONSTERS AND WIN SOME GLAMOROUS PRIZES!!
THAT WOULD MAKE A PERFECT VIDEO!!

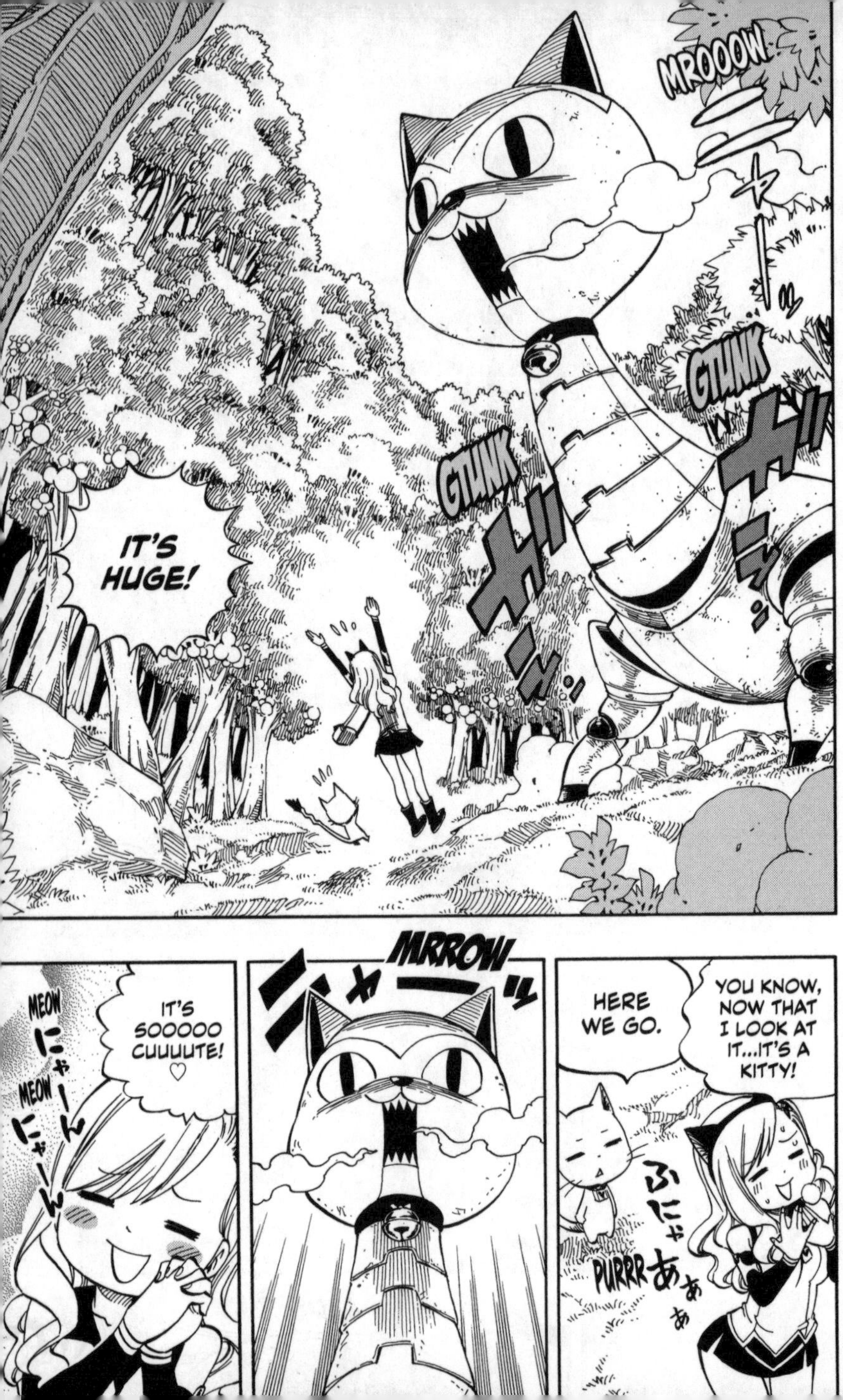
MROOOW
GTUNK
GTUNK
IT'S HUGE!
YOU KNOW, NOW THAT I LOOK AT IT...IT'S A KITTY!
HERE WE GO.
ふにゃあぁぁ
PURRR
MRROW
ニャーッ
IT'S SOOOOO CUUUUTE! ♡
にゃーん
MEOW
にゃーん
MEOW

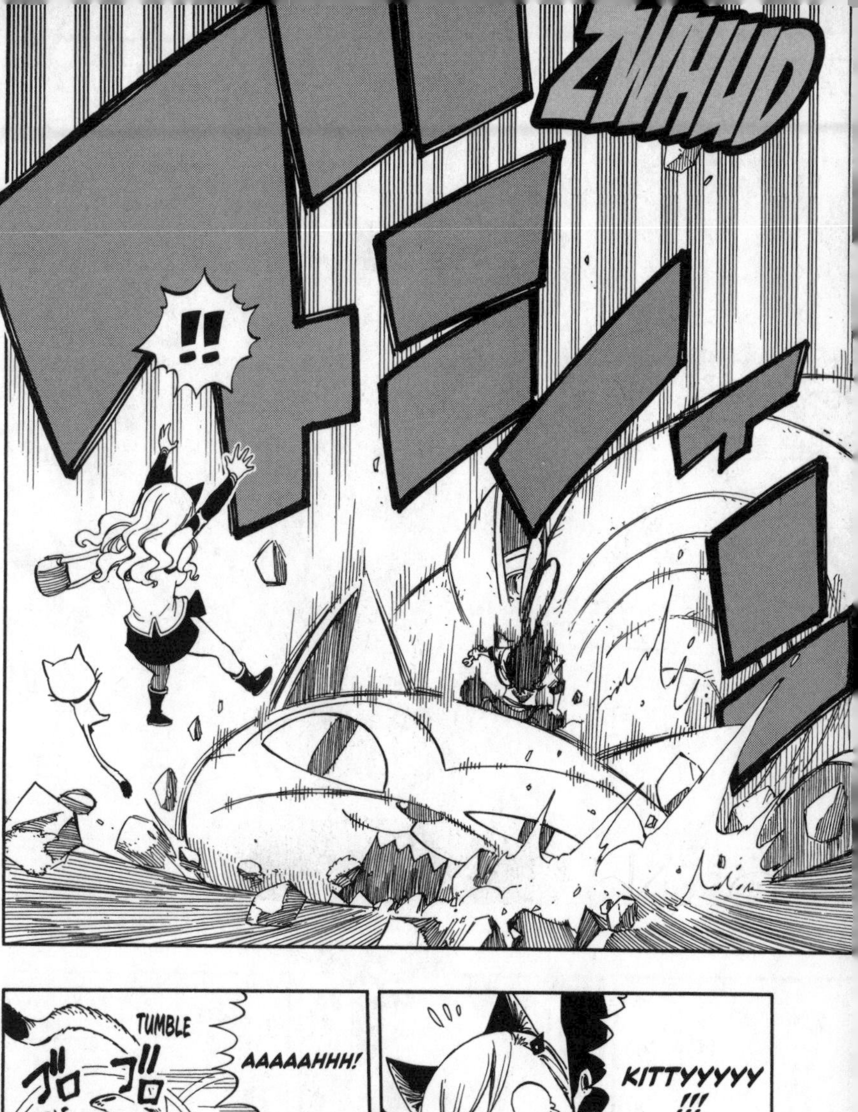
ZWHUD
!!
KITTYYYYY
!!!
TUMBLE
AAAAAHHH!
ゴロ ゴロ
TUMBLE
ゴロ
TUMBLE
ゴロ
TUMBLE

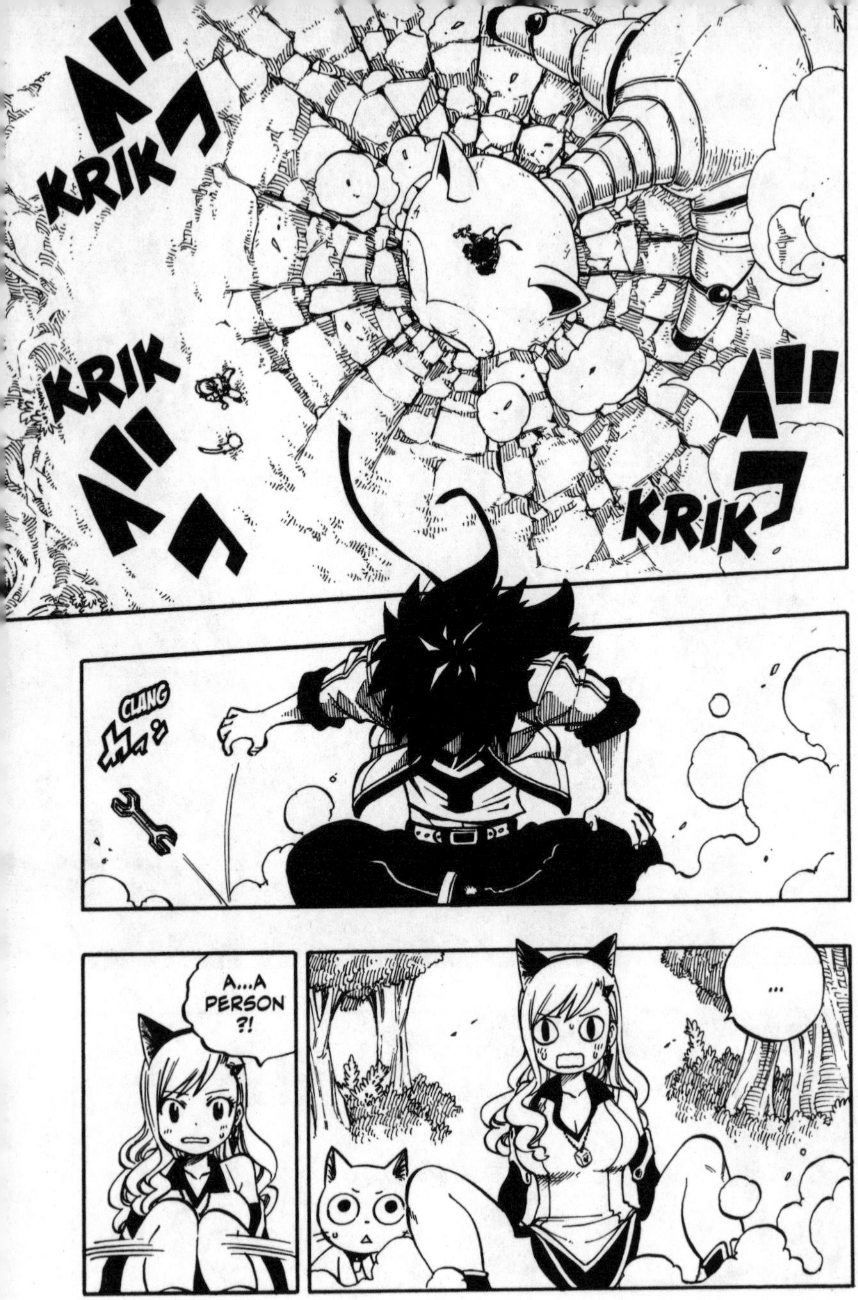
KRIK
KRIK
KRIK
CLANG
...
A...A PERSON ?!

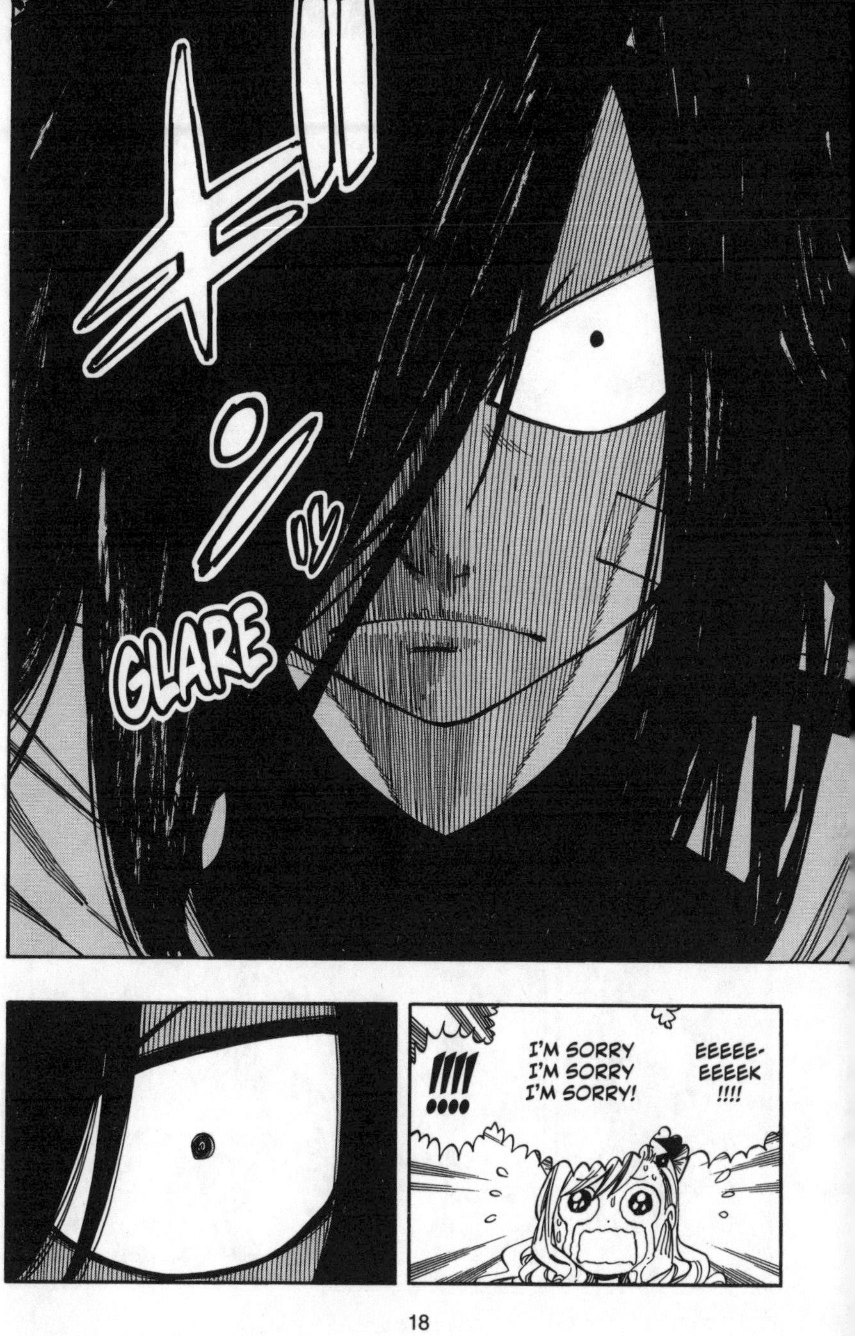
GLARE
EEEEE-
EEEEK
!!!!
I'M SORRY
I'M SORRY
I'M SORRY!
!!!!

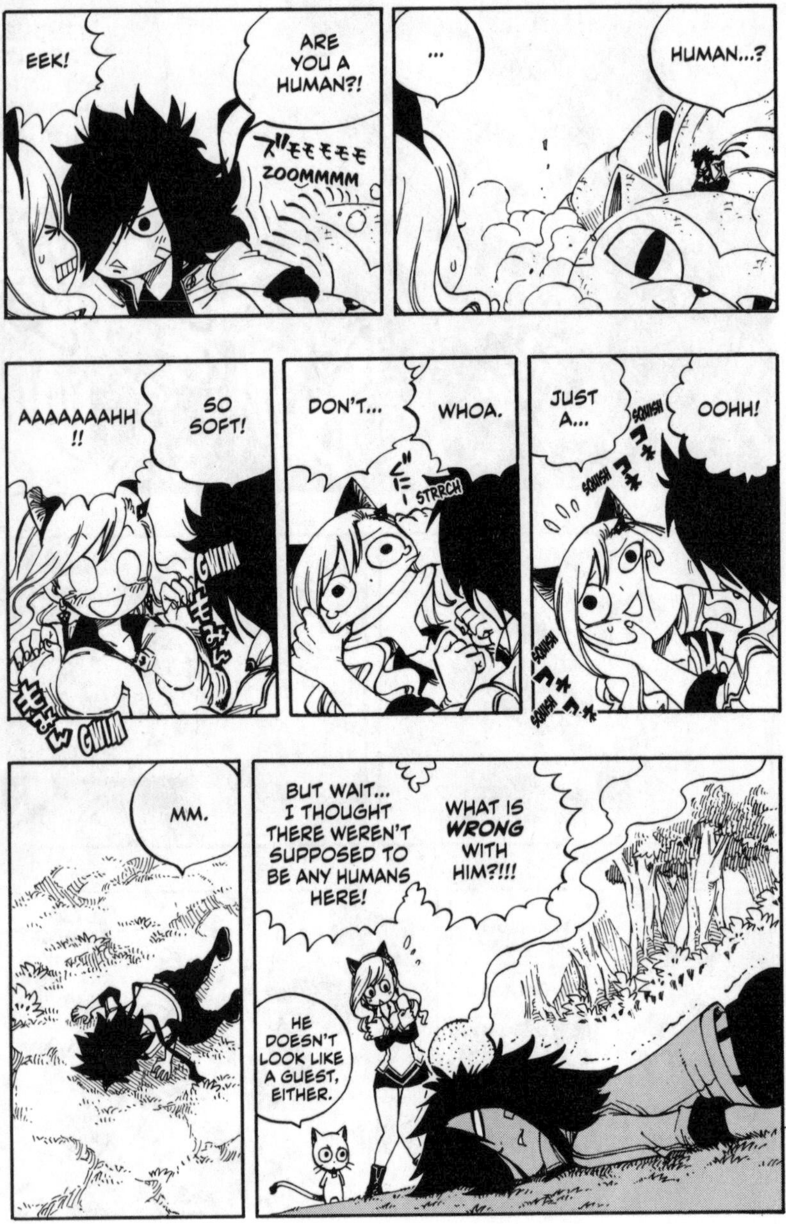
HUMAN...?
...
ARE YOU A HUMAN?!
ZOOMMMM
EEK!
OOHH!
JUST A...
SQUISH
SQUISH
WHOA.
DON'T...
STRRCH
SO SOFT!
AAAAAAAHH!!
GWIM
GWIM
WHAT IS **WRONG** WITH HIM?!!!
BUT WAIT... I THOUGHT THERE WEREN'T SUPPOSED TO BE ANY HUMANS HERE!
HE DOESN'T LOOK LIKE A GUEST, EITHER.
MM.

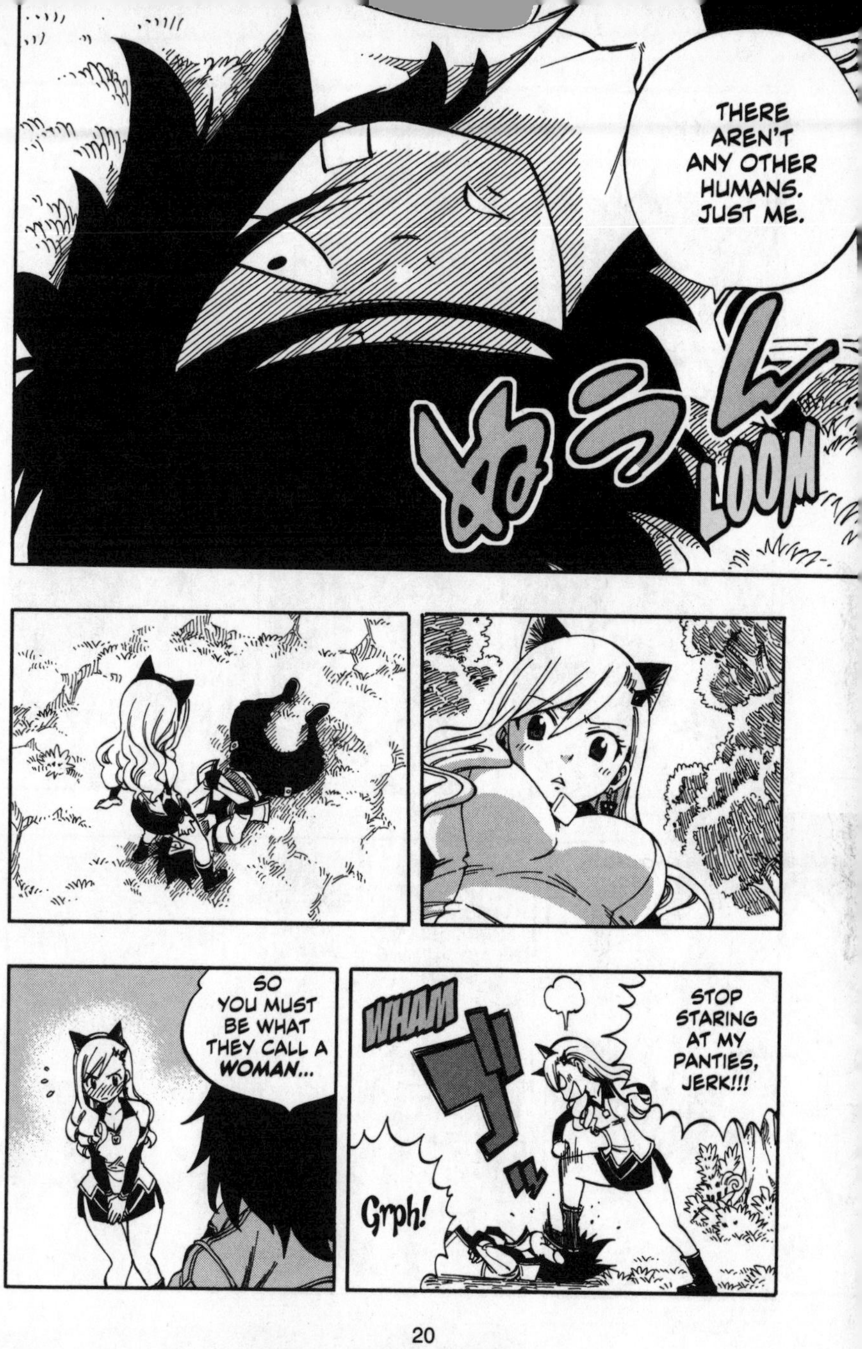
THERE AREN'T ANY OTHER HUMANS. JUST ME.
ぬうん
LOOM
STOP STARING AT MY PANTIES, JERK!!!
WHAM
Grph!
SO YOU MUST BE WHAT THEY CALL A WOMAN...

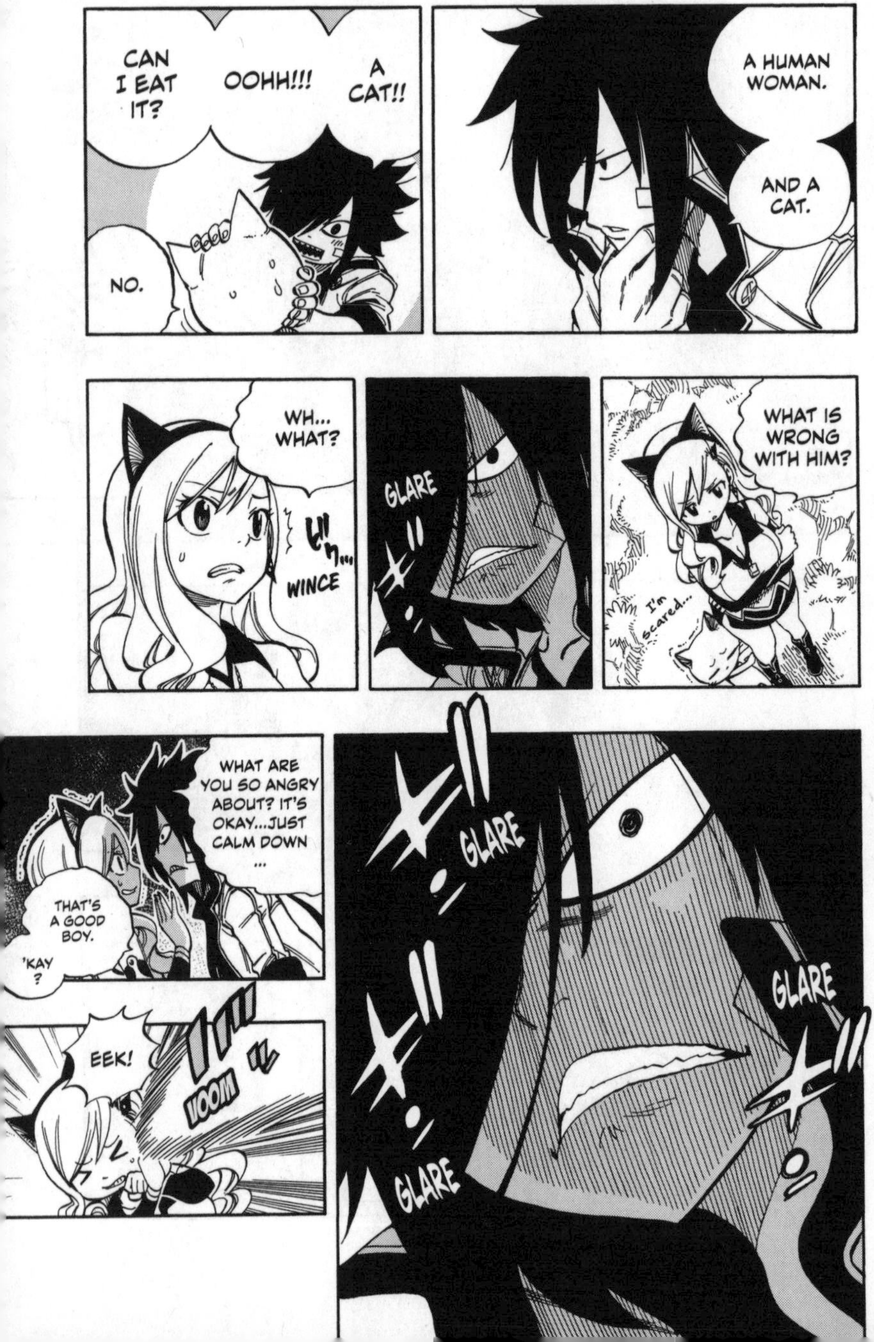
A HUMAN WOMAN.
AND A CAT.
A CAT!!
OOHH!!!
CAN I EAT IT?
NO.
WHAT IS WRONG WITH HIM?
I'm scared...
GLARE
WH... WHAT?
WINCE
GLARE
GLARE
GLARE
WHAT ARE YOU SO ANGRY ABOUT? IT'S OKAY...JUST CALM DOWN ...
THAT'S A GOOD BOY.
'KAY ?
VOOM
EEK!

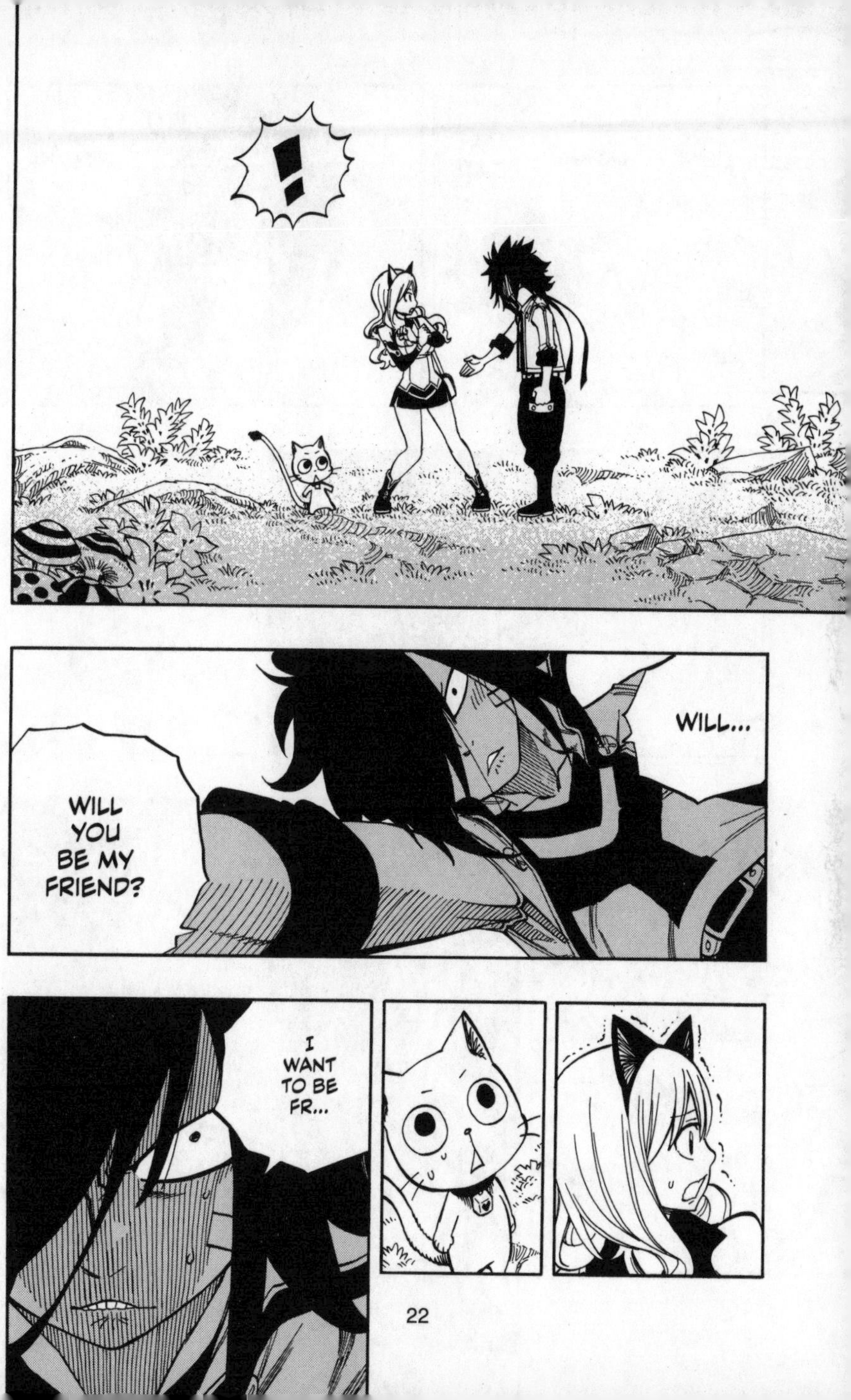
!!
WILL...
WILL YOU BE MY FRIEND?
I WANT TO BE FR...

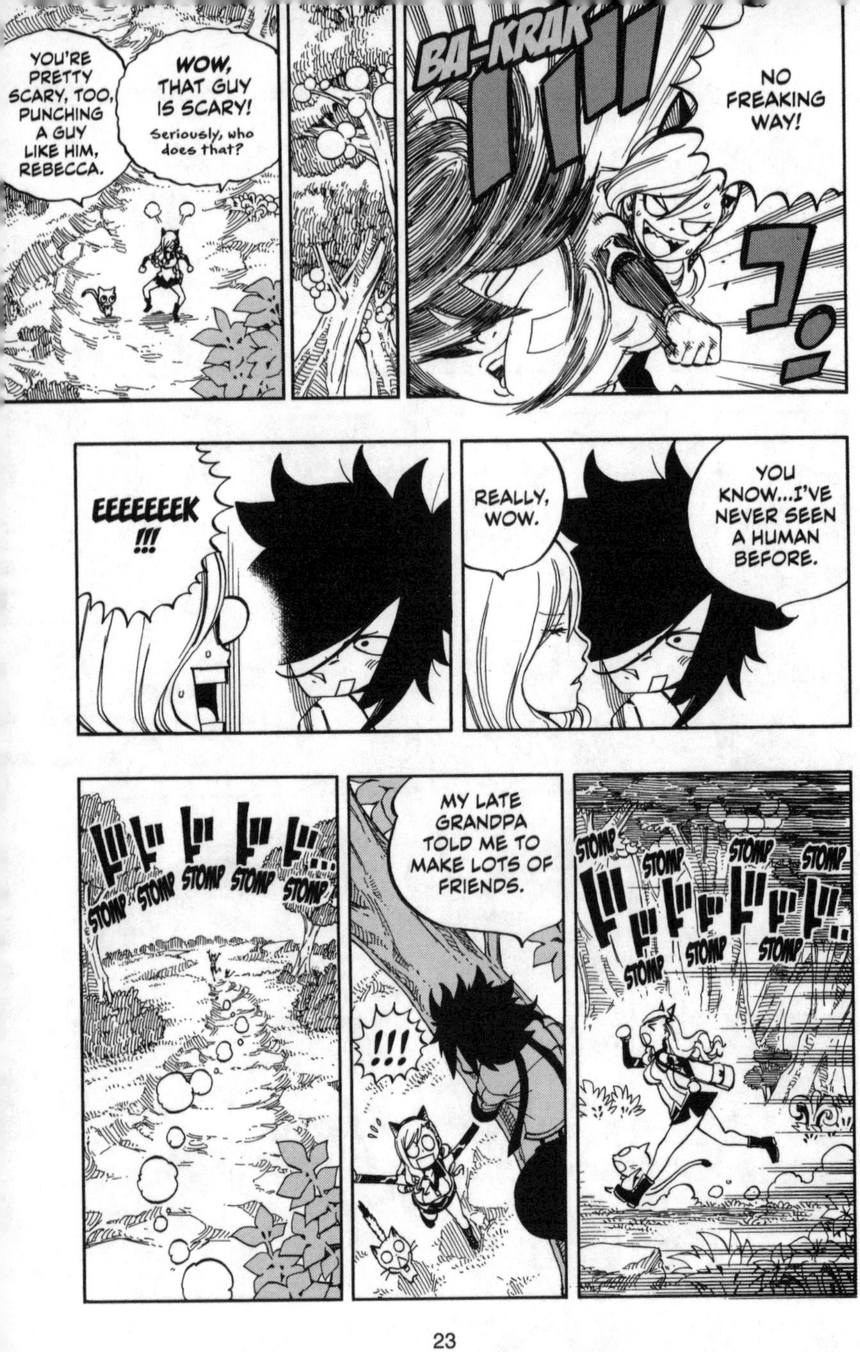
BA-KRAK
NO FREAKING WAY!
WOW, THAT GUY IS SCARY! Seriously, who does that?
YOU'RE PRETTY SCARY, TOO, PUNCHING A GUY LIKE HIM, REBECCA.
YOU KNOW...I'VE NEVER SEEN A HUMAN BEFORE.
REALLY, WOW.
EEEEEEEK!!!
STOMP STOMP STOMP STOMP STOMP STOMP STOMP
MY LATE GRANDPA TOLD ME TO MAKE LOTS OF FRIENDS.
!!!
STOMP STOMP STOMP STOMP STOMP

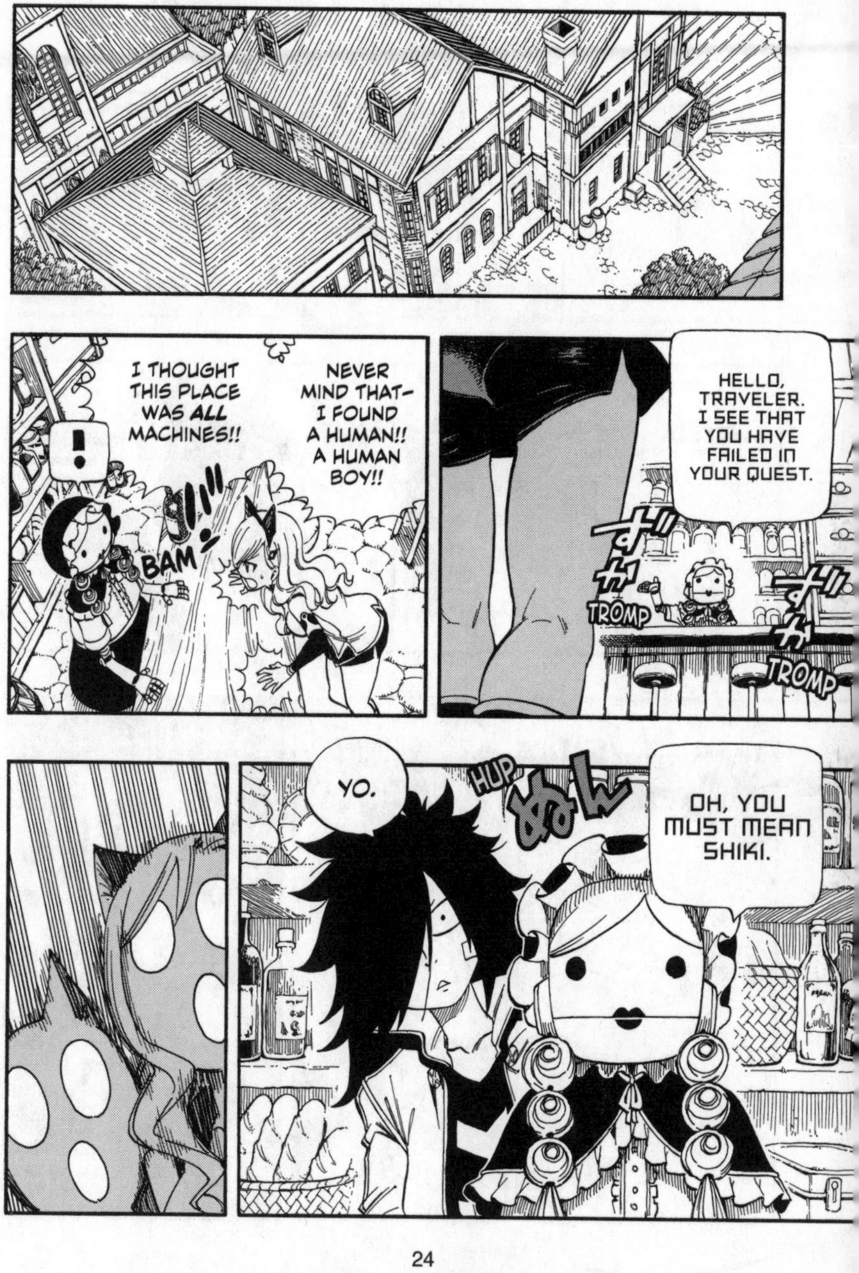
HELLO, TRAVELER. I SEE THAT YOU HAVE FAILED IN YOUR QUEST.
TROMP
TROMP
NEVER MIND THAT— I FOUND A HUMAN!! A HUMAN BOY!!
I THOUGHT THIS PLACE WAS ALL MACHINES!!
!
BAM
OH, YOU MUST MEAN SHIKI.
HUP
YO.

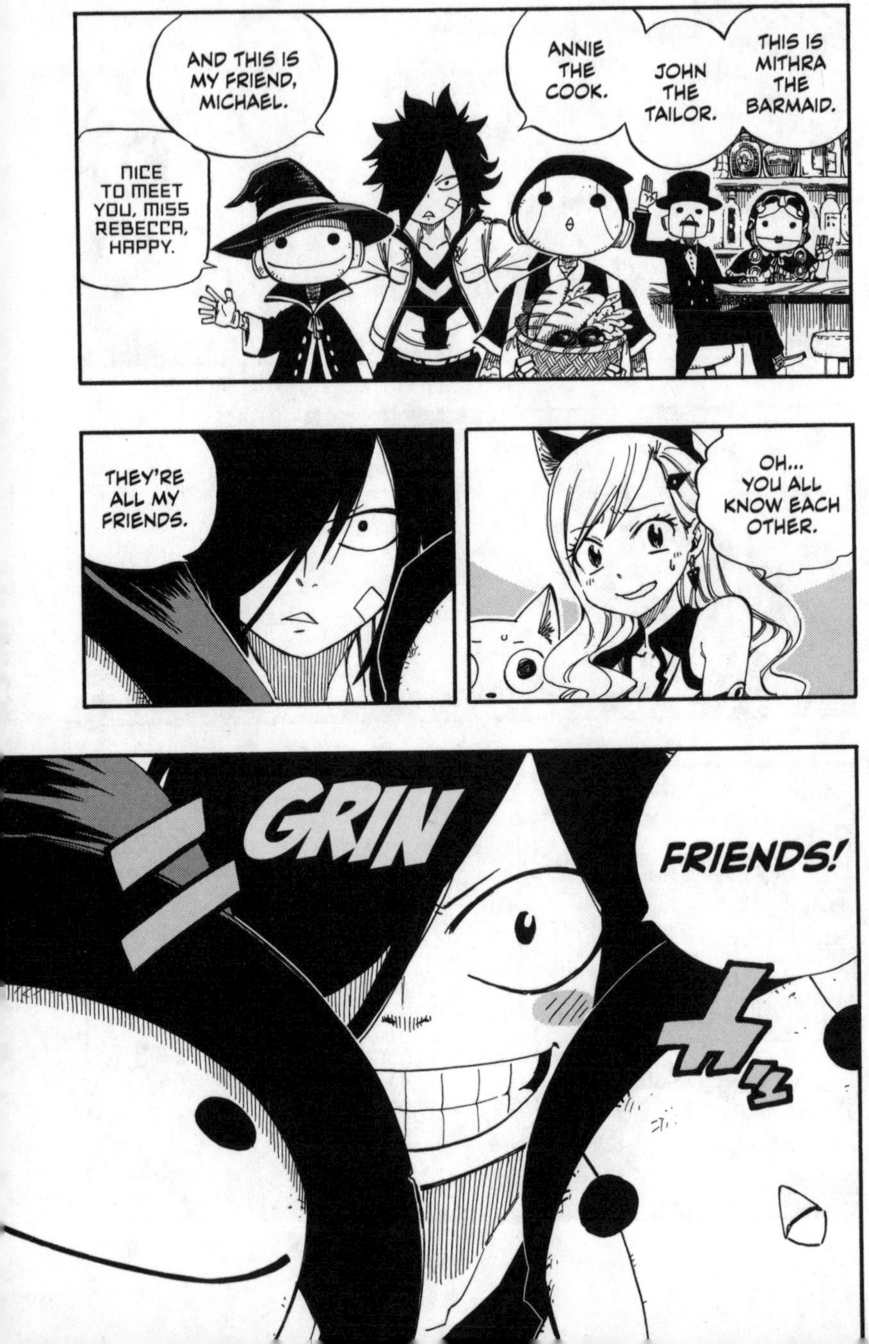
THIS IS MITHRA THE BARMAID.
JOHN THE TAILOR.
ANNIE THE COOK.
AND THIS IS MY FRIEND, MICHAEL.
NICE TO MEET YOU, MISS REBECCA, HAPPY.
OH... YOU ALL KNOW EACH OTHER.
THEY'RE ALL MY FRIENDS.
FRIENDS!
GRIN

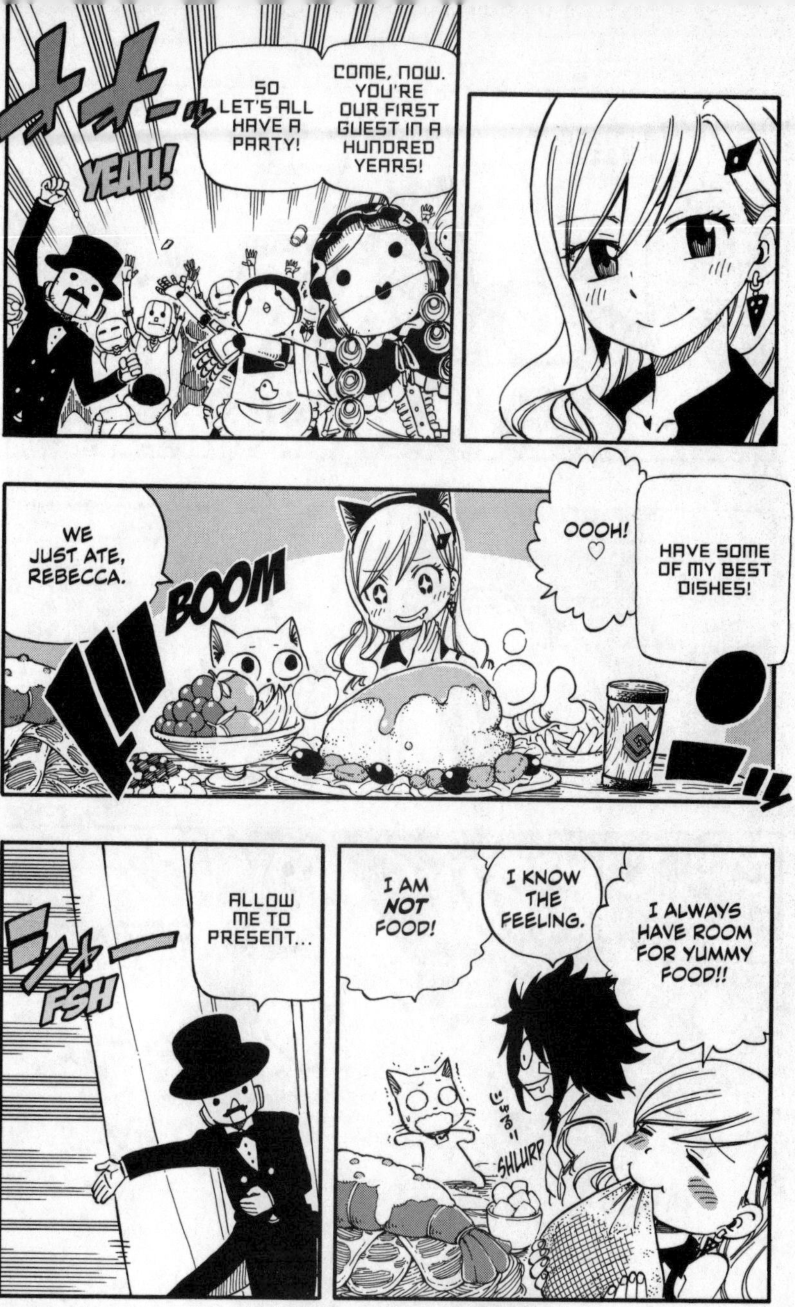
COME, NOW. YOU'RE OUR FIRST GUEST IN A HUNDRED YEARS!
SO LET'S ALL HAVE A PARTY!
YEAH!
HAVE SOME OF MY BEST DISHES!
OOOH! ♡
BOOM
WE JUST ATE, REBECCA.
I ALWAYS HAVE ROOM FOR YUMMY FOOD!!
I KNOW THE FEELING.
I AM *NOT* FOOD!
SHLURP
ALLOW ME TO PRESENT...
FSH

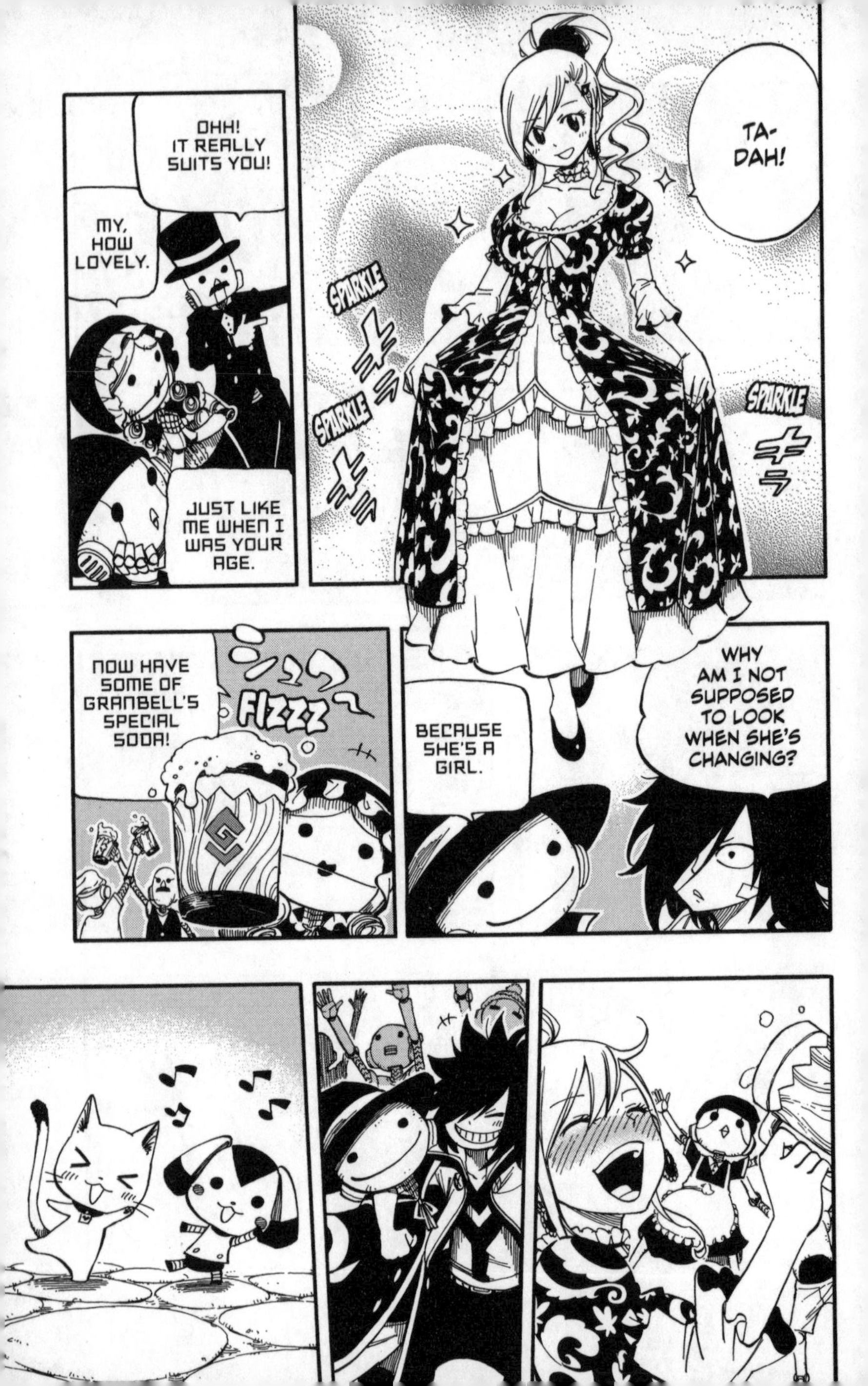
TA-DAH!
SPARKLE
SPARKLE
SPARKLE
OHH! IT REALLY SUITS YOU!
MY, HOW LOVELY.
JUST LIKE ME WHEN I WAS YOUR AGE.
WHY AM I NOT SUPPOSED TO LOOK WHEN SHE'S CHANGING?
BECAUSE SHE'S A GIRL.
NOW HAVE SOME OF GRANBELL'S SPECIAL SODA!
FIZZZ

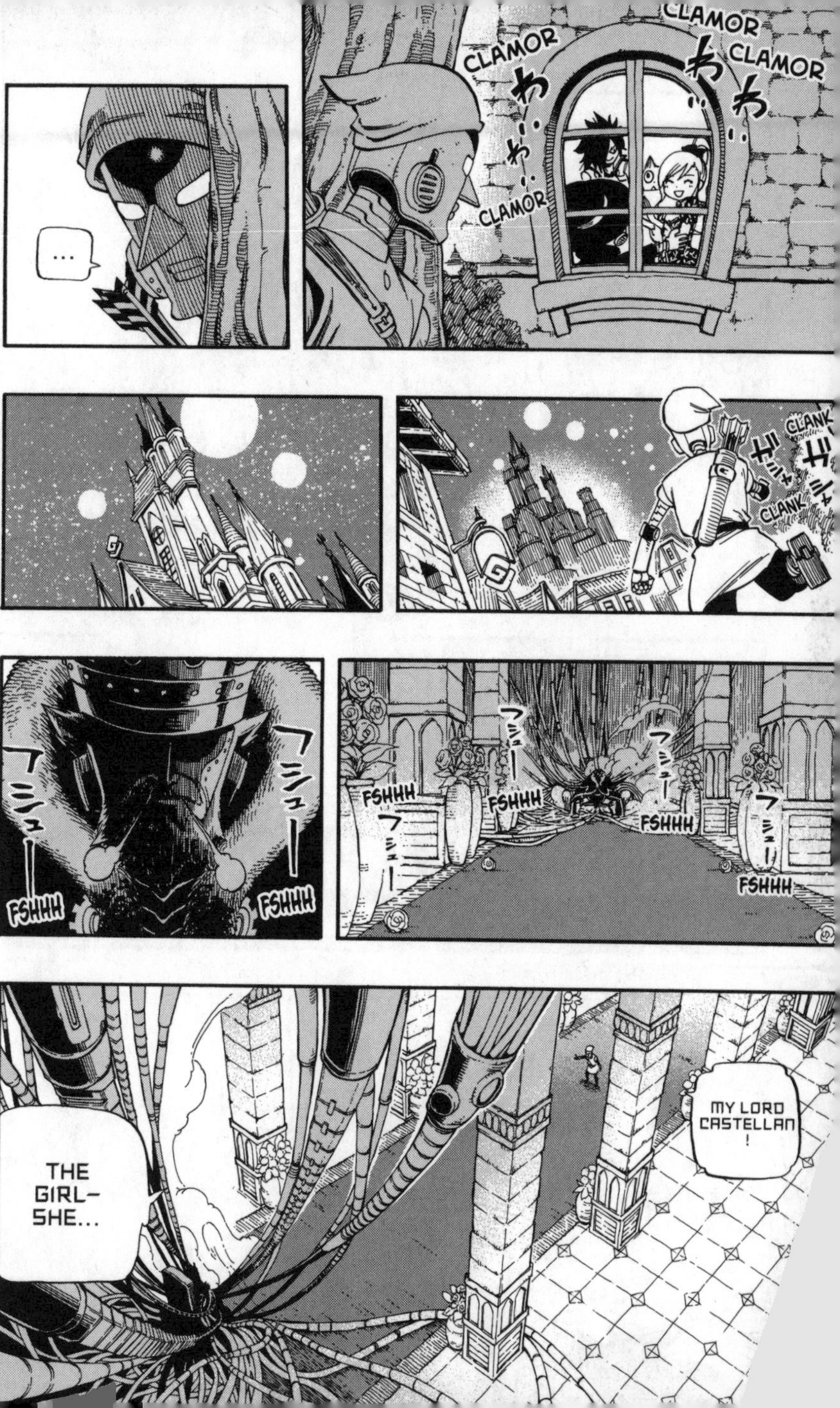
CLAMOR
CLAMOR
CLAMOR
CLAMOR
...
CLANK
CLANK
FSHHH
FSHHH
FSHHH
FSHHH
FSHHH
FSHHH
MY LORD CASTELLAN!
THE GIRL— SHE...

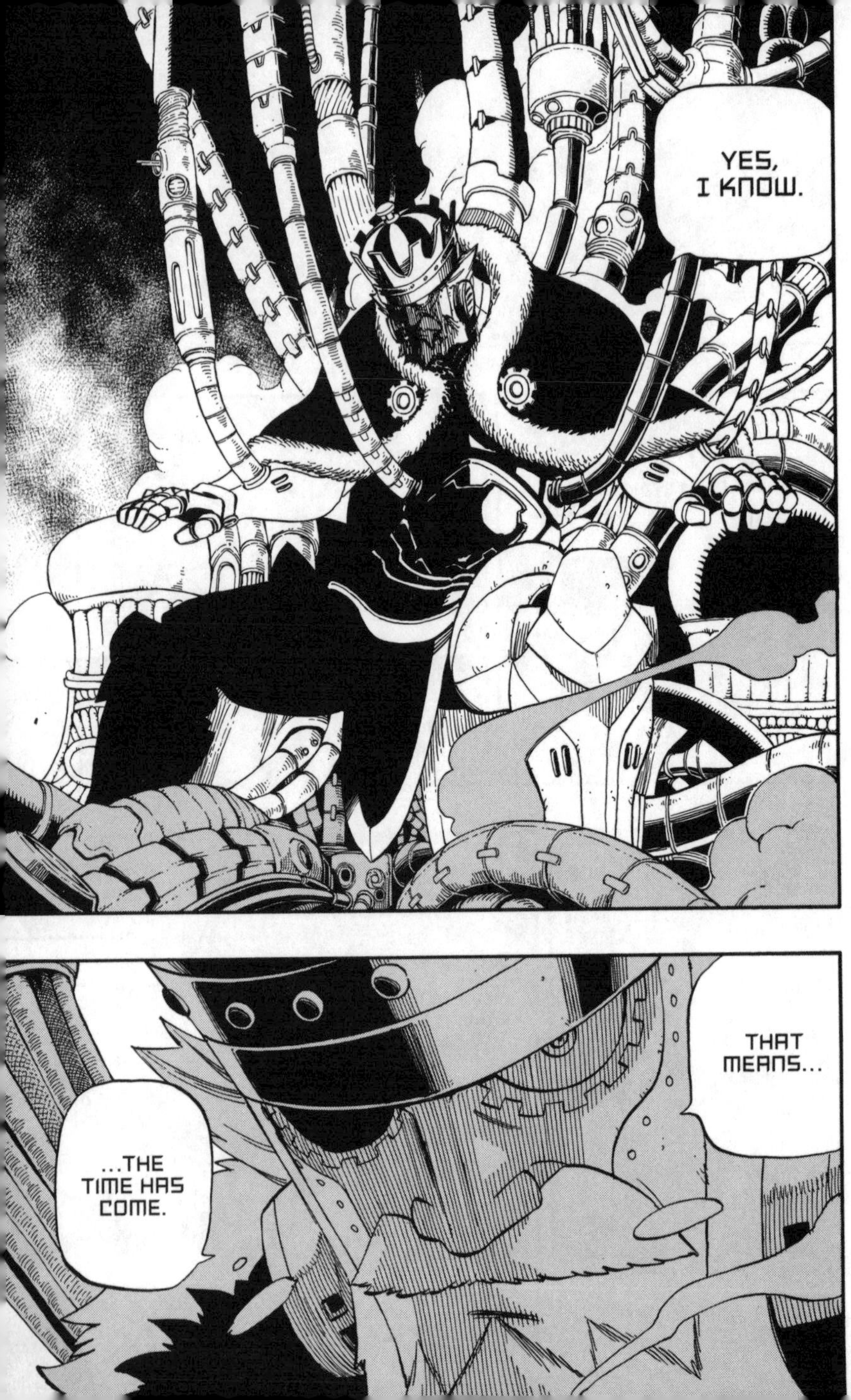
YES, I KNOW.
THAT MEANS...
...THE TIME HAS COME.

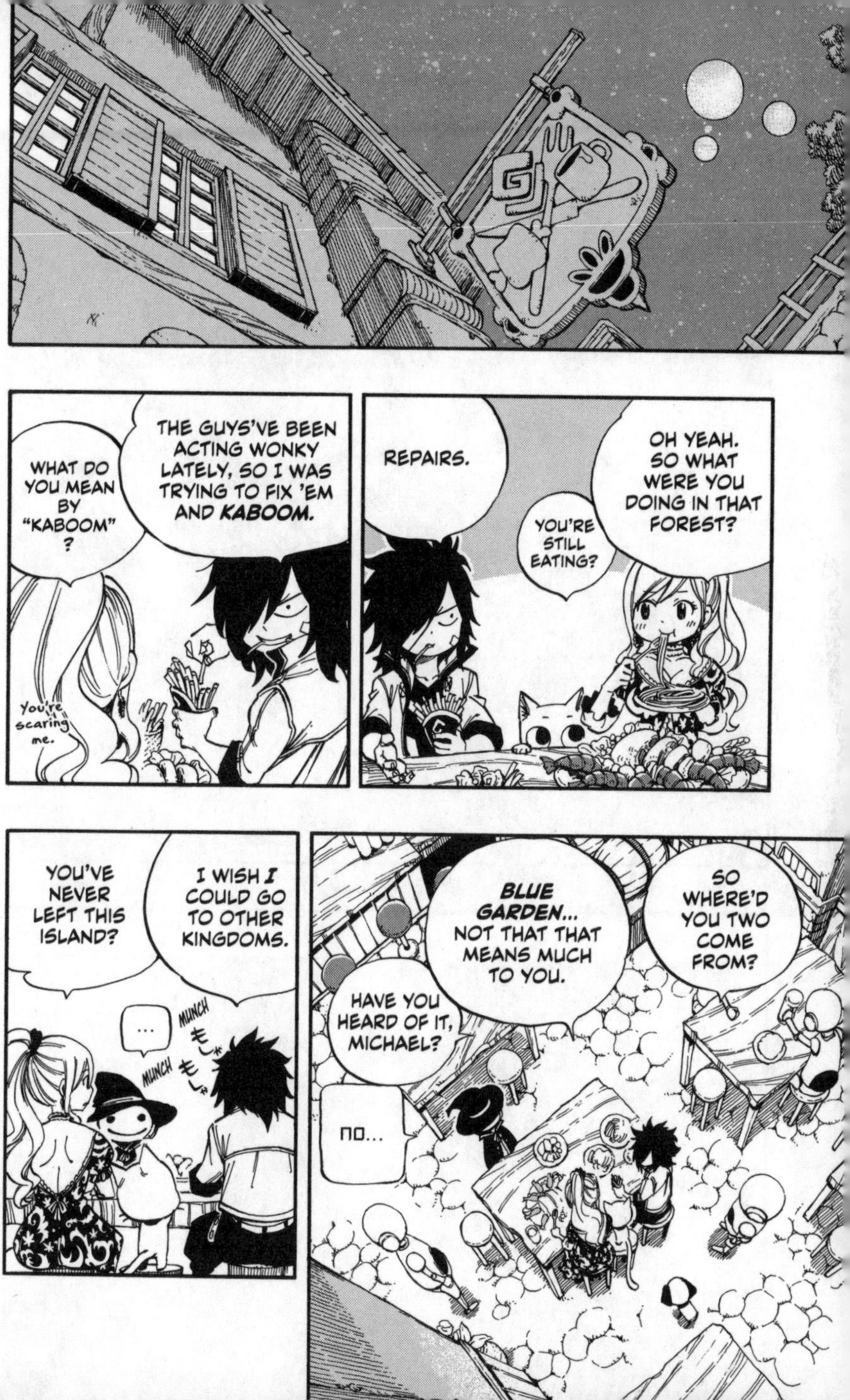
OH YEAH. SO WHAT WERE YOU DOING IN THAT FOREST?
YOU'RE STILL EATING?
REPAIRS.
THE GUYS'VE BEEN ACTING WONKY LATELY, SO I WAS TRYING TO FIX 'EM AND ***KABOOM.***
WHAT DO YOU MEAN BY "KABOOM"?
You're scaring me.
SO WHERE'D YOU TWO COME FROM?
BLUE GARDEN... NOT THAT THAT MEANS MUCH TO YOU.
HAVE YOU HEARD OF IT, MICHAEL?
no...
I WISH ***I*** COULD GO TO OTHER KINGDOMS.
YOU'VE NEVER LEFT THIS ISLAND?
...
MUNCH
MUNCH

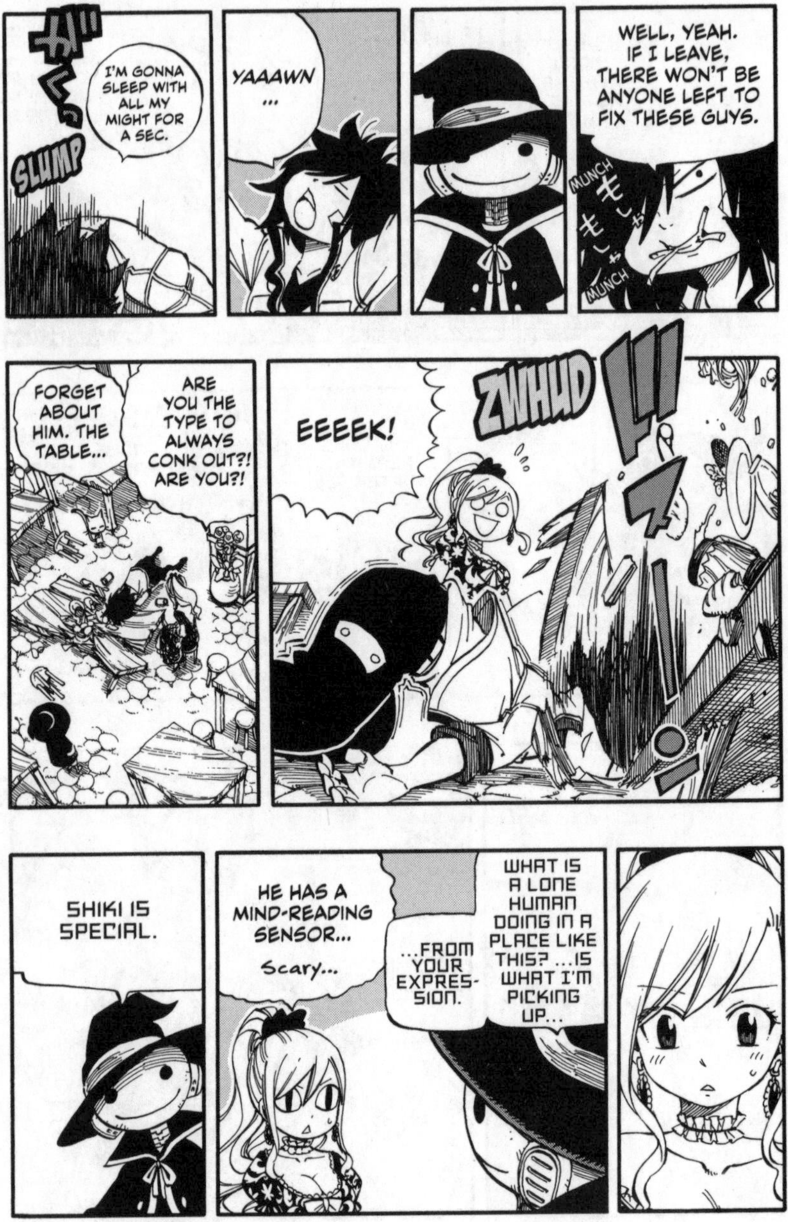
WELL, YEAH. IF I LEAVE, THERE WON'T BE ANYONE LEFT TO FIX THESE GUYS.
MUNCH
MUNCH
YAAAWN ...
I'M GONNA SLEEP WITH ALL MY MIGHT FOR A SEC.
SLUMP
ZWHUD
EEEEK!
ARE YOU THE TYPE TO ALWAYS CONK OUT?! ARE YOU?!
FORGET ABOUT HIM. THE TABLE...
WHAT IS A LONE HUMAN DOING IN A PLACE LIKE THIS? ...IS WHAT I'M PICKING UP...
...FROM YOUR EXPRESSION.
HE HAS A MIND-READING SENSOR...
Scary...
SHIKI IS SPECIAL.

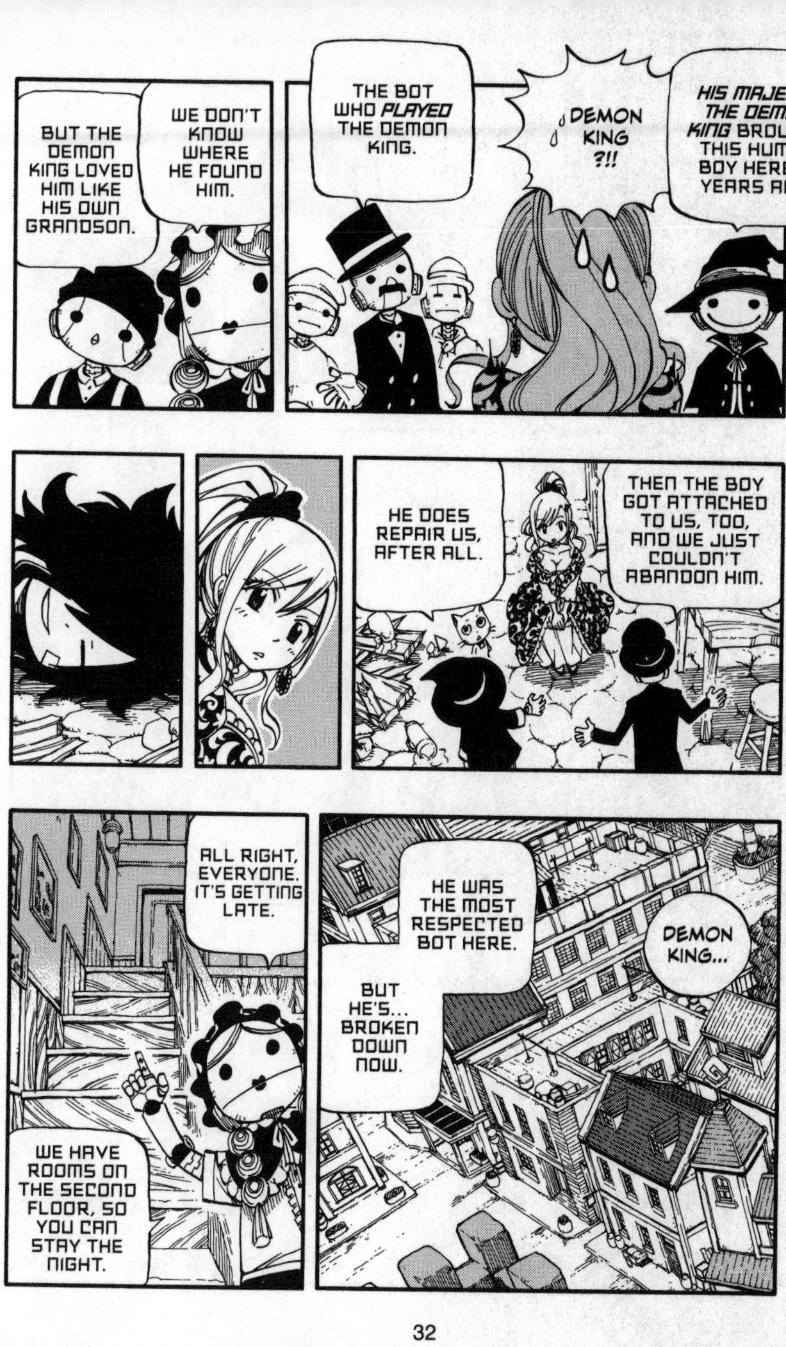
HIS MAJESTY THE DEMON KING BROUGHT THIS HUMAN BOY HERE 10 YEARS AGO.
DEMON KING ?!!
THE BOT WHO PLAYED THE DEMON KING.
WE DON'T KNOW WHERE HE FOUND HIM.
BUT THE DEMON KING LOVED HIM LIKE HIS OWN GRANDSON.
THEN THE BOY GOT ATTACHED TO US, TOO, AND WE JUST COULDN'T ABANDON HIM.
HE DOES REPAIR US, AFTER ALL.
DEMON KING...
HE WAS THE MOST RESPECTED BOT HERE.
BUT HE'S... BROKEN DOWN NOW.
ALL RIGHT, EVERYONE. IT'S GETTING LATE.
WE HAVE ROOMS ON THE SECOND FLOOR, SO YOU CAN STAY THE NIGHT.

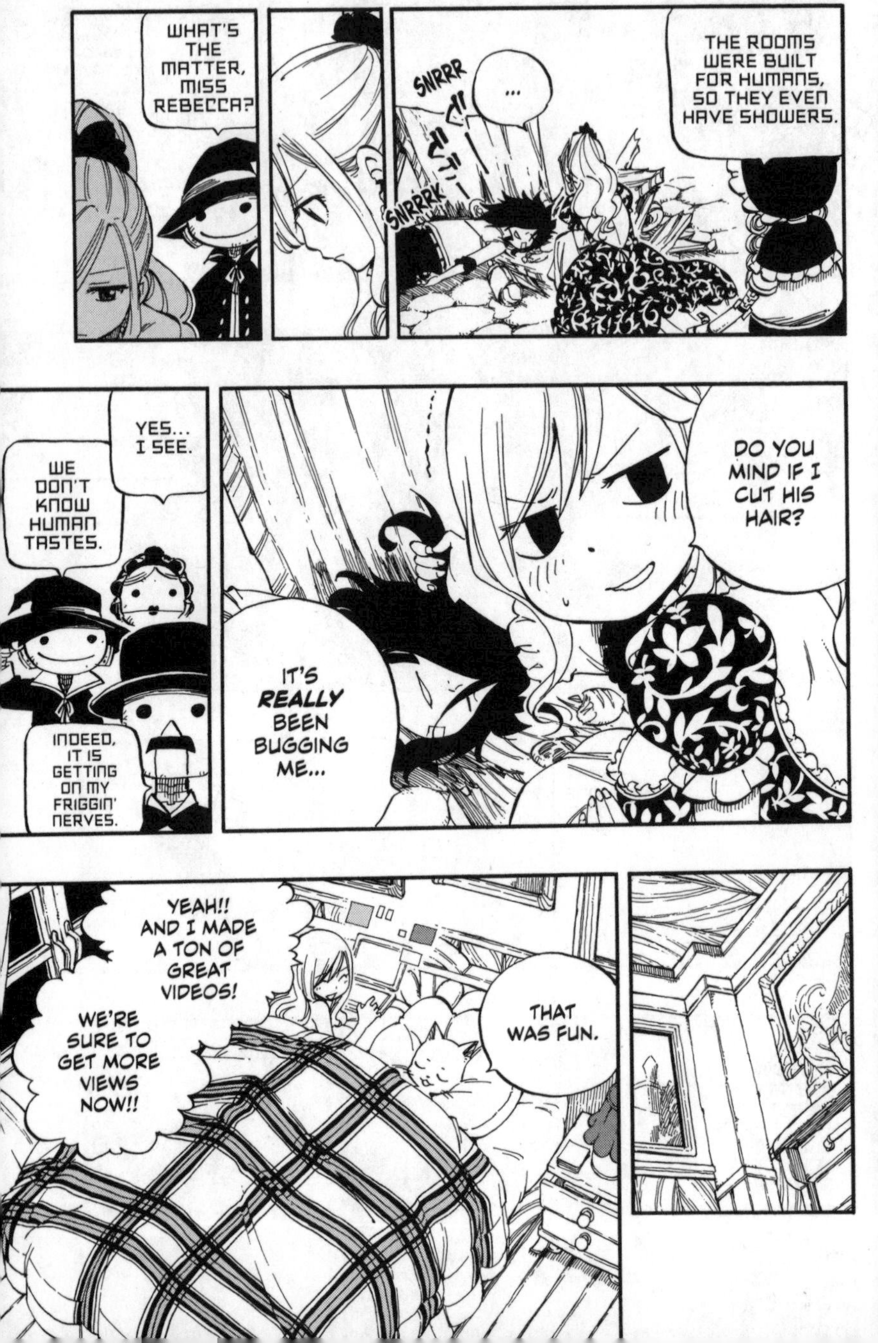
THE ROOMS WERE BUILT FOR HUMANS, SO THEY EVEN HAVE SHOWERS.
...
SNRRR
SNRRRK
WHAT'S THE MATTER, MISS REBECCA?
DO YOU MIND IF I CUT HIS HAIR?
IT'S *REALLY* BEEN BUGGING ME...
YES... I SEE.
WE DON'T KNOW HUMAN TASTES.
INDEED, IT IS GETTING ON MY FRIGGIN' NERVES.
THAT WAS FUN.
YEAH!! AND I MADE A TON OF GREAT VIDEOS!
WE'RE SURE TO GET MORE VIEWS NOW!!

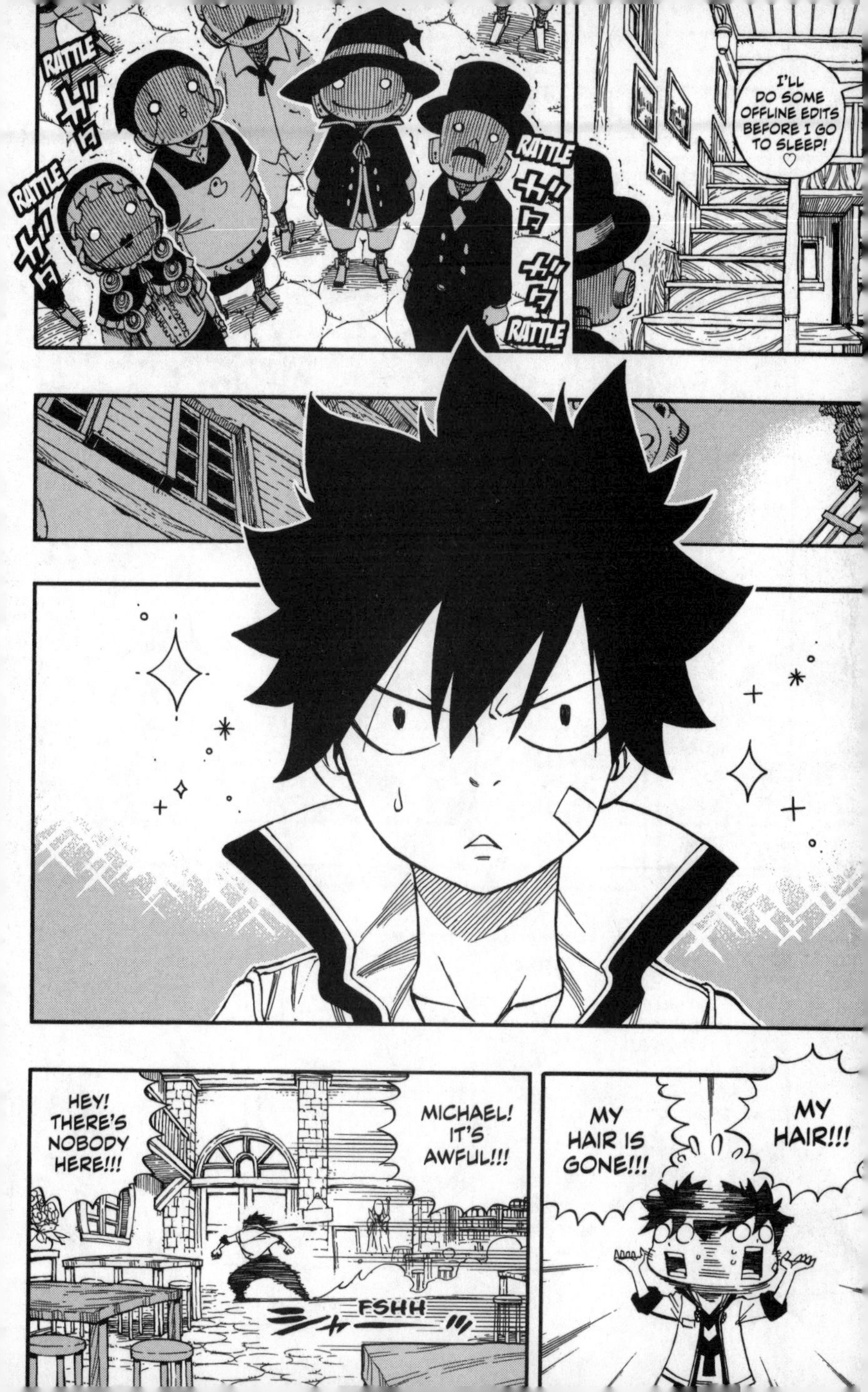
I'LL DO SOME OFFLINE EDITS BEFORE I GO TO SLEEP! ♡
RATTLE
RATTLE
RATTLE
RATTLE
MY HAIR!!!
MY HAIR IS GONE!!!
MICHAEL! IT'S AWFUL!!!
HEY! THERE'S NOBODY HERE!!!
FSHH

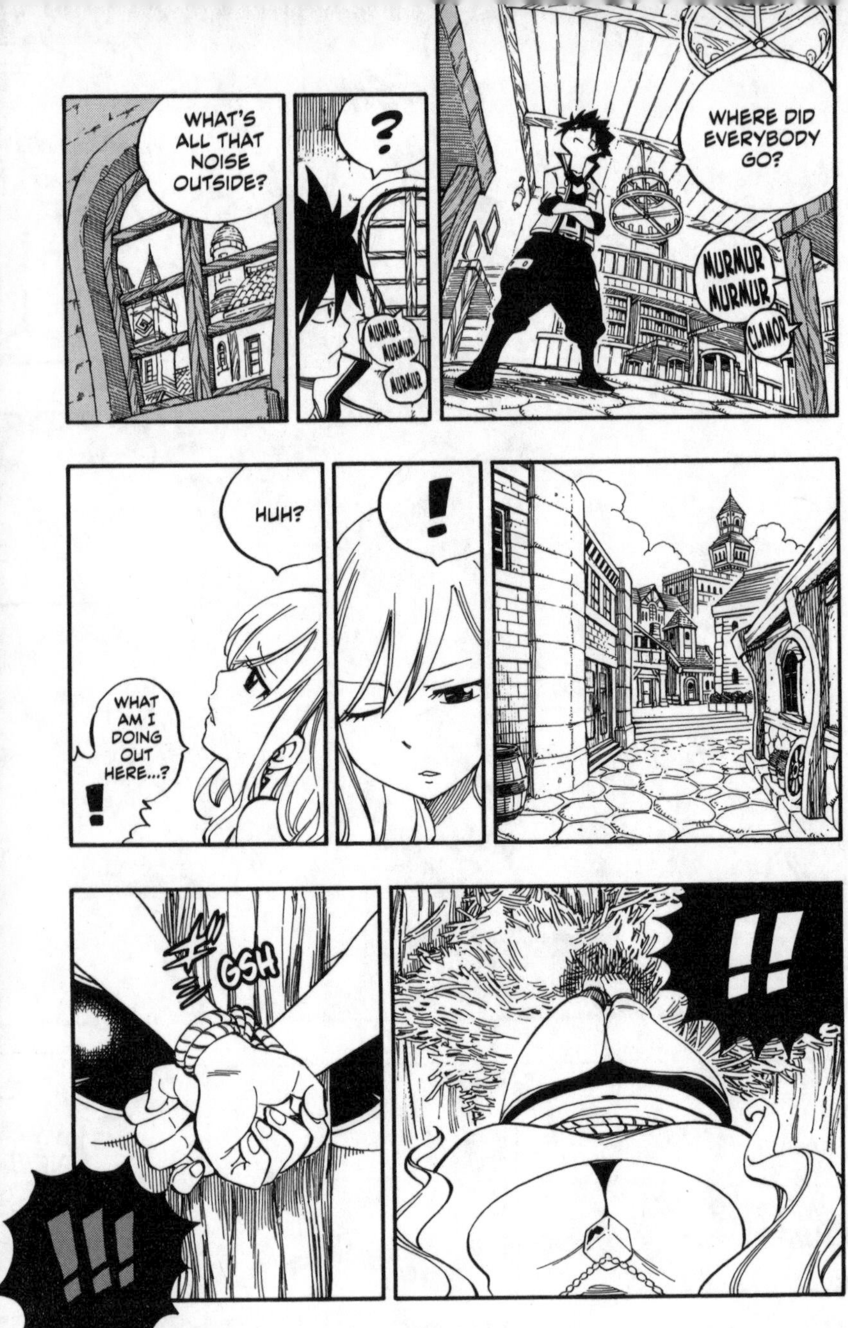
WHERE DID EVERYBODY GO?
MURMUR MURMUR
CLAMOR
?
MURMUR MURMUR
MURMUR
WHAT'S ALL THAT NOISE OUTSIDE?
!
HUH?
WHAT AM I DOING OUT HERE...?
!
!!
GSH
!!!

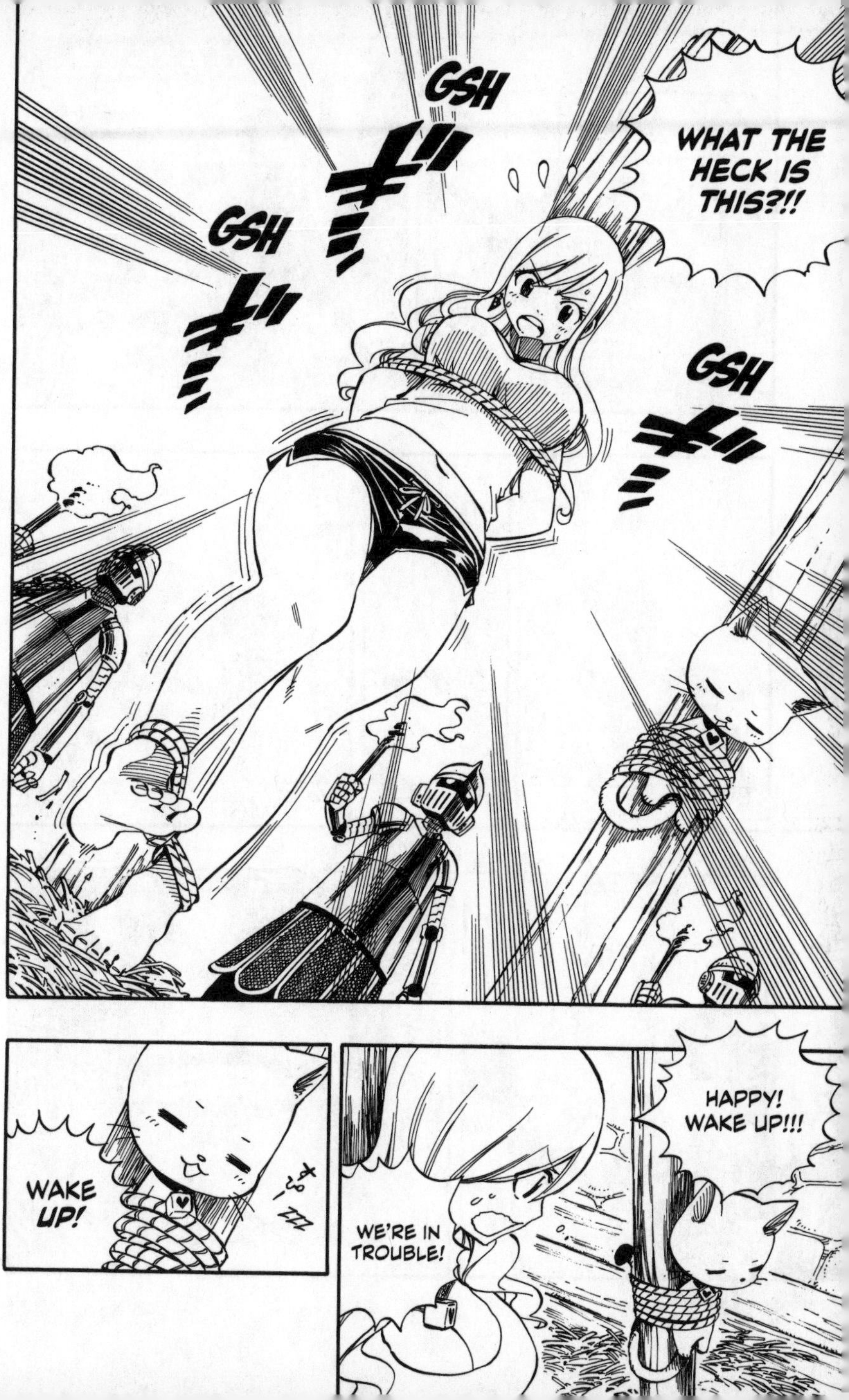
WHAT THE HECK IS THIS?!!
GSH
GSH
GSH
HAPPY! WAKE UP!!!
WE'RE IN TROUBLE!
WAKE UP!
ZZZ

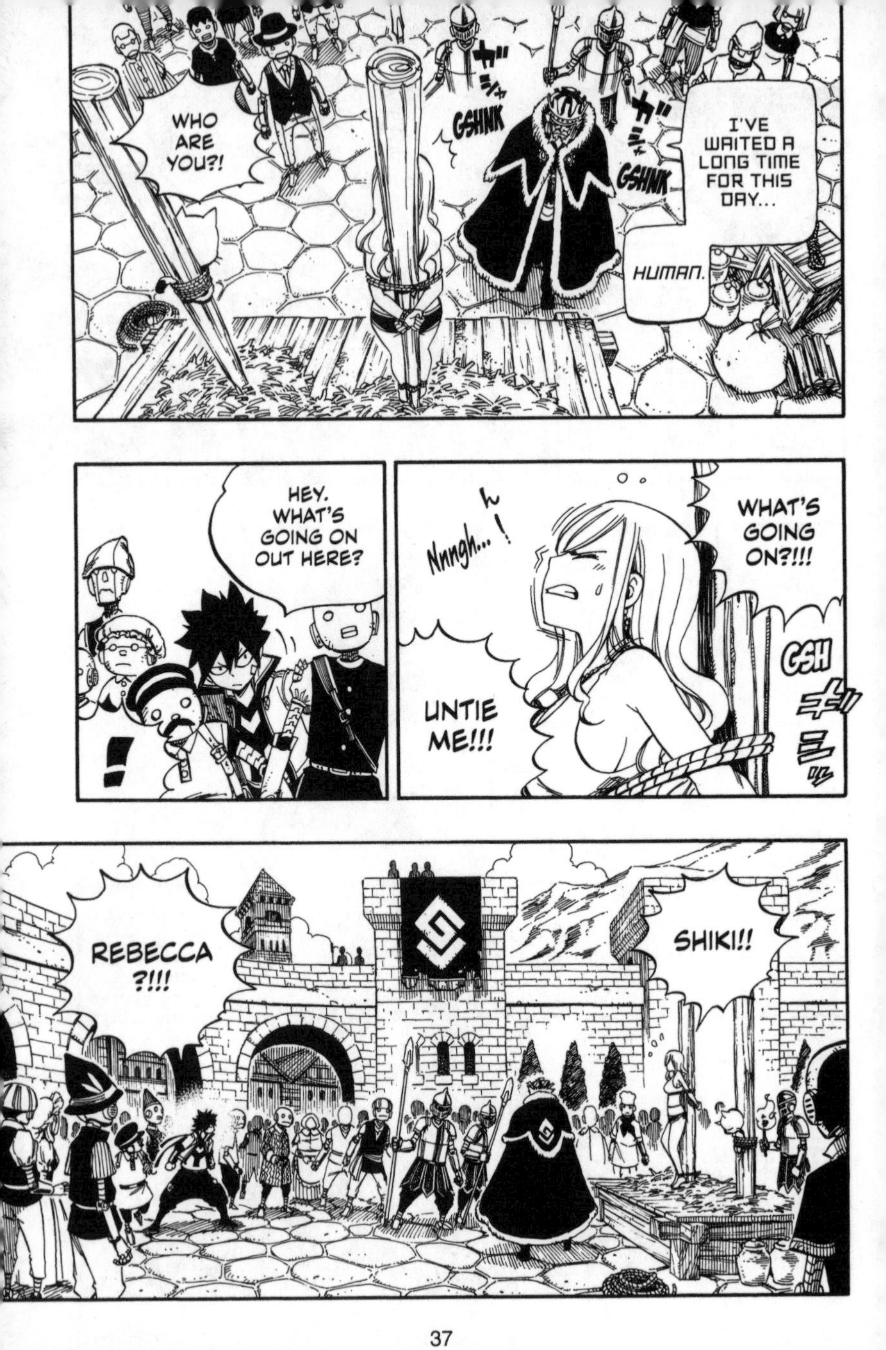
I'VE WAITED A LONG TIME FOR THIS DAY...
HUMAN.
GSHNK
GSHNK
WHO ARE YOU?!
WHAT'S GOING ON?!!!
GSH
Nnngh...!
UNTIE ME!!!
HEY. WHAT'S GOING ON OUT HERE?
SHIKI!!
REBECCA ?!!!

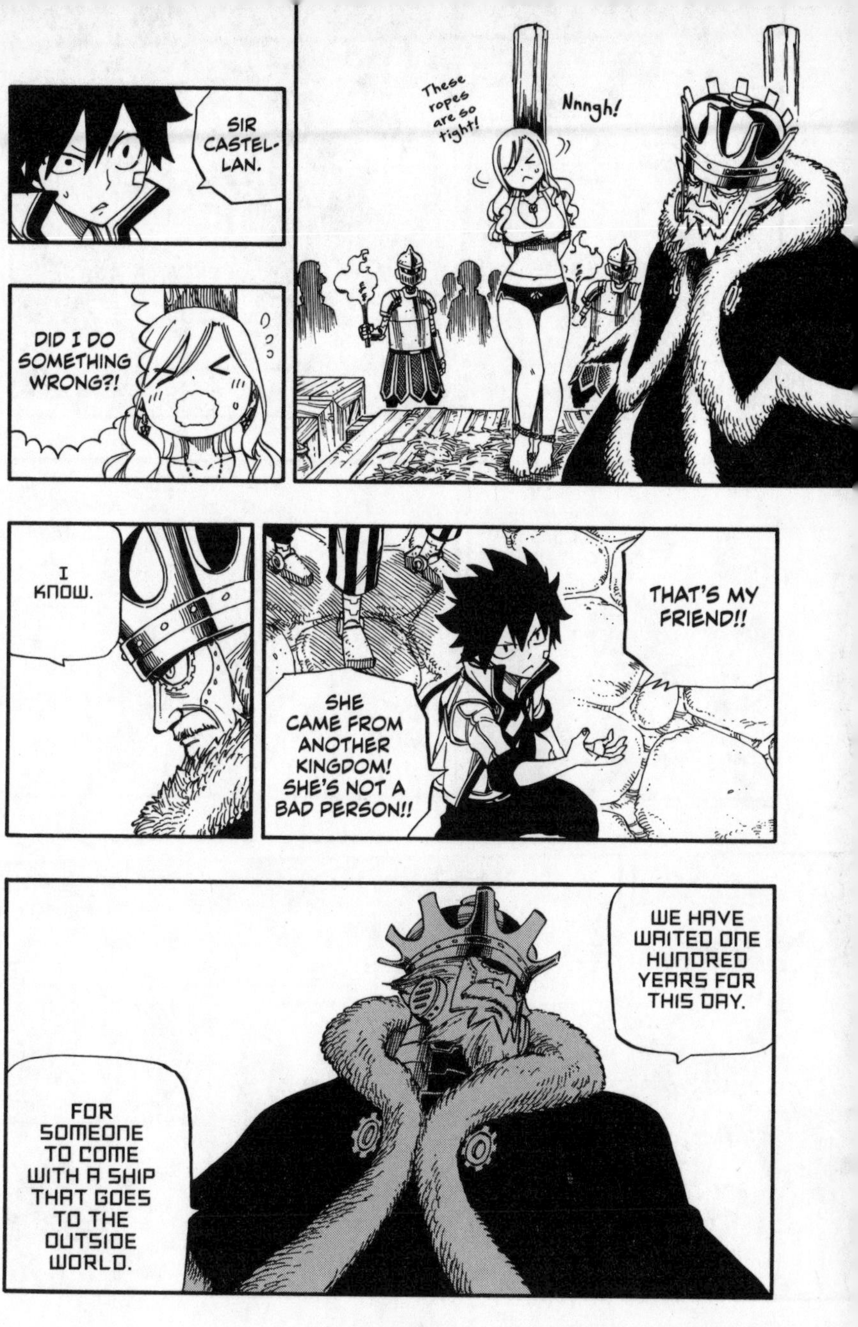
Nnngh!
These ropes are so tight!
SIR CASTEL-LAN.
DID I DO SOMETHING WRONG?!
THAT'S MY FRIEND!!
SHE CAME FROM ANOTHER KINGDOM! SHE'S NOT A BAD PERSON!!
I KNOW.
WE HAVE WAITED ONE HUNDRED YEARS FOR THIS DAY.
FOR SOMEONE TO COME WITH A SHIP THAT GOES TO THE OUTSIDE WORLD.

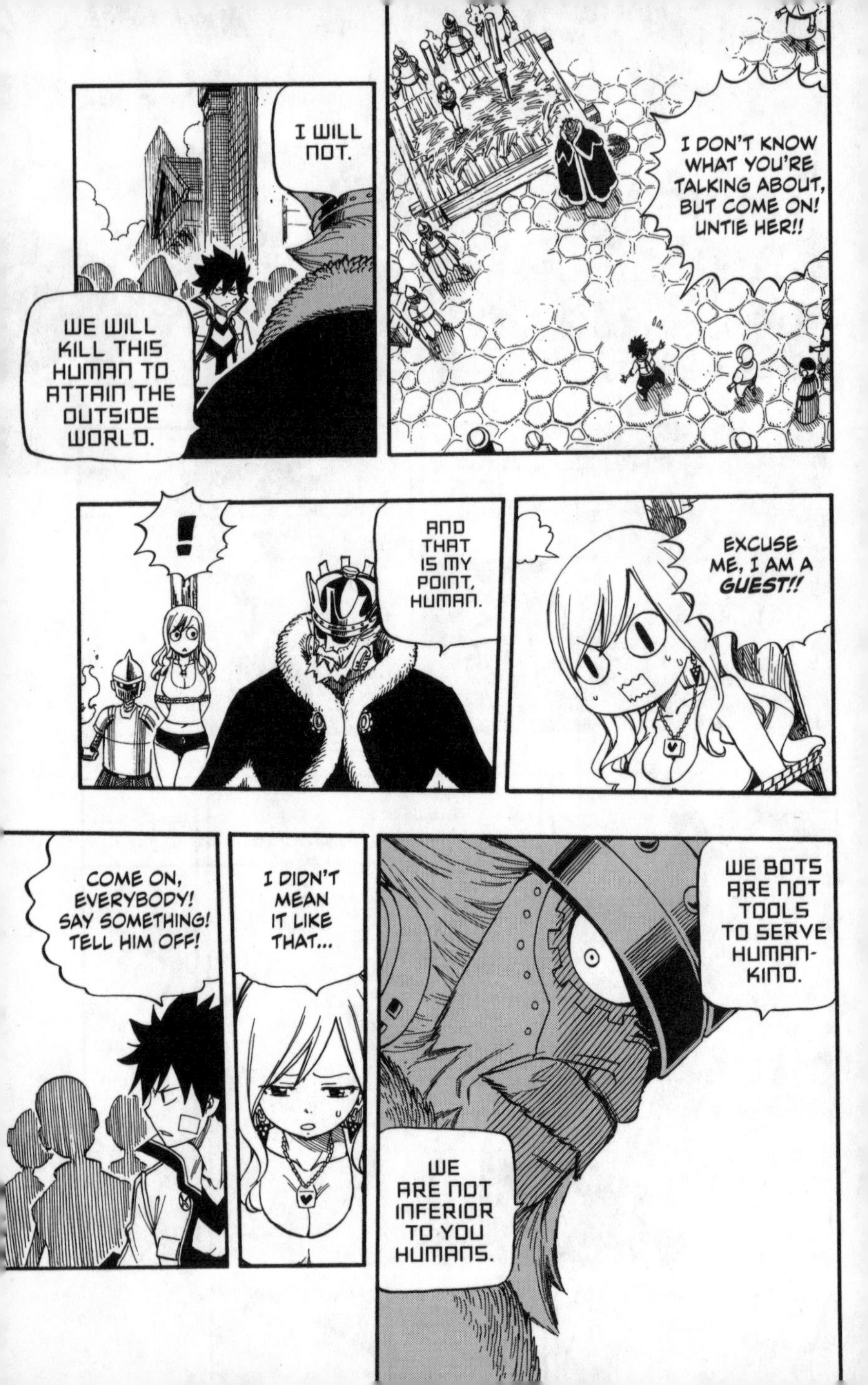
I DON'T KNOW WHAT YOU'RE TALKING ABOUT, BUT COME ON! UNTIE HER!!
I WILL NOT.
WE WILL KILL THIS HUMAN TO ATTAIN THE OUTSIDE WORLD.
EXCUSE ME, I AM A *GUEST!!*
AND THAT IS MY POINT, HUMAN.
!
WE BOTS ARE NOT TOOLS TO SERVE HUMAN-KIND.
WE ARE NOT INFERIOR TO YOU HUMANS.
I DIDN'T MEAN IT LIKE THAT...
COME ON, EVERYBODY! SAY SOMETHING! TELL HIM OFF!

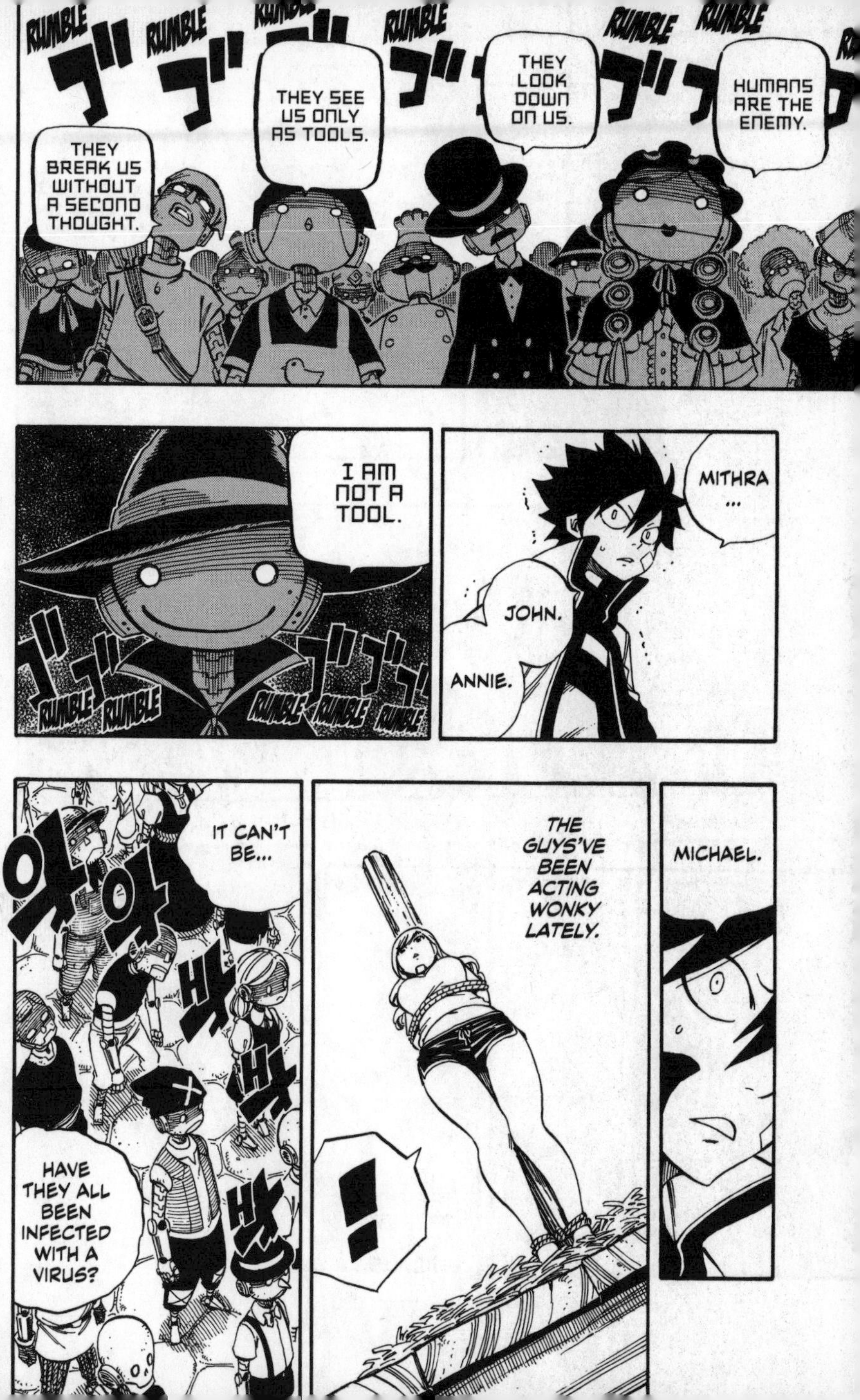
RUMBLE RUMBLE RUMBLE RUMBLE RUMBLE RUMBLE
HUMANS ARE THE ENEMY.
THEY LOOK DOWN ON US.
THEY SEE US ONLY AS TOOLS.
THEY BREAK US WITHOUT A SECOND THOUGHT.
MITHRA...
JOHN.
ANNIE.
I AM NOT A TOOL.
RUMBLE RUMBLE RUMBLE RUMBLE RUMBLE
MICHAEL.
THE GUYS'VE BEEN ACTING WONKY LATELY.
!
IT CAN'T BE...
HAVE THEY ALL BEEN INFECTED WITH A VIRUS?

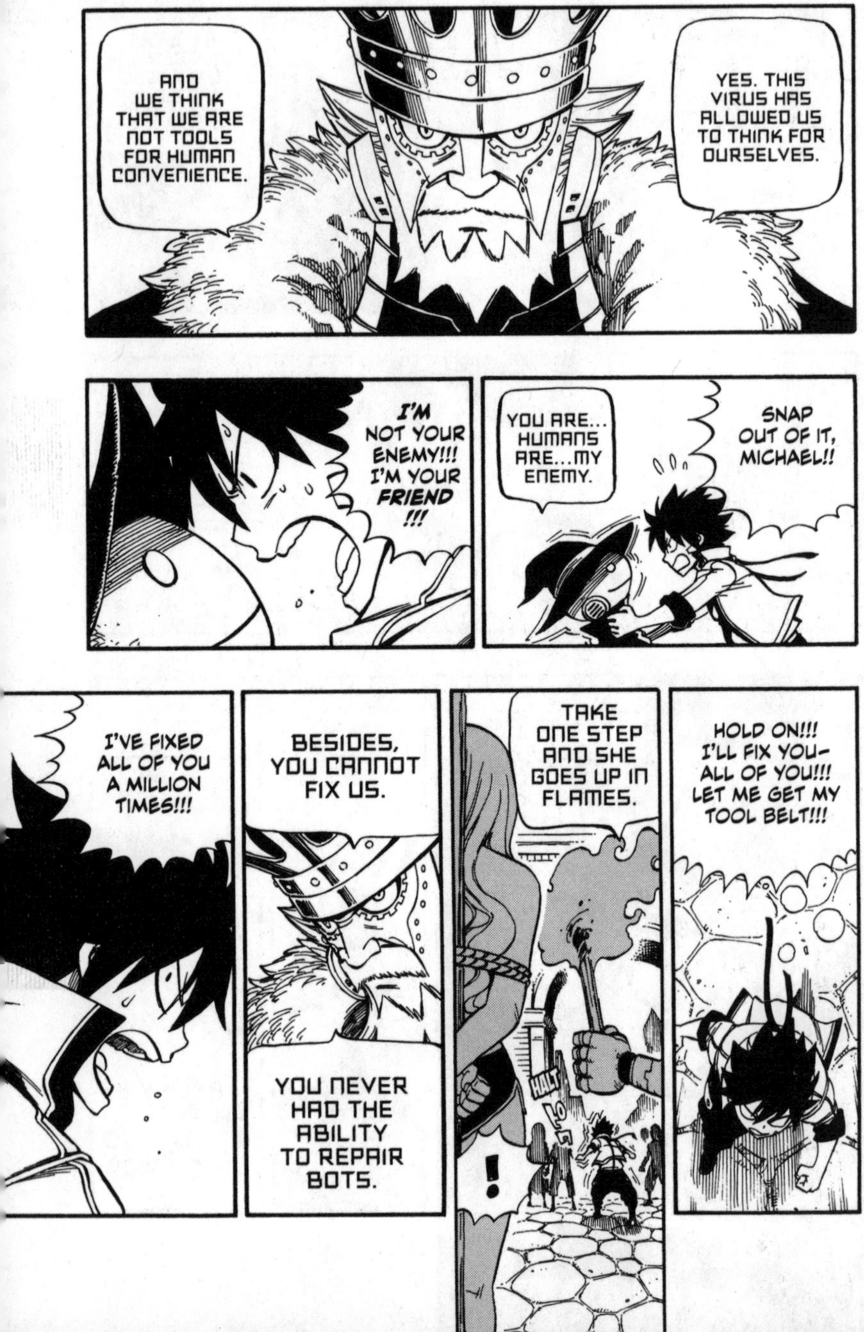
YES. THIS VIRUS HAS ALLOWED US TO THINK FOR OURSELVES.
AND WE THINK THAT WE ARE NOT TOOLS FOR HUMAN CONVENIENCE.
SNAP OUT OF IT, MICHAEL!!
YOU ARE... HUMANS ARE...MY ENEMY.
I'M NOT YOUR ENEMY!!! I'M YOUR FRIEND!!!
HOLD ON!!! I'LL FIX YOU— ALL OF YOU!!! LET ME GET MY TOOL BELT!!!
TAKE ONE STEP AND SHE GOES UP IN FLAMES.
BESIDES, YOU CANNOT FIX US.
YOU NEVER HAD THE ABILITY TO REPAIR BOTS.
I'VE FIXED ALL OF YOU A MILLION TIMES!!!

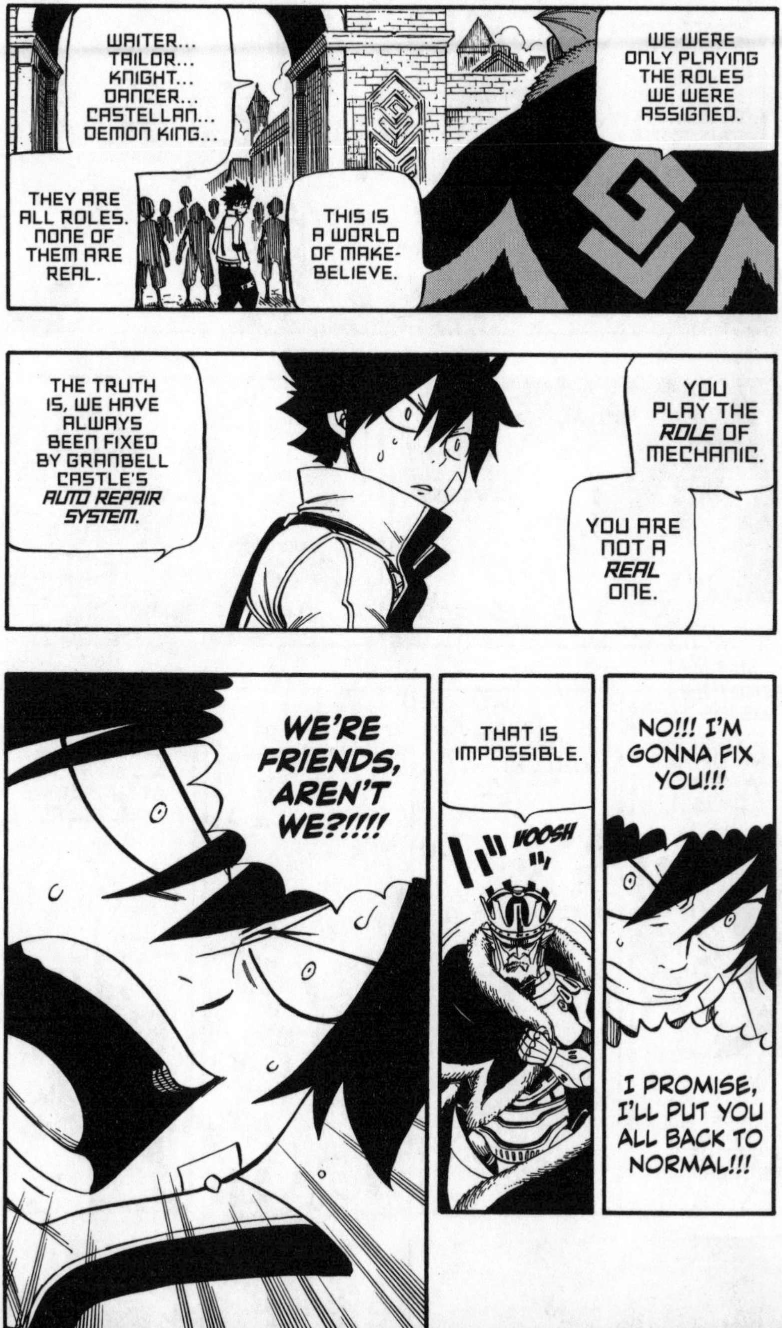
WE WERE ONLY PLAYING THE ROLES WE WERE ASSIGNED.
WAITER... TAILOR... KNIGHT... DANCER... CASTELLAN... DEMON KING...
THIS IS A WORLD OF MAKE-BELIEVE.
THEY ARE ALL ROLES. NONE OF THEM ARE REAL.
YOU PLAY THE *ROLE* OF MECHANIC.
YOU ARE NOT A *REAL* ONE.
THE TRUTH IS, WE HAVE ALWAYS BEEN FIXED BY GRANBELL CASTLE'S *AUTO REPAIR SYSTEM.*
NO!!! I'M GONNA FIX YOU!!!
I PROMISE, I'LL PUT YOU ALL BACK TO NORMAL!!!
THAT IS IMPOSSIBLE.
VOOSH
WE'RE FRIENDS, AREN'T WE?!!!!

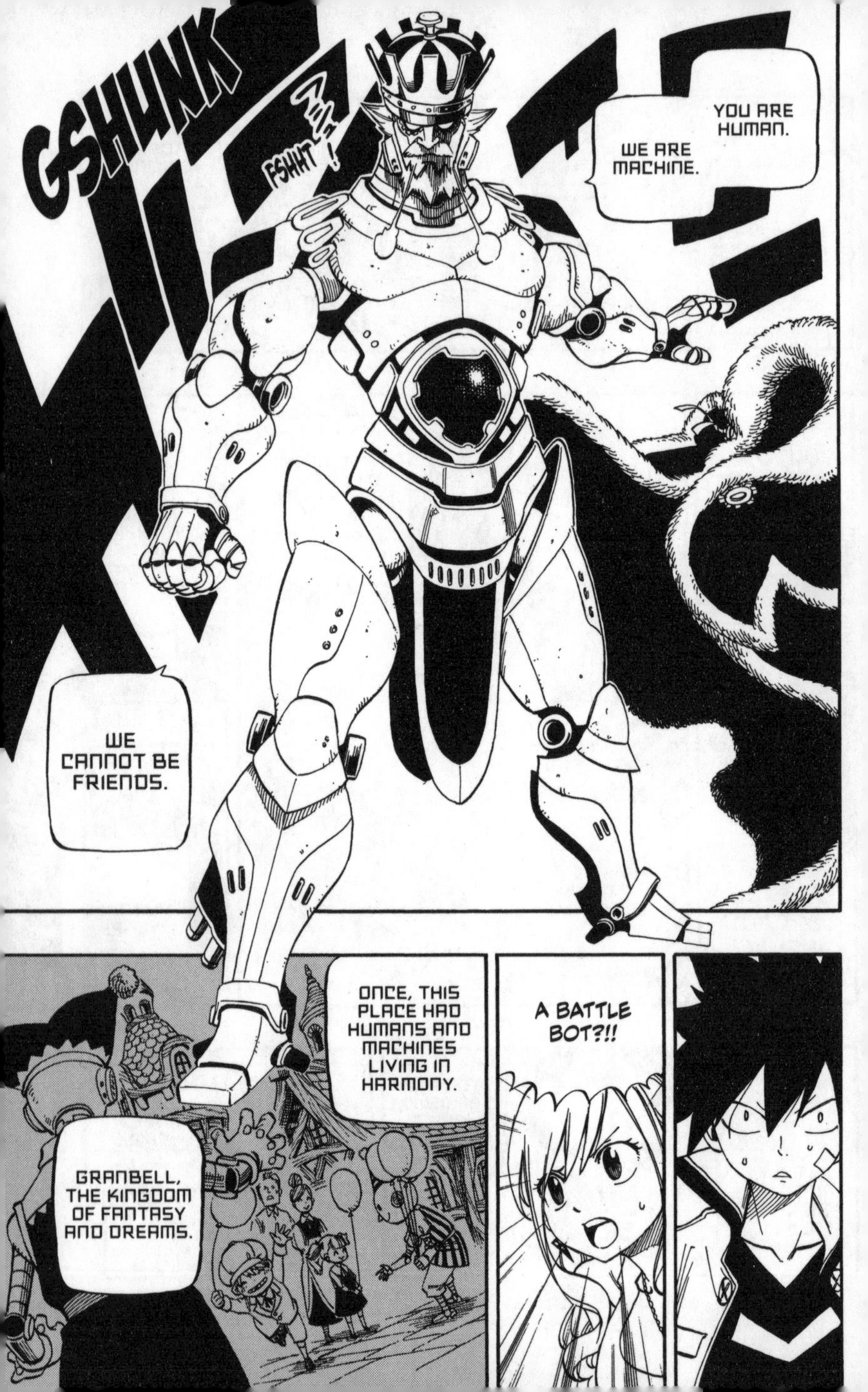
YOU ARE HUMAN.
WE ARE MACHINE.
FSHHT!
GSHUNK
WE CANNOT BE FRIENDS.
A BATTLE BOT?!!
ONCE, THIS PLACE HAD HUMANS AND MACHINES LIVING IN HARMONY.
GRANBELL, THE KINGDOM OF FANTASY AND DREAMS.

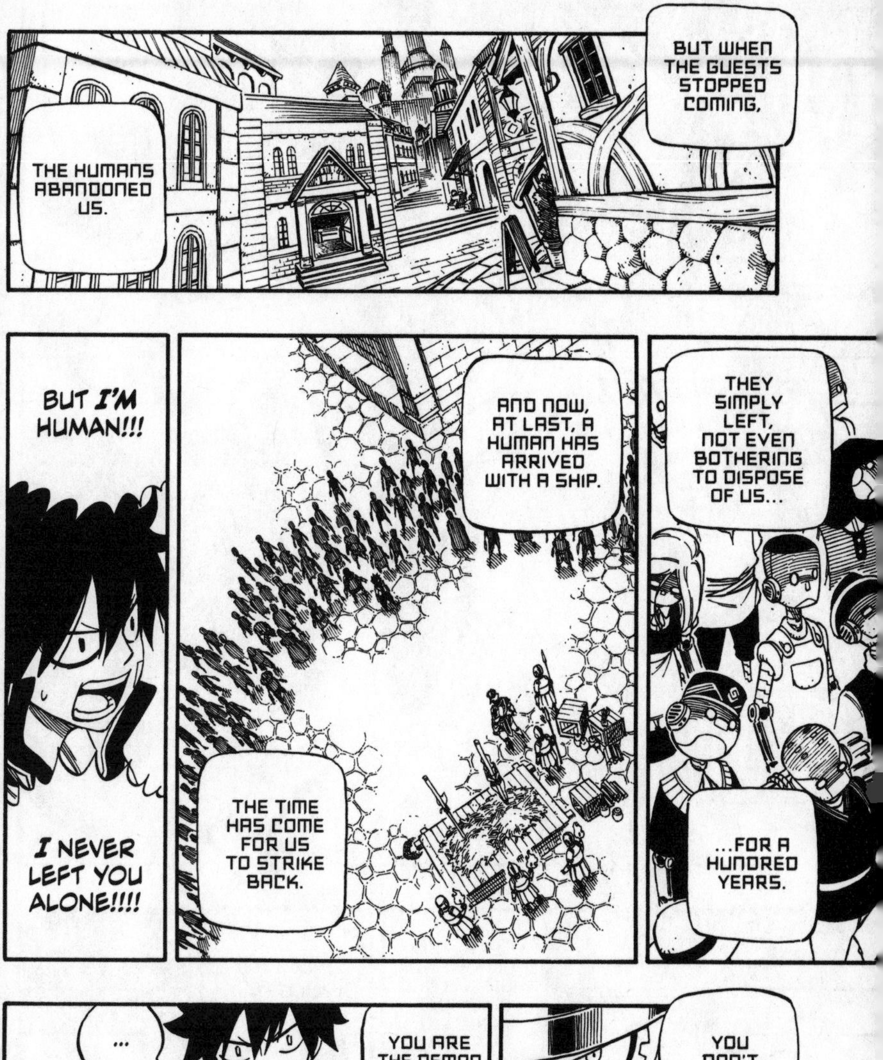
BUT WHEN THE GUESTS STOPPED COMING,
THE HUMANS ABANDONED US.
THEY SIMPLY LEFT, NOT EVEN BOTHERING TO DISPOSE OF US...
...FOR A HUNDRED YEARS.
AND NOW, AT LAST, A HUMAN HAS ARRIVED WITH A SHIP.
THE TIME HAS COME FOR US TO STRIKE BACK.
BUT I'M HUMAN!!!
I NEVER LEFT YOU ALONE!!!!
YOU DON'T HAVE A SHIP.
YOU ARE THE DEMON KING'S WHELP.
...
WE SIMPLY DIDN'T BOTHER TO KILL YOU.

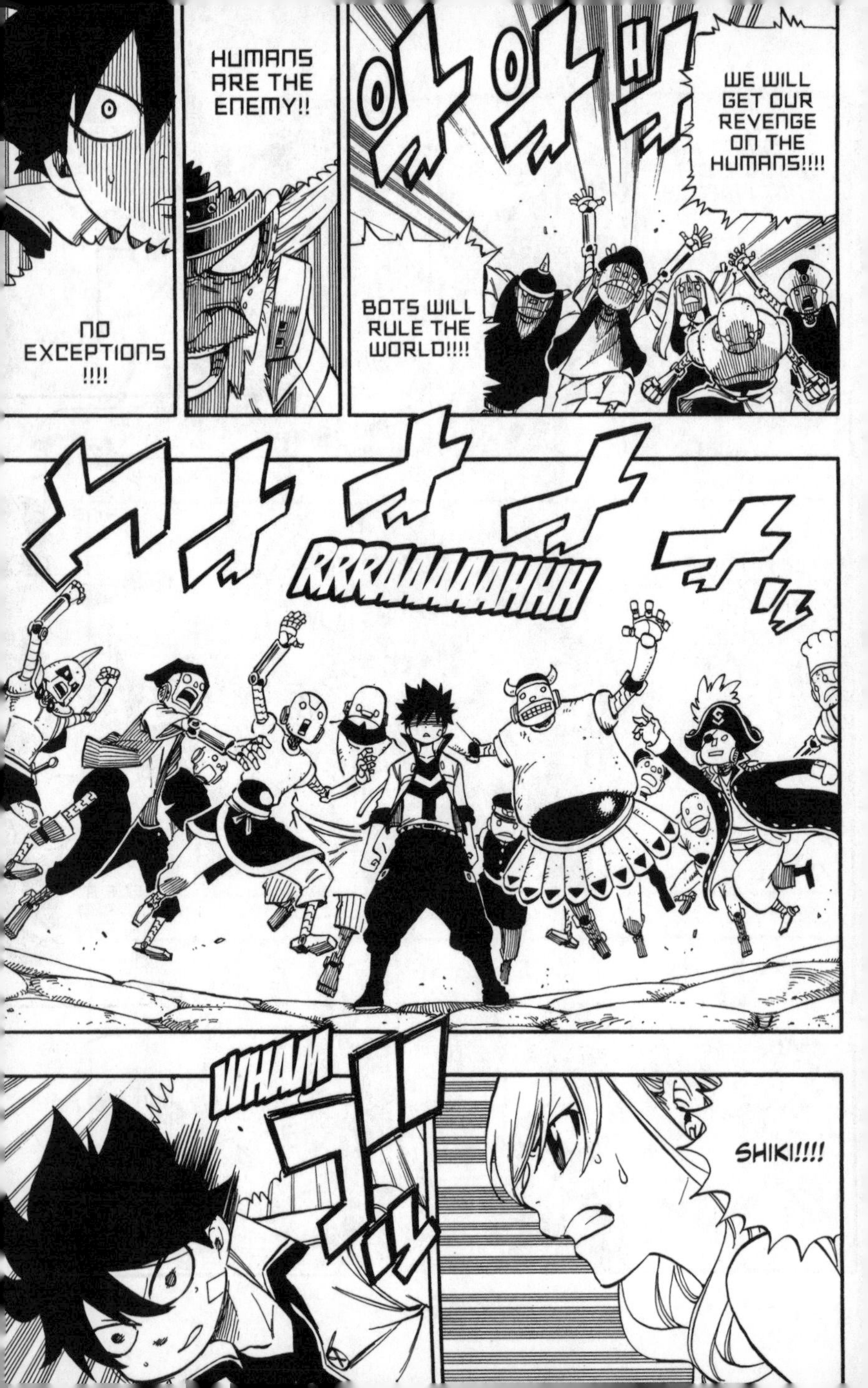
WE WILL GET OUR REVENGE ON THE HUMANS!!!!
BOTS WILL RULE THE WORLD!!!!
HUMANS ARE THE ENEMY!!
NO EXCEPTIONS !!!!
RRRAAAAAAHHH
SHIKI!!!!
WHAM

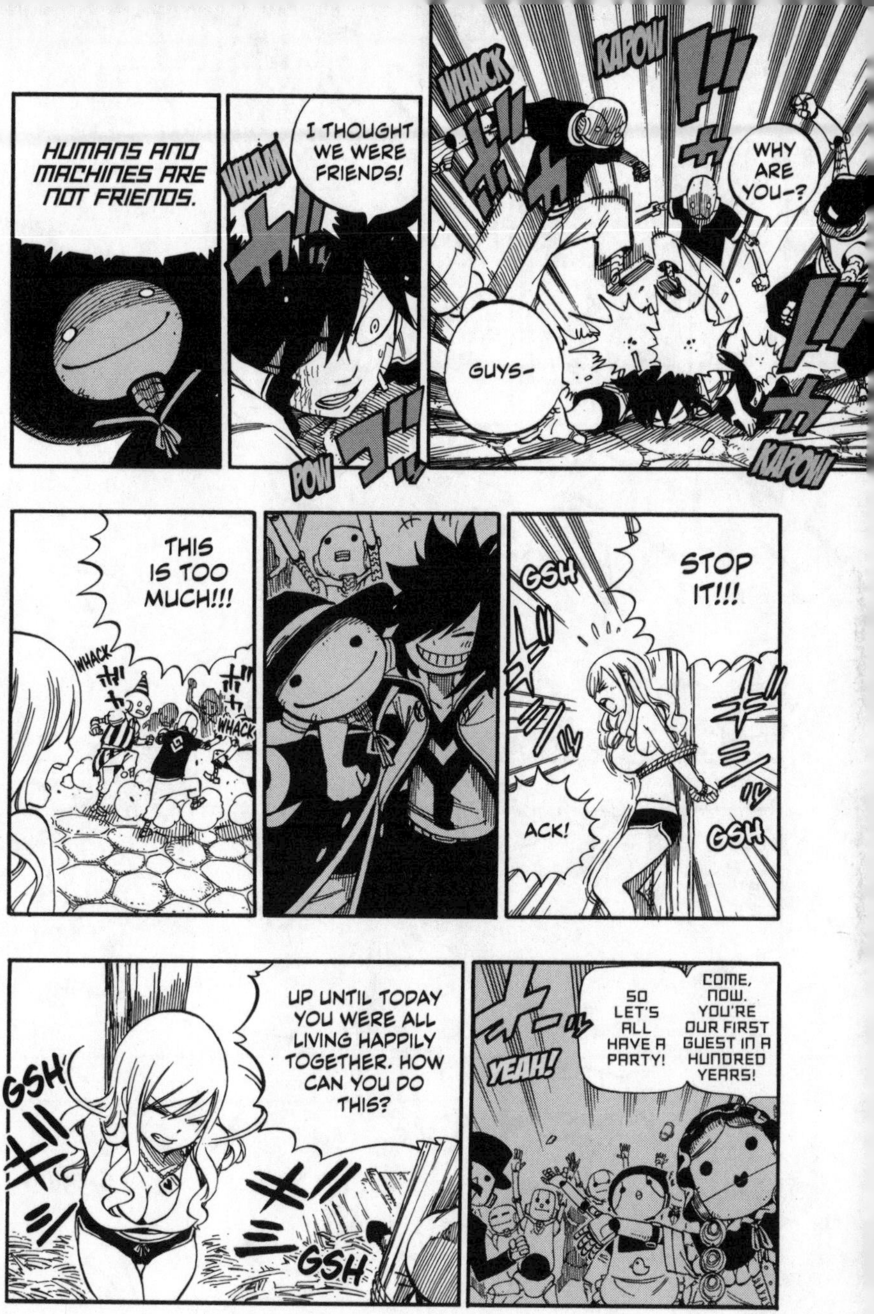
KAPOW
WHACK
WHY ARE YOU-?
GUYS-
KAPOW
WHAM
I THOUGHT WE WERE FRIENDS!
POW
HUMANS AND MACHINES ARE NOT FRIENDS.
GSH
STOP IT!!!
ACK!
GSH
THIS IS TOO MUCH!!!
WHACK
WHACK
COME, NOW. YOU'RE OUR FIRST GUEST IN A HUNDRED YEARS!
SO LET'S ALL HAVE A PARTY!
YEAH!
UP UNTIL TODAY YOU WERE ALL LIVING HAPPILY TOGETHER. HOW CAN YOU DO THIS?
GSH
GSH

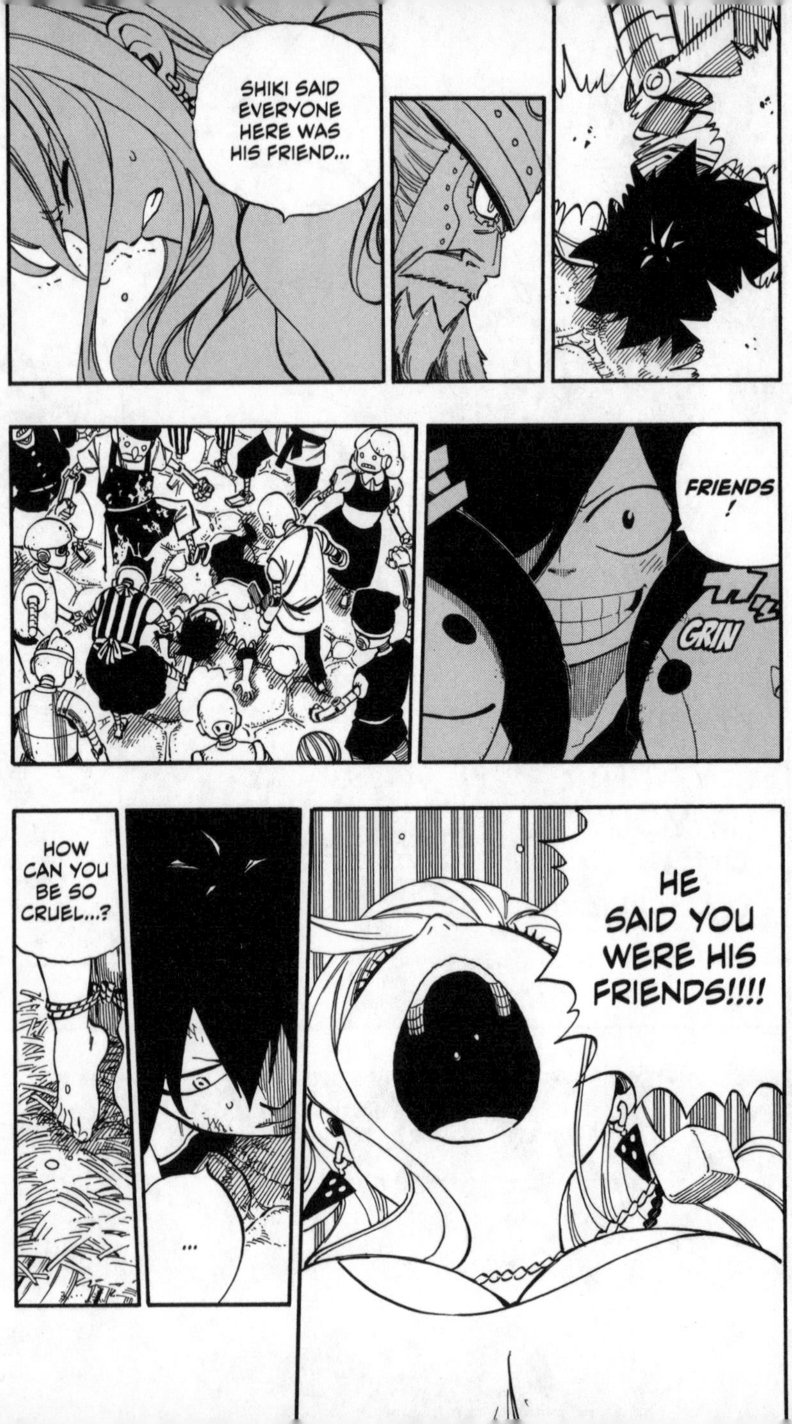
SHIKI SAID EVERYONE HERE WAS HIS FRIEND...
FRIENDS!
GRIN
HE SAID YOU WERE HIS FRIENDS!!!!
...
HOW CAN YOU BE SO CRUEL...?

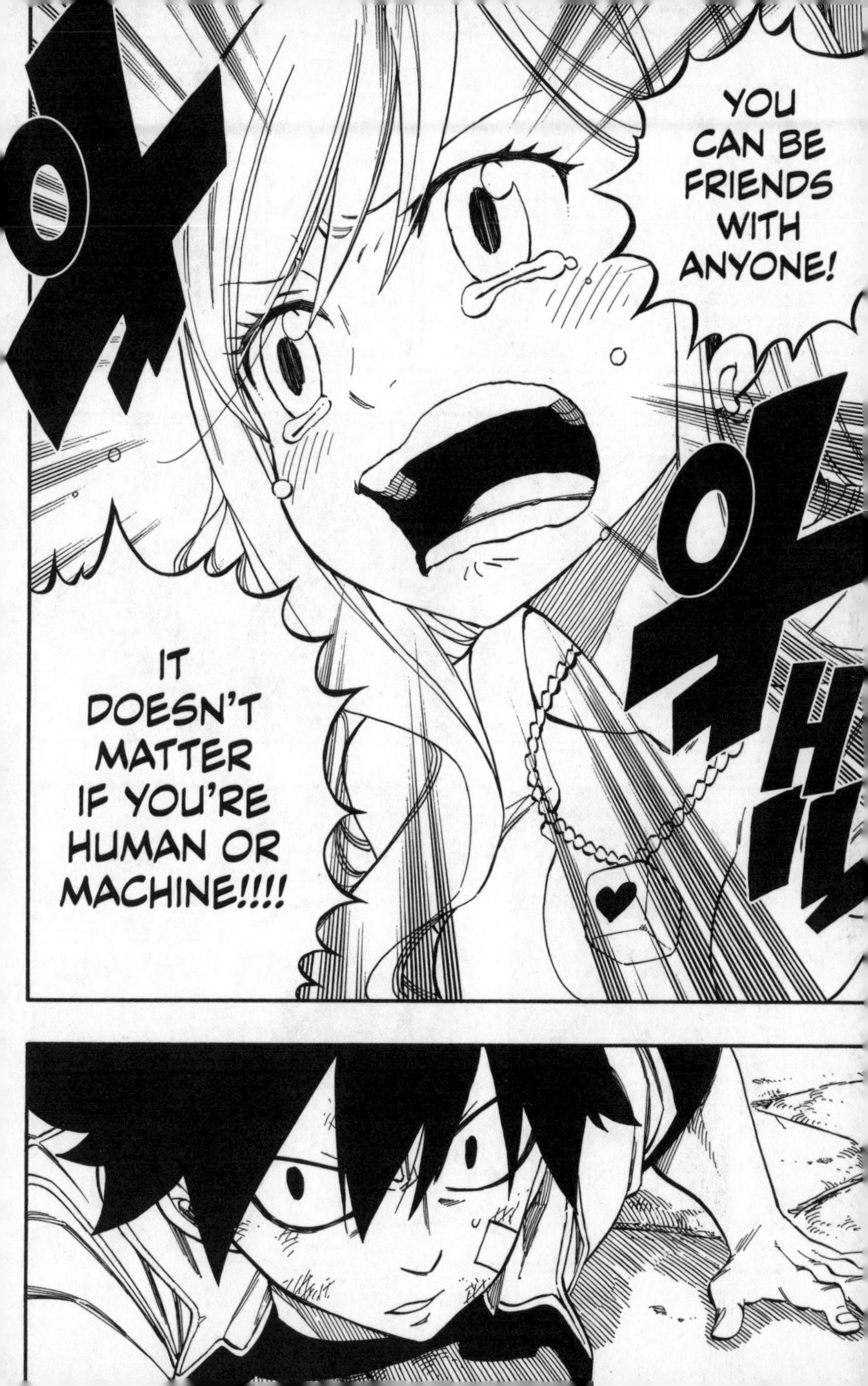
YOU CAN BE FRIENDS WITH ANYONE!
IT DOESN'T MATTER IF YOU'RE HUMAN OR MACHINE!!!!

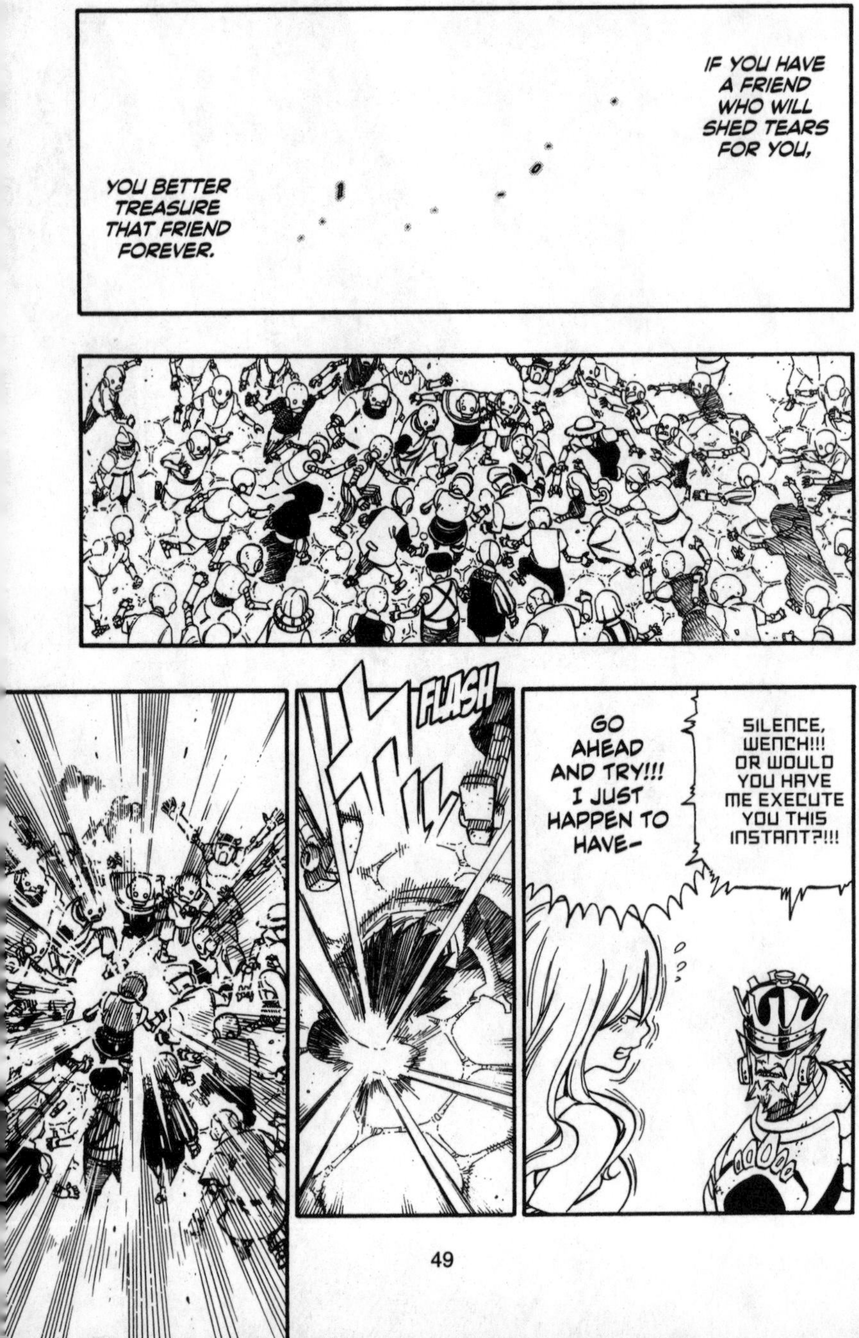
IF YOU HAVE A FRIEND WHO WILL SHED TEARS FOR YOU,
YOU BETTER TREASURE THAT FRIEND FOREVER.
SILENCE, WENCH!!! OR WOULD YOU HAVE ME EXECUTE YOU THIS INSTANT?!!!
GO AHEAD AND TRY!!! I JUST HAPPEN TO HAVE-
FLASH

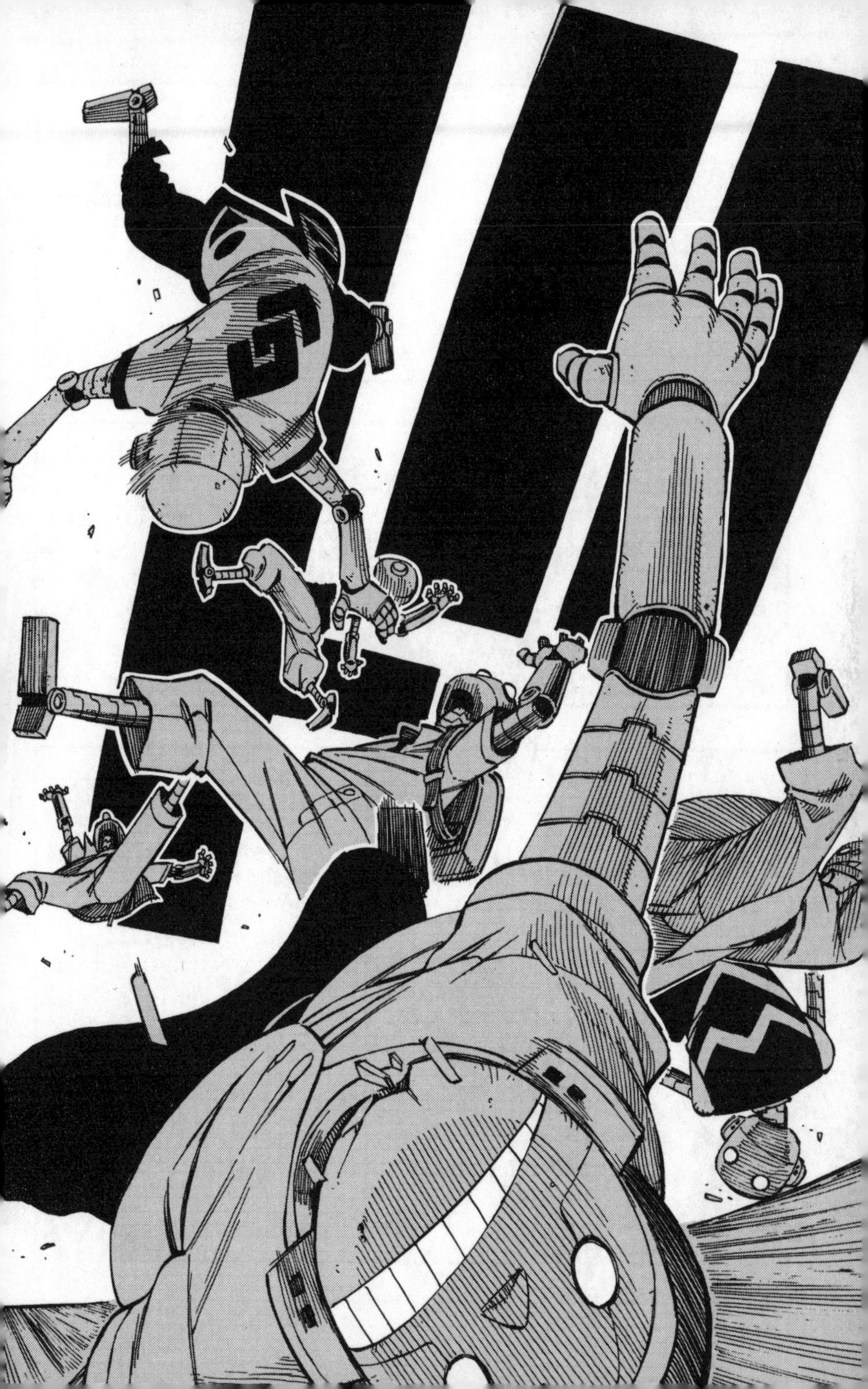

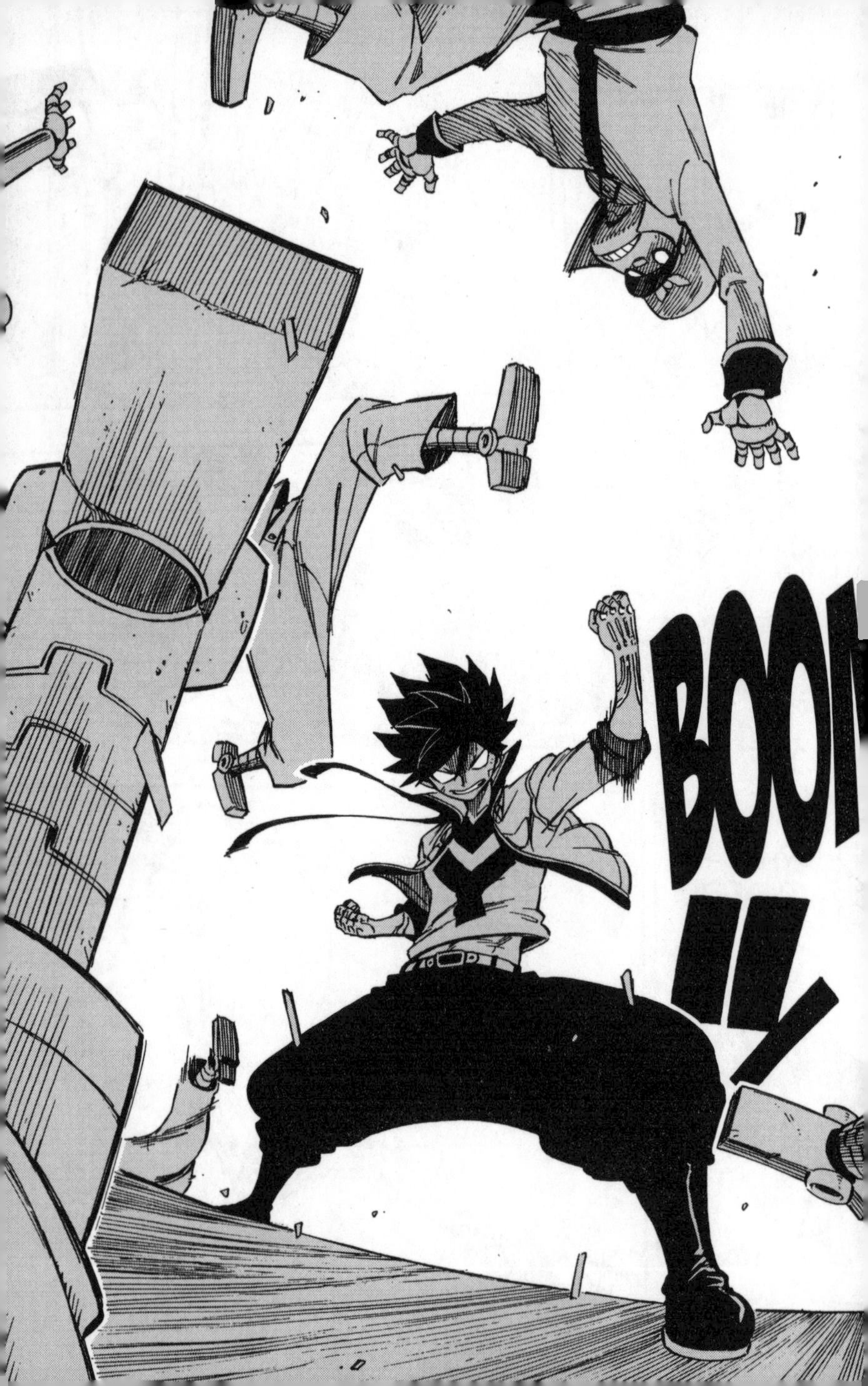
BOOOM!!

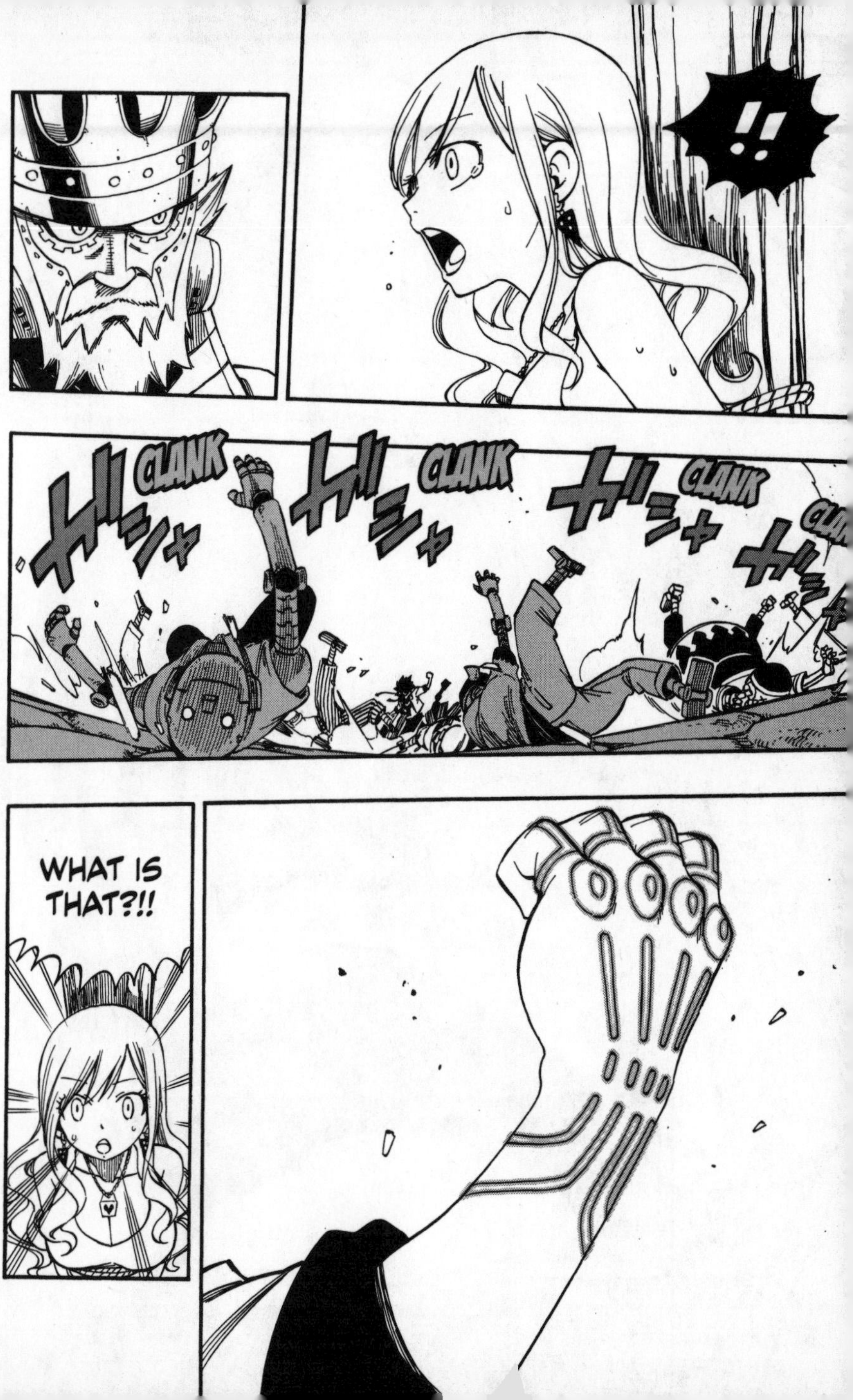
!!
CLANK
CLANK
CLANK
WHAT IS THAT?!!

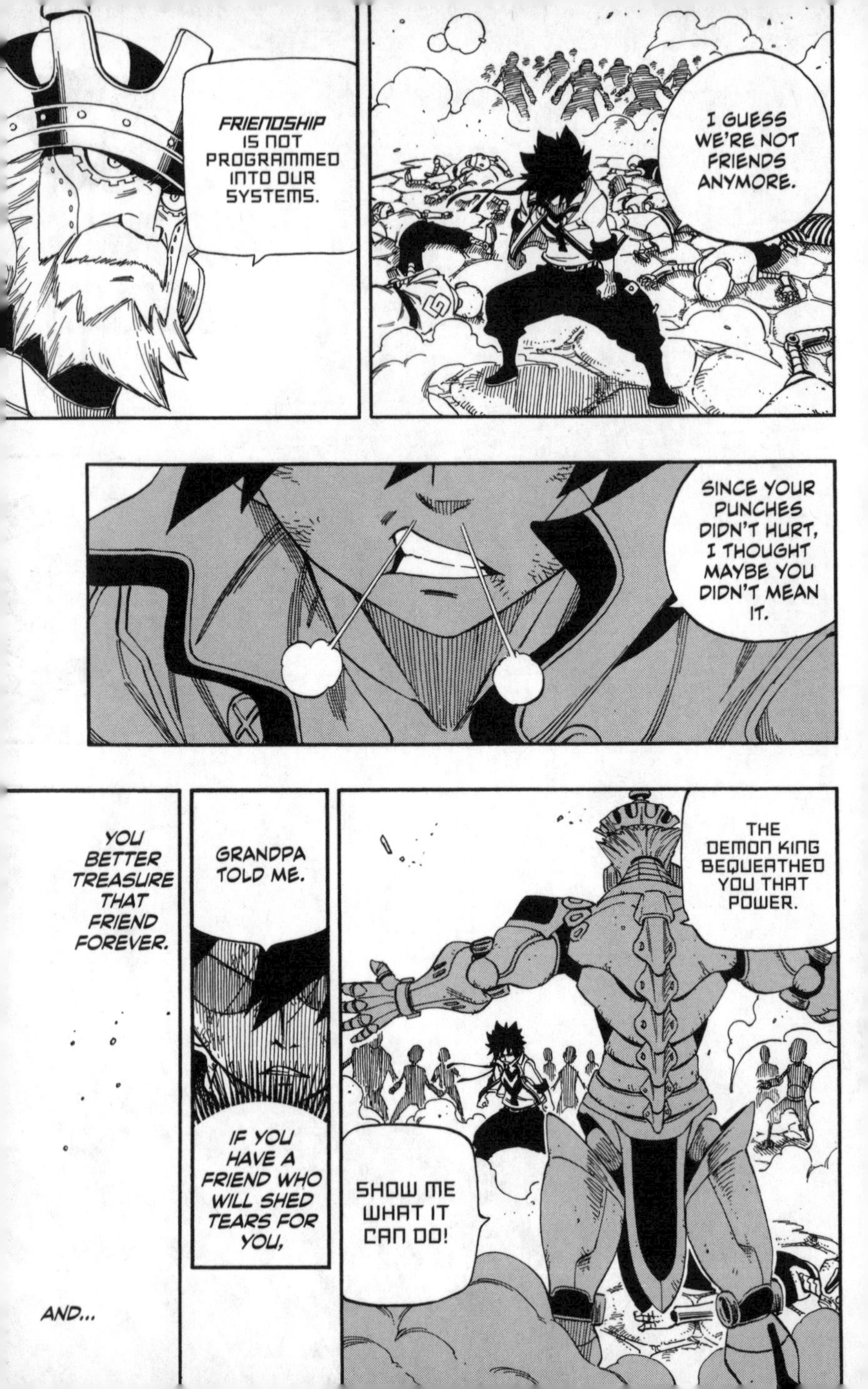
I GUESS WE'RE NOT FRIENDS ANYMORE.
FRIENDSHIP IS NOT PROGRAMMED INTO OUR SYSTEMS.
SINCE YOUR PUNCHES DIDN'T HURT, I THOUGHT MAYBE YOU DIDN'T MEAN IT.
THE DEMON KING BEQUEATHED YOU THAT POWER.
SHOW ME WHAT IT CAN DO!
GRANDPA TOLD ME.
IF YOU HAVE A FRIEND WHO WILL SHED TEARS FOR YOU,
YOU BETTER TREASURE THAT FRIEND FOREVER.
AND...

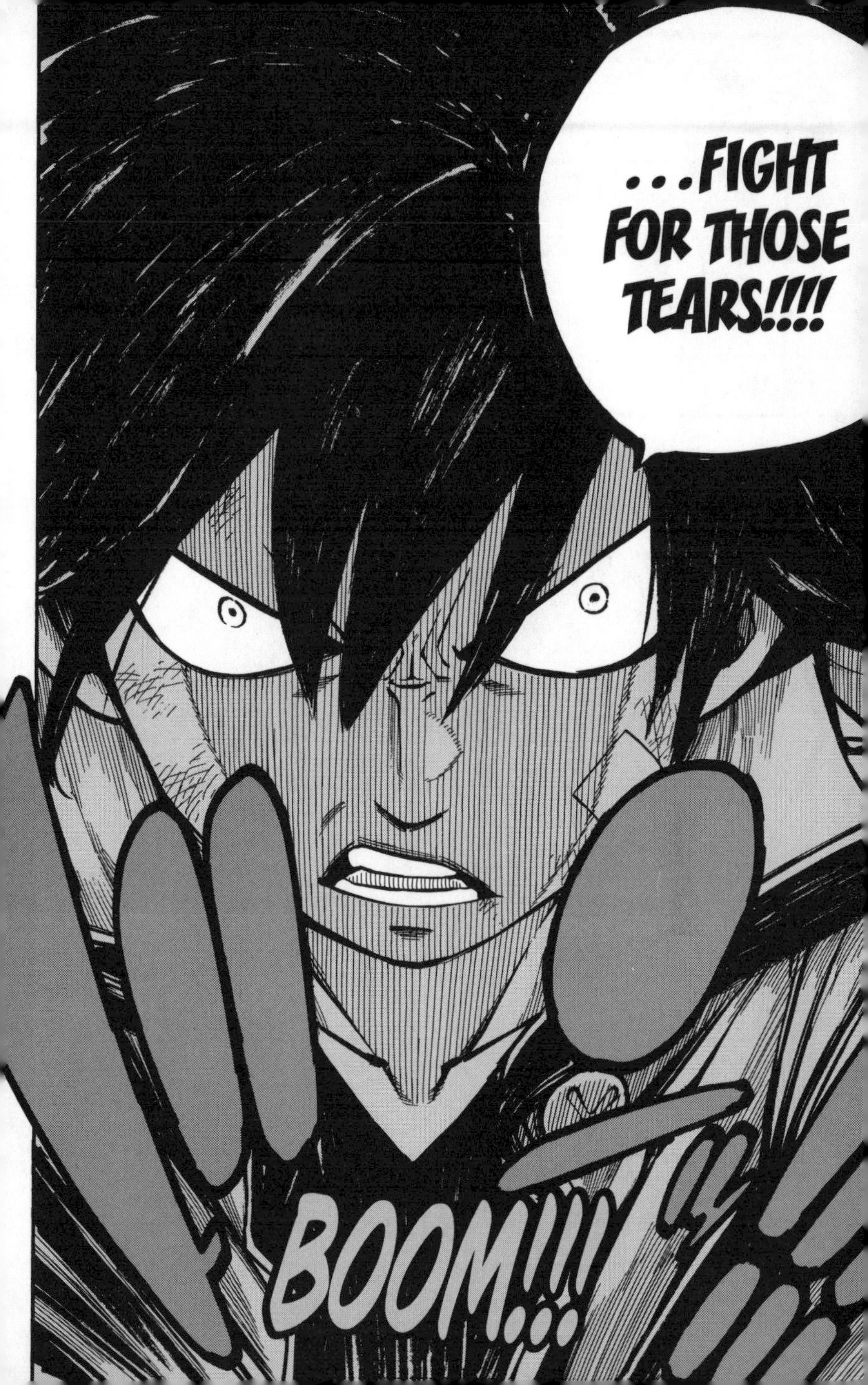
...FIGHT FOR THOSE TEARS!!!!
BOOM!!!

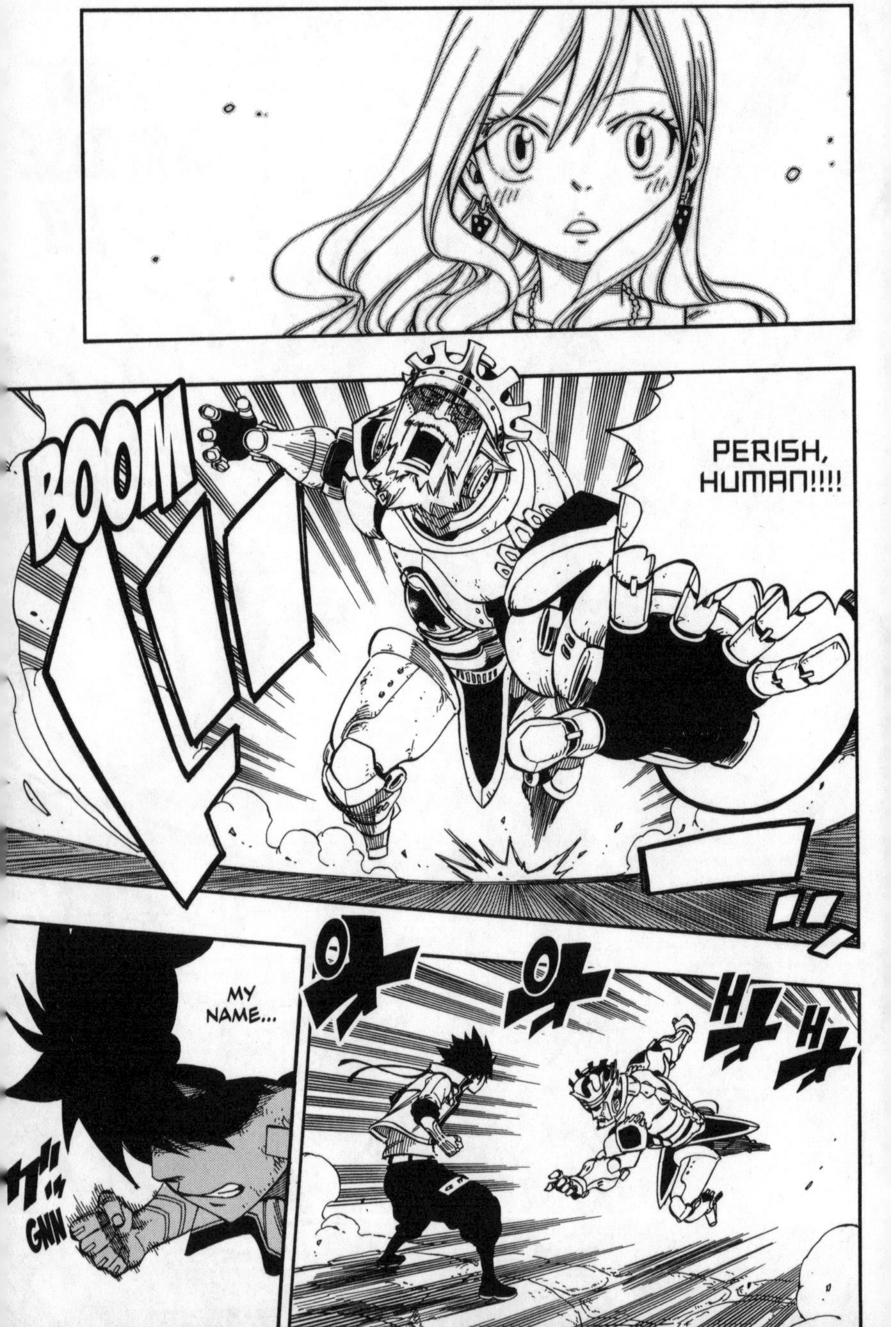
PERISH, HUMAN!!!!
BOOM
MY NAME...
GNN

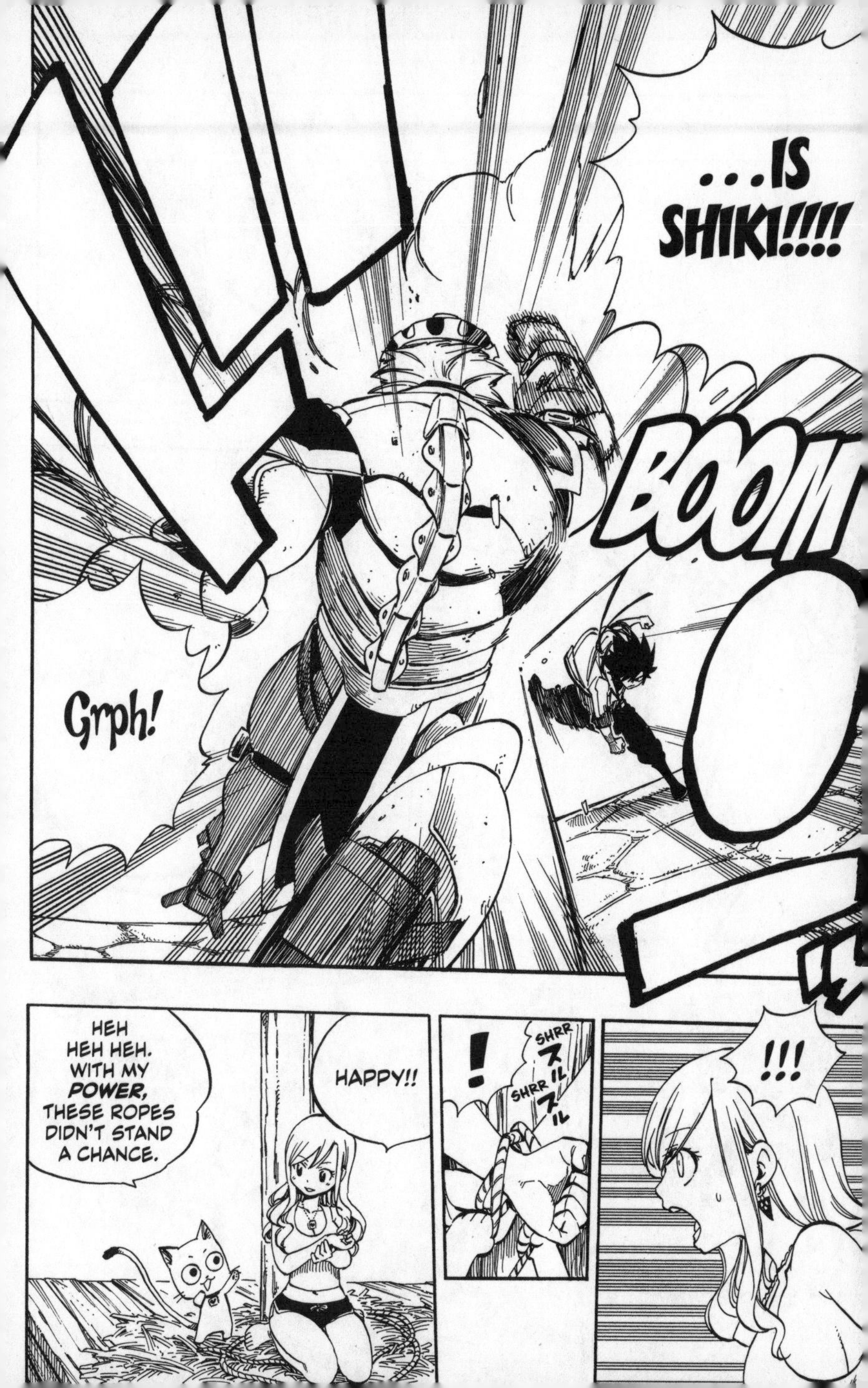
...IS SHIKI!!!!
BOOM
Grph!
!!!
SHRR
SHRR
!
HAPPY!!
HEH HEH HEH. WITH MY *POWER,* THESE ROPES DIDN'T STAND A CHANCE.

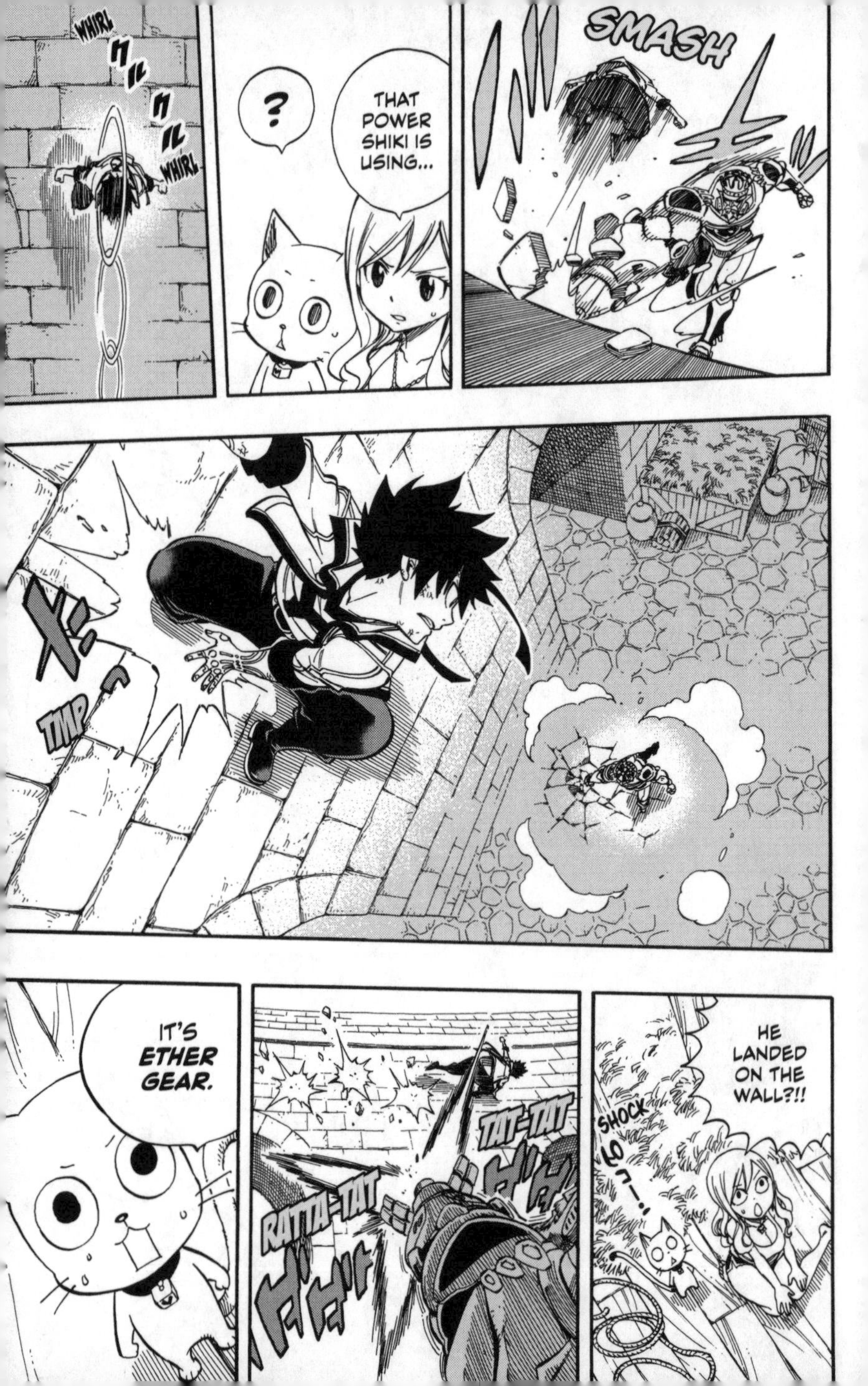
SMASH
THAT POWER SHIKI IS USING...
?
WHIRL
WHIRL
TMP
HE LANDED ON THE WALL?!!
SHOCK
TAT-TAT
RATTA-TAT
IT'S ETHER GEAR.

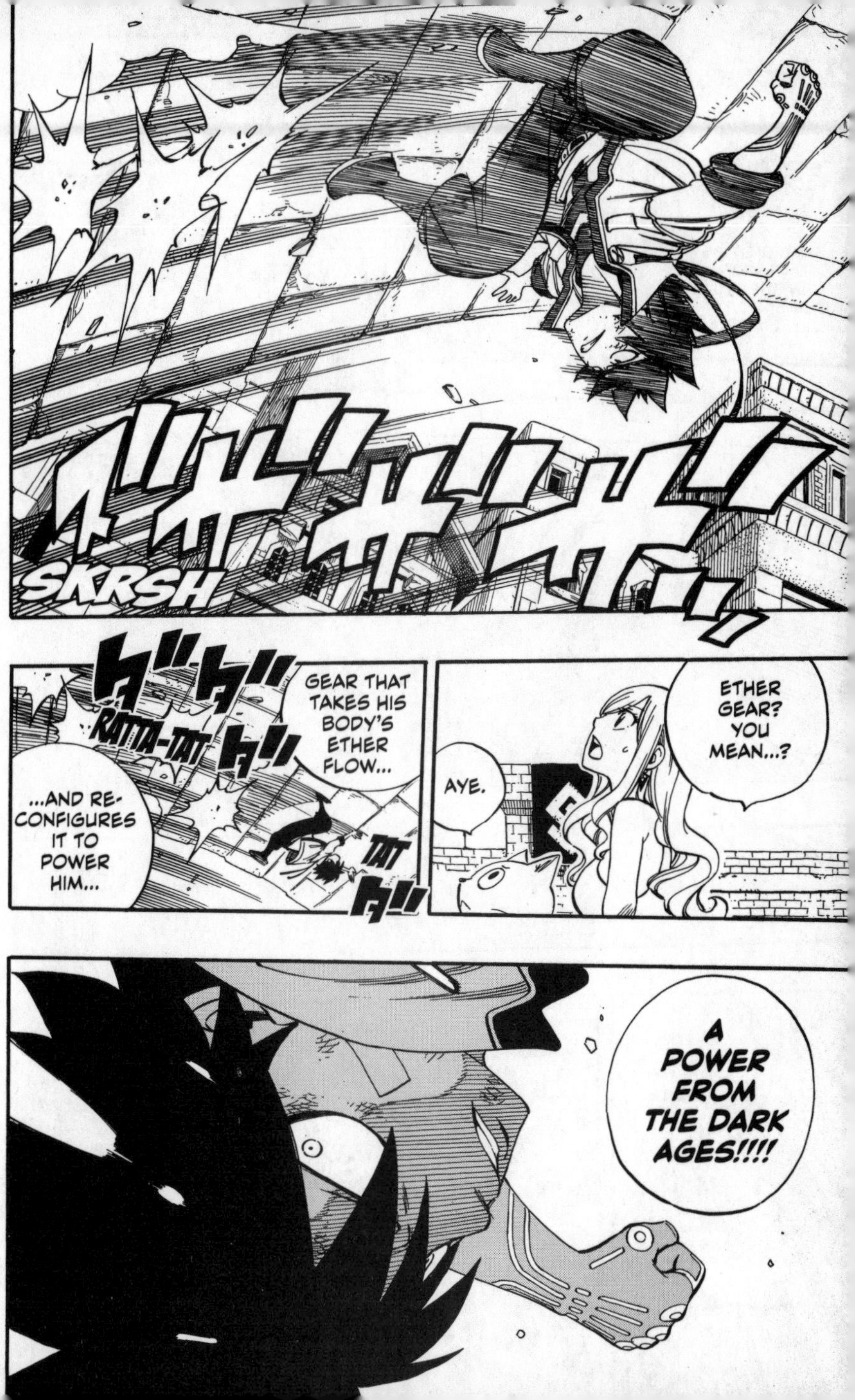
SKRSH
ETHER GEAR? YOU MEAN...?
AYE.
GEAR THAT TAKES HIS BODY'S ETHER FLOW...
RATTA-TAT
TAT
...AND RE-CONFIGURES IT TO POWER HIM...
A POWER FROM THE DARK AGES!!!!

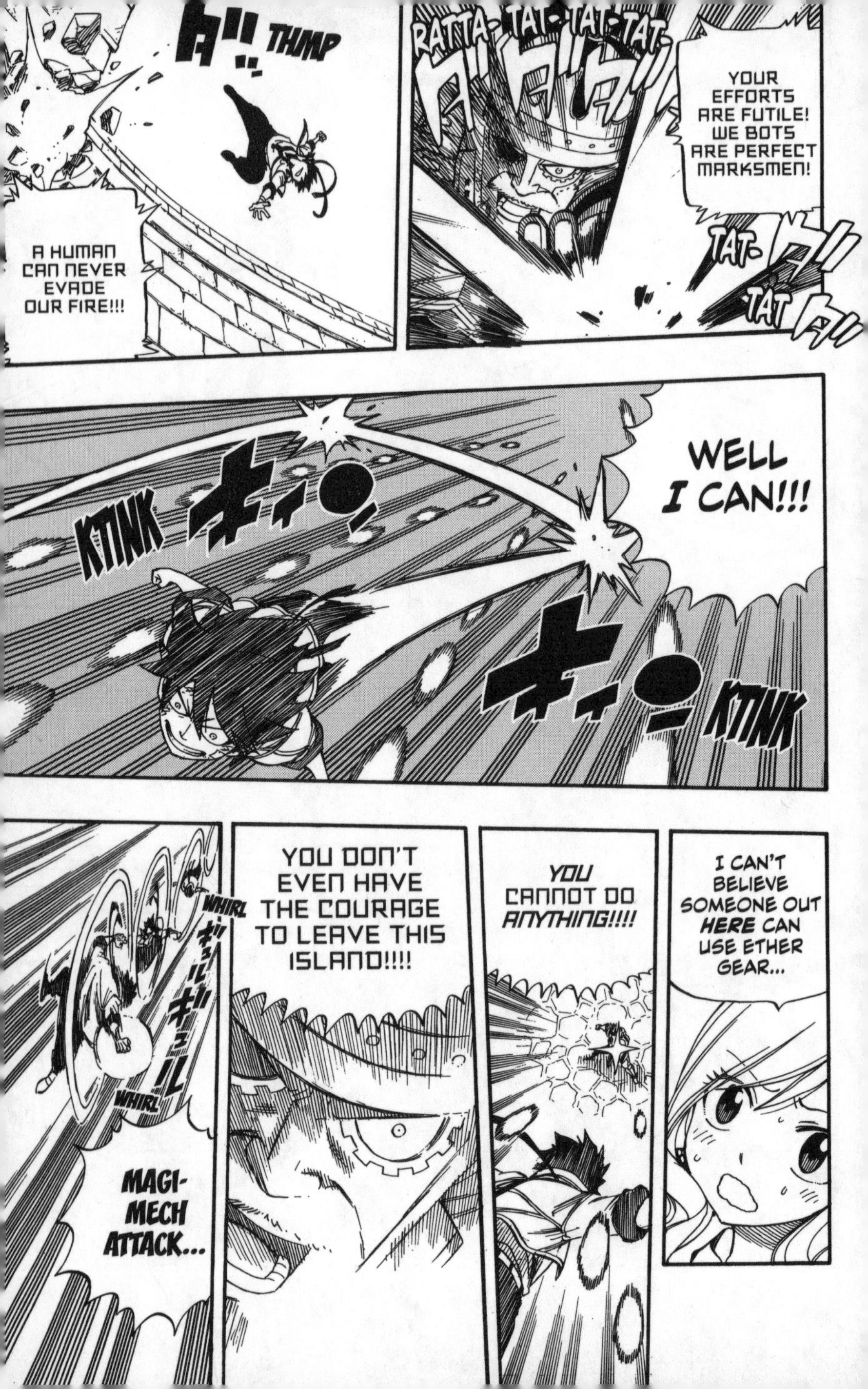
RATTA-TAT-TAT-TAT
YOUR EFFORTS ARE FUTILE! WE BOTS ARE PERFECT MARKSMEN!
TAT-
TAT
THMP
A HUMAN CAN NEVER EVADE OUR FIRE!!!
WELL I CAN!!!
KTINK
KTINK
I CAN'T BELIEVE SOMEONE OUT HERE CAN USE ETHER GEAR...
YOU CANNOT DO ANYTHING!!!!
YOU DON'T EVEN HAVE THE COURAGE TO LEAVE THIS ISLAND!!!!
WHIRL
WHIRL
MAGI-MECH ATTACK...

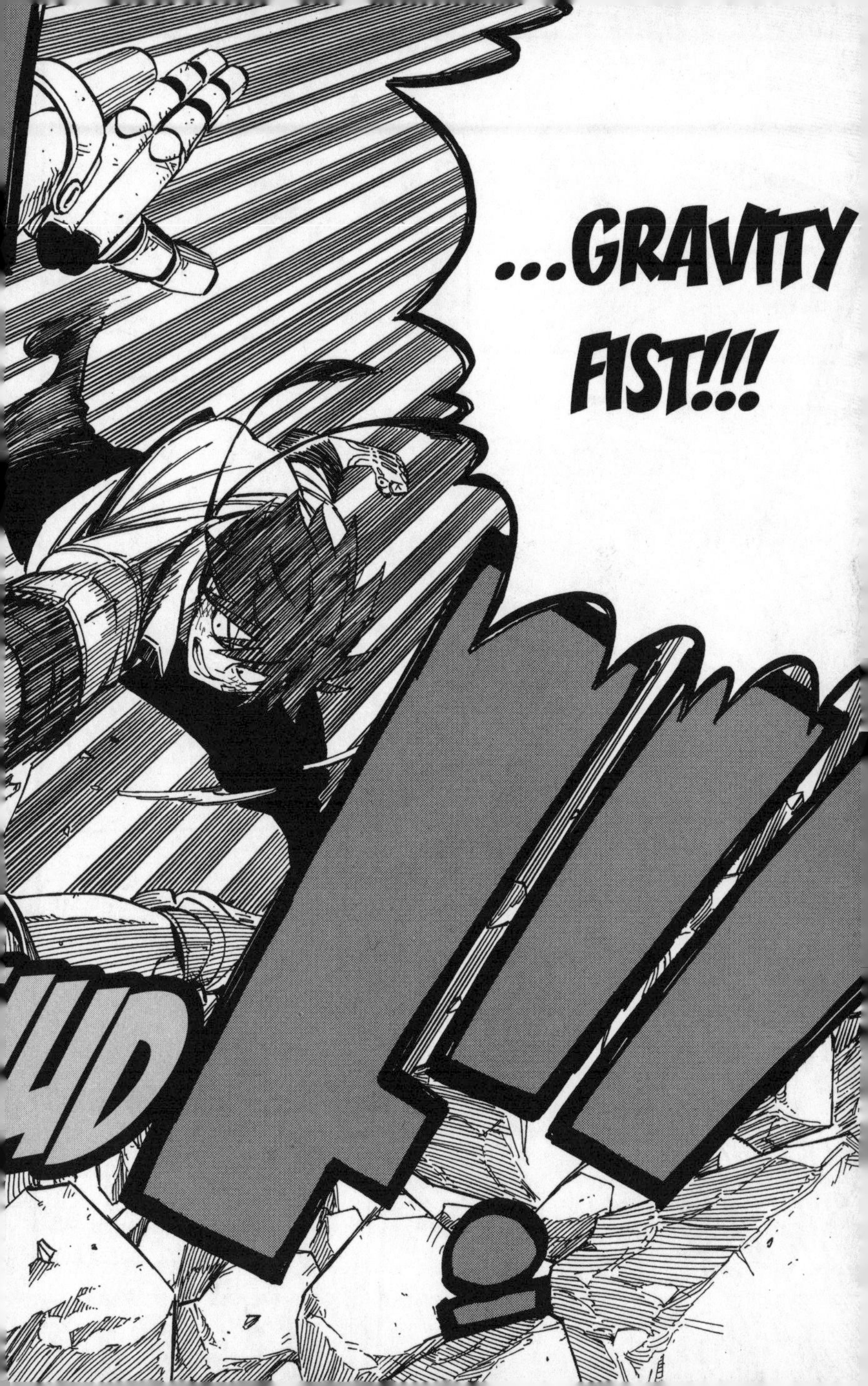
...GRAVITY FIST!!!

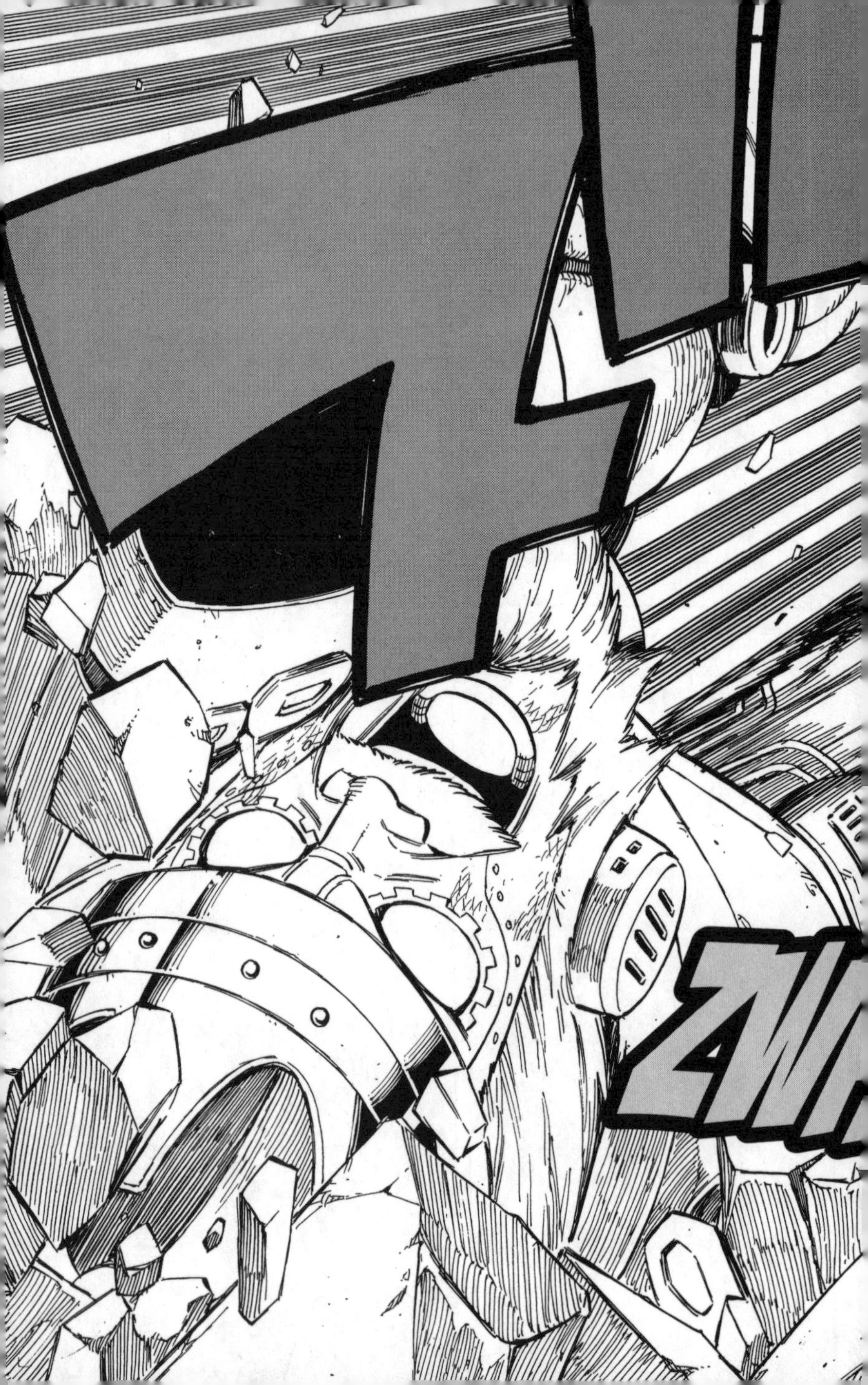

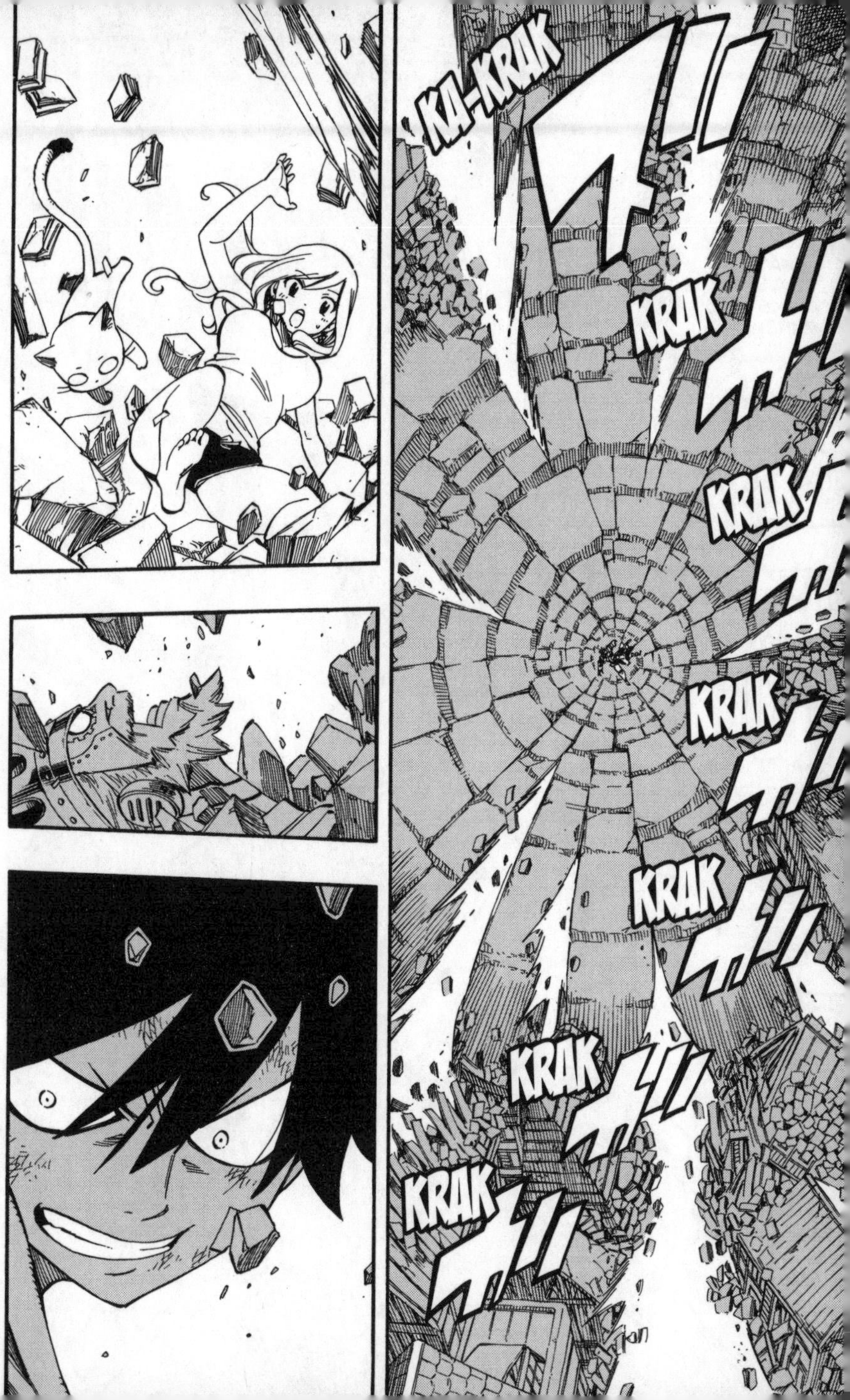
KA-KRAK
KRAK
KRAK
KRAK
KRAK
KRAK
KRAK

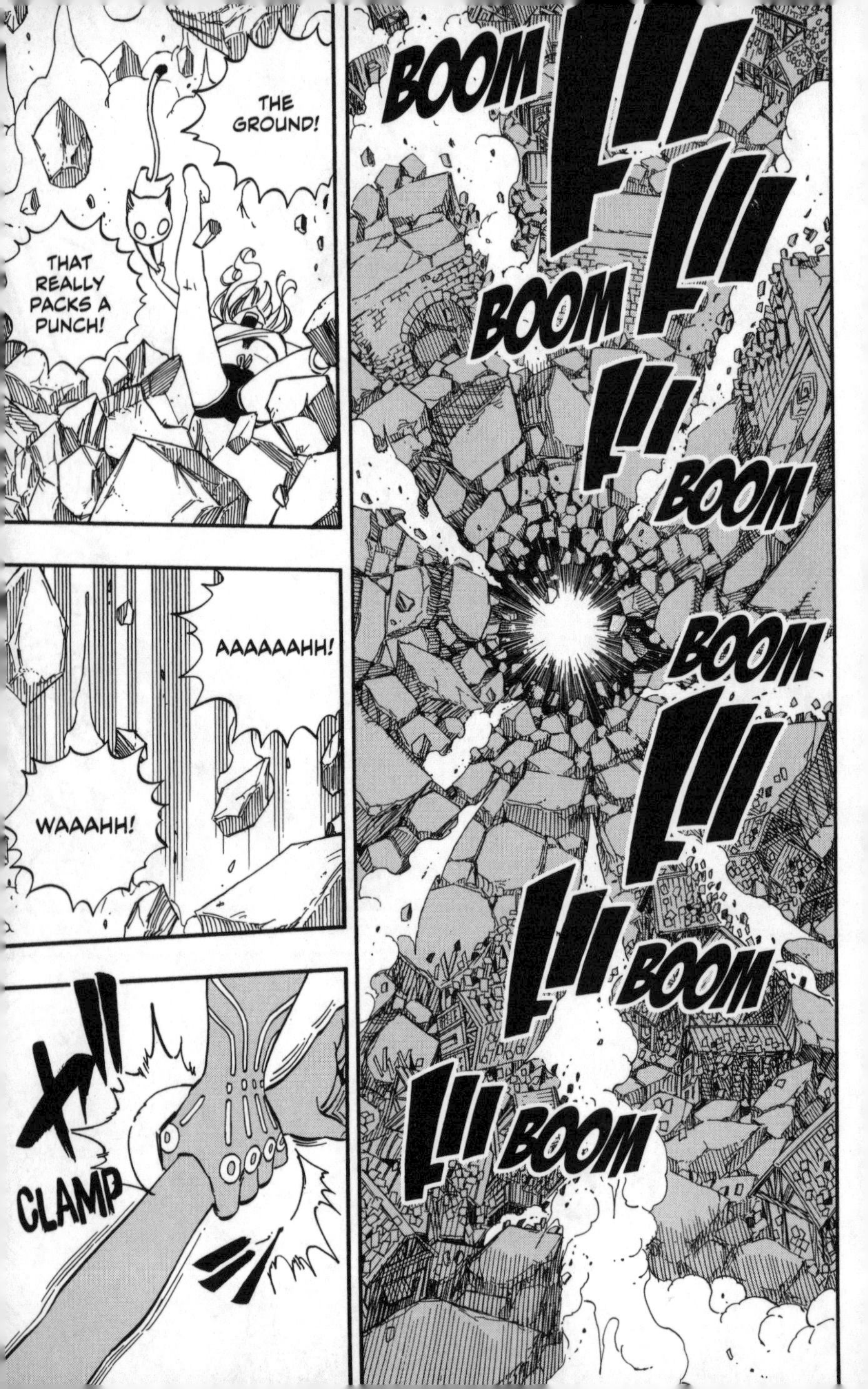
BOOM!!
BOOM!!
BOOM!!
BOOM!!
BOOM!!
BOOM!!
THE GROUND!
THAT REALLY PACKS A PUNCH!
AAAAAAHH!
WAAAHH!
CLAMP

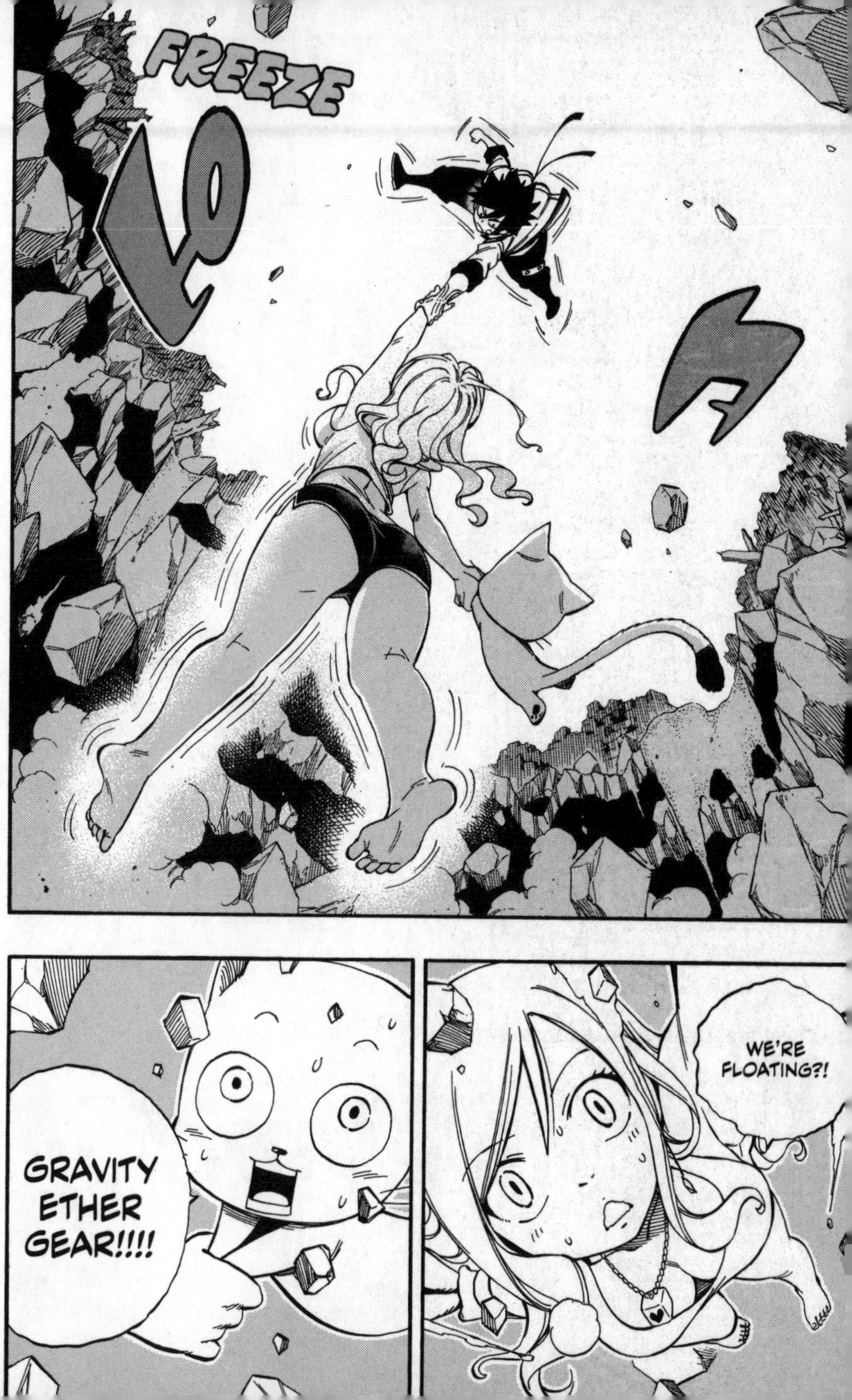
FREEZE
WE'RE FLOATING?!
GRAVITY ETHER GEAR!!!!

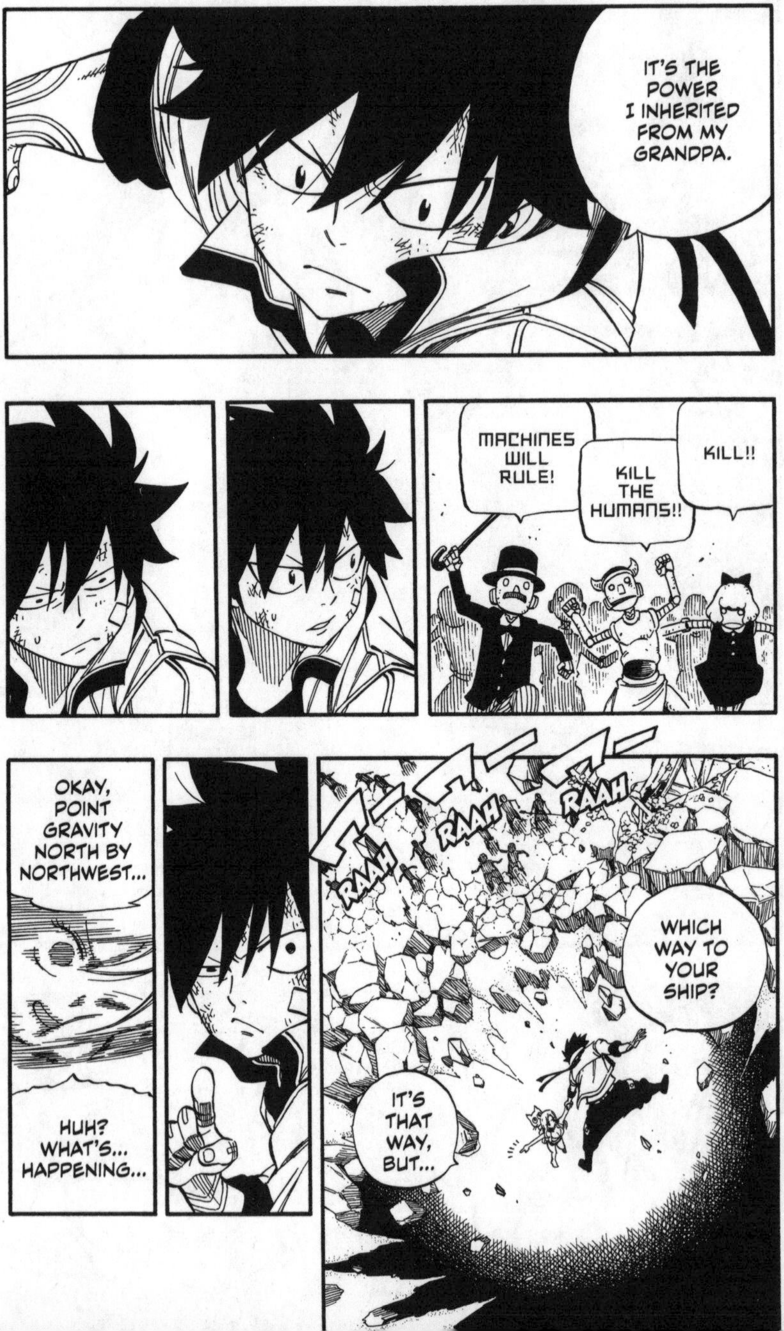
IT'S THE POWER I INHERITED FROM MY GRANDPA.
KILL!!
KILL THE HUMANS!!
MACHINES WILL RULE!
RAAH
RAAH
RAAH
WHICH WAY TO YOUR SHIP?
IT'S THAT WAY, BUT...
OKAY, POINT GRAVITY NORTH BY NORTHWEST...
HUH? WHAT'S... HAPPENING...

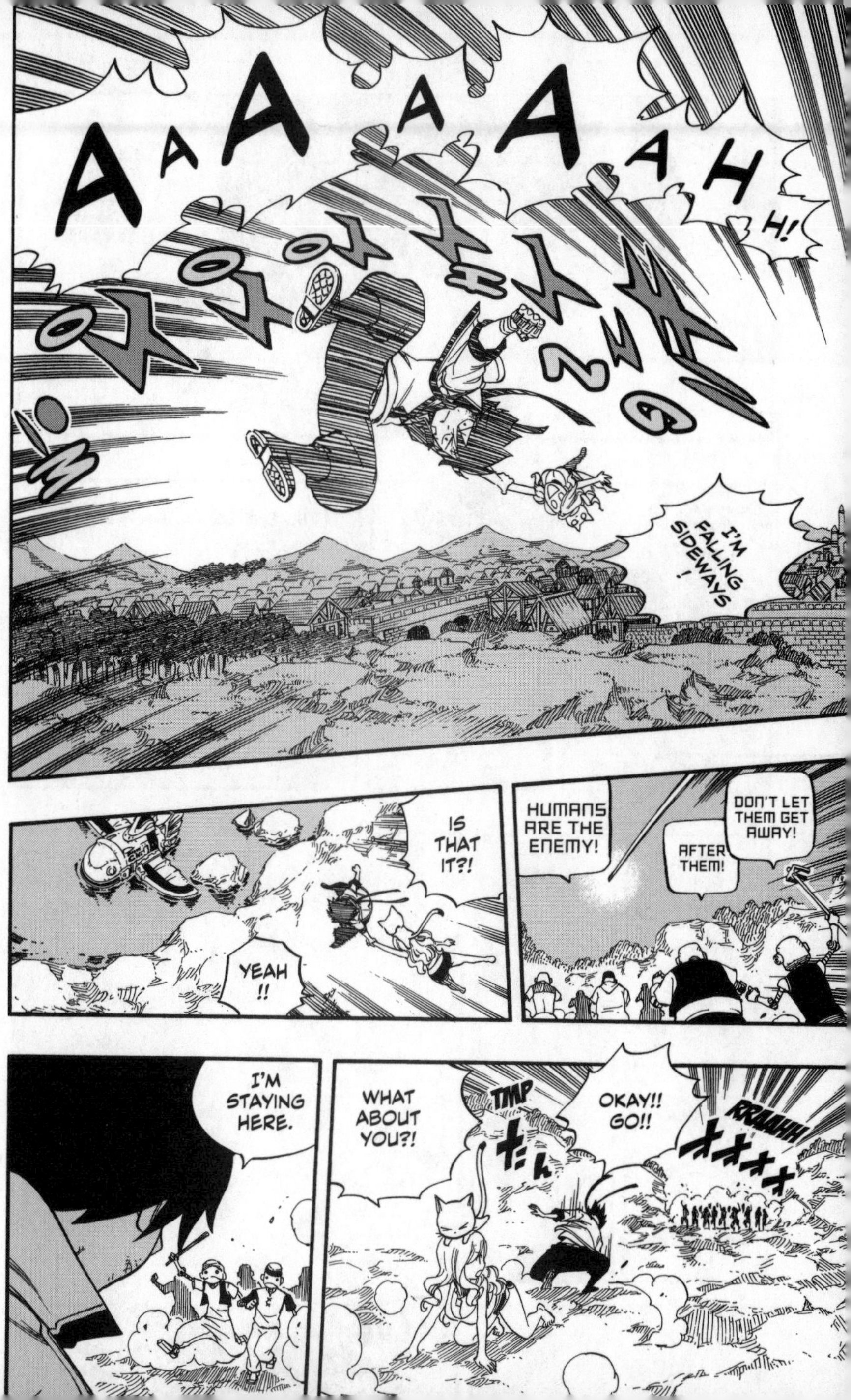

AAAAAAAAH
H!
I'M FALLING SIDEWAYS!
DON'T LET THEM GET AWAY!
AFTER THEM!
HUMANS ARE THE ENEMY!
IS THAT IT?!
YEAH!!
RRAAAHH!
OKAY!! GO!!
TMP
WHAT ABOUT YOU?!
I'M STAYING HERE.

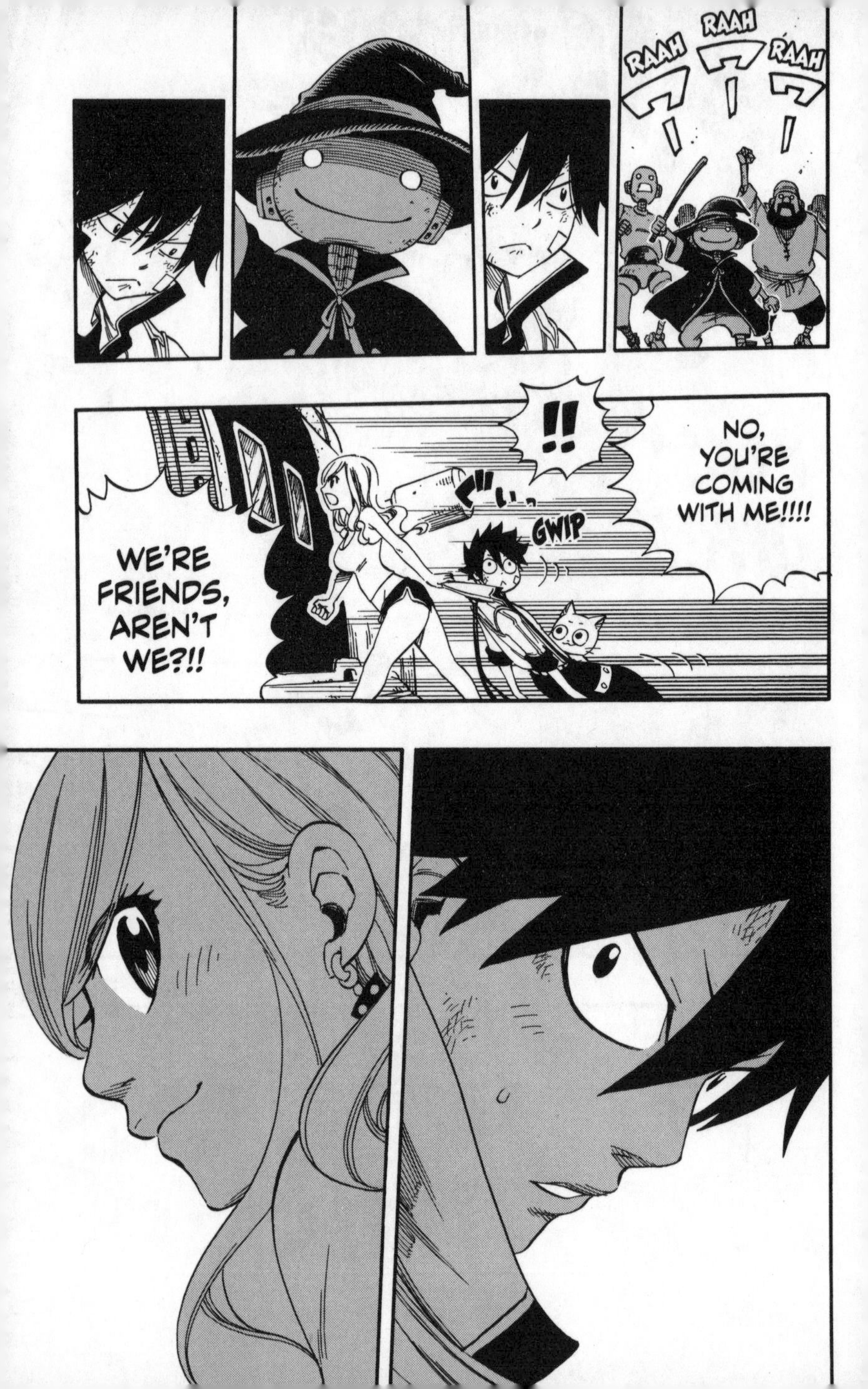
RAAH
RAAH
RAAH
NO, YOU'RE COMING WITH ME!!!!
!!
GWIP
WE'RE FRIENDS, AREN'T WE?!!

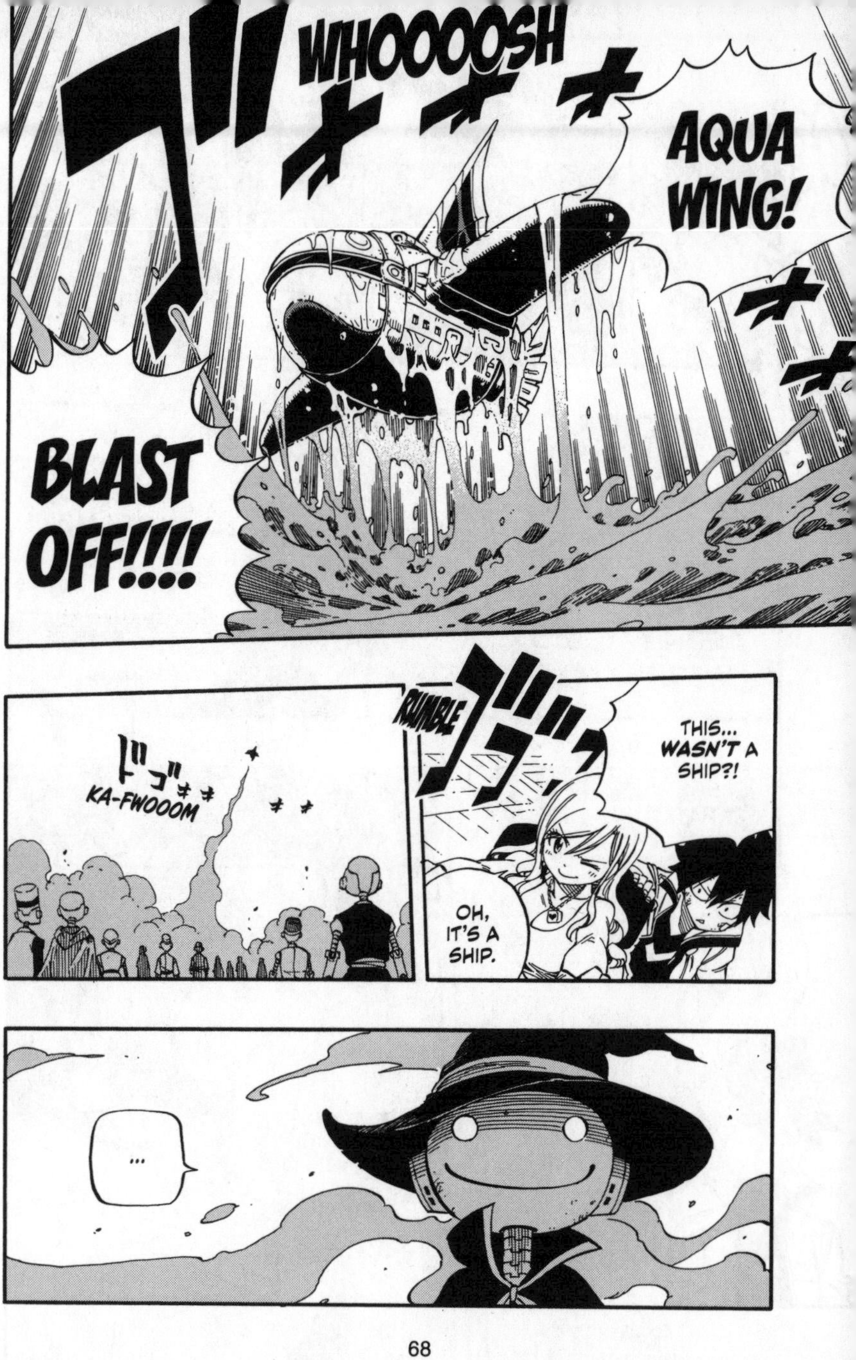
WHOOOOSH
AQUA WING!
BLAST OFF!!!!!
RUMBLE
THIS... WASN'T A SHIP?!
OH, IT'S A SHIP.
KA-FWOOOM
...

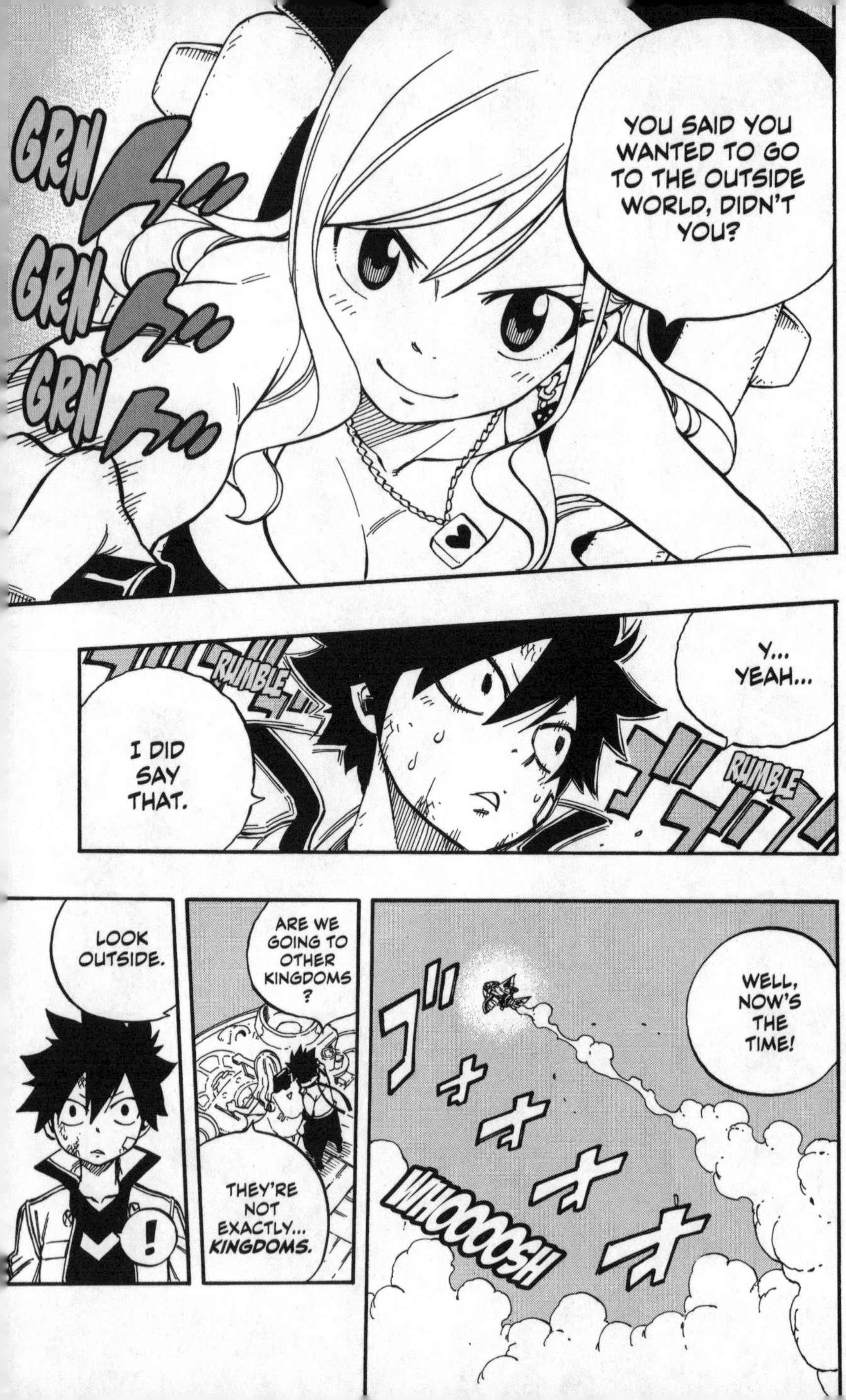
YOU SAID YOU WANTED TO GO TO THE OUTSIDE WORLD, DIDN'T YOU?
GRN
GRN
GRN
Y... YEAH...
RUMBLE
RUMBLE
I DID SAY THAT.
WELL, NOW'S THE TIME!
WHOOOOSH
ARE WE GOING TO OTHER KINGDOMS?
THEY'RE NOT EXACTLY... KINGDOMS.
LOOK OUTSIDE.
!

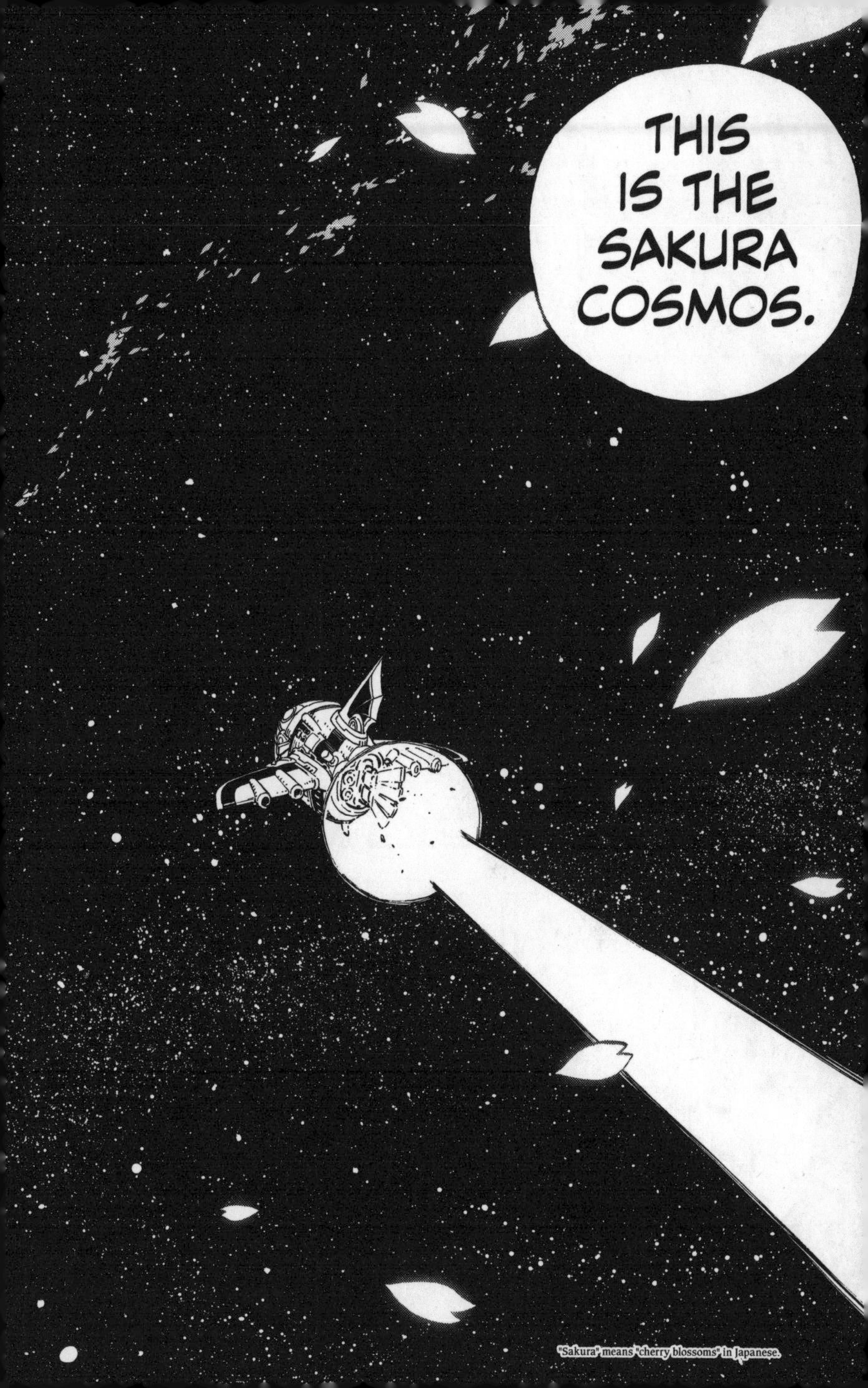
THIS IS THE SAKURA COSMOS.
"Sakura" means "cherry blossoms" in Japanese.

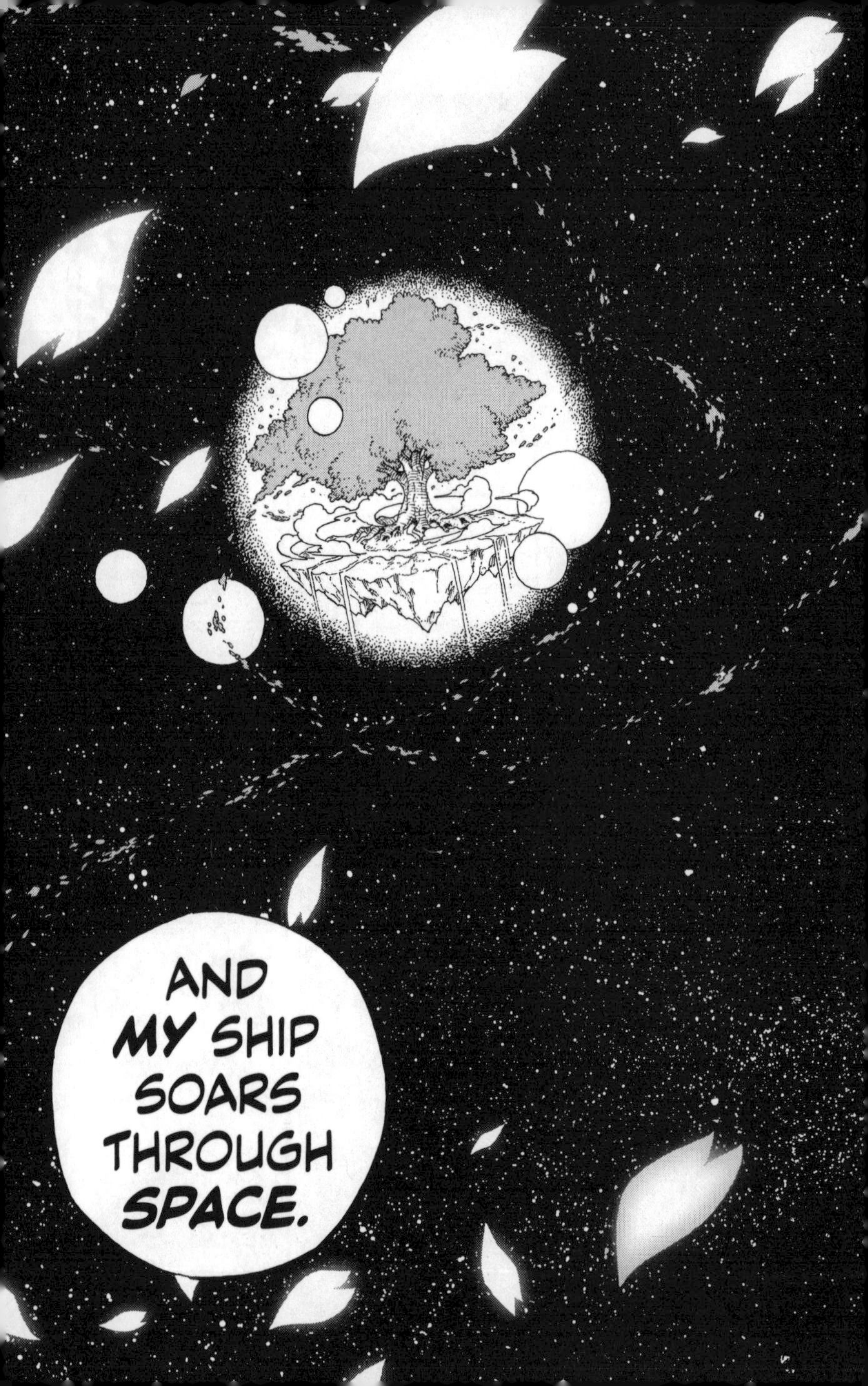
AND MY SHIP SOARS THROUGH SPACE.

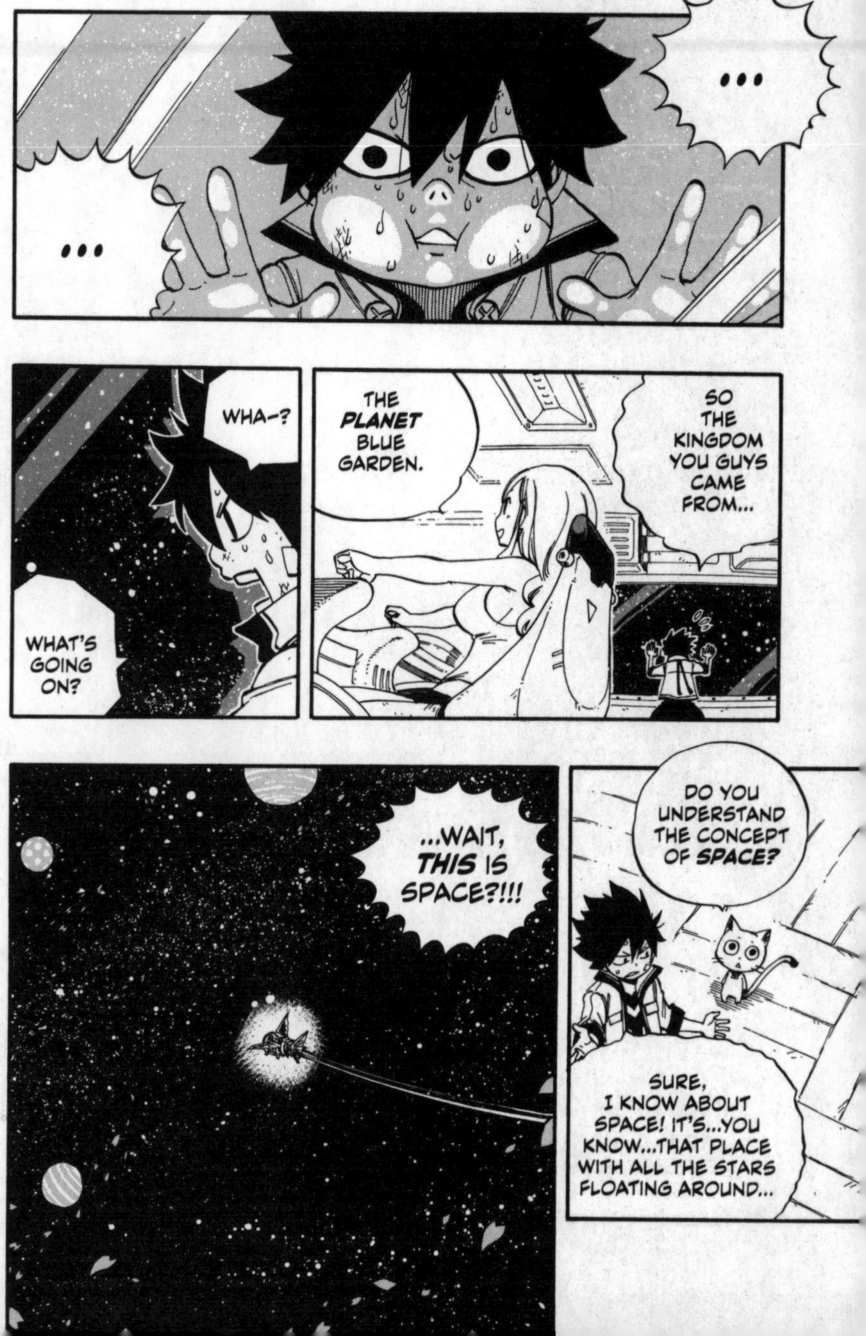
...
...
SO THE KINGDOM YOU GUYS CAME FROM...
THE PLANET BLUE GARDEN.
WHA-?
WHAT'S GOING ON?
DO YOU UNDERSTAND THE CONCEPT OF SPACE?
SURE, I KNOW ABOUT SPACE! IT'S...YOU KNOW...THAT PLACE WITH ALL THE STARS FLOATING AROUND...
...WAIT, THIS IS SPACE?!!!

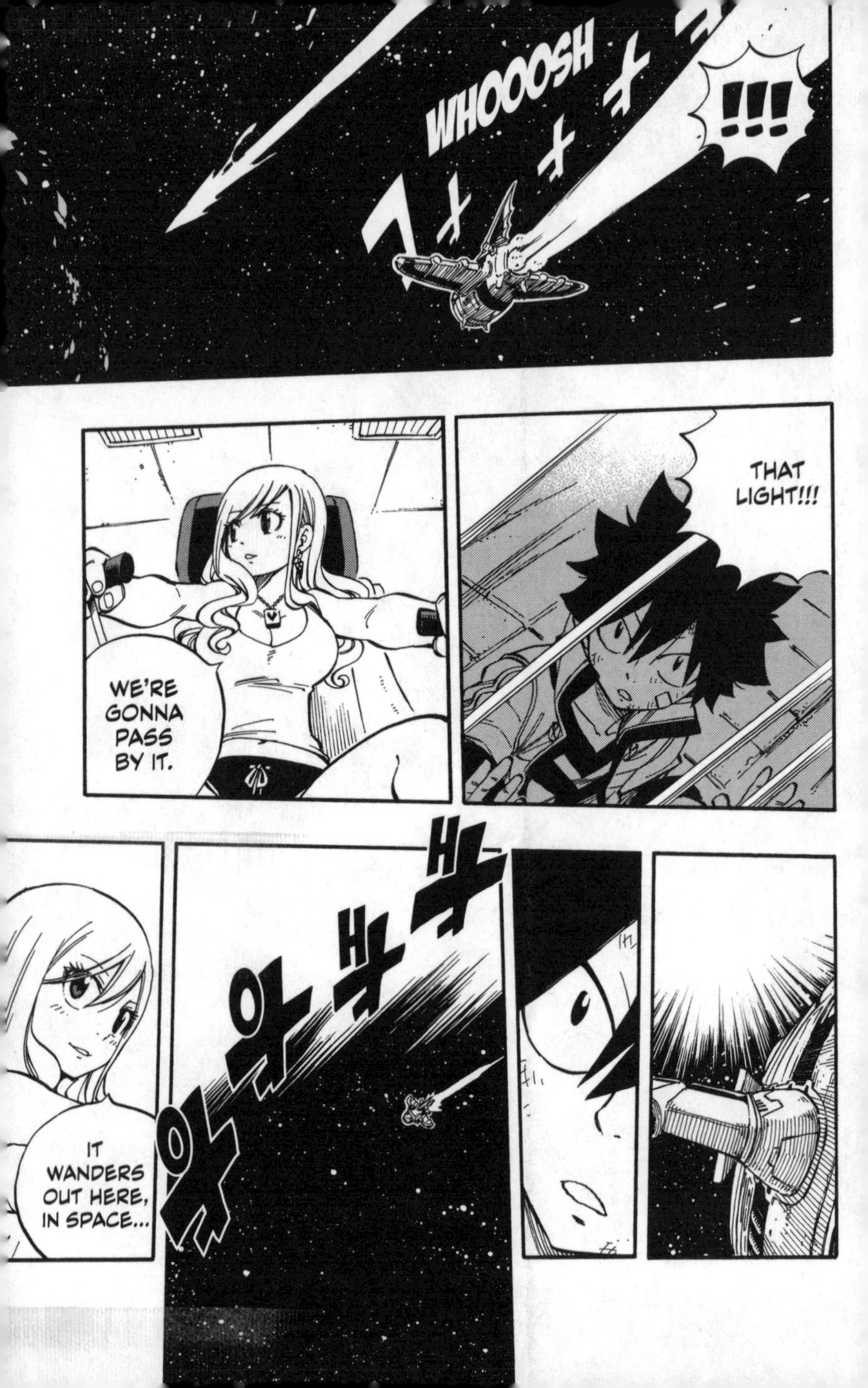
!!!
WHOOOSH
THAT LIGHT!!!
WE'RE GONNA PASS BY IT.
IT WANDERS OUT HERE, IN SPACE...

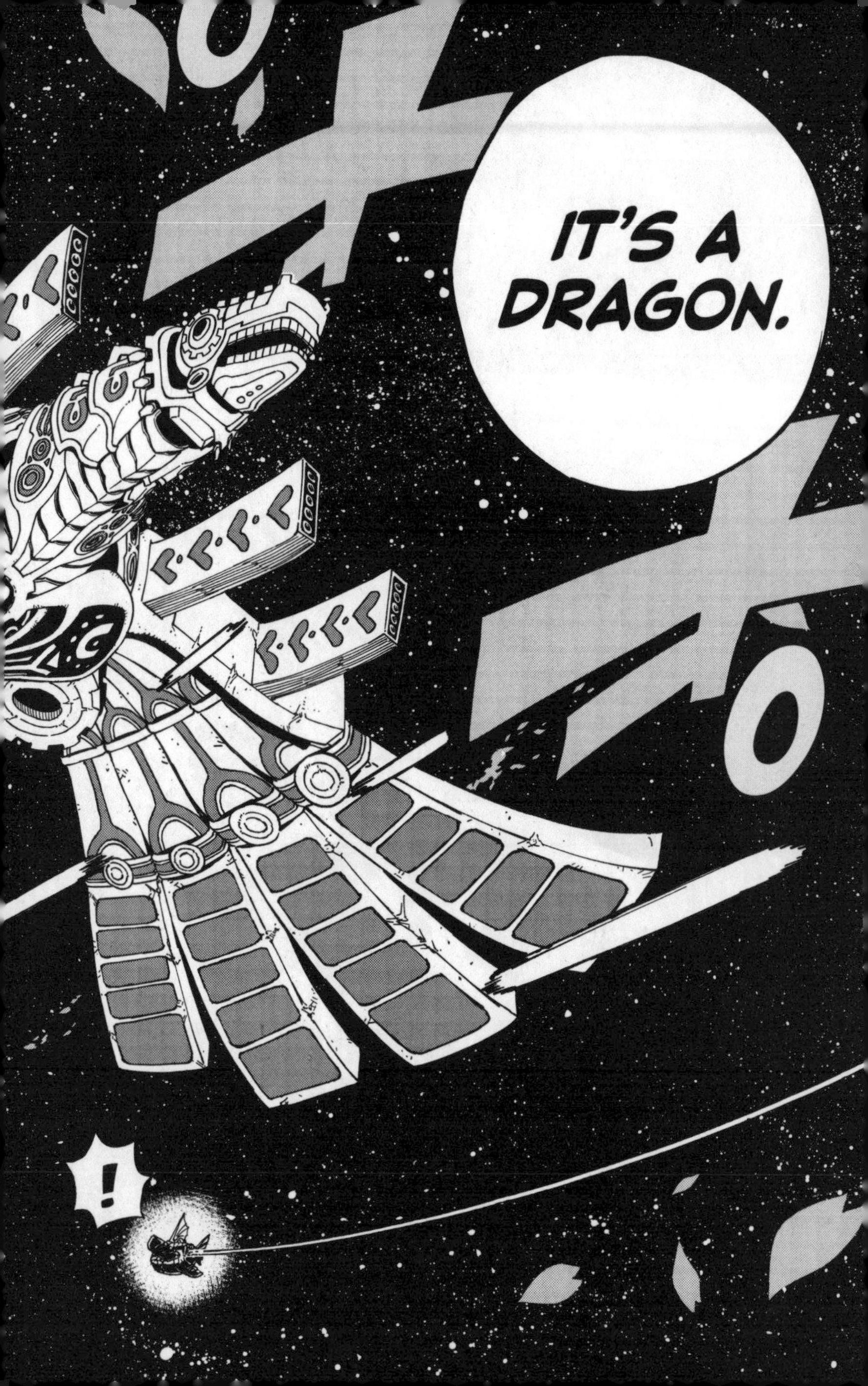
IT'S A DRAGON.
!

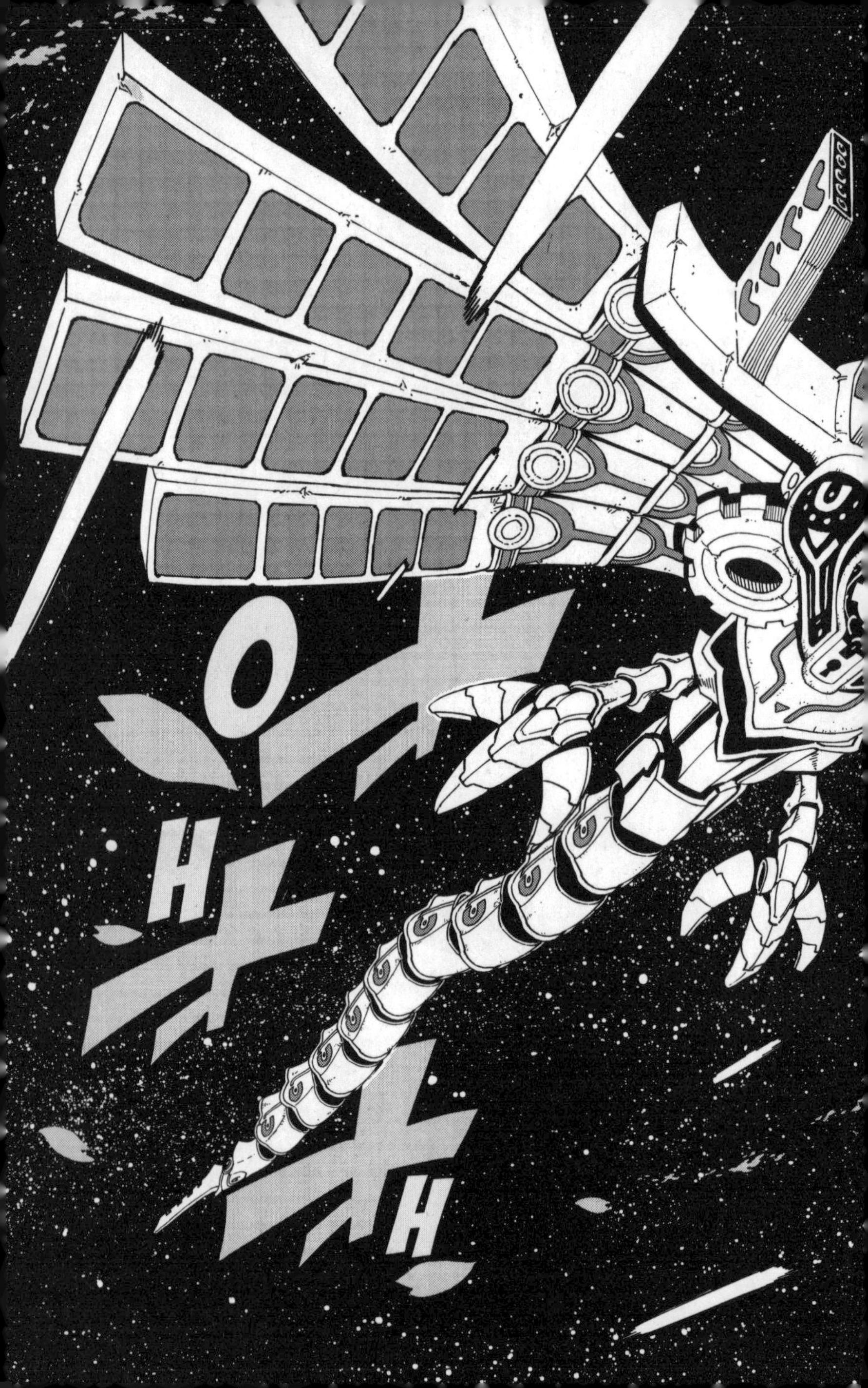

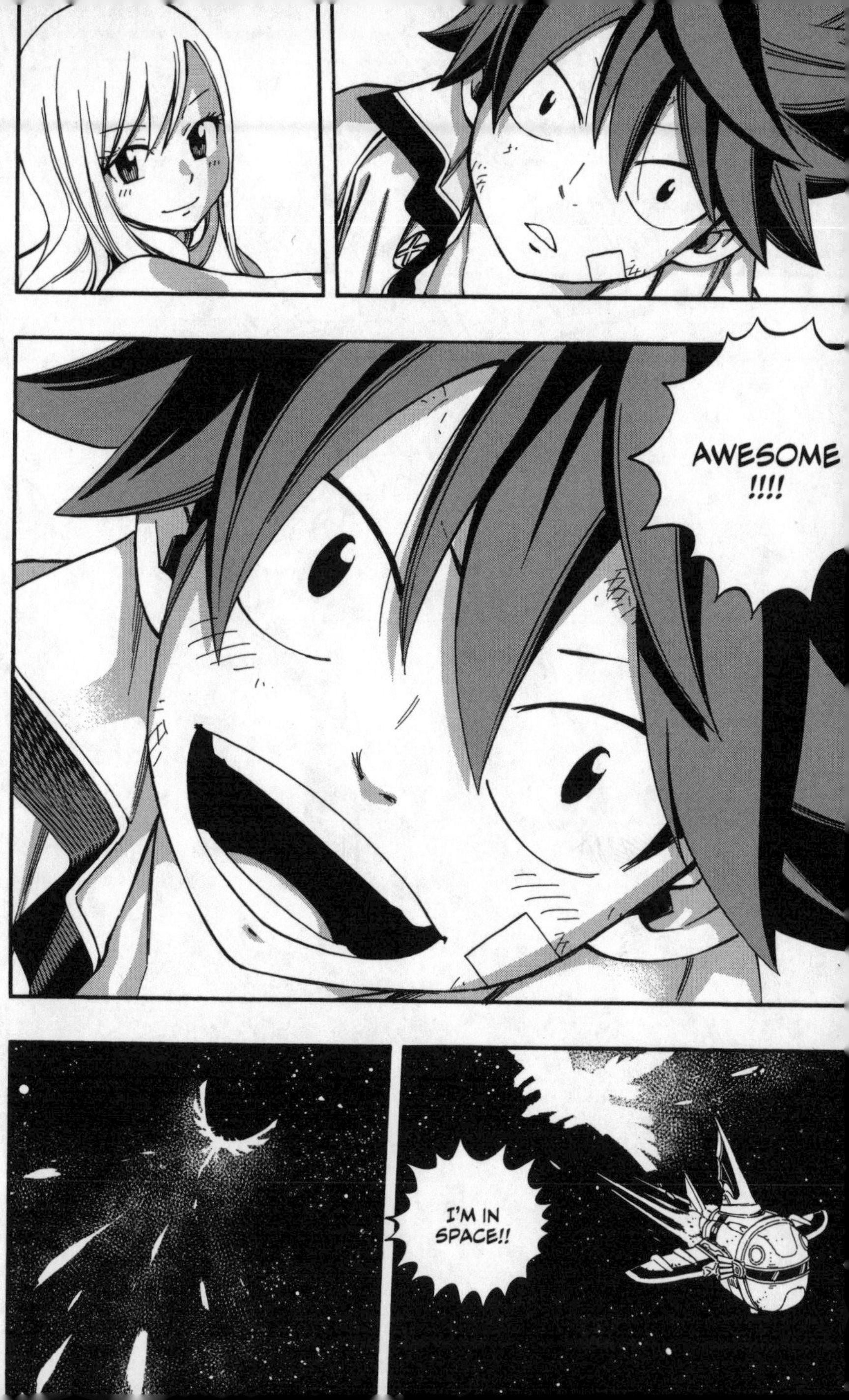
AWESOME !!!!
I'M IN SPACE!!

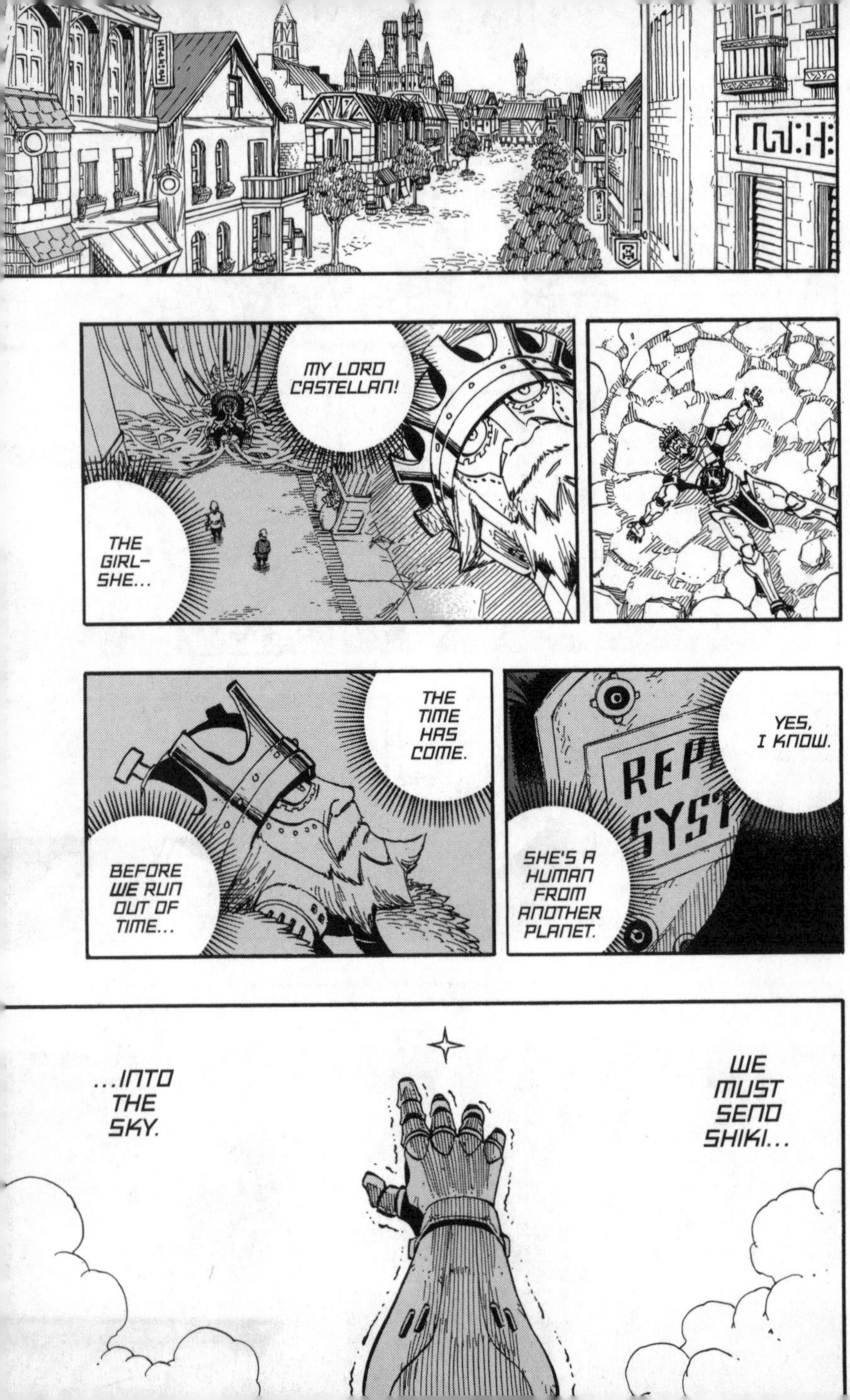
MY LORD CASTELLAN!
THE GIRL— SHE...
YES, I KNOW.
SHE'S A HUMAN FROM ANOTHER PLANET.
THE TIME HAS COME.
BEFORE WE RUN OUT OF TIME...
WE MUST SEND SHIKI...
...INTO THE SKY.

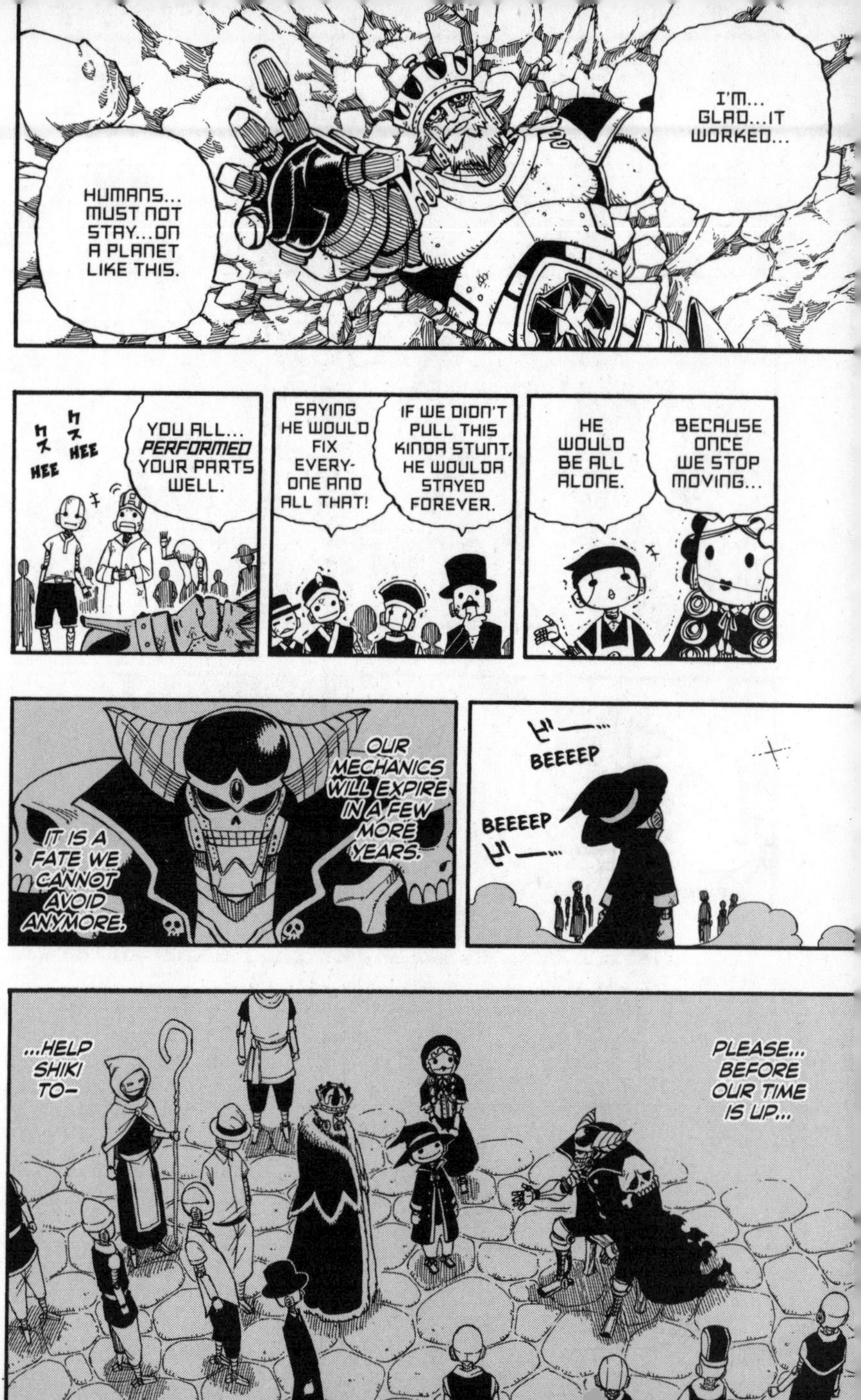
I'M... GLAD...IT WORKED...
HUMANS... MUST NOT STAY...ON A PLANET LIKE THIS.
BECAUSE ONCE WE STOP MOVING...
HE WOULD BE ALL ALONE.
IF WE DIDN'T PULL THIS KINDA STUNT, HE WOULDA STAYED FOREVER.
SAYING HE WOULD FIX EVERYONE AND ALL THAT!
YOU ALL... PERFORMED YOUR PARTS WELL.
クス HEE
クス HEE
ビー… BEEEEP
ビー… BEEEEP
OUR MECHANICS WILL EXPIRE IN A FEW MORE YEARS.
IT IS A FATE WE CANNOT AVOID ANYMORE.
PLEASE... BEFORE OUR TIME IS UP...
...HELP SHIKI TO-

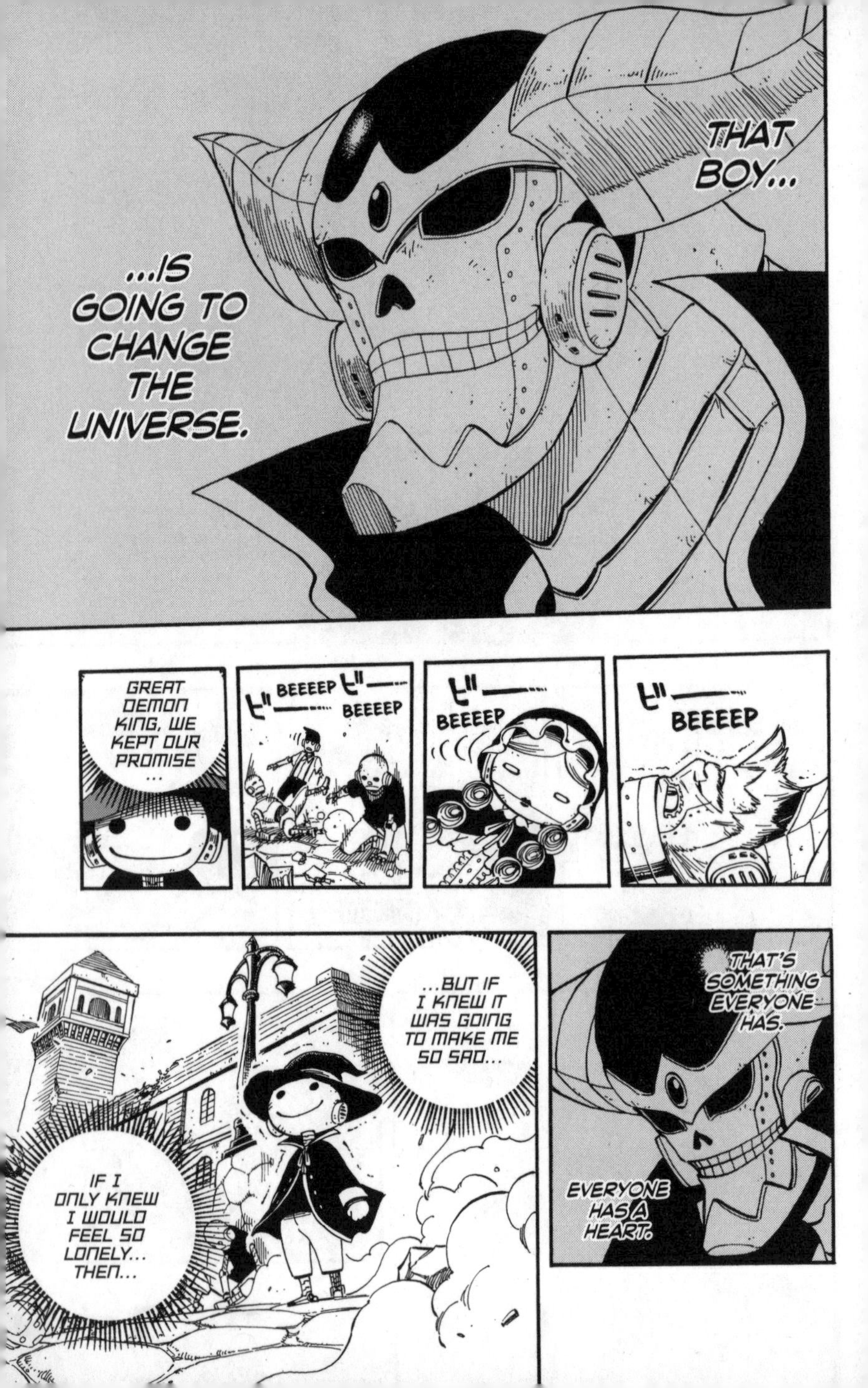
THAT BOY...
...IS GOING TO CHANGE THE UNIVERSE.
ビー
BEEEEP
ビー
BEEEEP
ビー
BEEEEP
ビー
BEEEEP
GREAT DEMON KING, WE KEPT OUR PROMISE ...
THAT'S SOMETHING EVERYONE HAS.
EVERYONE HAS A HEART.
...BUT IF I KNEW IT WAS GOING TO MAKE ME SO SAD...
IF I ONLY KNEW I WOULD FEEL SO LONELY... THEN...

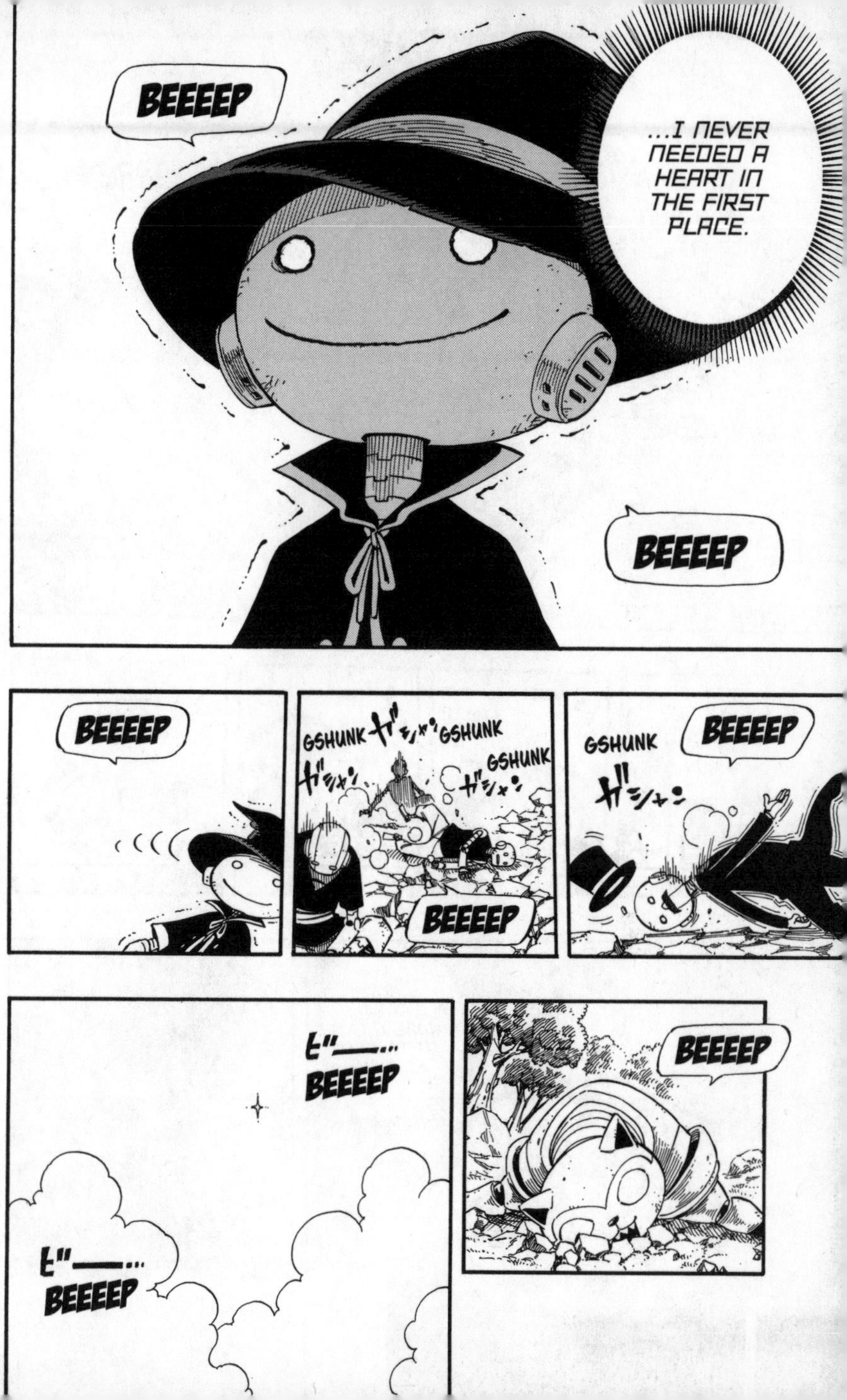
...I NEVER NEEDED A HEART IN THE FIRST PLACE.
BEEEEP
BEEEEP
BEEEEP
GSHUNK
ガシャン
GSHUNK
GSHUNK
GSHUNK
ガシャン
ガシャン
ガシャン
BEEEEP
BEEEEP
BEEEEP
ビ"——…
BEEEEP
ビ"——…
BEEEEP

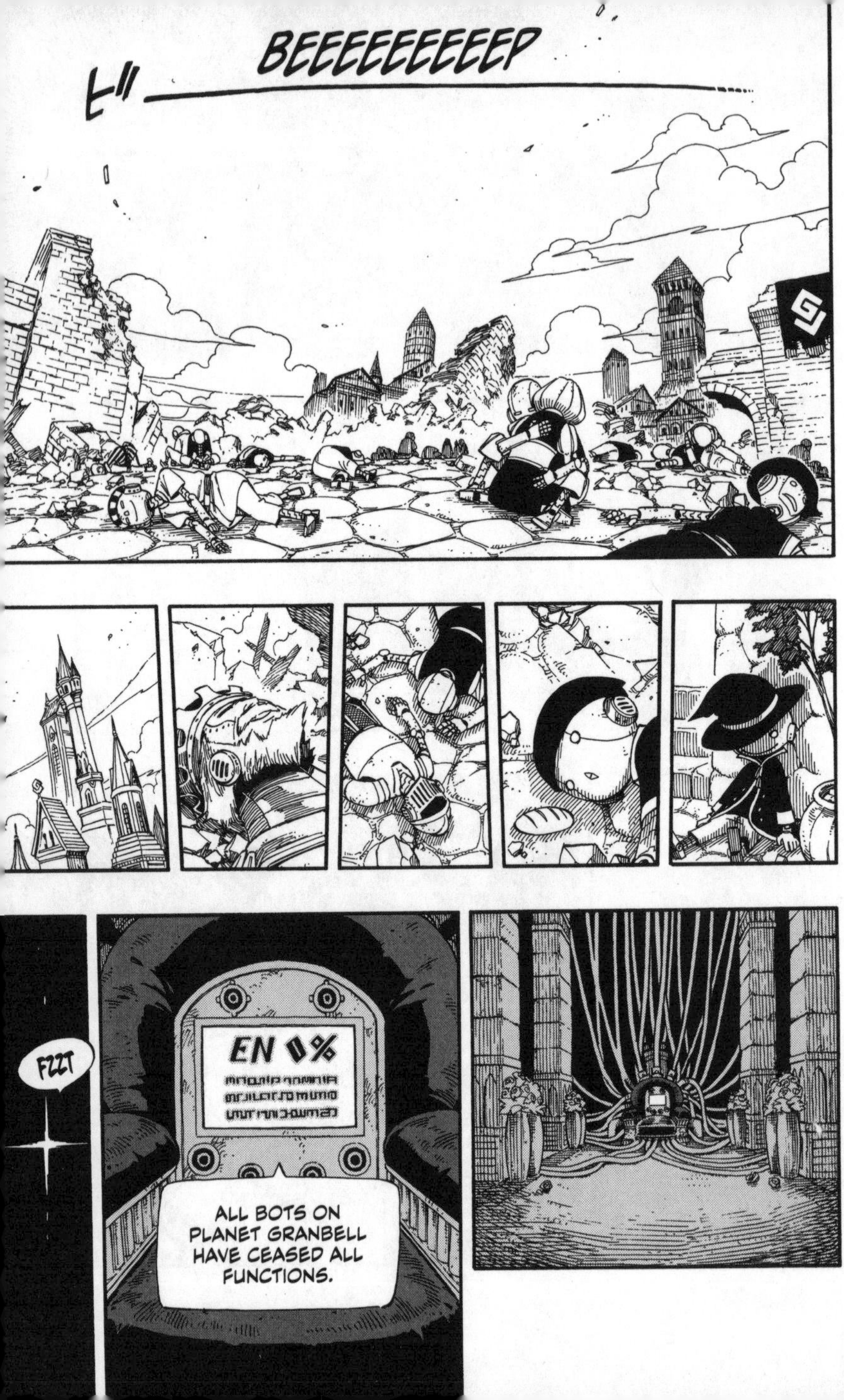
ビ
BEEEEEEEEEEP
EN 0%
FZZT
ALL BOTS ON PLANET GRANBELL HAVE CEASED ALL FUNCTIONS.

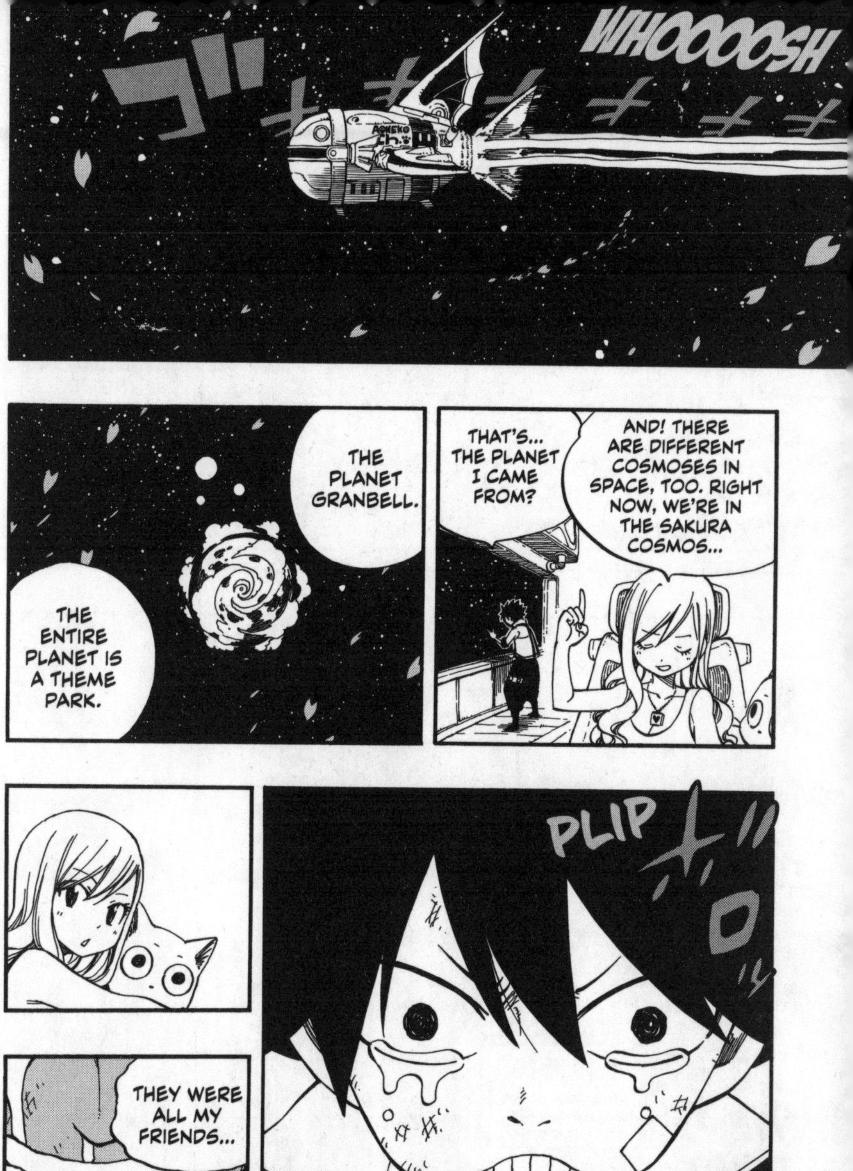
WHOOOOSH
AND! THERE ARE DIFFERENT COSMOSES IN SPACE, TOO. RIGHT NOW, WE'RE IN THE SAKURA COSMOS...
THAT'S... THE PLANET I CAME FROM?
THE PLANET GRANBELL.
THE ENTIRE PLANET IS A THEME PARK.
PLIP
THEY WERE ALL MY FRIENDS...

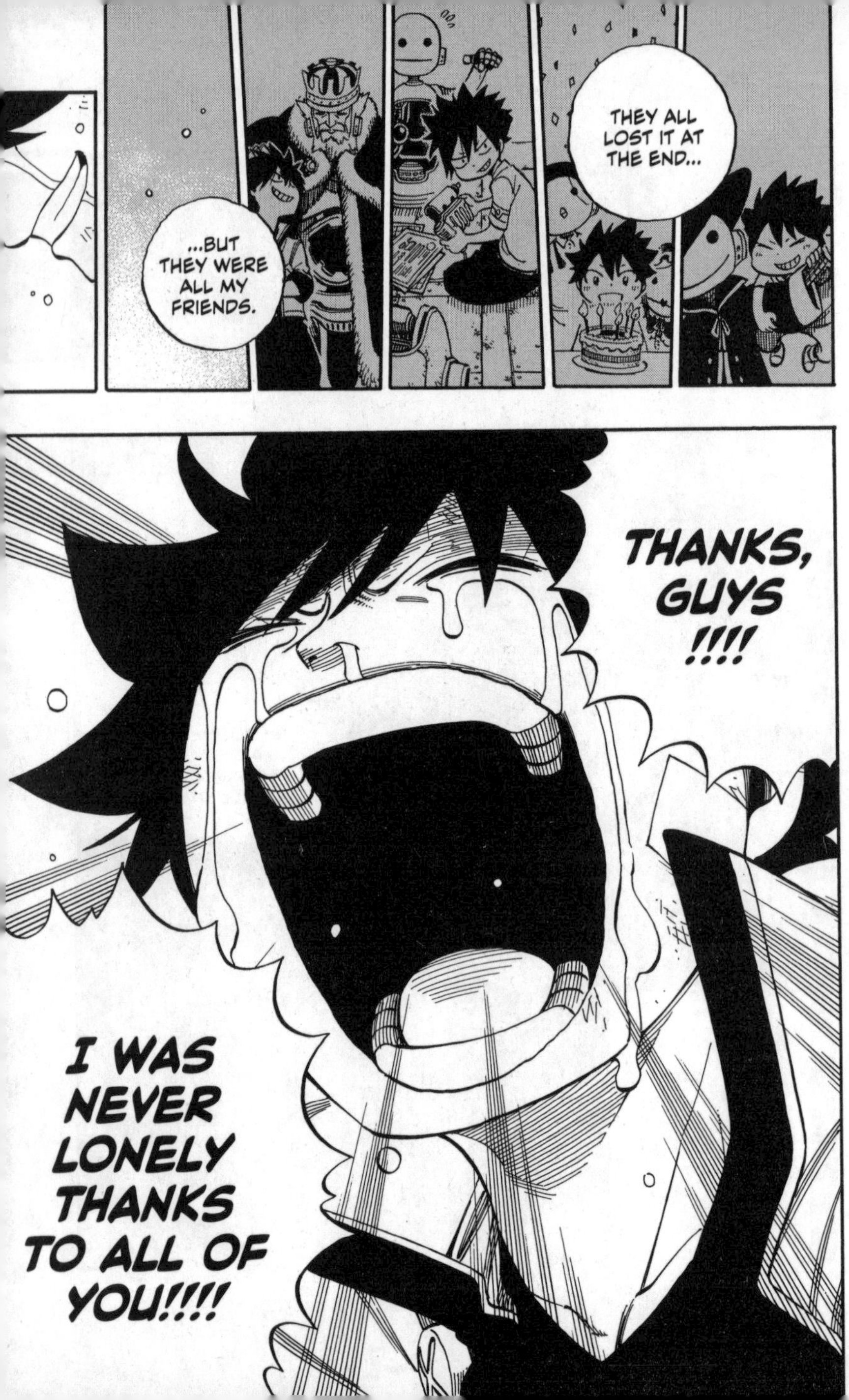
THEY ALL LOST IT AT THE END...
...BUT THEY WERE ALL MY FRIENDS.
THANKS, GUYS!!!!
I WAS NEVER LONELY THANKS TO ALL OF YOU!!!!

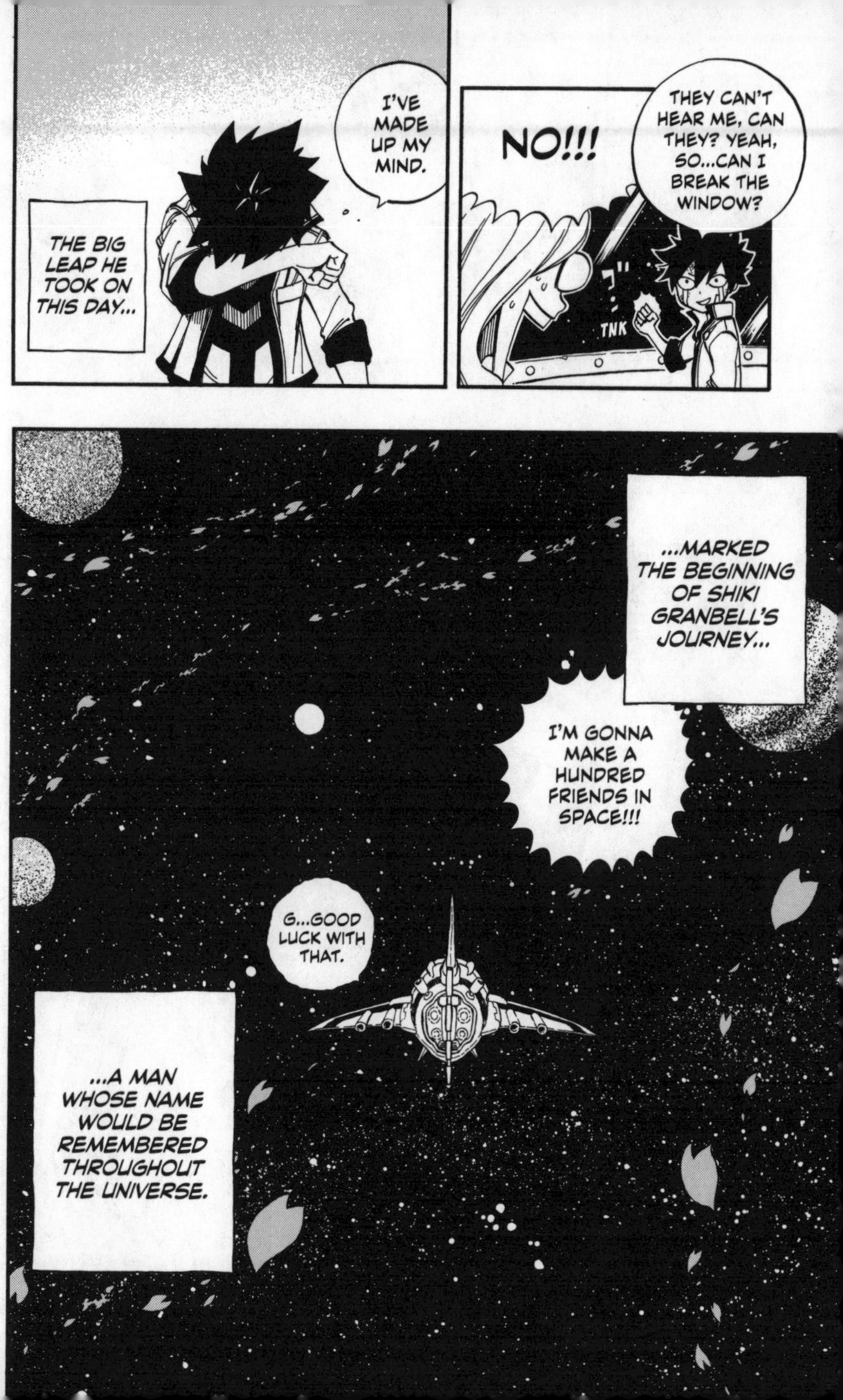
THEY CAN'T HEAR ME, CAN THEY? YEAH, SO...CAN I BREAK THE WINDOW?
NO!!!
TNK
I'VE MADE UP MY MIND.
THE BIG LEAP HE TOOK ON THIS DAY...
...MARKED THE BEGINNING OF SHIKI GRANBELL'S JOURNEY...
I'M GONNA MAKE A HUNDRED FRIENDS IN SPACE!!!
G...GOOD LUCK WITH THAT.
...A MAN WHOSE NAME WOULD BE REMEMBERED THROUGHOUT THE UNIVERSE.

EDENSZERO

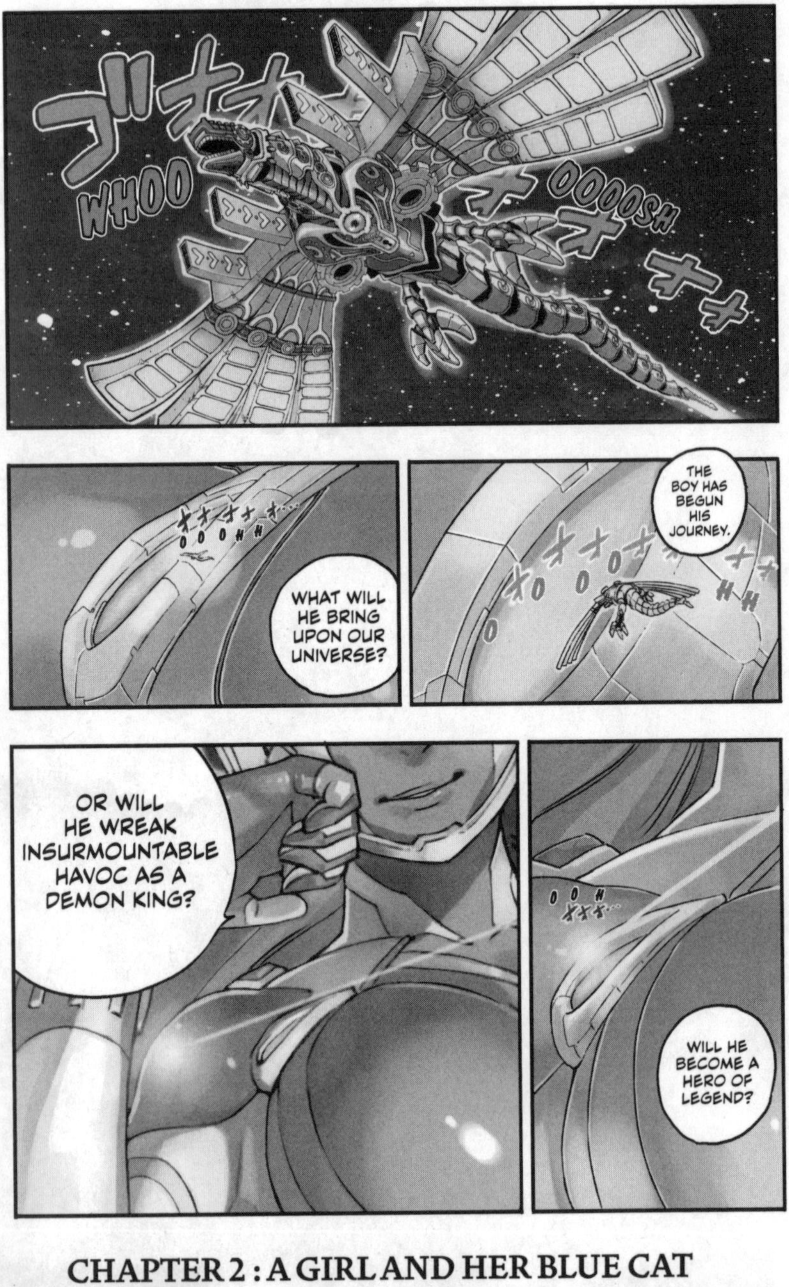

WHOO
OOOOOSH
THE BOY HAS BEGUN HIS JOURNEY.
WHAT WILL HE BRING UPON OUR UNIVERSE?
WILL HE BECOME A HERO OF LEGEND?
OR WILL HE WREAK INSURMOUNTABLE HAVOC AS A DEMON KING?

CHAPTER 2 : A GIRL AND HER BLUE CAT

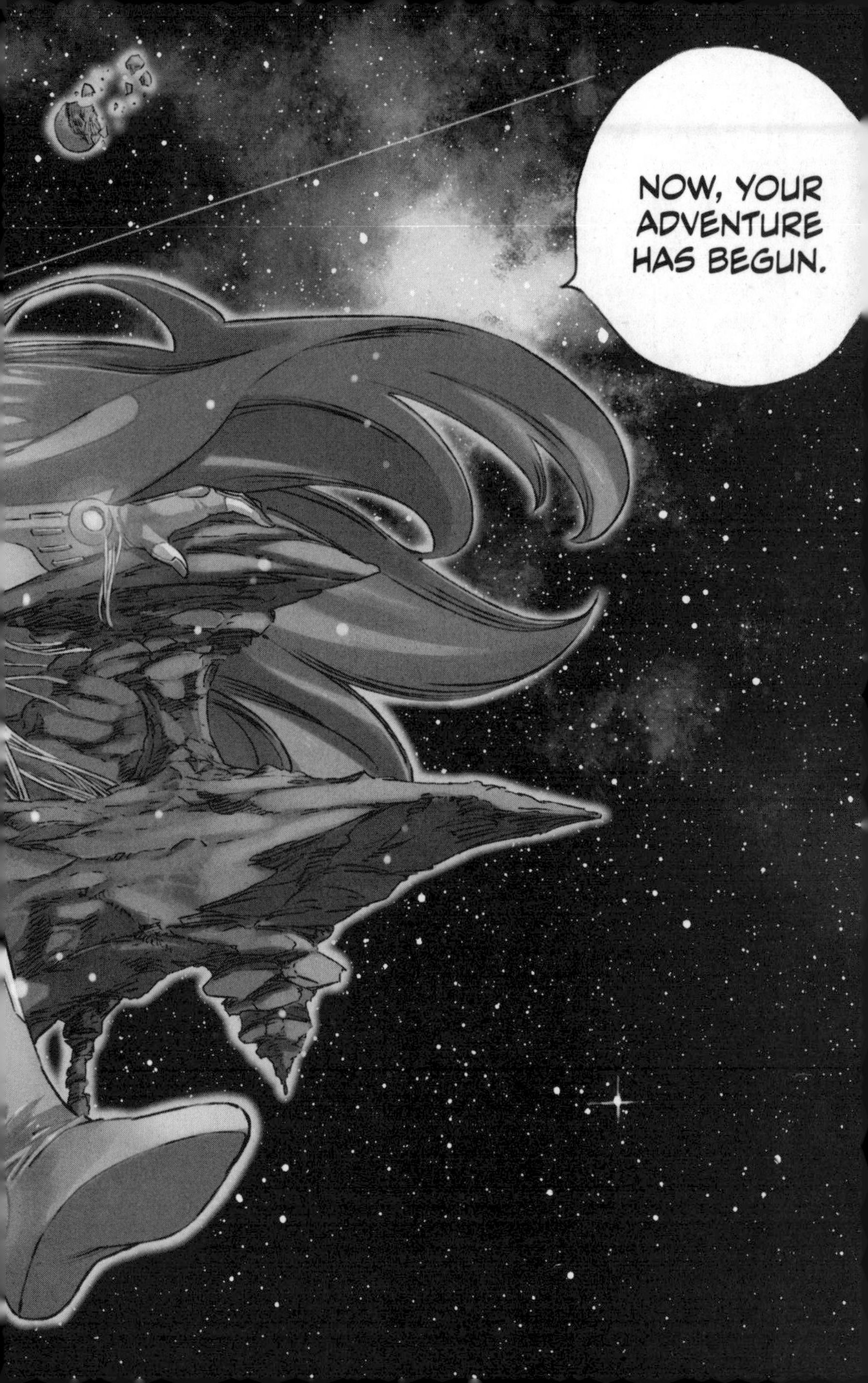
NOW, YOUR ADVENTURE HAS BEGUN.

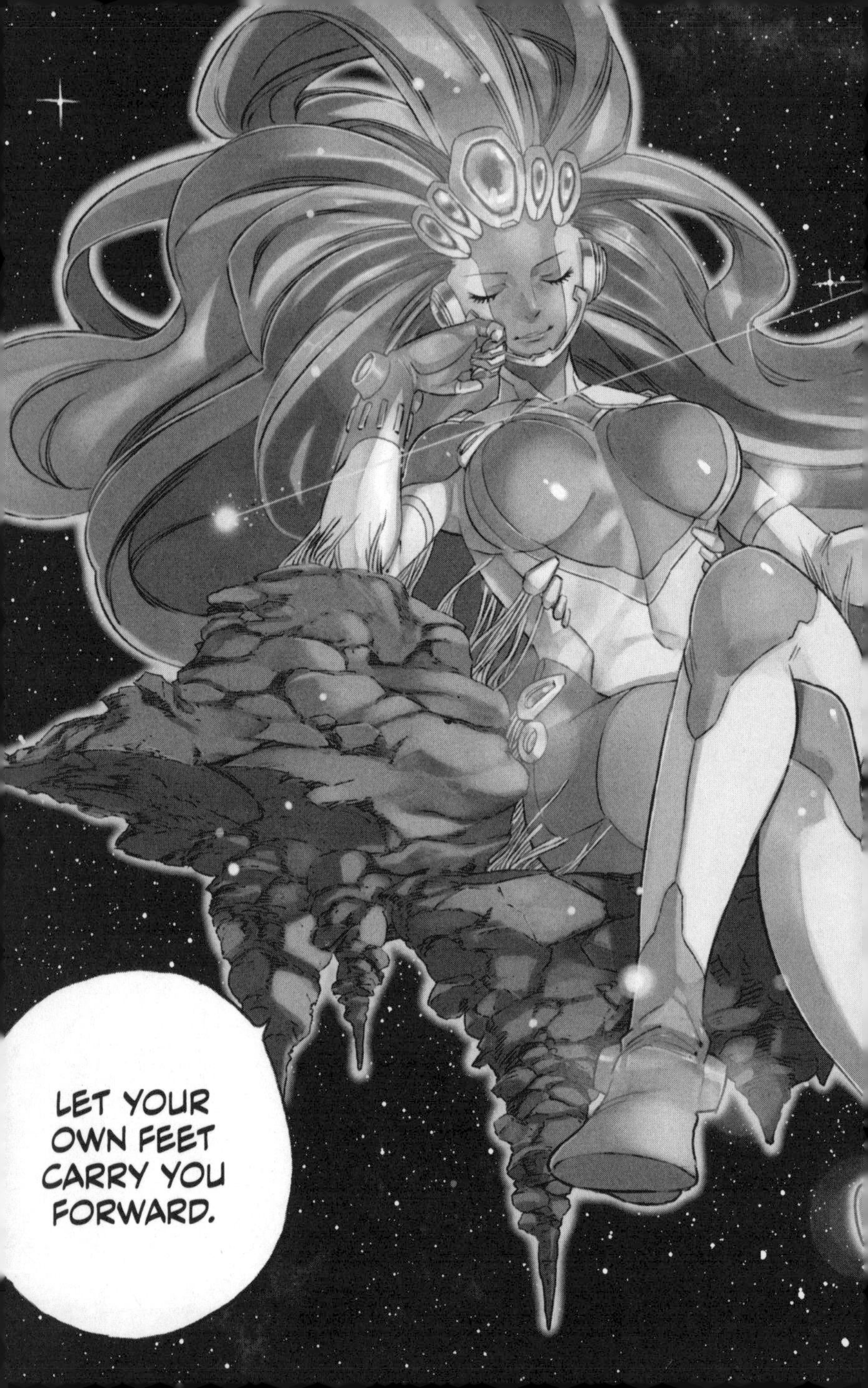
LET YOUR OWN FEET CARRY YOU FORWARD.

EDENSZERO

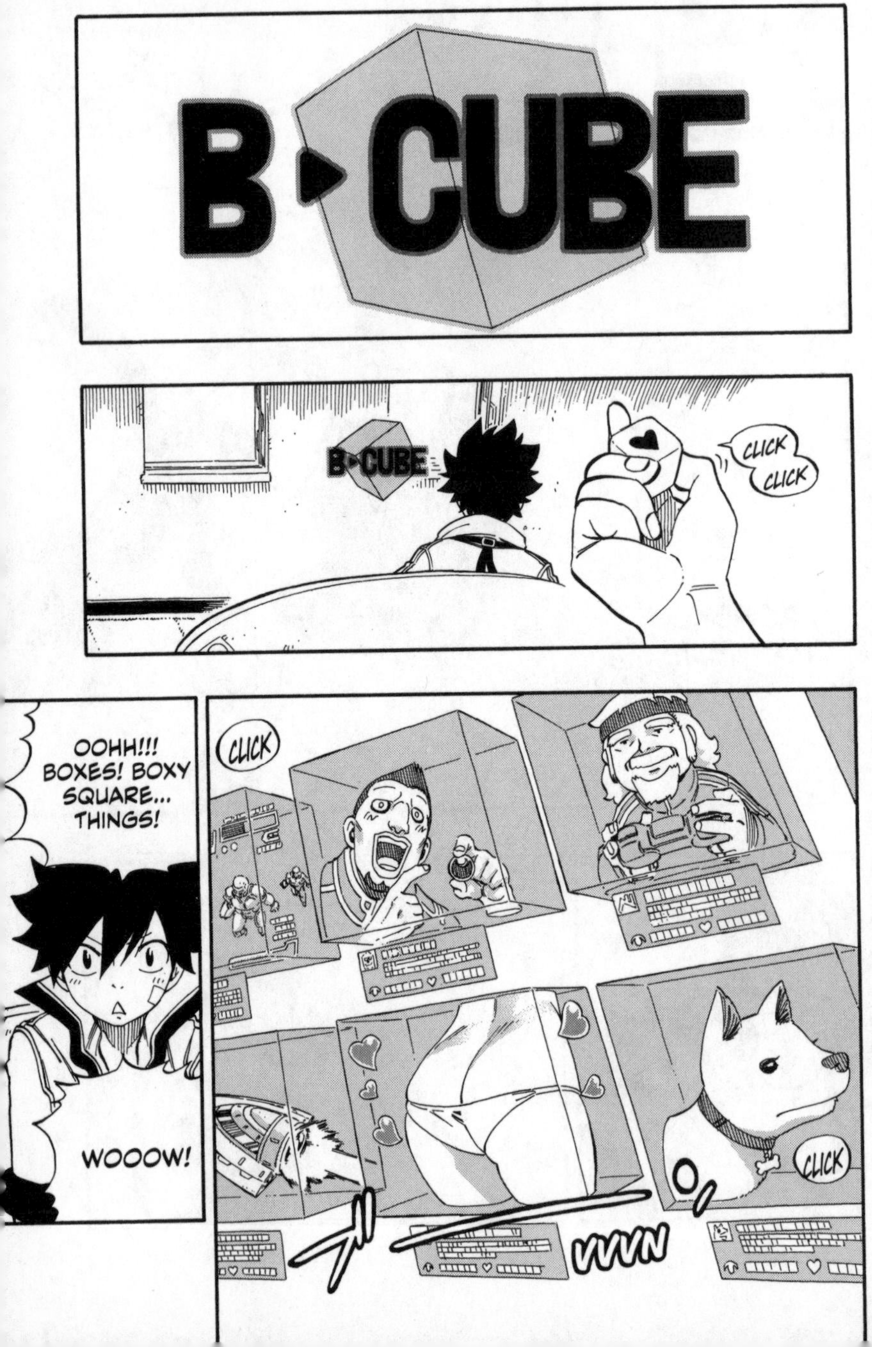
B▸CUBE
B▸CUBE
CLICK
CLICK
CLICK
CLICK
VVVN
OOHH!!! BOXES! BOXY SQUARE... THINGS!
WOOOW!

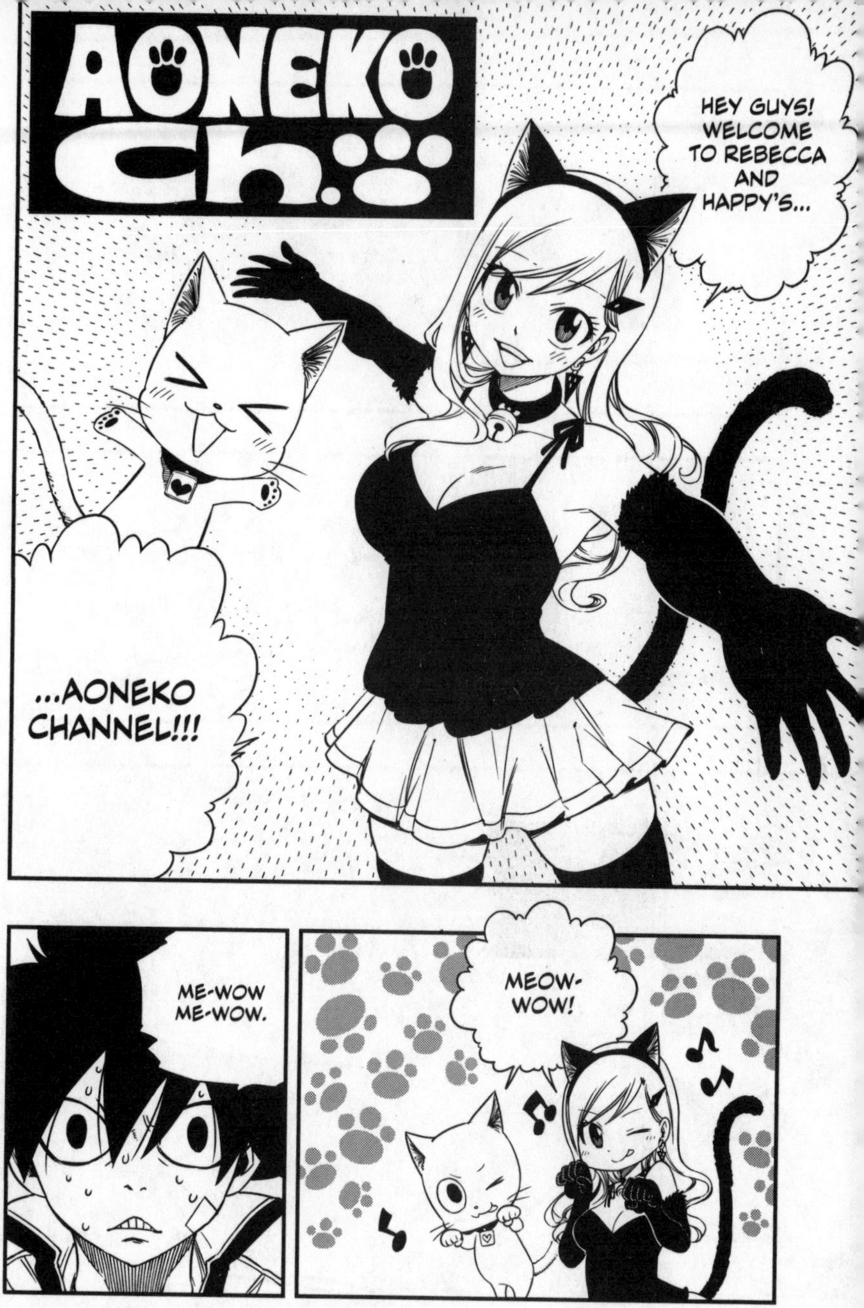
AONEKO Ch.
HEY GUYS! WELCOME TO REBECCA AND HAPPY'S...
...AONEKO CHANNEL!!!
MEOW-WOW!
ME-WOW ME-WOW.

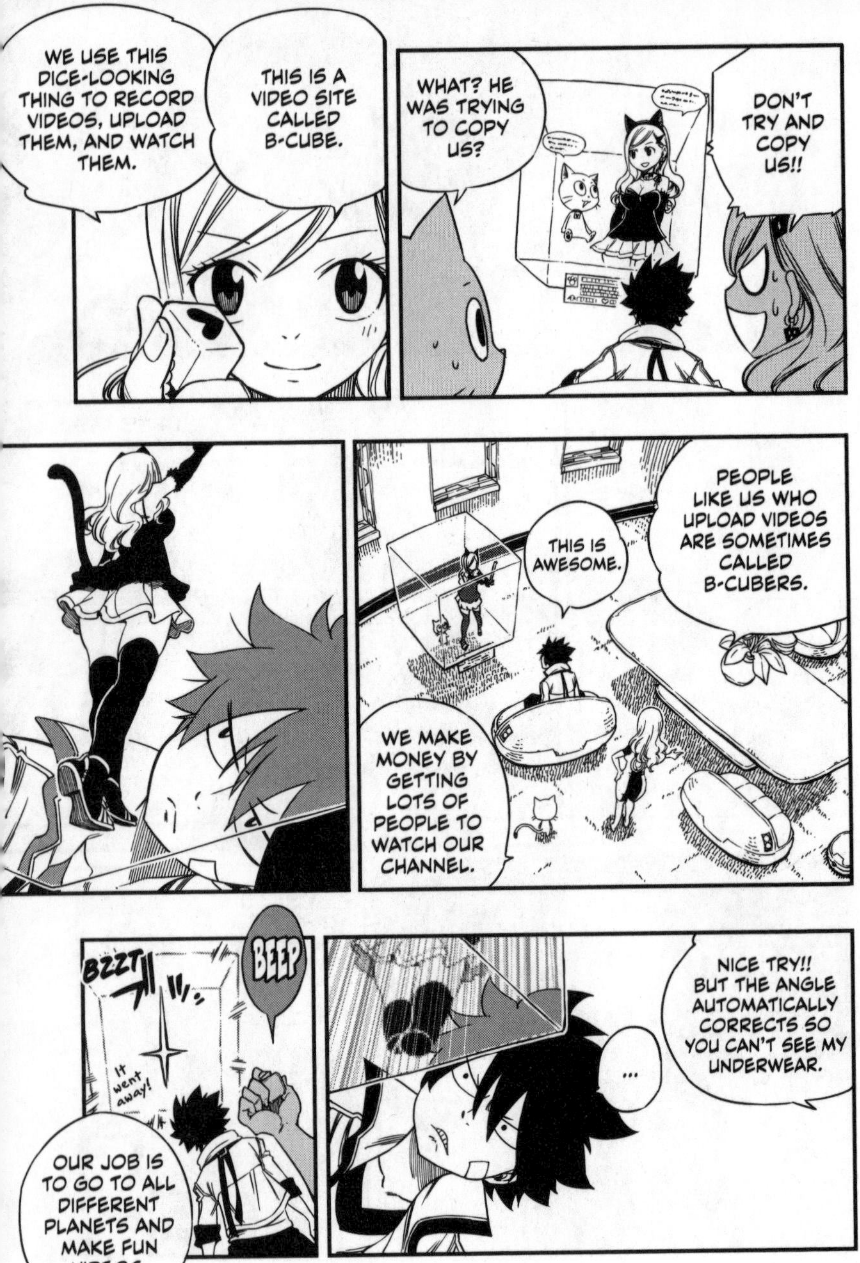
DON'T TRY AND COPY US!!
WHAT? HE WAS TRYING TO COPY US?
THIS IS A VIDEO SITE CALLED B-CUBE.
WE USE THIS DICE-LOOKING THING TO RECORD VIDEOS, UPLOAD THEM, AND WATCH THEM.
PEOPLE LIKE US WHO UPLOAD VIDEOS ARE SOMETIMES CALLED B-CUBERS.
THIS IS AWESOME.
WE MAKE MONEY BY GETTING LOTS OF PEOPLE TO WATCH OUR CHANNEL.
NICE TRY!! BUT THE ANGLE AUTOMATICALLY CORRECTS SO YOU CAN'T SEE MY UNDERWEAR.
...
BEEP
BZZT
It went away!
OUR JOB IS TO GO TO ALL DIFFERENT PLANETS AND MAKE FUN VIDEOS.

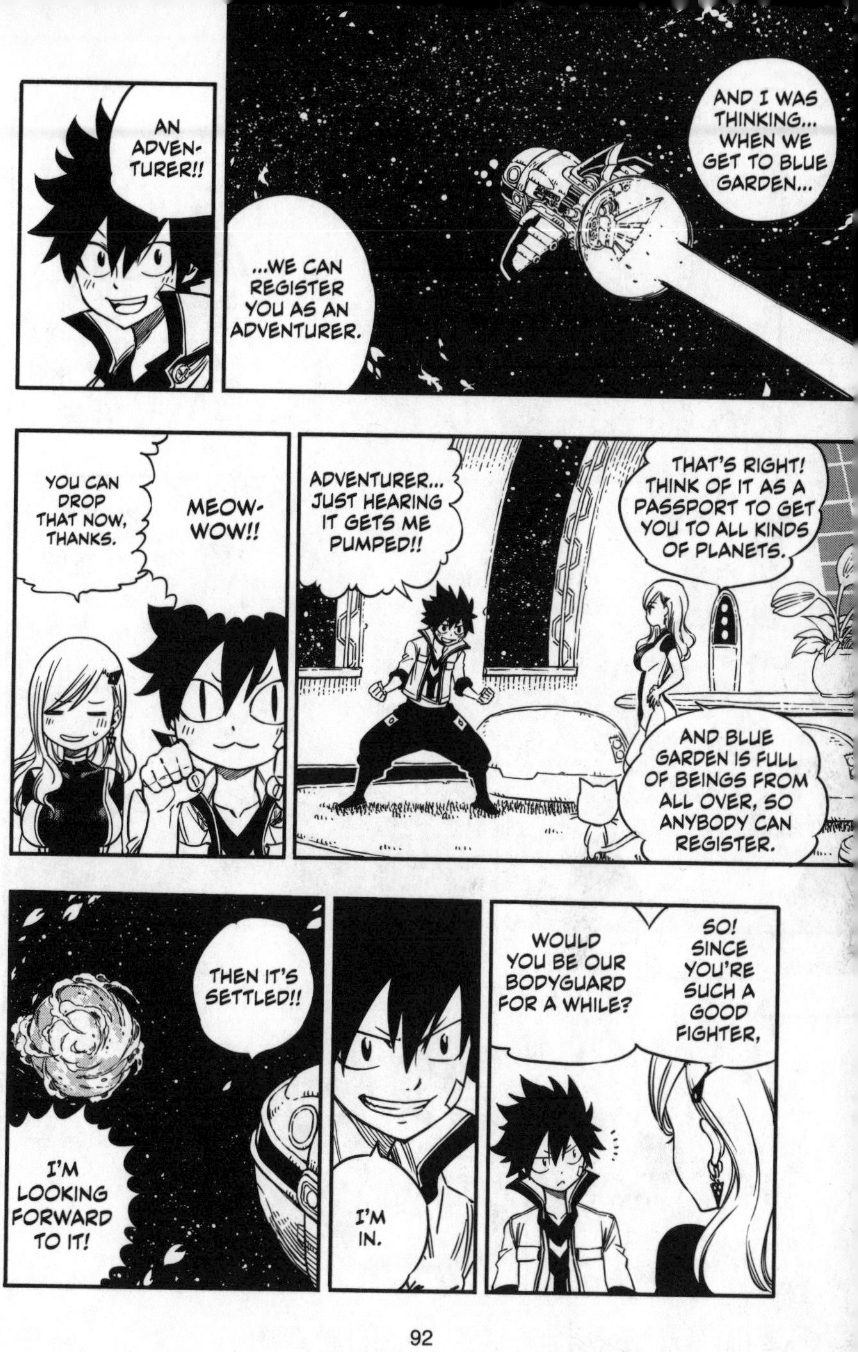
AND I WAS THINKING... WHEN WE GET TO BLUE GARDEN...
...WE CAN REGISTER YOU AS AN ADVENTURER.
AN ADVEN-TURER!!
THAT'S RIGHT! THINK OF IT AS A PASSPORT TO GET YOU TO ALL KINDS OF PLANETS.
ADVENTURER... JUST HEARING IT GETS ME PUMPED!!
AND BLUE GARDEN IS FULL OF BEINGS FROM ALL OVER, SO ANYBODY CAN REGISTER.
MEOW-WOW!!
YOU CAN DROP THAT NOW, THANKS.
SO! SINCE YOU'RE SUCH A GOOD FIGHTER,
WOULD YOU BE OUR BODYGUARD FOR A WHILE?
I'M IN.
THEN IT'S SETTLED!!
I'M LOOKING FORWARD TO IT!

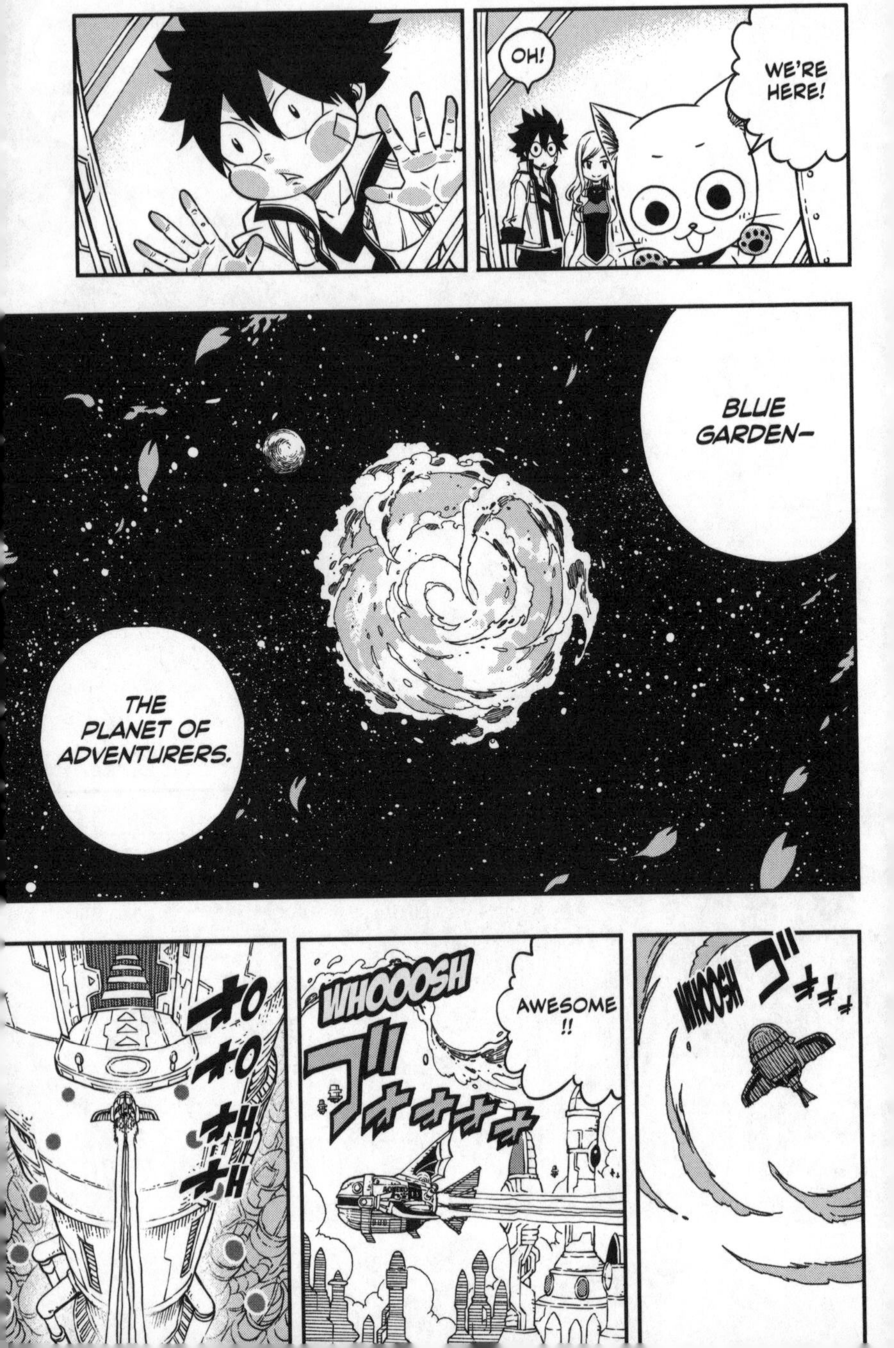
WE'RE HERE!
OH!
BLUE GARDEN—
THE PLANET OF ADVENTURERS.
WHOOSH
AWESOME!!
WHOOOSH

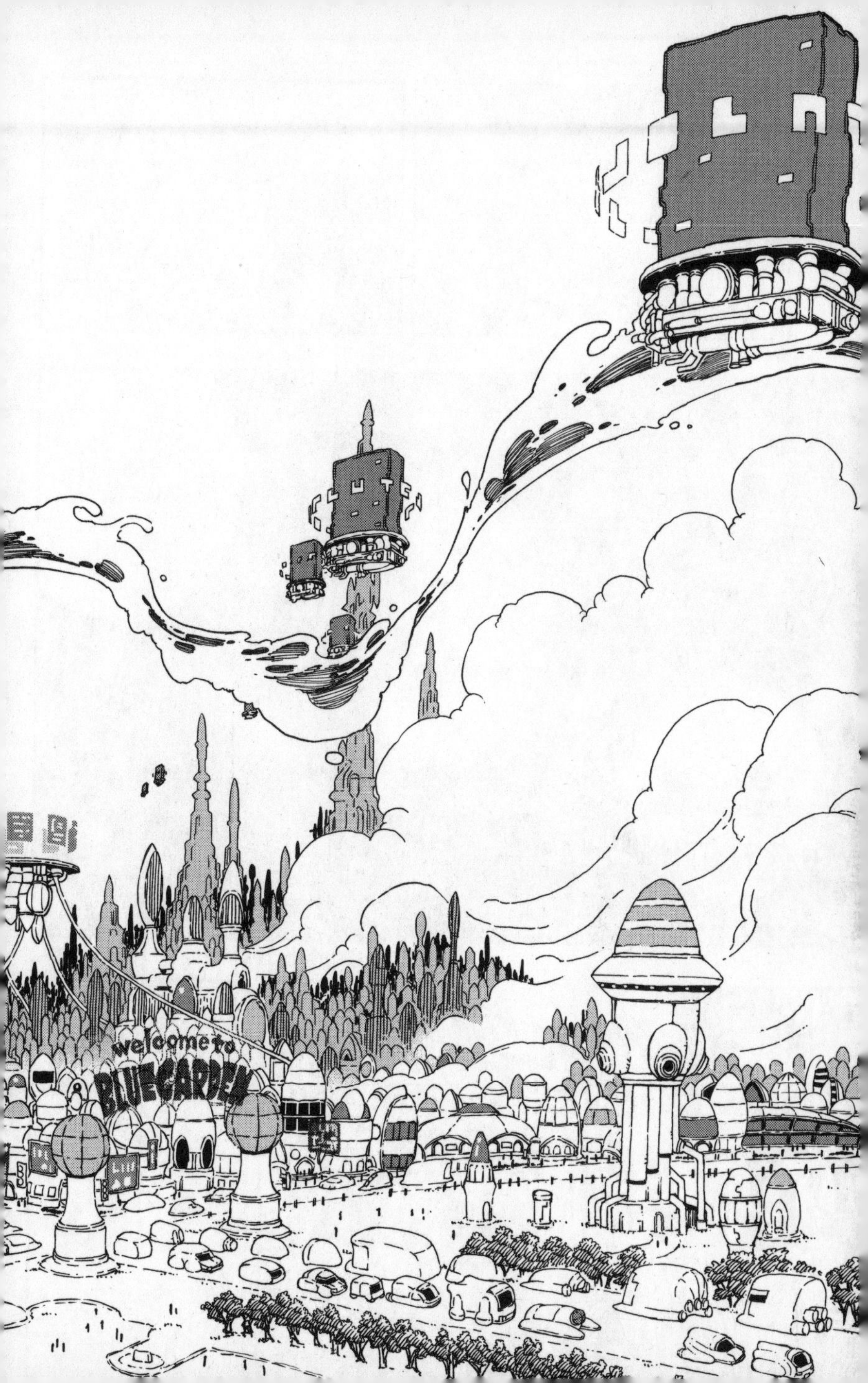
welcome to
BLUEGARDEN

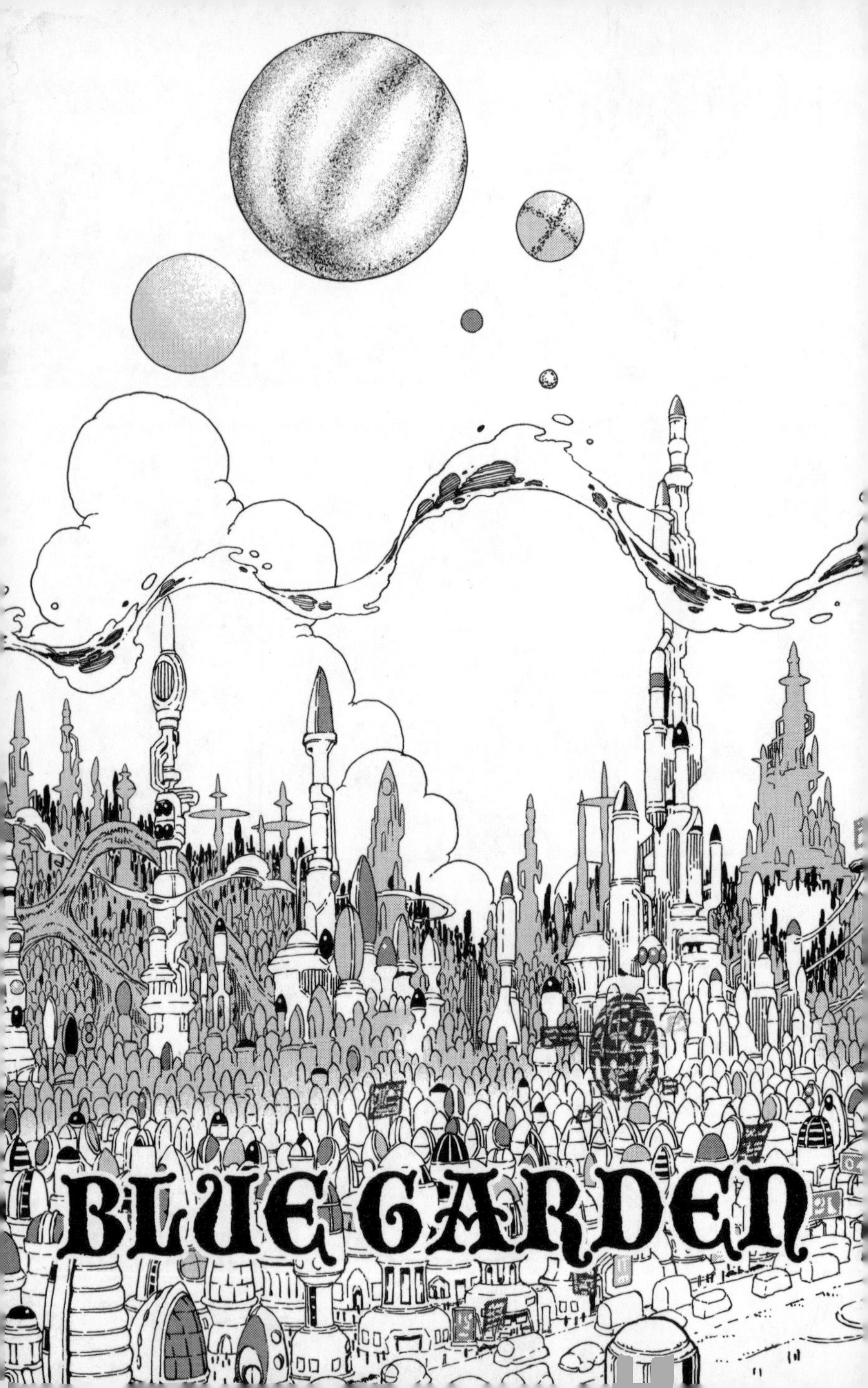
BLUE GARDEN

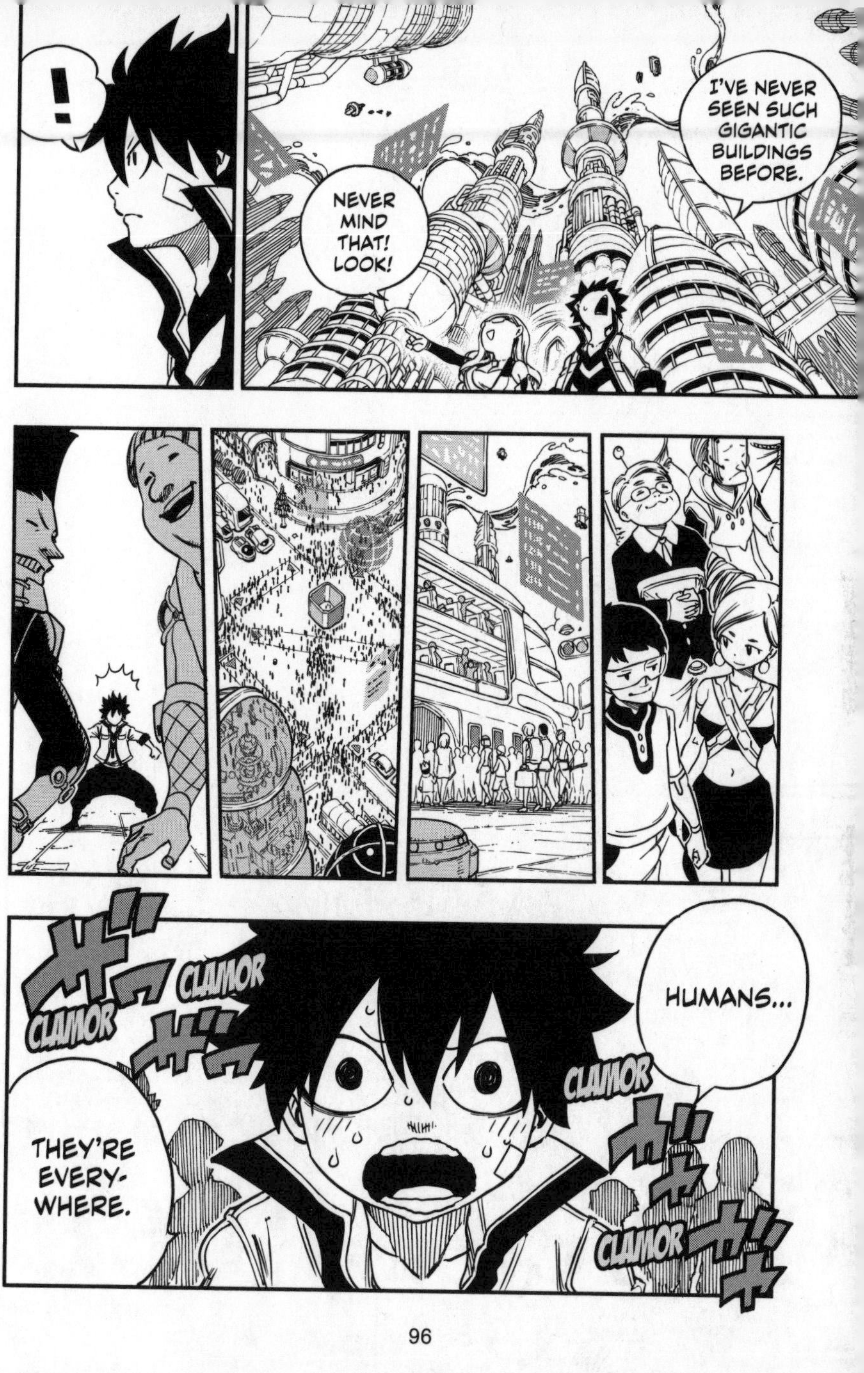
I'VE NEVER SEEN SUCH GIGANTIC BUILDINGS BEFORE.
NEVER MIND THAT! LOOK!
!
HUMANS...
CLAMOR
CLAMOR
THEY'RE EVERY-WHERE.
CLAMOR
CLAMOR

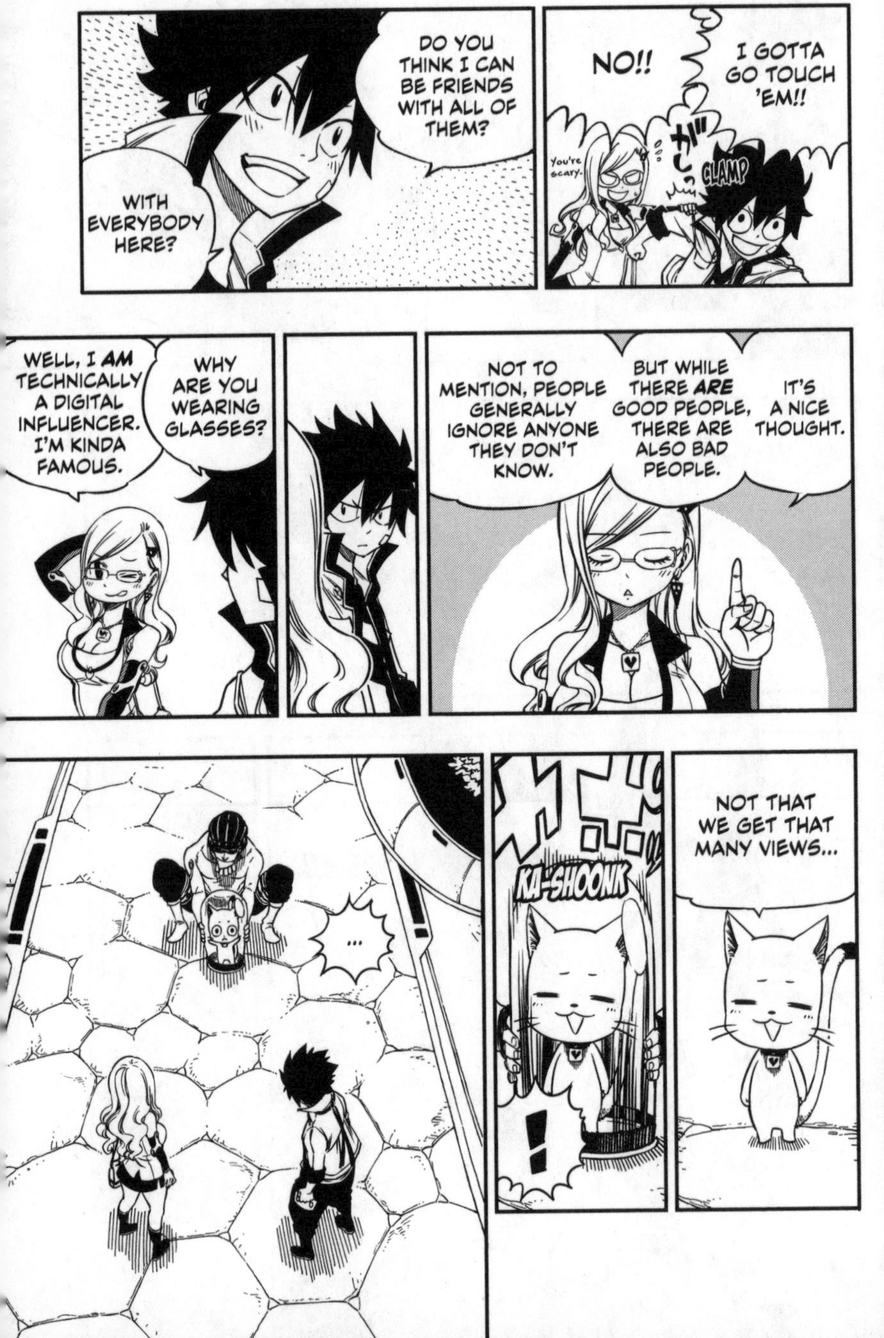
I GOTTA GO TOUCH 'EM!!
NO!!
CLAMP
You're scary.
DO YOU THINK I CAN BE FRIENDS WITH ALL OF THEM?
WITH EVERYBODY HERE?
IT'S A NICE THOUGHT.
BUT WHILE THERE ARE GOOD PEOPLE, THERE ARE ALSO BAD PEOPLE.
NOT TO MENTION, PEOPLE GENERALLY IGNORE ANYONE THEY DON'T KNOW.
WHY ARE YOU WEARING GLASSES?
WELL, I AM TECHNICALLY A DIGITAL INFLUENCER. I'M KINDA FAMOUS.
NOT THAT WE GET THAT MANY VIEWS...
KA-SHOONK
!
...

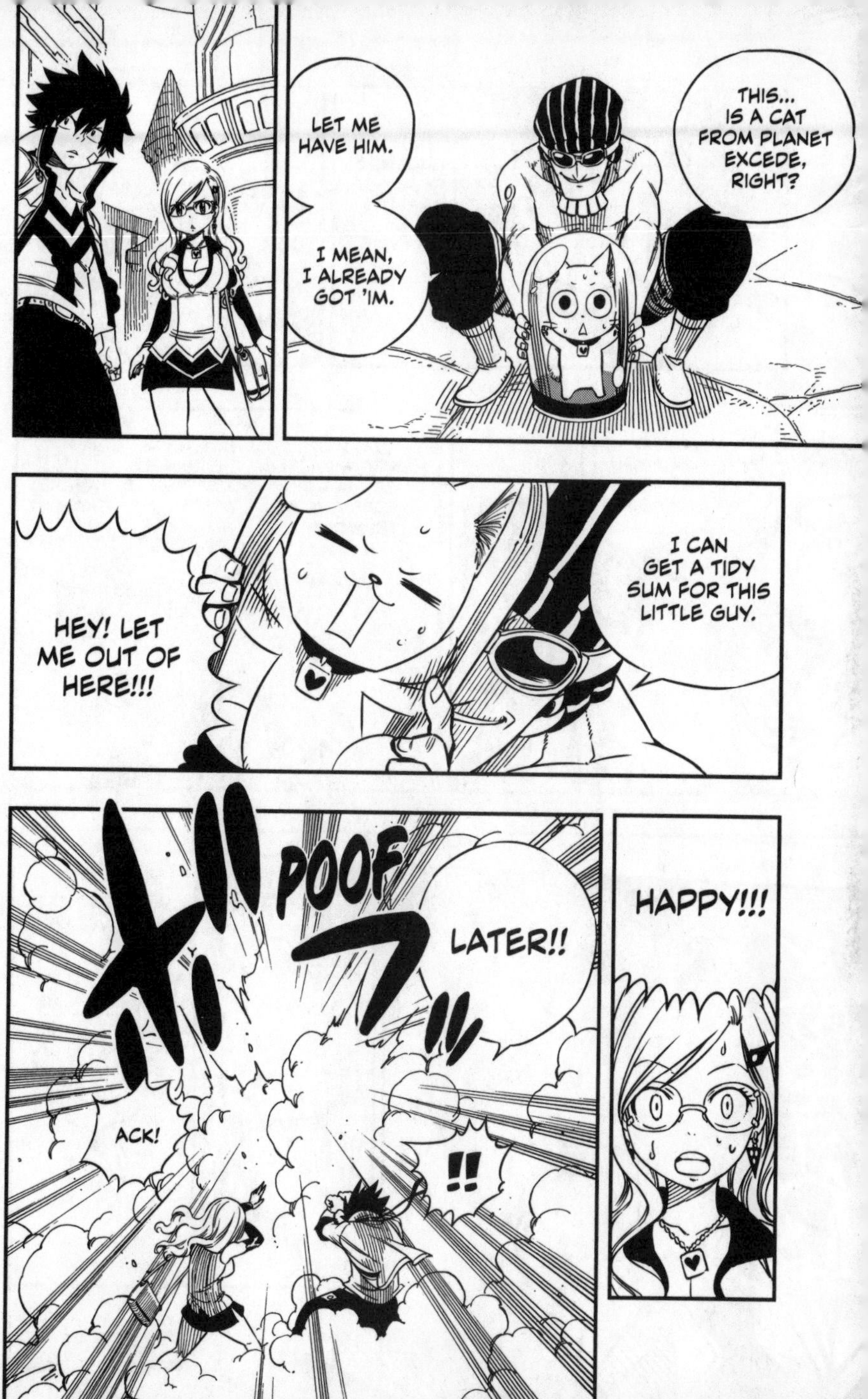
THIS... IS A CAT FROM PLANET EXCEDE, RIGHT?
LET ME HAVE HIM.
I MEAN, I ALREADY GOT 'IM.
I CAN GET A TIDY SUM FOR THIS LITTLE GUY.
HEY! LET ME OUT OF HERE!!!
HAPPY!!!
LATER!!
POOF
ACK!
!!

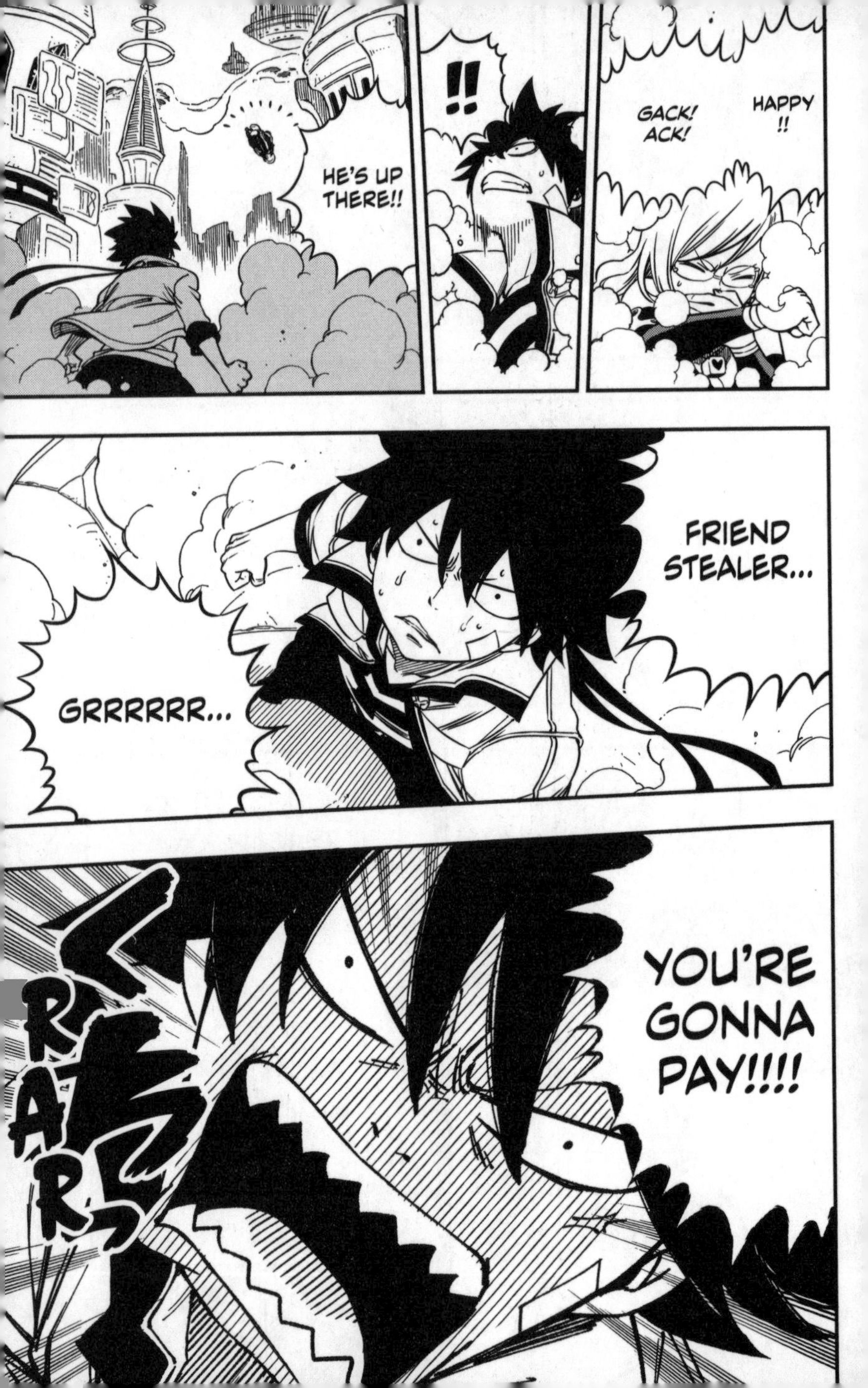
HAPPY !!
GACK! ACK!
!!
HE'S UP THERE!!
FRIEND STEALER...
GRRRRRR...
YOU'RE GONNA PAY!!!!
RAAR

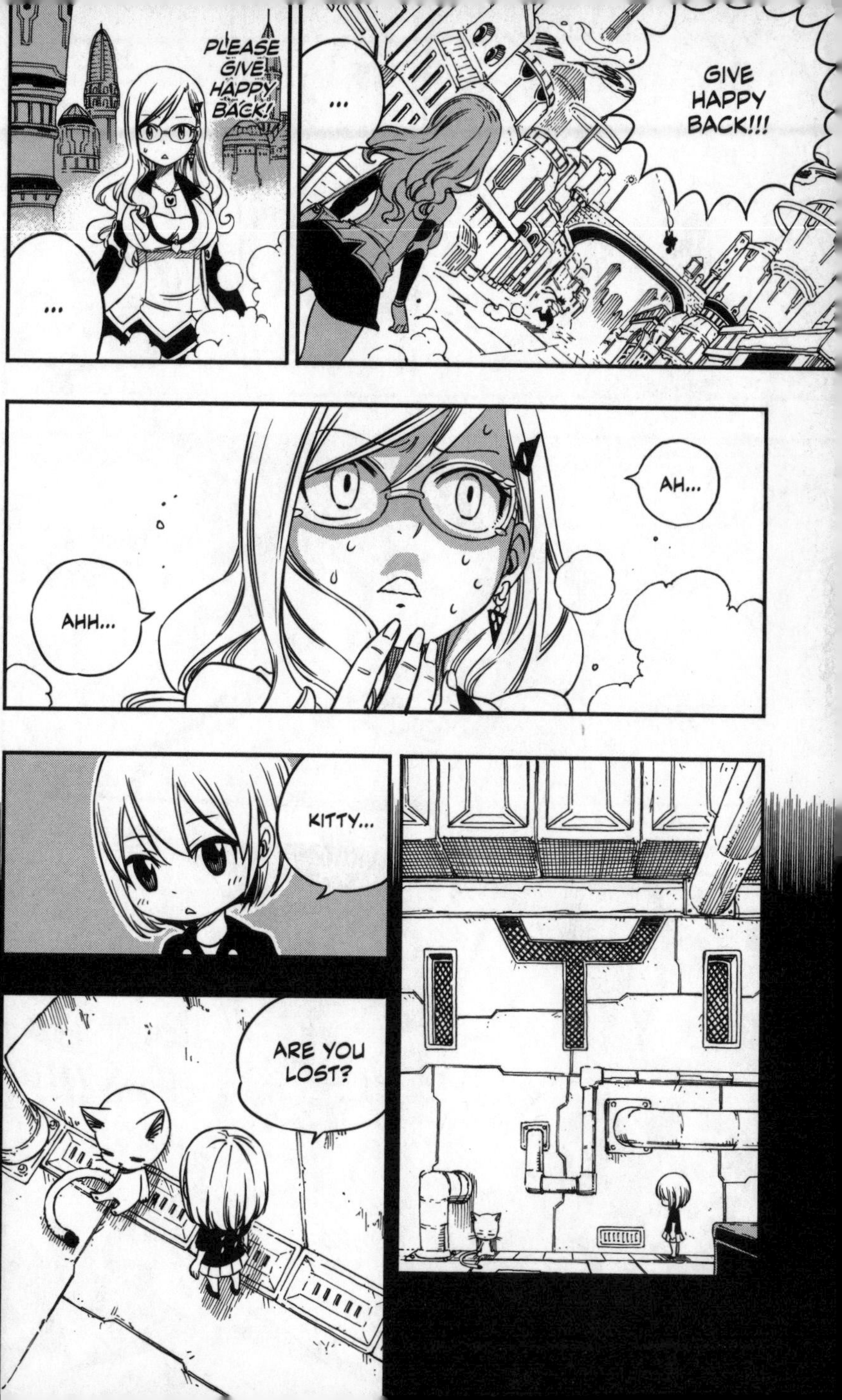
GIVE HAPPY BACK!!!
...
PLEASE GIVE HAPPY BACK!
...
AH...
AHH...
KITTY...
ARE YOU LOST?

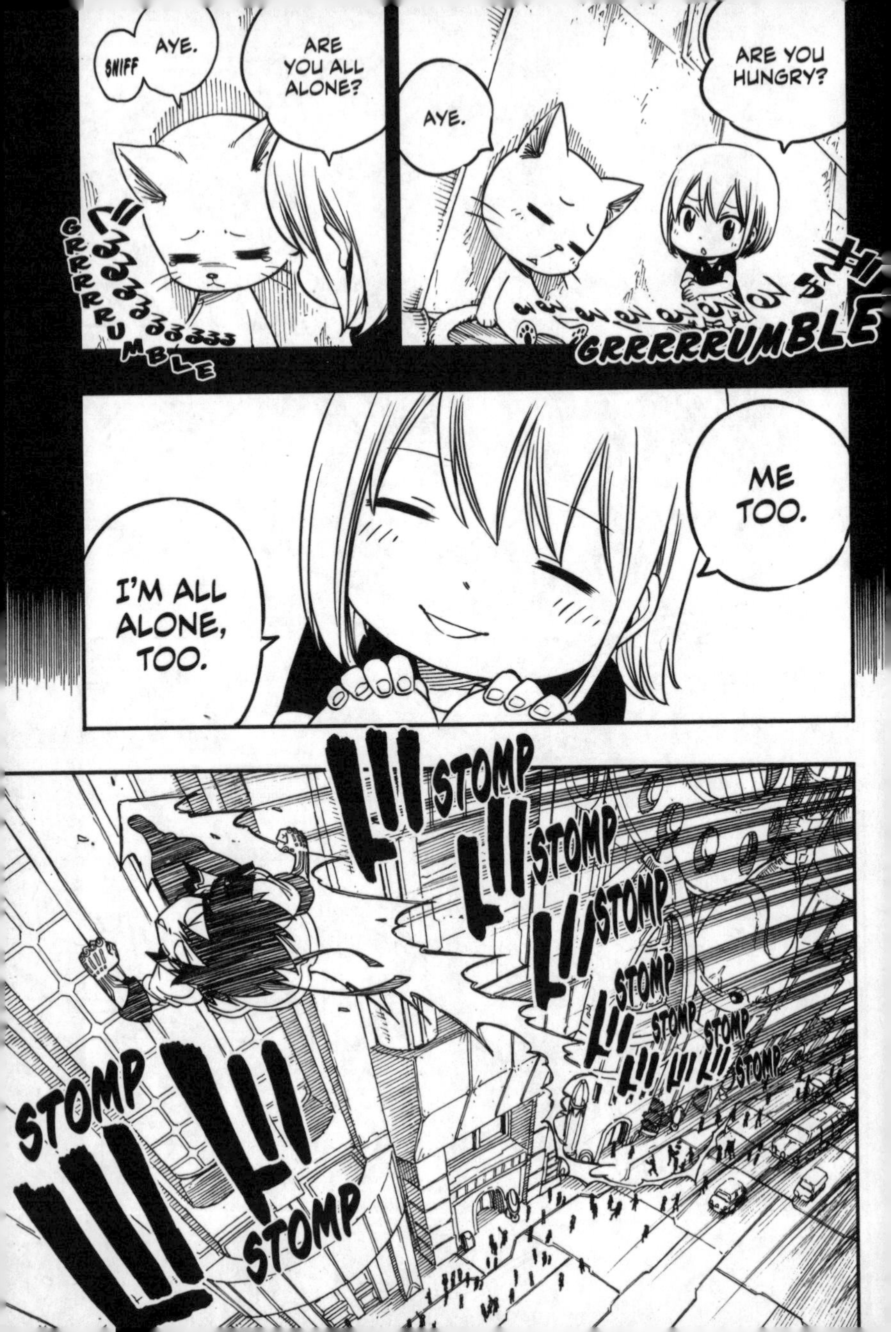
ARE YOU HUNGRY?
AYE.
GRRRRRUMBLE
ARE YOU ALL ALONE?
AYE.
SNIFF
GRRRRRUMBLE
ME TOO.
I'M ALL ALONE, TOO.
STOMP
STOMP
STOMP
STOMP
STOMP
STOMP
STOMP
STOMP
STOMP

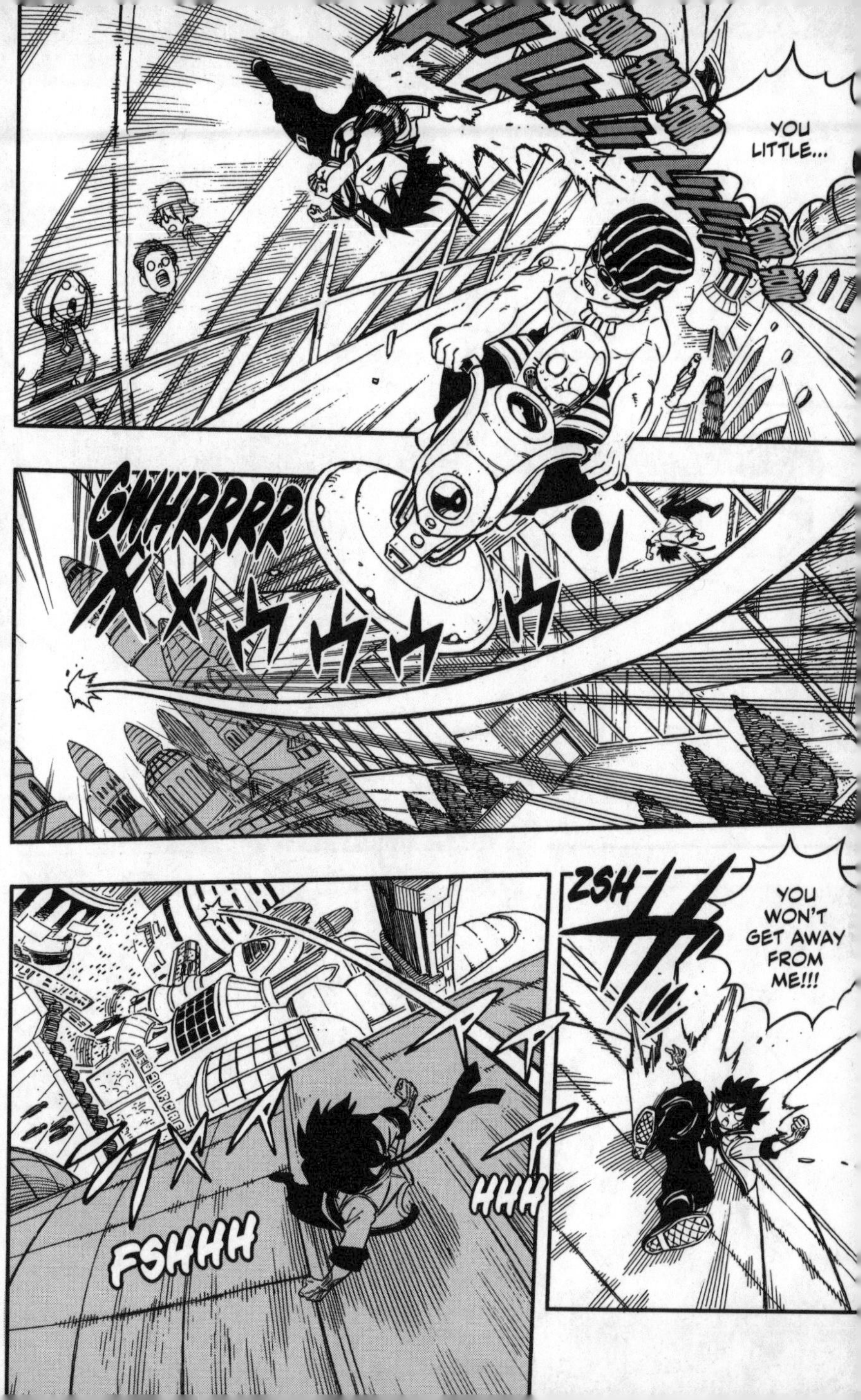
YOU LITTLE...
GWHRRRRR
ZSH
YOU WON'T GET AWAY FROM ME!!!
HHH
FSHHH

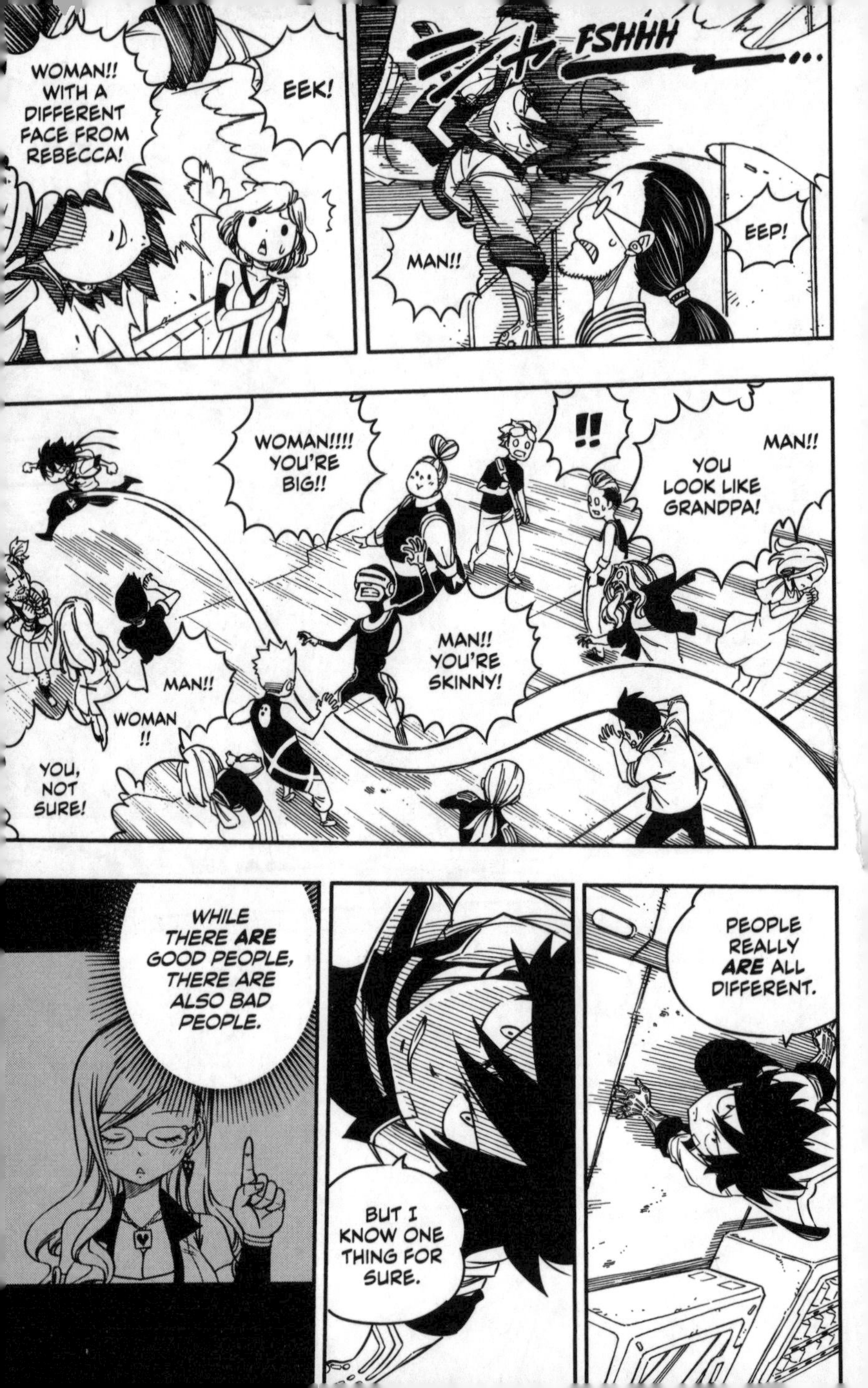
FSHHH...
EEP!
MAN!!
EEK!
WOMAN!! WITH A DIFFERENT FACE FROM REBECCA!
MAN!!
YOU LOOK LIKE GRANDPA!
!!
WOMAN!!!! YOU'RE BIG!!
MAN!! YOU'RE SKINNY!
MAN!!
WOMAN !!
YOU, NOT SURE!
PEOPLE REALLY ARE ALL DIFFERENT.
BUT I KNOW ONE THING FOR SURE.
WHILE THERE ARE GOOD PEOPLE, THERE ARE ALSO BAD PEOPLE.

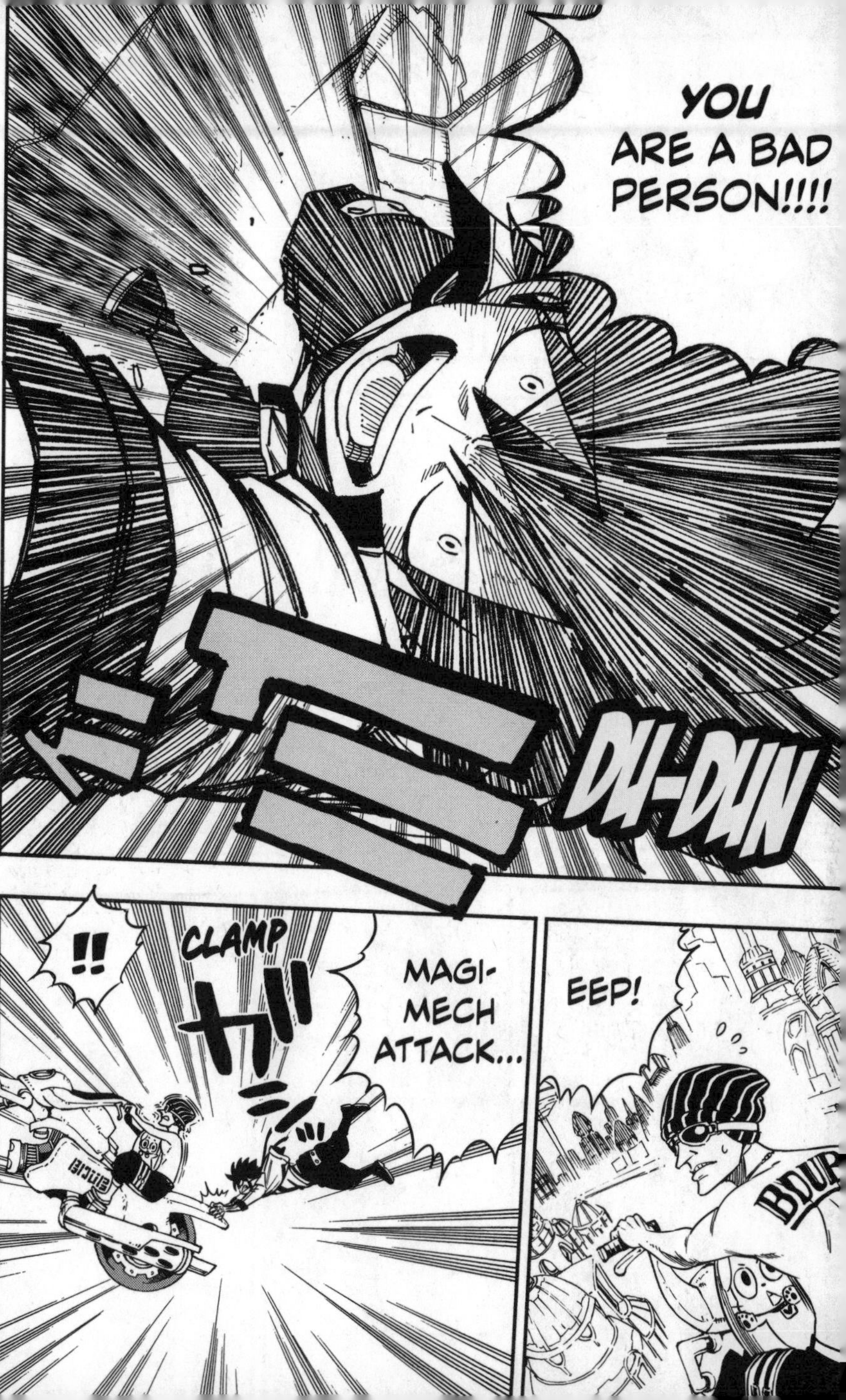
YOU ARE A BAD PERSON!!!!
DU-DUN
EEP!
MAGI-MECH ATTACK...
CLAMP
ガッ
!!

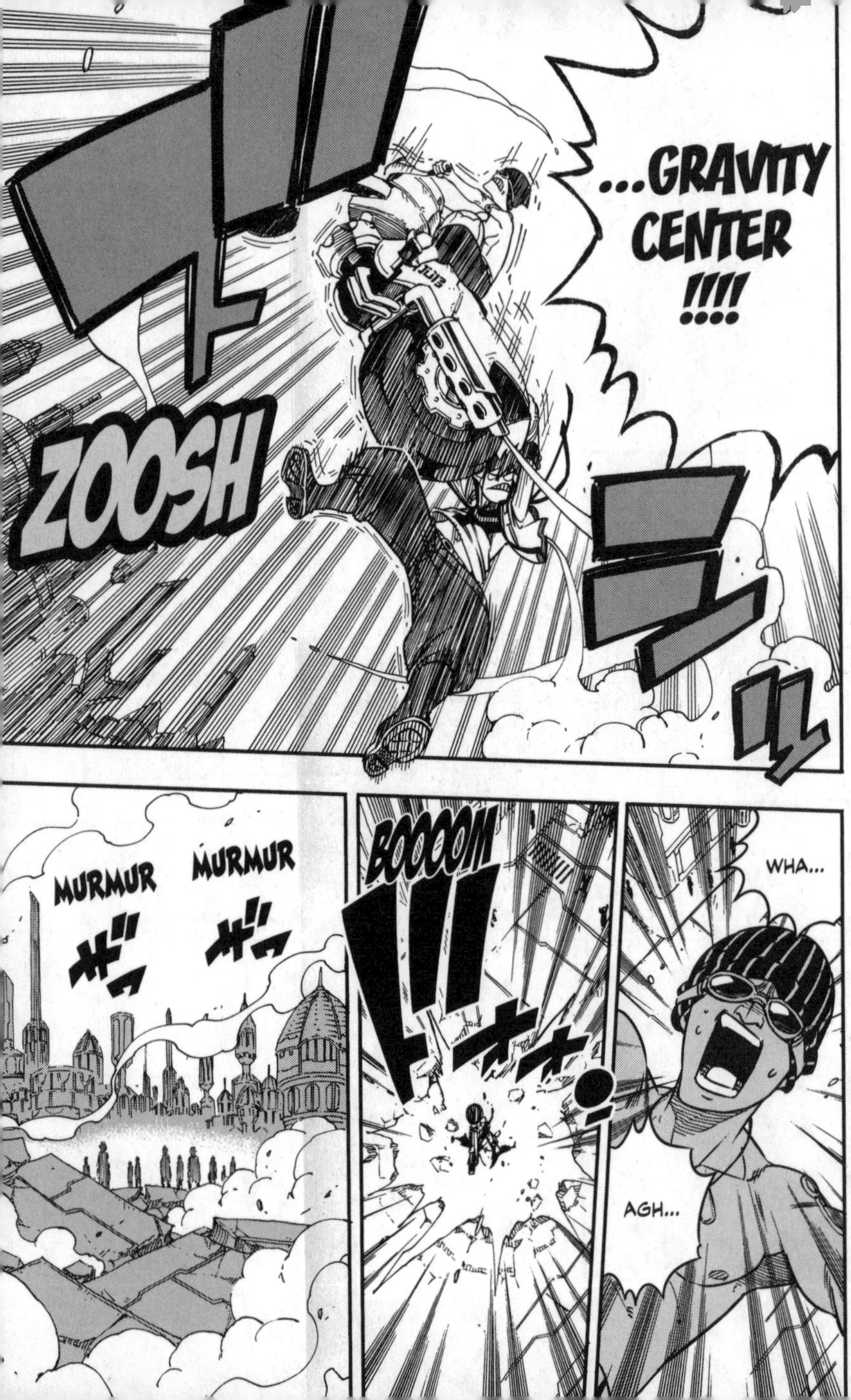
...GRAVITY CENTER !!!!
ZOOSH
WHA...
AGH...
BOOOOM
MURMUR
MURMUR

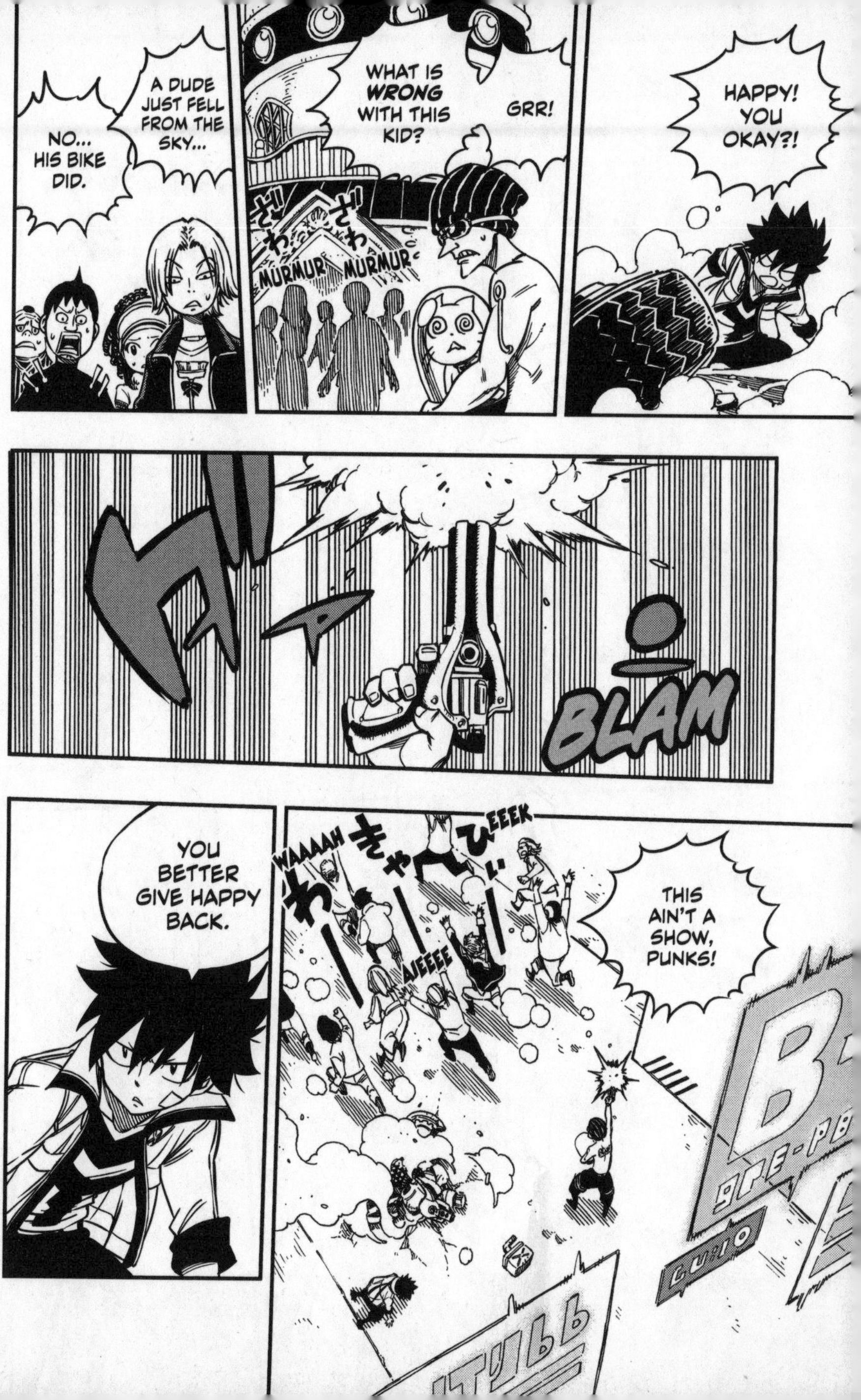
HAPPY! YOU OKAY?!
GRR!
WHAT IS WRONG WITH THIS KID?
ざわ ざわ
MURMUR MURMUR
A DUDE JUST FELL FROM THE SKY...
NO... HIS BIKE DID.
BLAM
THIS AIN'T A SHOW, PUNKS!
ひぃ EEEK
きゃ
わ WAAAAH
AIEEEE
YOU BETTER GIVE HAPPY BACK.

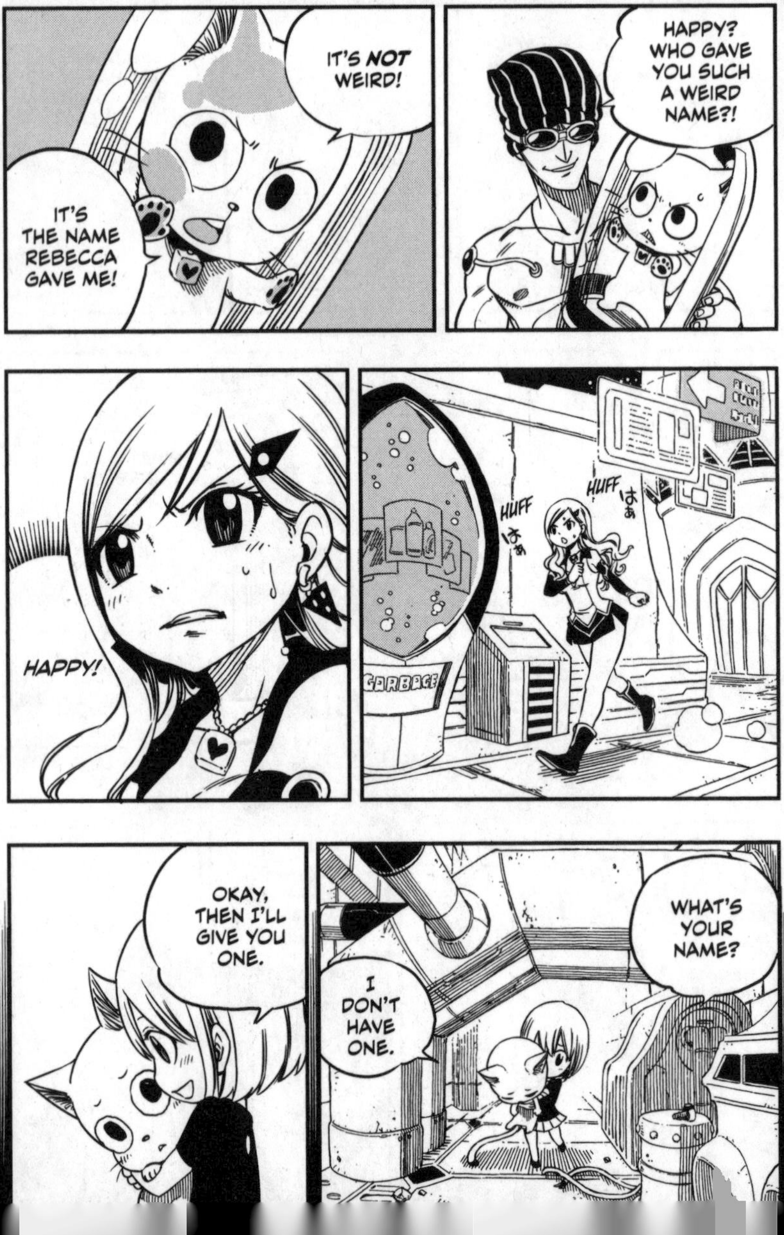
HAPPY? WHO GAVE YOU SUCH A WEIRD NAME?!
IT'S NOT WEIRD!
IT'S THE NAME REBECCA GAVE ME!
HUFF はぁ
HUFF はぁ
GARBAGE
HAPPY!
WHAT'S YOUR NAME?
I DON'T HAVE ONE.
OKAY, THEN I'LL GIVE YOU ONE.

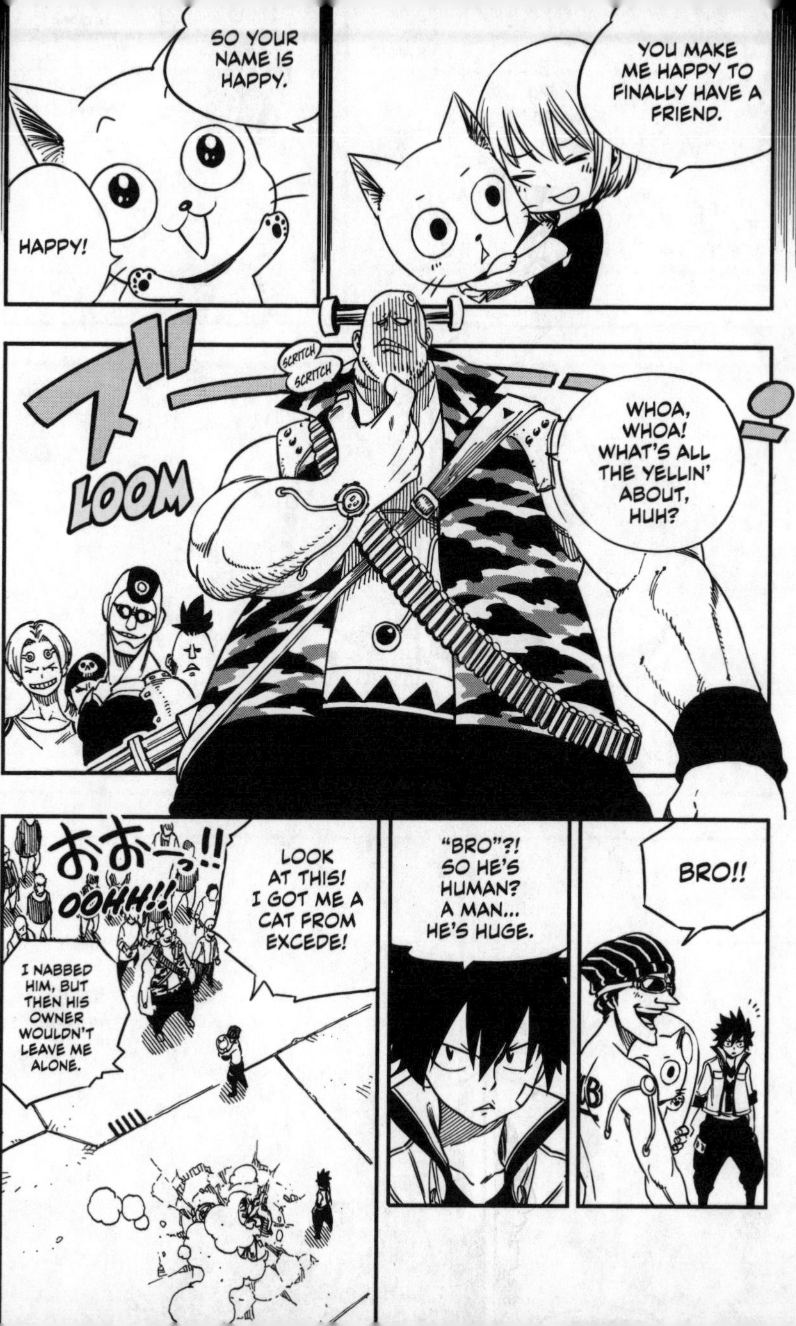
YOU MAKE ME HAPPY TO FINALLY HAVE A FRIEND.
SO YOUR NAME IS HAPPY.
HAPPY!
WHOA, WHOA! WHAT'S ALL THE YELLIN' ABOUT, HUH?
ズーッ
LOOM
SCRITCH
SCRITCH
BRO!!
"BRO"?! SO HE'S HUMAN? A MAN... HE'S HUGE.
LOOK AT THIS! I GOT ME A CAT FROM EXCEDE!
おおーっ!!
OOHH!!
I NABBED HIM, BUT THEN HIS OWNER WOULDN'T LEAVE ME ALONE.

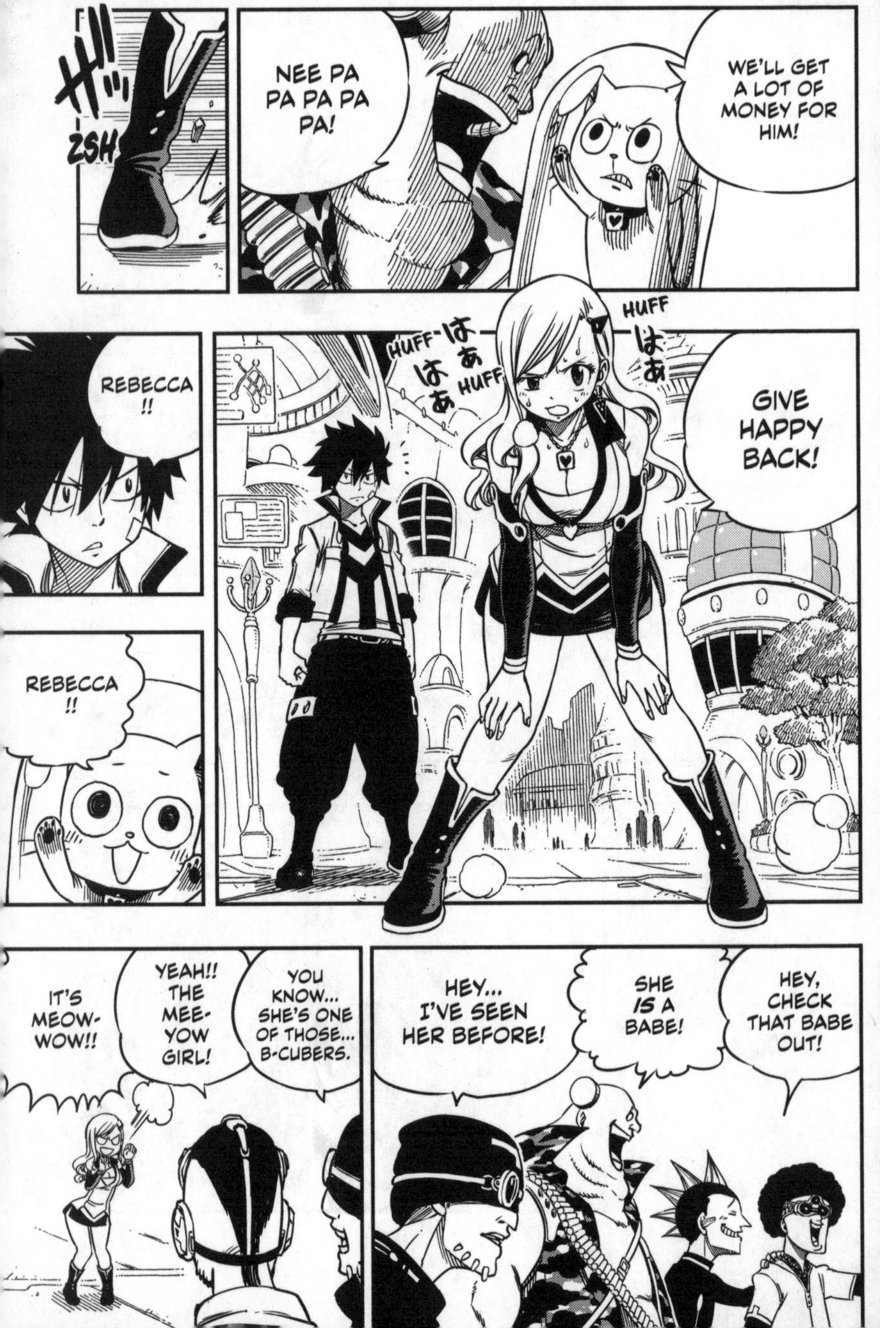

WE'LL GET A LOT OF MONEY FOR HIM!
NEE PA PA PA PA PA!
ザッ
ZSH
GIVE HAPPY BACK!
HUFF はあ
HUFF はあ
HUFF はあ
REBECCA!!
REBECCA!!
HEY, CHECK THAT BABE OUT!
SHE *IS* A BABE!
HEY... I'VE SEEN HER BEFORE!
YOU KNOW... SHE'S ONE OF THOSE... B-CUBERS.
YEAH!! THE MEE-YOW GIRL!
IT'S MEOW-WOW!!

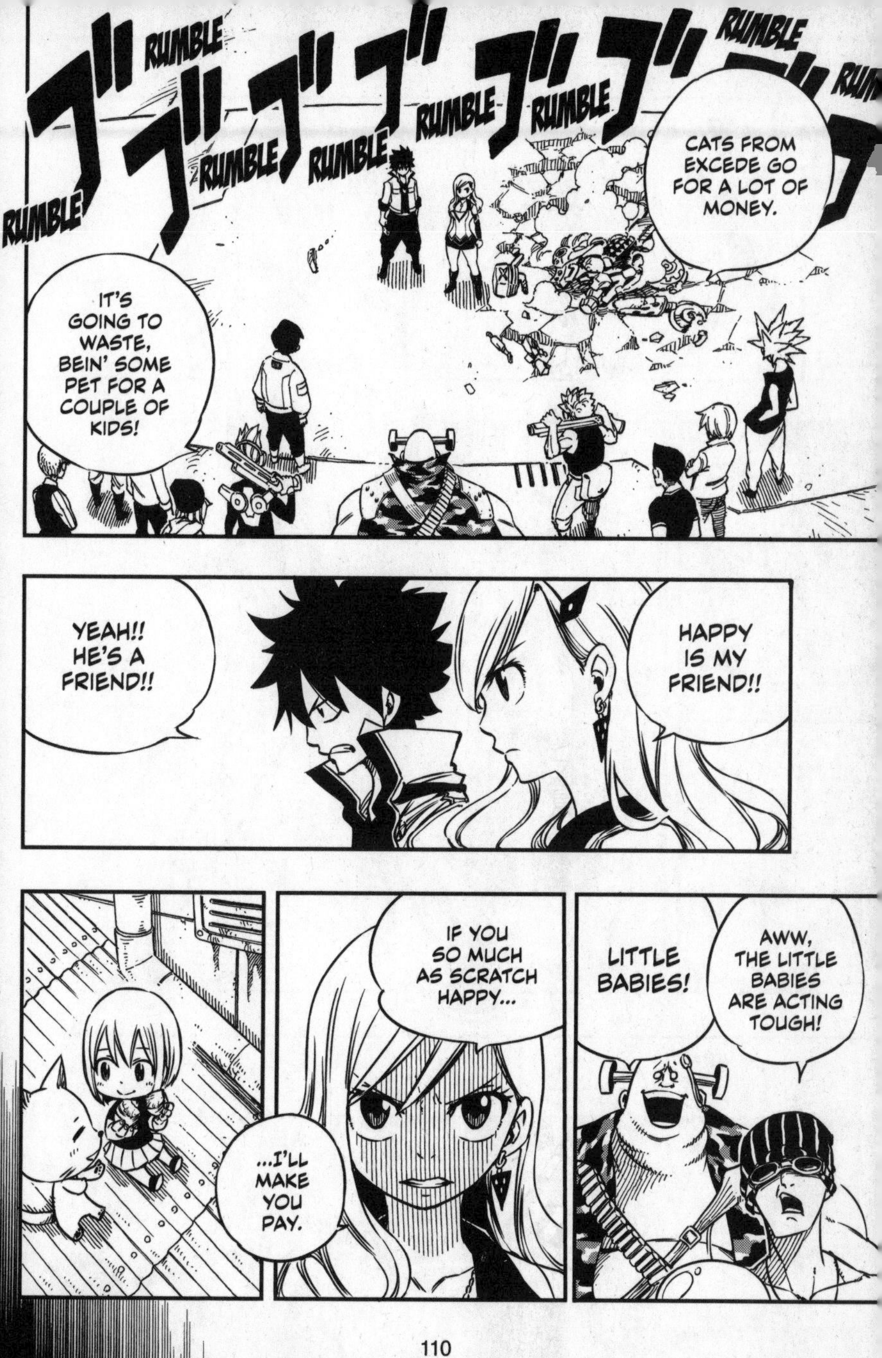
RUMBLE RUMBLE RUMBLE RUMBLE RUMBLE RUMBLE RUMBLE RUMBLE RUMBLE
CATS FROM EXCEDE GO FOR A LOT OF MONEY.
IT'S GOING TO WASTE, BEIN' SOME PET FOR A COUPLE OF KIDS!
HAPPY IS MY FRIEND!!
YEAH!! HE'S A FRIEND!!
AWW, THE LITTLE BABIES ARE ACTING TOUGH!
LITTLE BABIES!
IF YOU SO MUCH AS SCRATCH HAPPY...
...I'LL MAKE YOU PAY.

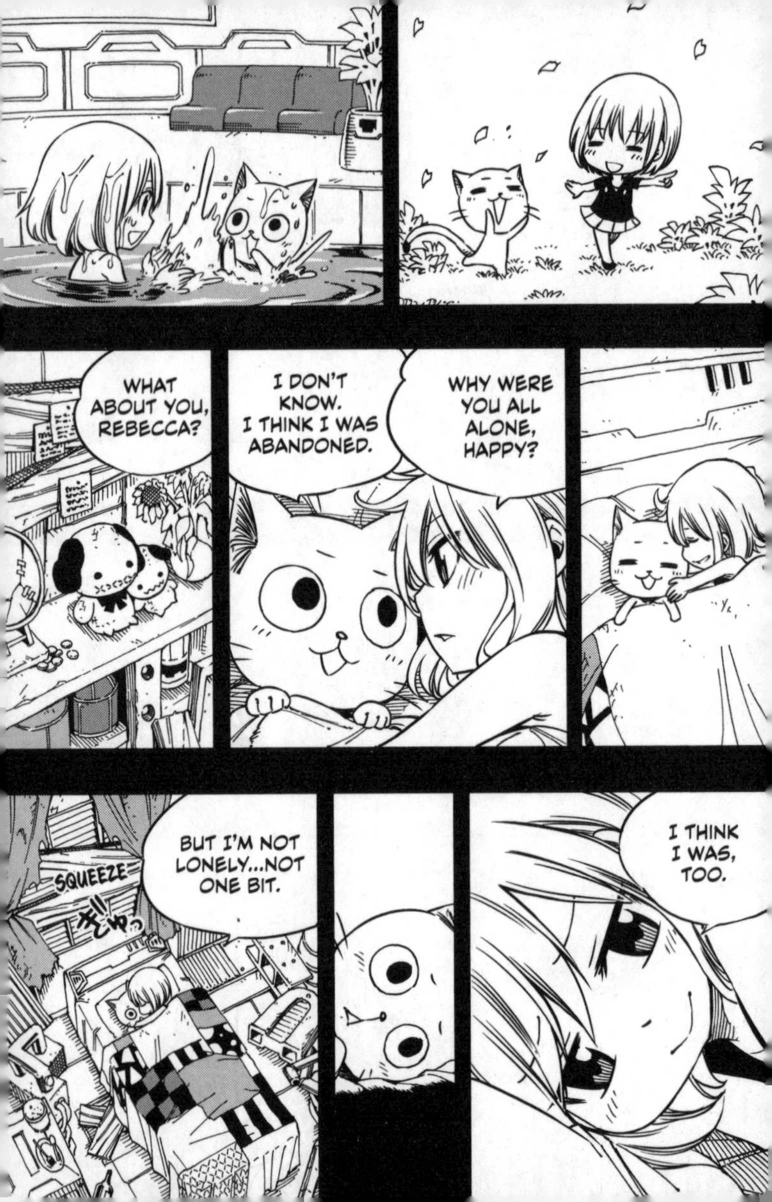
WHY WERE YOU ALL ALONE, HAPPY?
I DON'T KNOW. I THINK I WAS ABANDONED.
WHAT ABOUT YOU, REBECCA?
I THINK I WAS, TOO.
BUT I'M NOT LONELY...NOT ONE BIT.
SQUEEZE

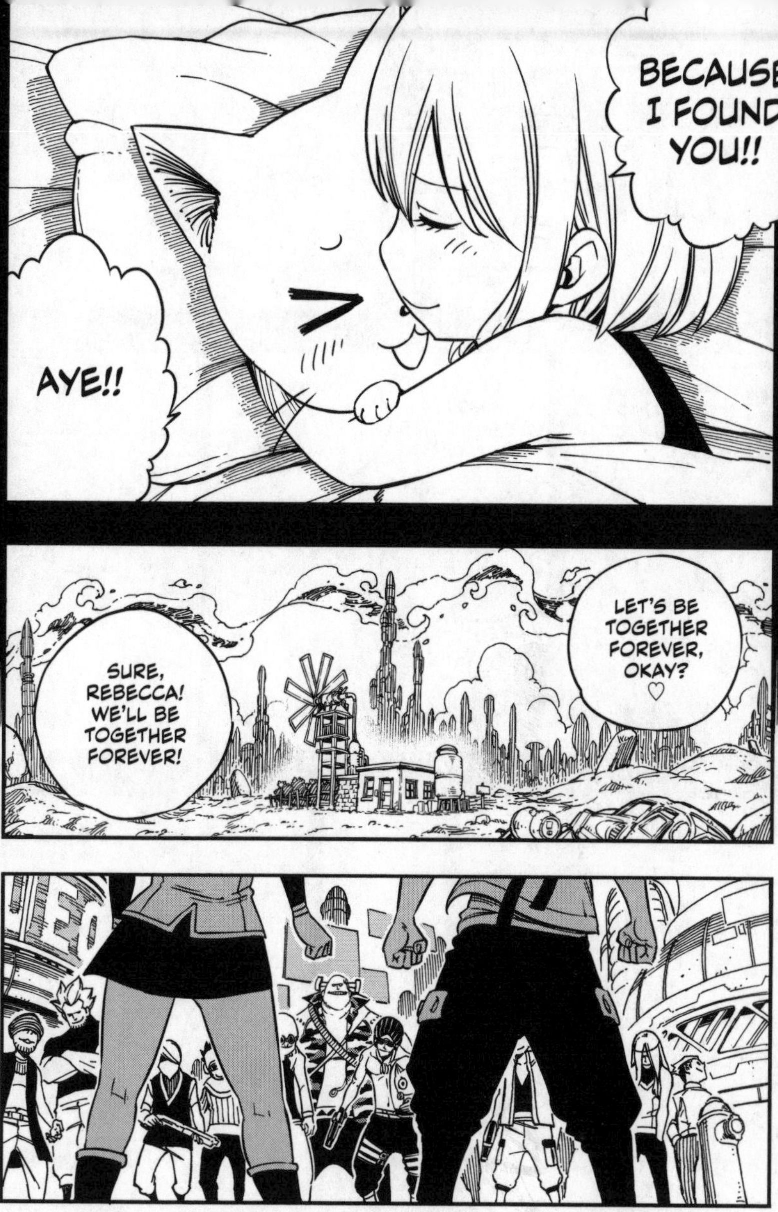
BECAUSE I FOUND YOU!!
AYE!!
LET'S BE TOGETHER FOREVER, OKAY? ♡
SURE, REBECCA! WE'LL BE TOGETHER FOREVER!

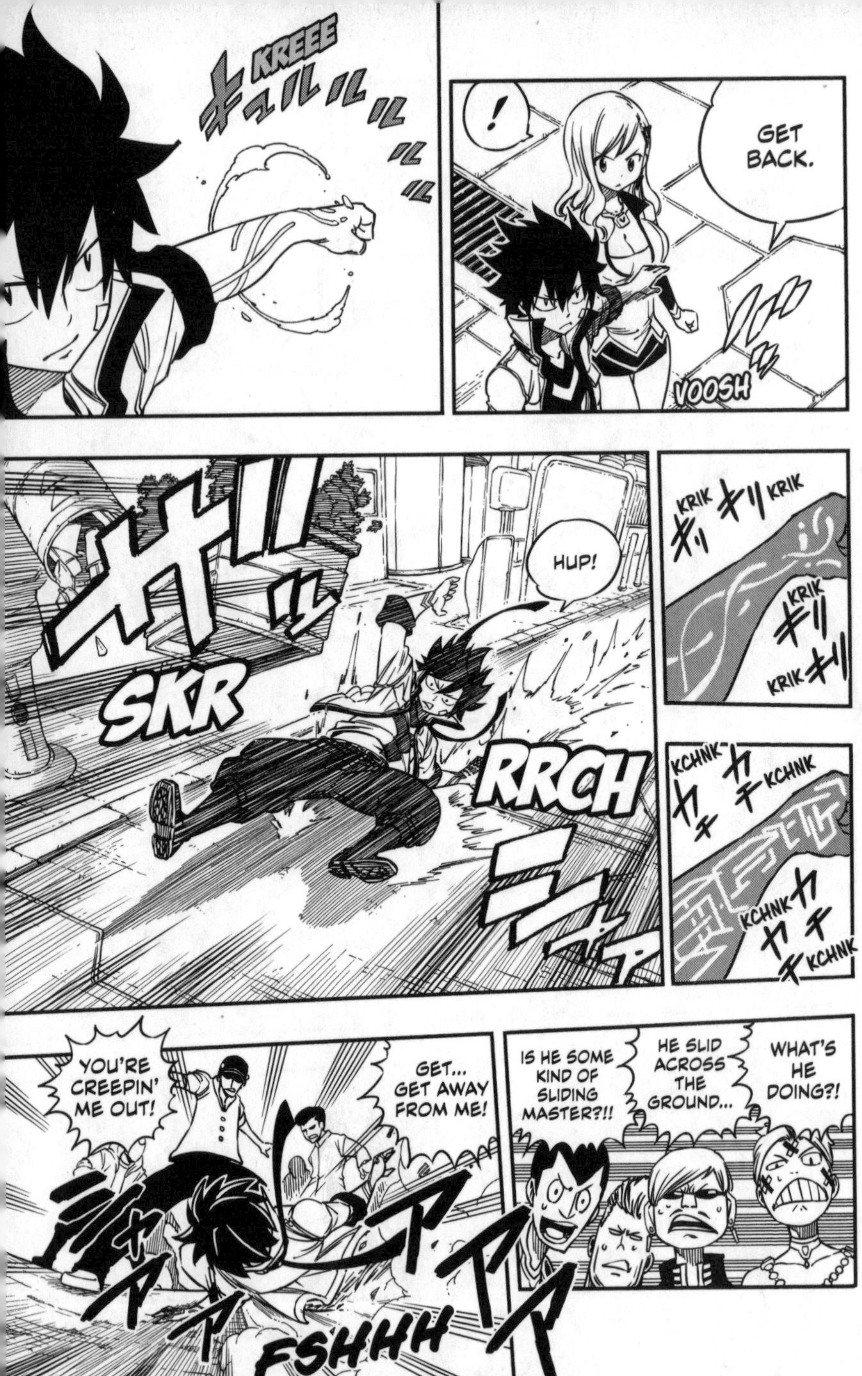
!
GET BACK.
VOOSH
KREEE
KRIK
KRIK
KRIK
KRIK
KCHNK
KCHNK
KCHNK
KCHNK
HUP!
SKR
RRCH
WHAT'S HE DOING?!
HE SLID ACROSS THE GROUND...
IS HE SOME KIND OF SLIDING MASTER?!!
GET... GET AWAY FROM ME!
YOU'RE CREEPIN' ME OUT!
FSHHH

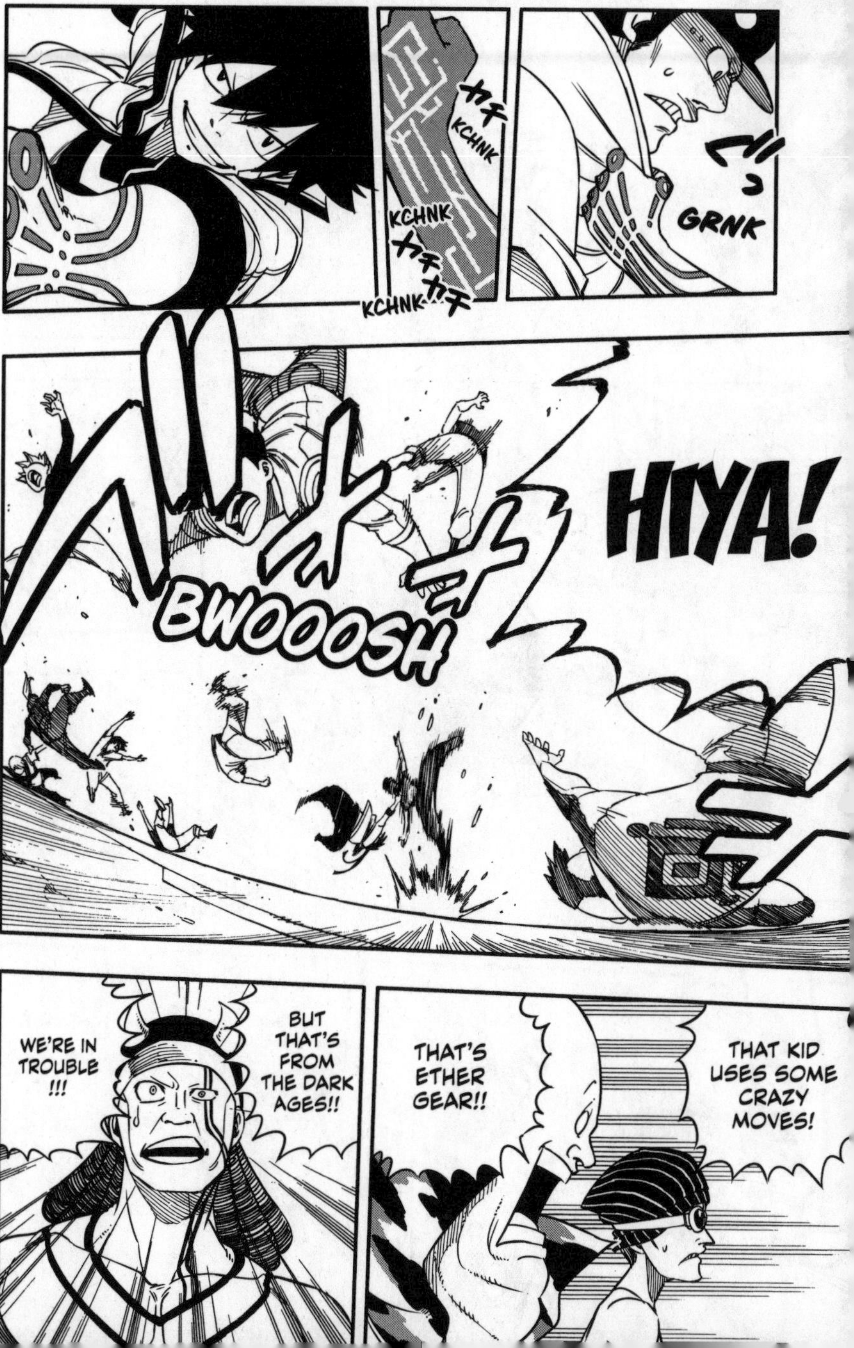

GRNK
カチ
KCHNK
KCHNK
カチ
カチ
KCHNK
HIYA!
BWOOOSH
THAT KID USES SOME CRAZY MOVES!
THAT'S ETHER GEAR!!
BUT THAT'S FROM THE DARK AGES!!
WE'RE IN TROUBLE !!!

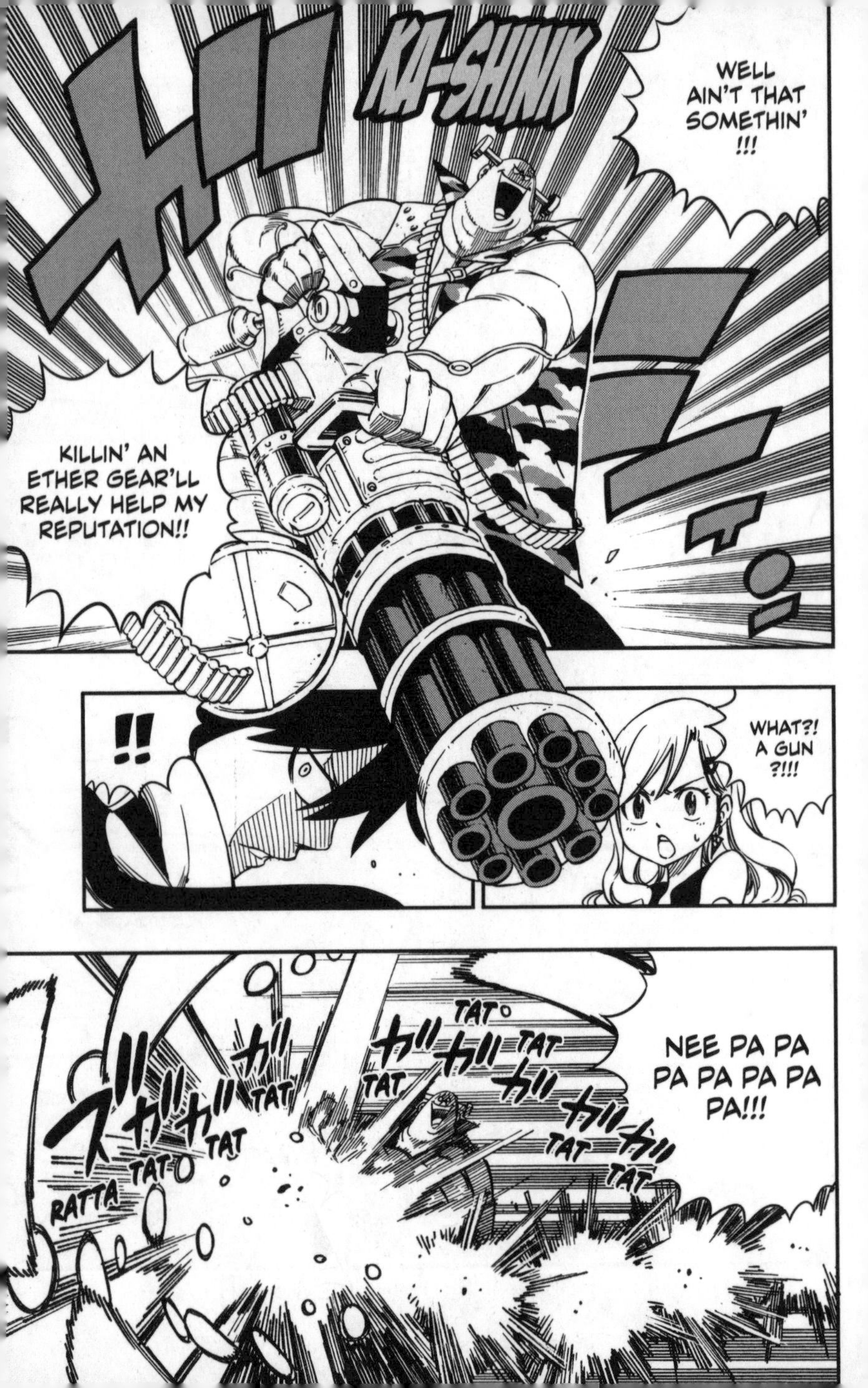
WELL AIN'T THAT SOMETHIN' !!!
KA-SHINK
KILLIN' AN ETHER GEAR'LL REALLY HELP MY REPUTATION!!
WHAT?! A GUN ?!!!
!!
NEE PA PA PA PA PA PA PA!!!
TAT
TAT
TAT
TAT
TAT
TAT
TAT
TAT
RATTA

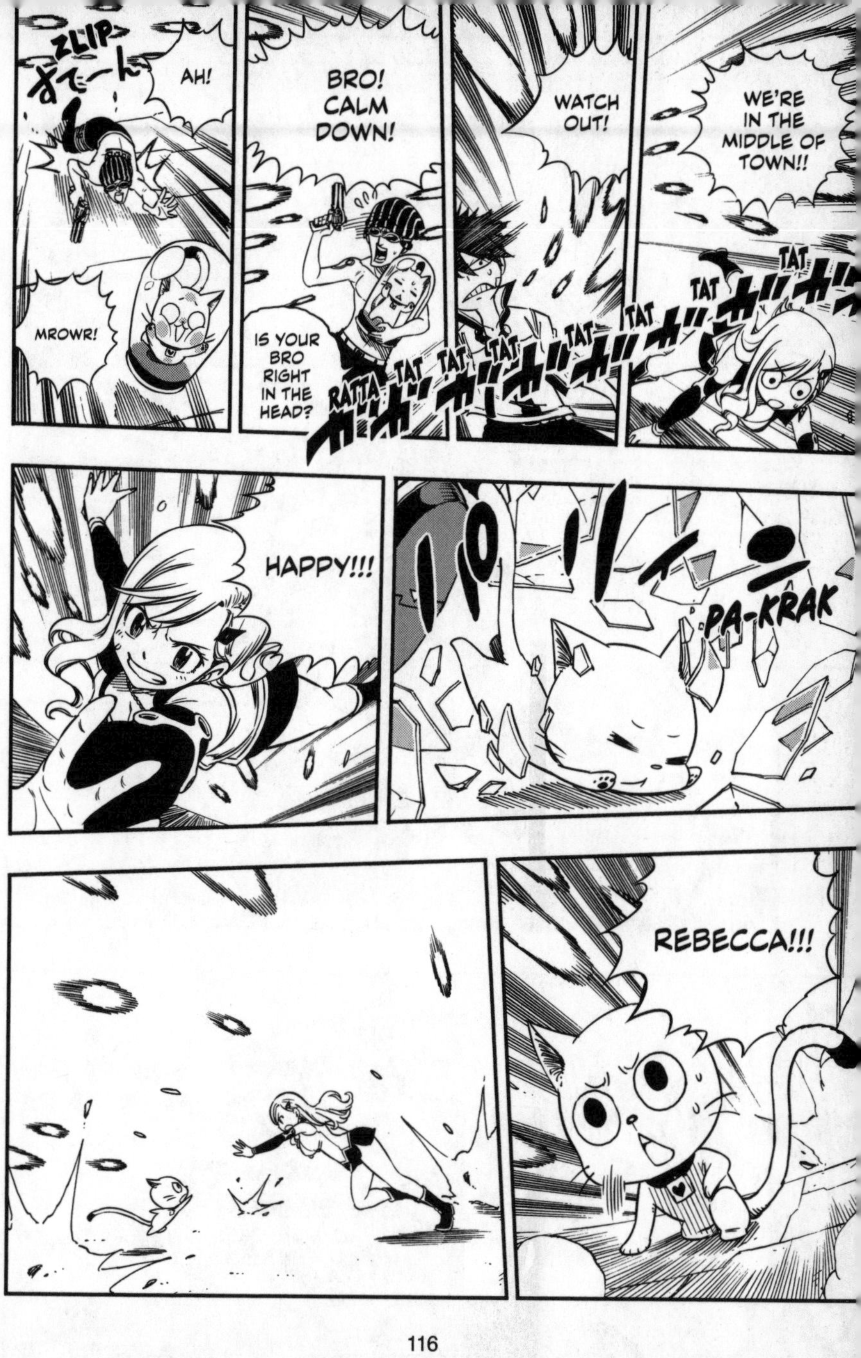
WE'RE IN THE MIDDLE OF TOWN!!
TAT TAT
WATCH OUT!
RATTA TAT TAT TAT TAT TAT
BRO! CALM DOWN!
IS YOUR BRO RIGHT IN THE HEAD?
ZLIP
すてーん
AH!
MROWR!
PA-KRAK
HAPPY!!!
REBECCA!!!

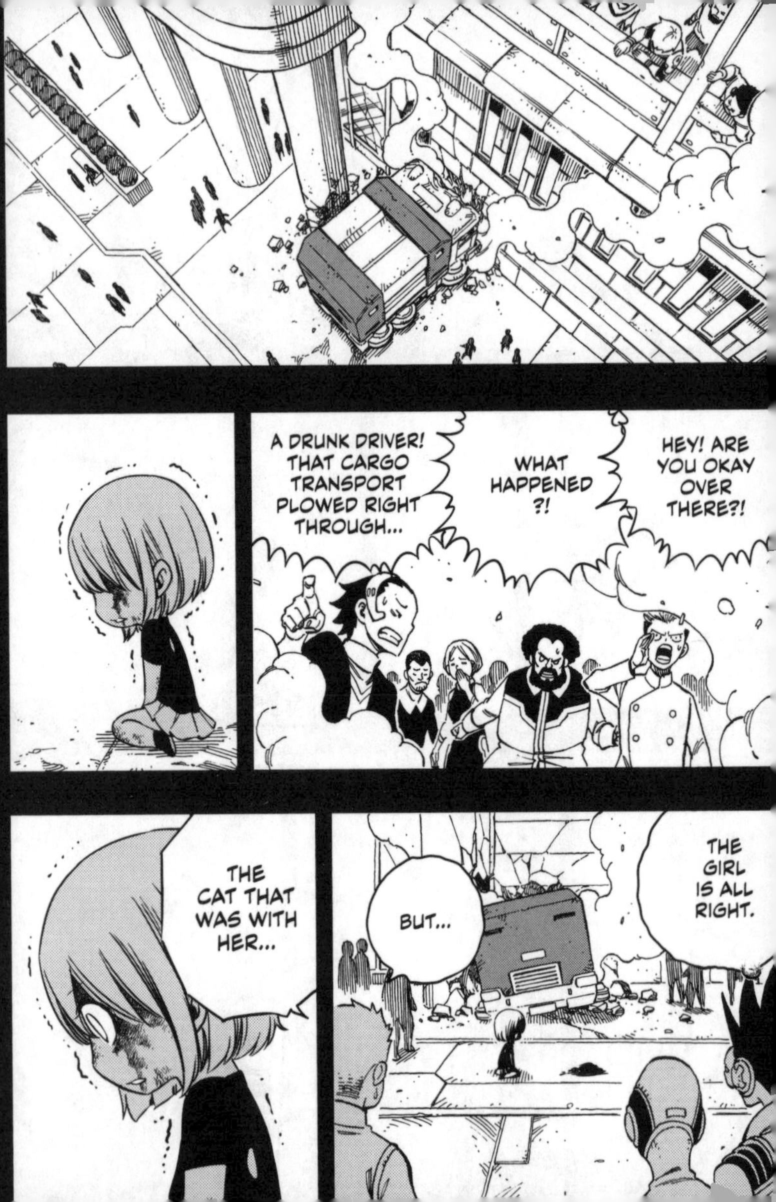
HEY! ARE YOU OKAY OVER THERE?!
WHAT HAPPENED?!
A DRUNK DRIVER! THAT CARGO TRANSPORT PLOWED RIGHT THROUGH...
THE GIRL IS ALL RIGHT.
BUT...
THE CAT THAT WAS WITH HER...

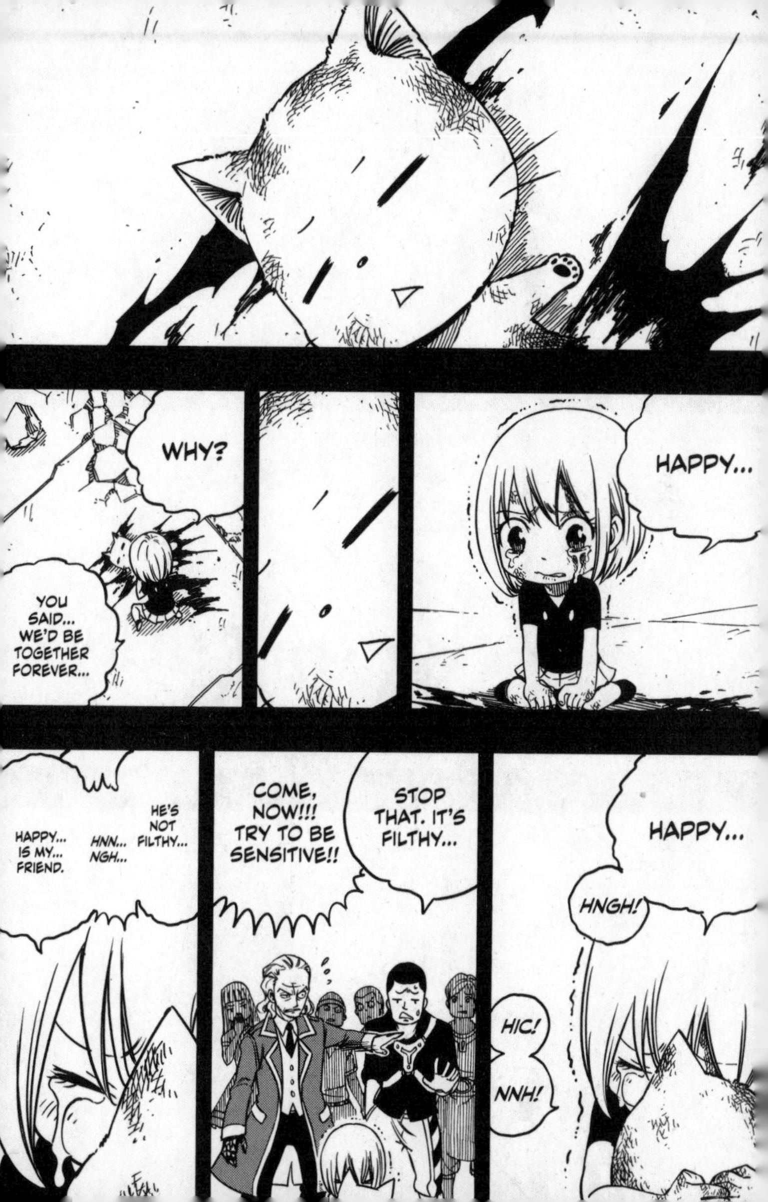
HAPPY...
WHY?
YOU SAID... WE'D BE TOGETHER FOREVER...
HAPPY...
HNGH!
HIC!
NNH!
STOP THAT. IT'S FILTHY...
COME, NOW!!! TRY TO BE SENSITIVE!!
HE'S NOT FILTHY...
HNN... NGH...
HAPPY... IS MY... FRIEND.

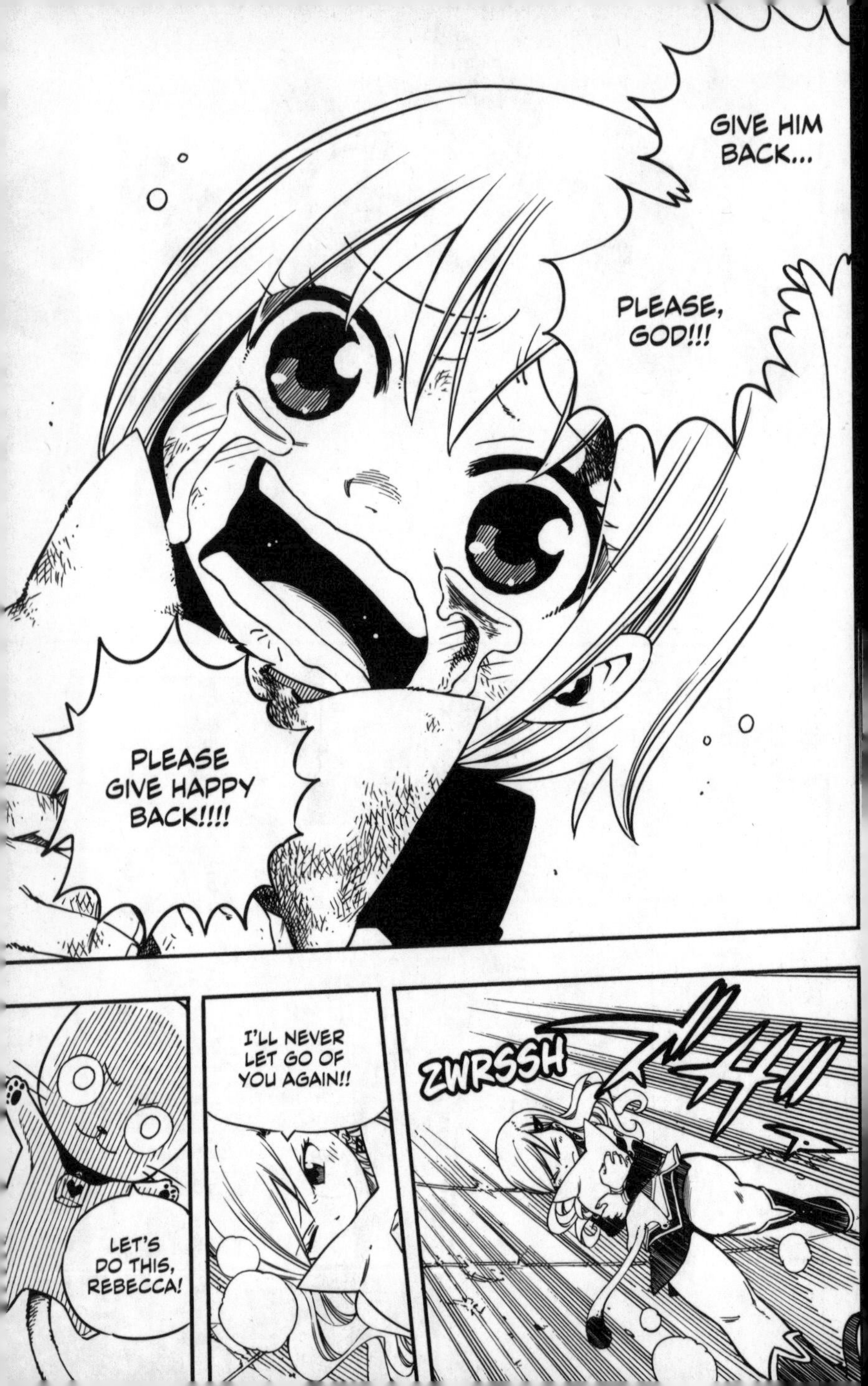
GIVE HIM BACK...
PLEASE, GOD!!!
PLEASE GIVE HAPPY BACK!!!!
ZWRSSH
I'LL NEVER LET GO OF YOU AGAIN!!
LET'S DO THIS, REBECCA!

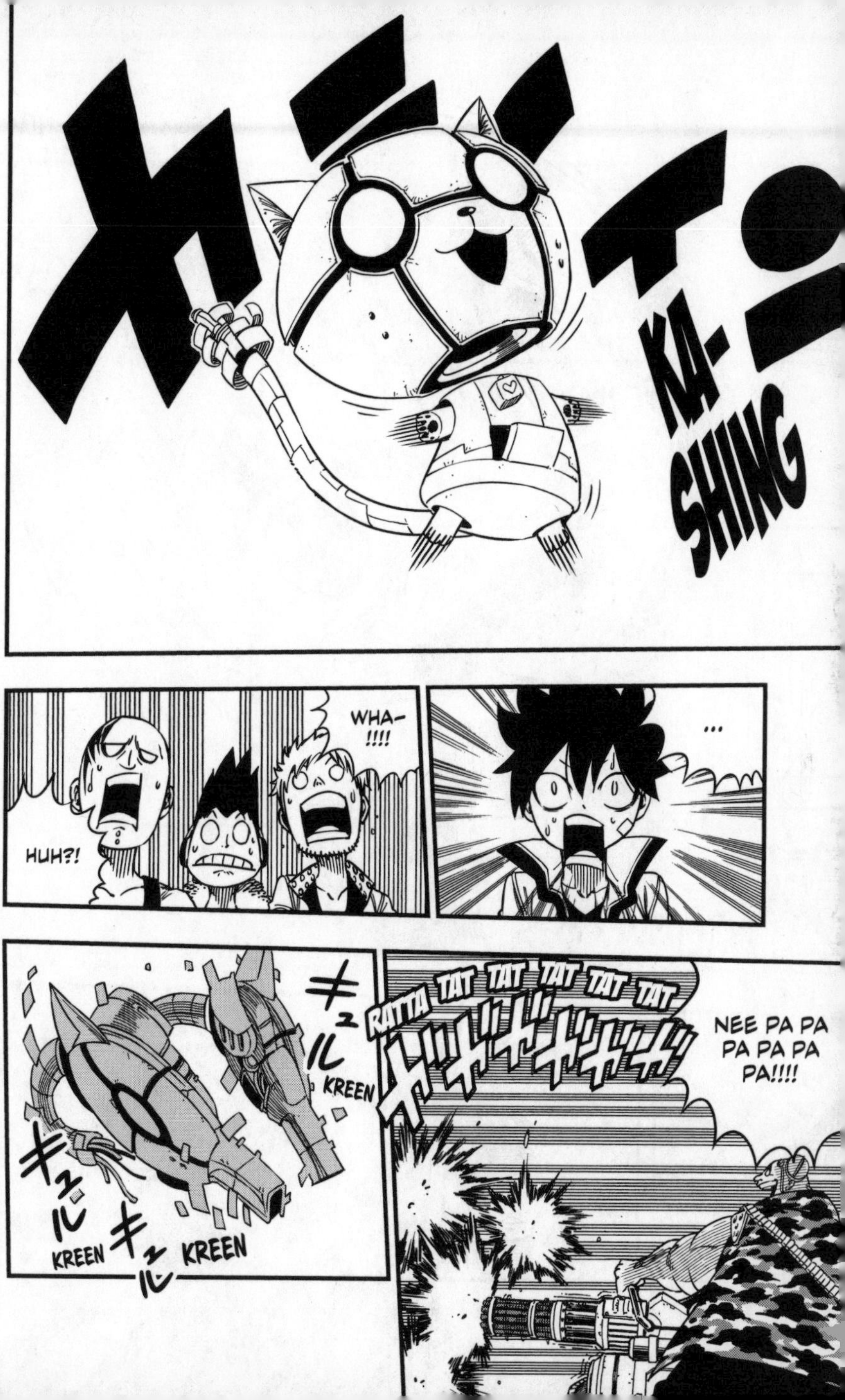
KA-SHING
...
WHA-!!!!
HUH?!
NEE PA PA PA PA PA PA!!!!
RATTA TAT TAT TAT TAT TAT
KREEN
KREEN
KREEN

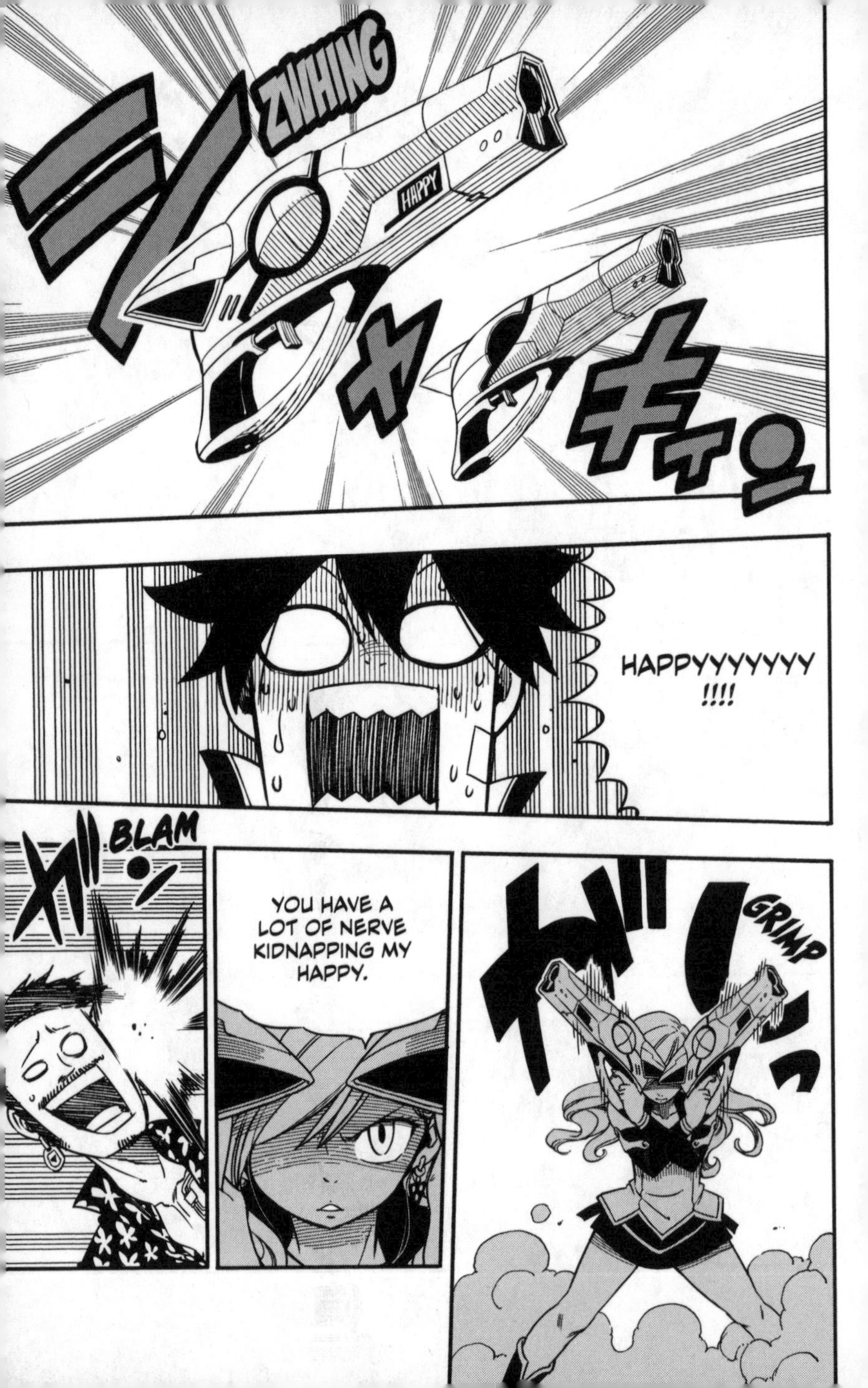
ZWHING
HAPPY
HAPPYYYYYYY !!!!
GRIMP
YOU HAVE A LOT OF NERVE KIDNAPPING MY HAPPY.
BLAM

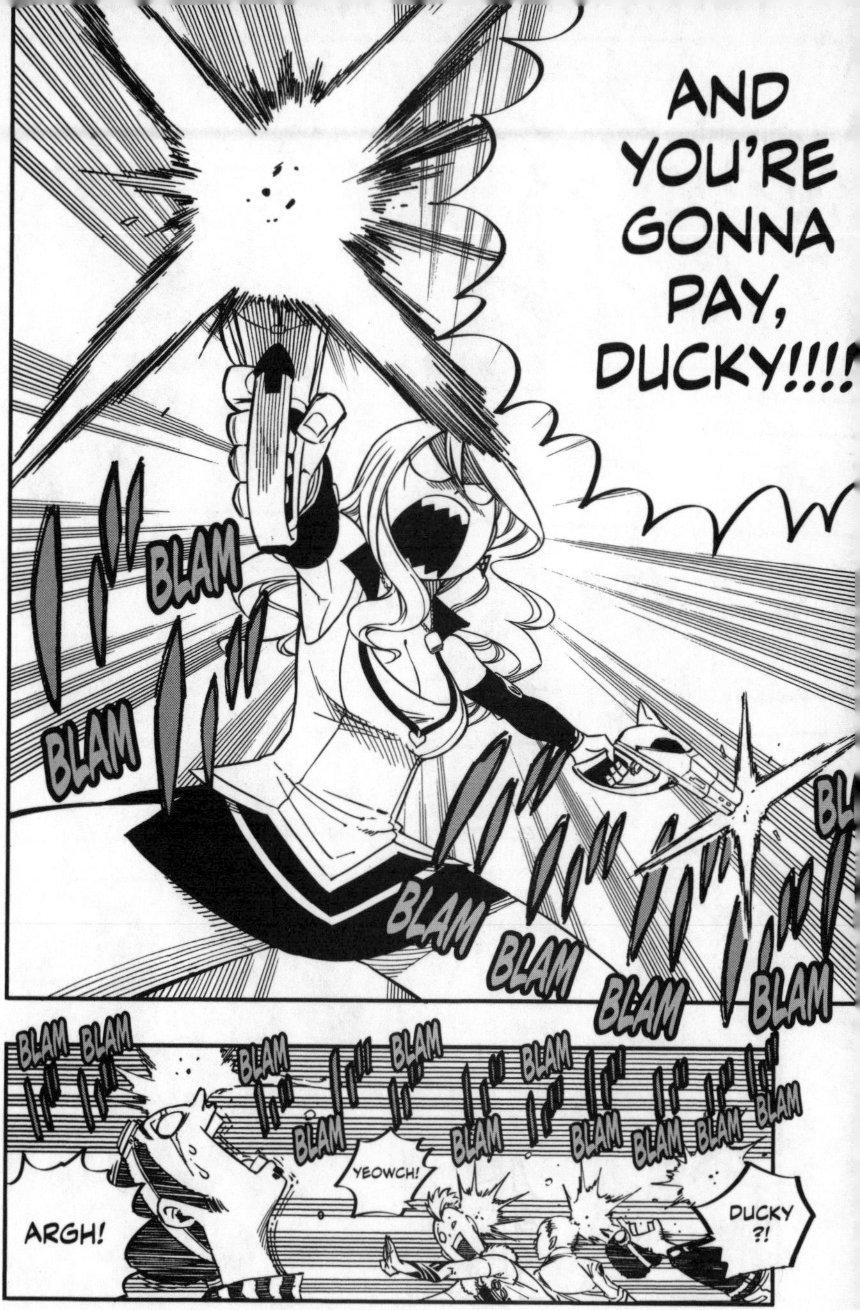
AND YOU'RE GONNA PAY, DUCKY!!!!
BLAM
BLAM
BLAM
BLAM
BLAM
BLAM
BLAM BLAM BLAM BLAM BLAM BLAM BLAM BLAM BLAM BLAM BLAM BLAM BLAM BLAM
DUCKY ?!
YEOWCH!
ARGH!

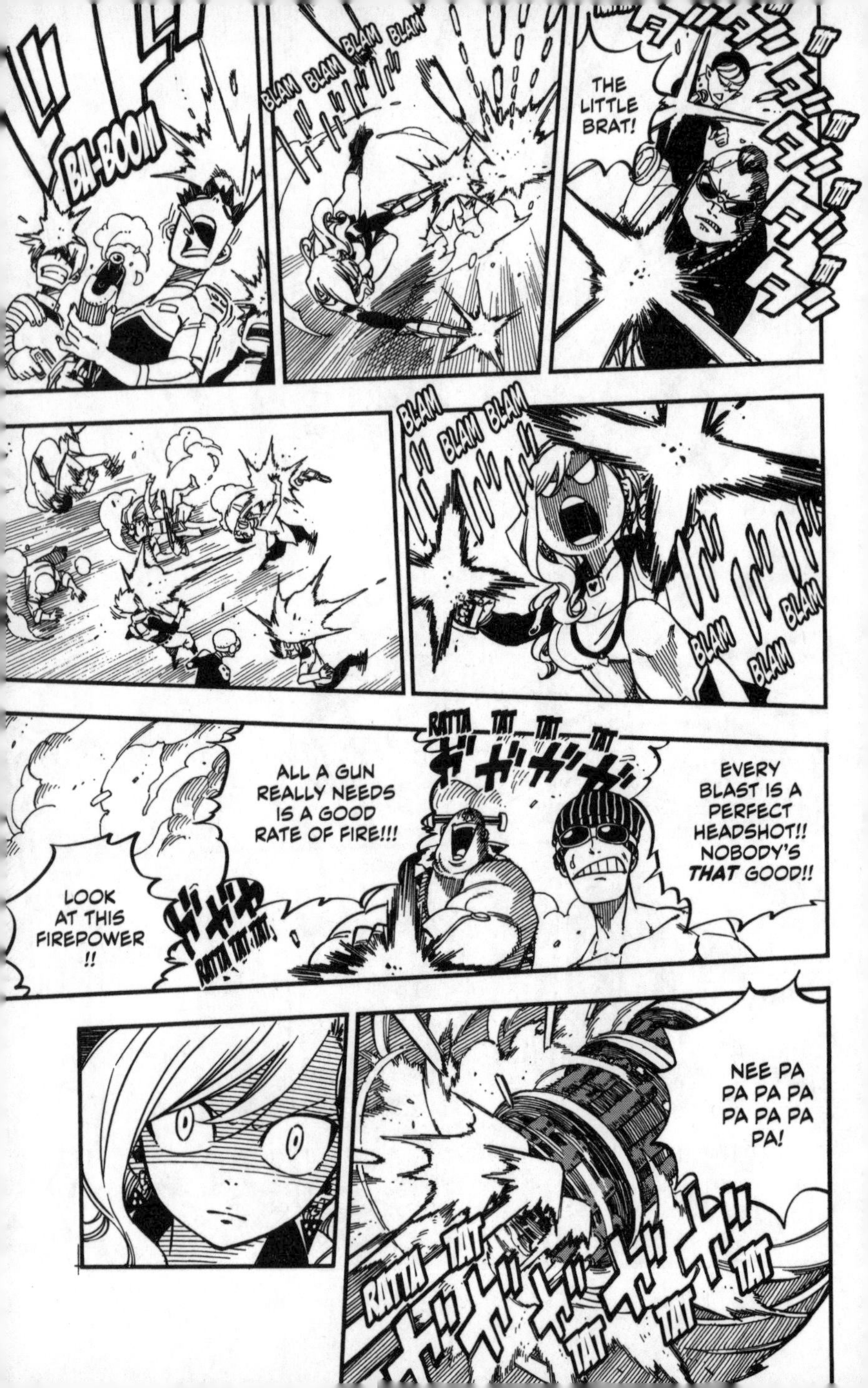

TAT TAT TAT TAT
THE LITTLE BRAT!
BLAM BLAM BLAM BLAM
BA-BOOM
BLAM BLAM BLAM
BLAM BLAM BLAM
EVERY BLAST IS A PERFECT HEADSHOT!! NOBODY'S *THAT* GOOD!!
RATTA TAT TAT TAT
ALL A GUN REALLY NEEDS IS A GOOD RATE OF FIRE!!!
RATTA TAT TAT
LOOK AT THIS FIREPOWER !!
NEE PA PA PA PA PA PA PA PA PA PA!
RATTA TAT TAT TAT TAT TAT

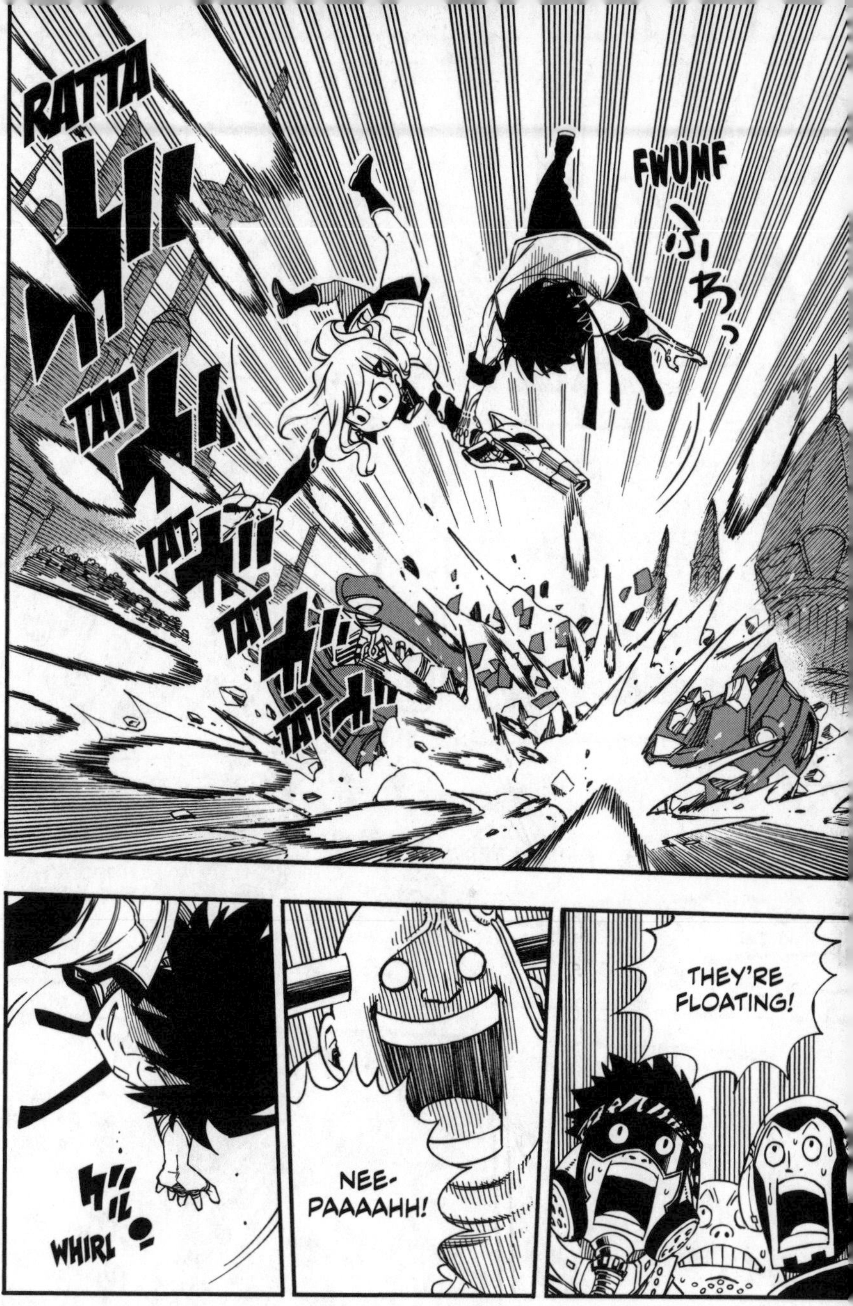
FWUMF
ふわっ
RATTA
TAT
TAT
TAT
TAT
THEY'RE FLOATING!
NEE-PAAAAHH!
WHIRL

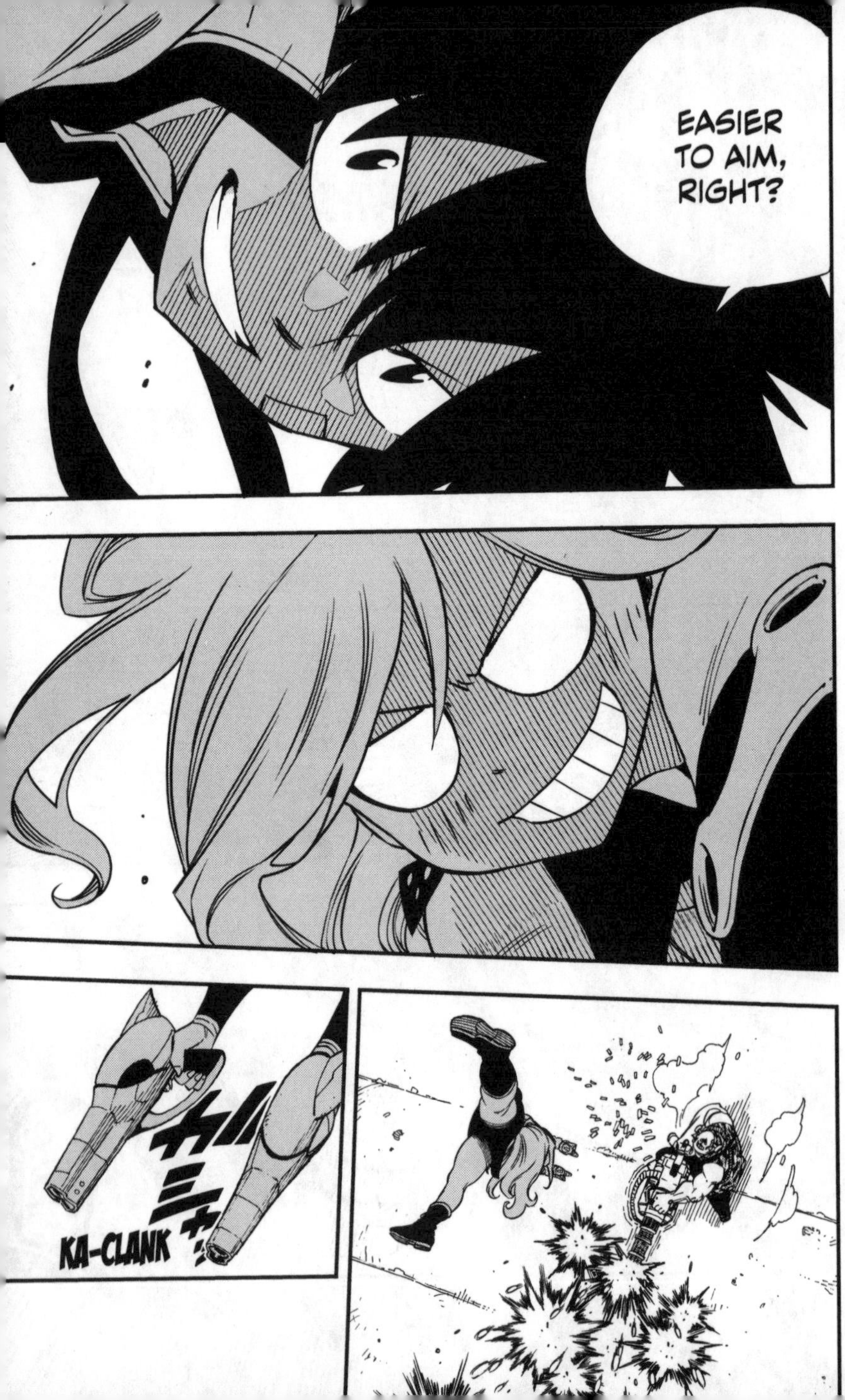
EASIER TO AIM, RIGHT?
KA-CLANK

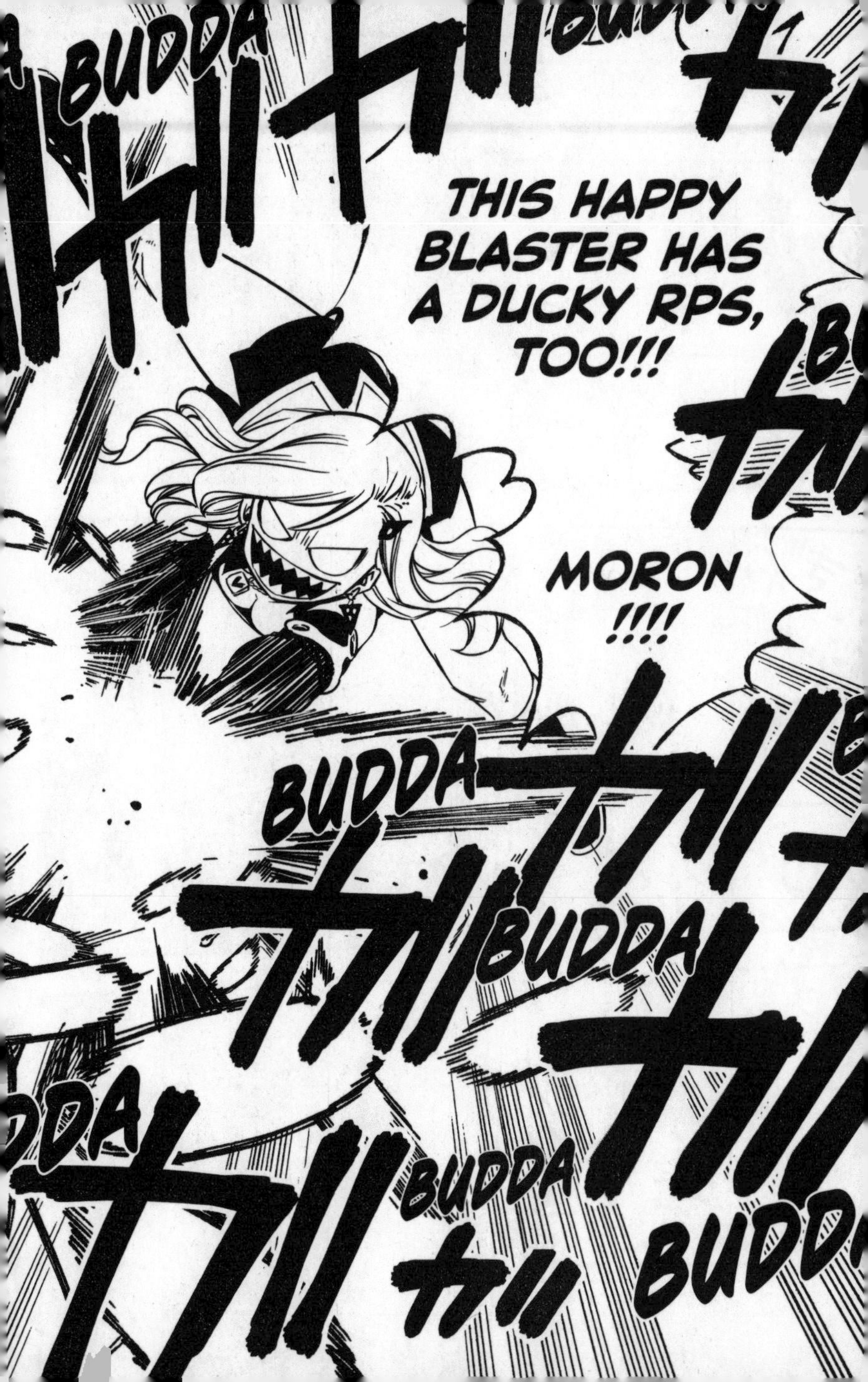
BUDDA
THIS HAPPY BLASTER HAS A DUCKY RPS, TOO!!!
MORON !!!!
BUDDA
BUDDA
BUDDA

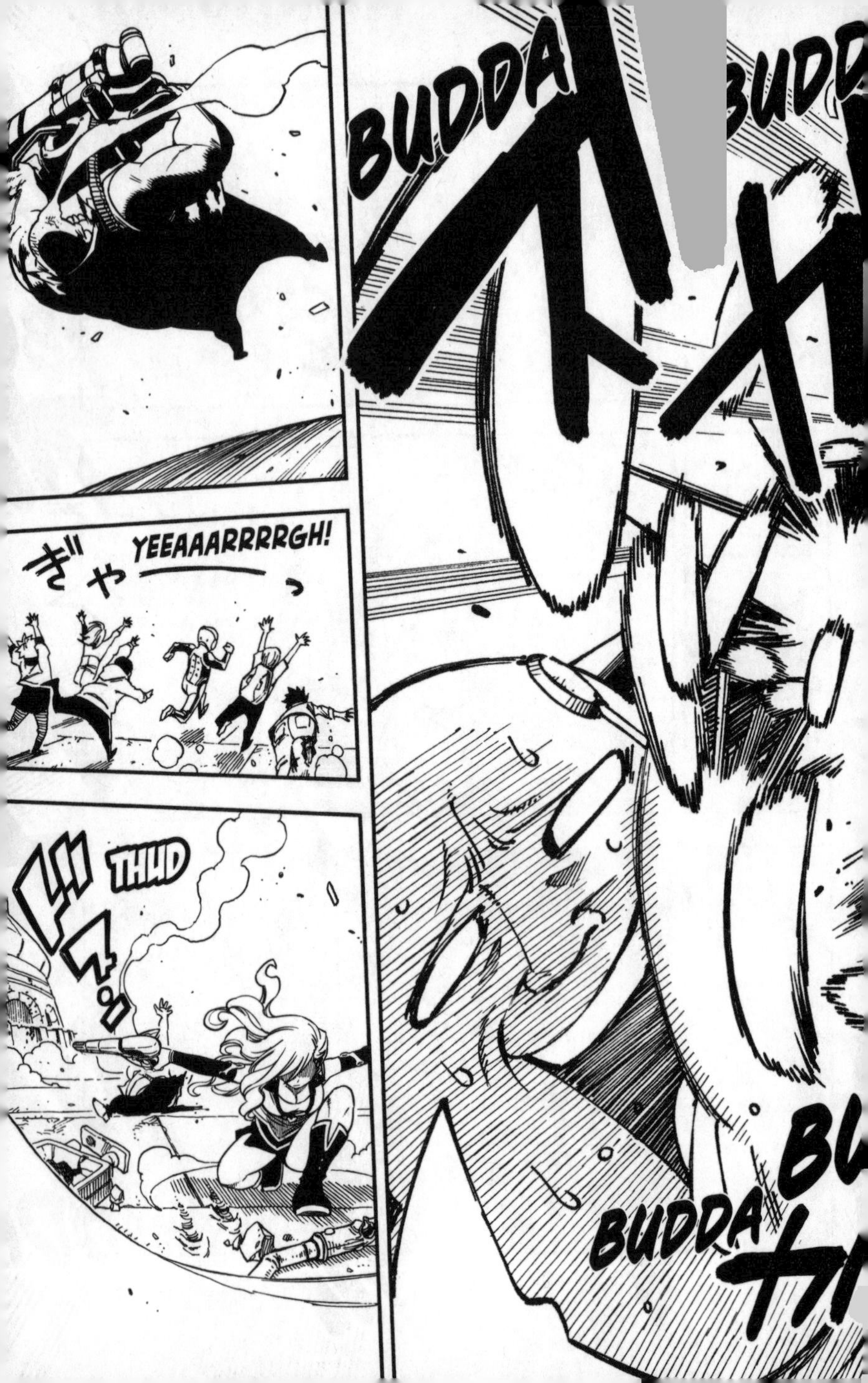
BUDD
BUDDA
BU
BUDDA
ぎゃーっ
YEEAAARRRGH!
THUD

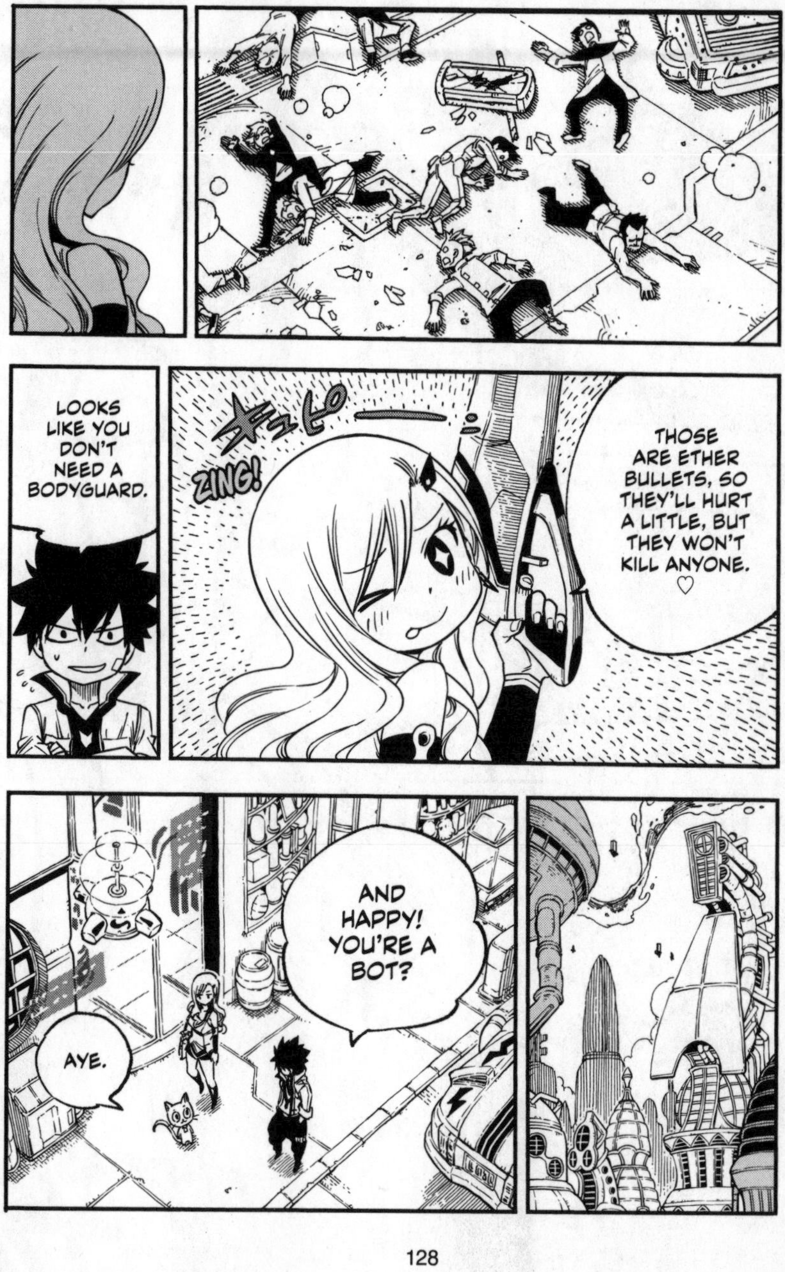
THOSE ARE ETHER BULLETS, SO THEY'LL HURT A LITTLE, BUT THEY WON'T KILL ANYONE. ♡
ZING!
LOOKS LIKE YOU DON'T NEED A BODYGUARD.
AND HAPPY! YOU'RE A BOT?
AYE.

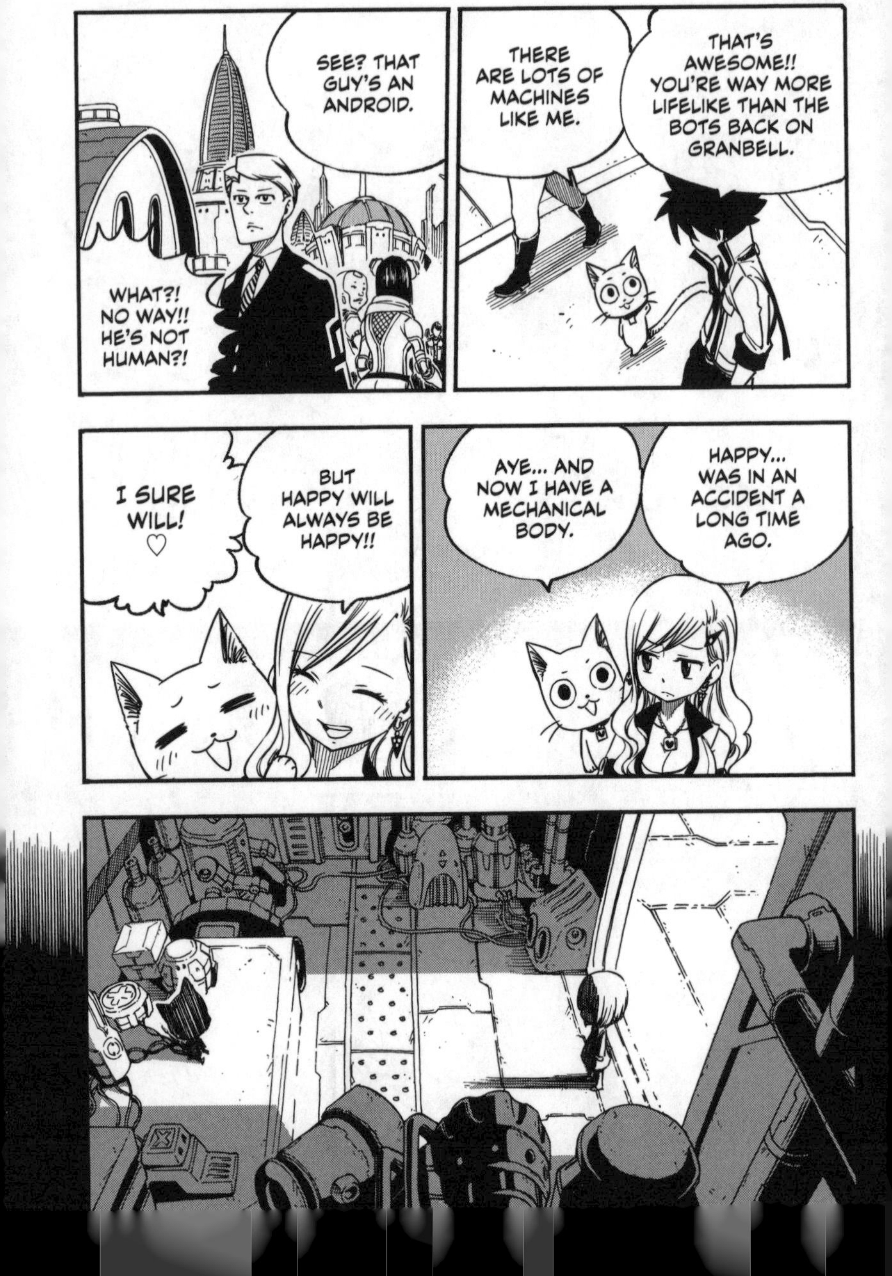
THAT'S AWESOME!! YOU'RE WAY MORE LIFELIKE THAN THE BOTS BACK ON GRANBELL.
THERE ARE LOTS OF MACHINES LIKE ME.
SEE? THAT GUY'S AN ANDROID.
WHAT?! NO WAY!! HE'S NOT HUMAN?!
HAPPY... WAS IN AN ACCIDENT A LONG TIME AGO.
AYE... AND NOW I HAVE A MECHANICAL BODY.
BUT HAPPY WILL ALWAYS BE HAPPY!!
I SURE WILL! ♡

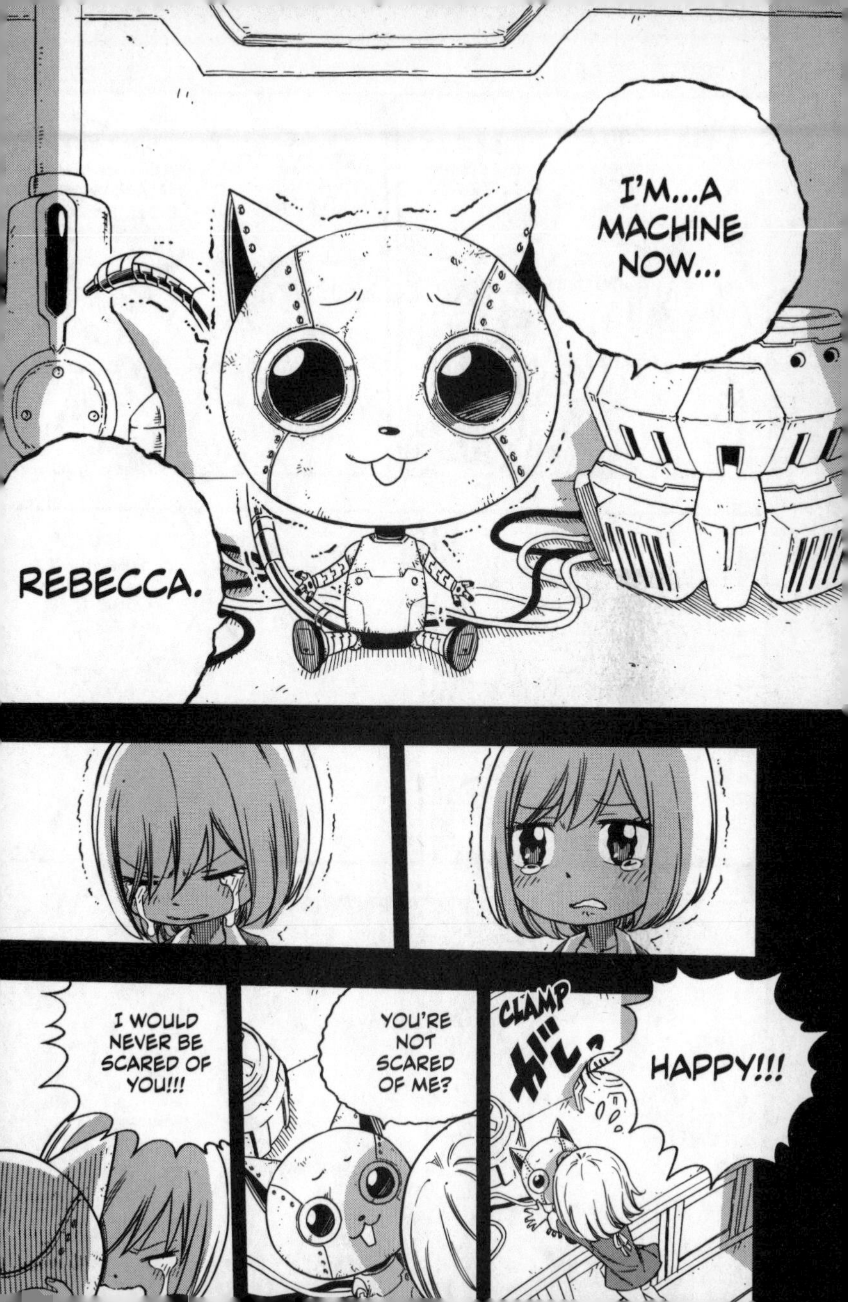
I'M...A MACHINE NOW...
REBECCA.
CLAMP
HAPPY!!!
YOU'RE NOT SCARED OF ME?
I WOULD NEVER BE SCARED OF YOU!!!

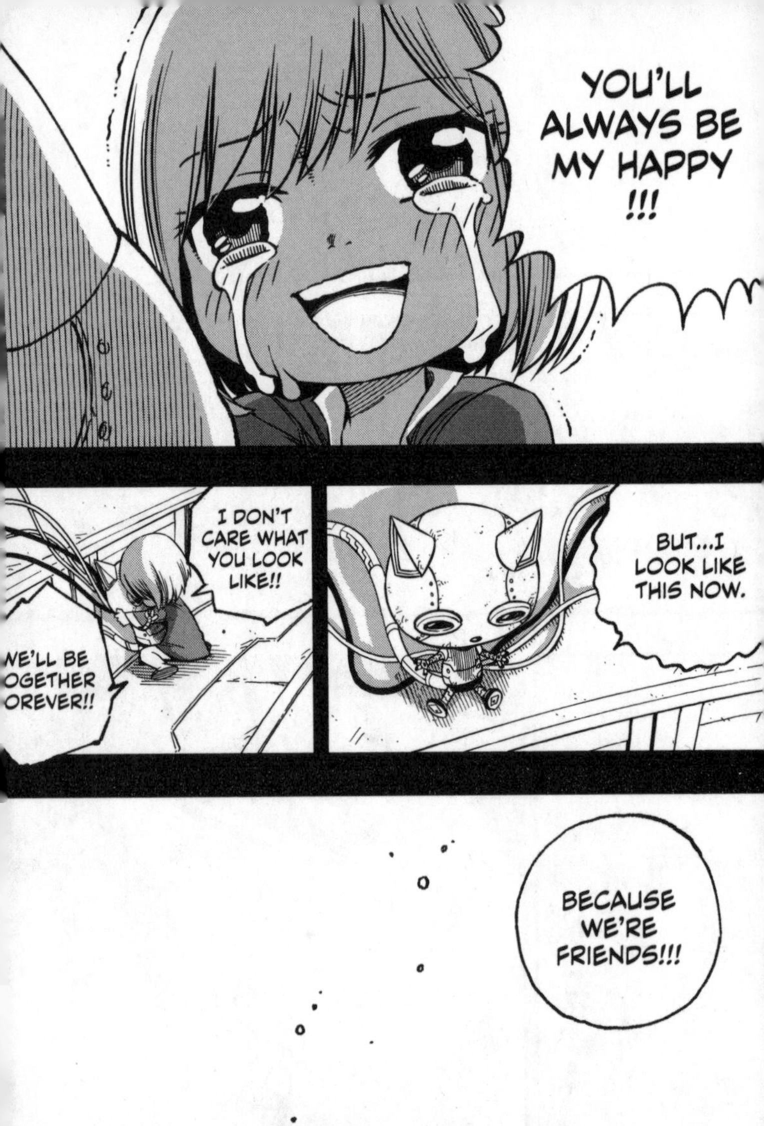
YOU'LL ALWAYS BE MY HAPPY !!!
BUT...I LOOK LIKE THIS NOW.
I DON'T CARE WHAT YOU LOOK LIKE!!
WE'LL BE OGETHER OREVER!!
BECAUSE WE'RE FRIENDS!!!

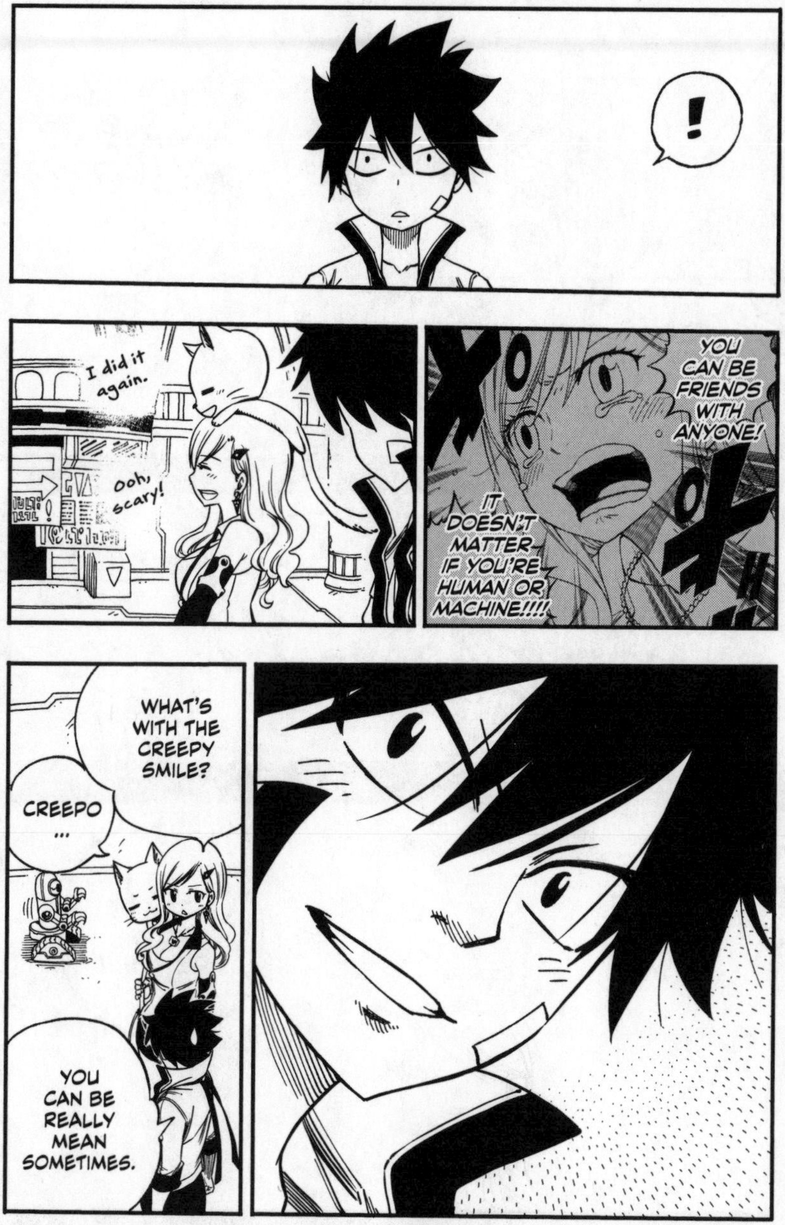
!
YOU CAN BE FRIENDS WITH ANYONE!
IT DOESN'T MATTER IF YOU'RE HUMAN OR MACHINE!!!!
I did it again.
Ooh, scary!
WHAT'S WITH THE CREEPY SMILE?
CREEPO ...
YOU CAN BE REALLY MEAN SOMETIMES.

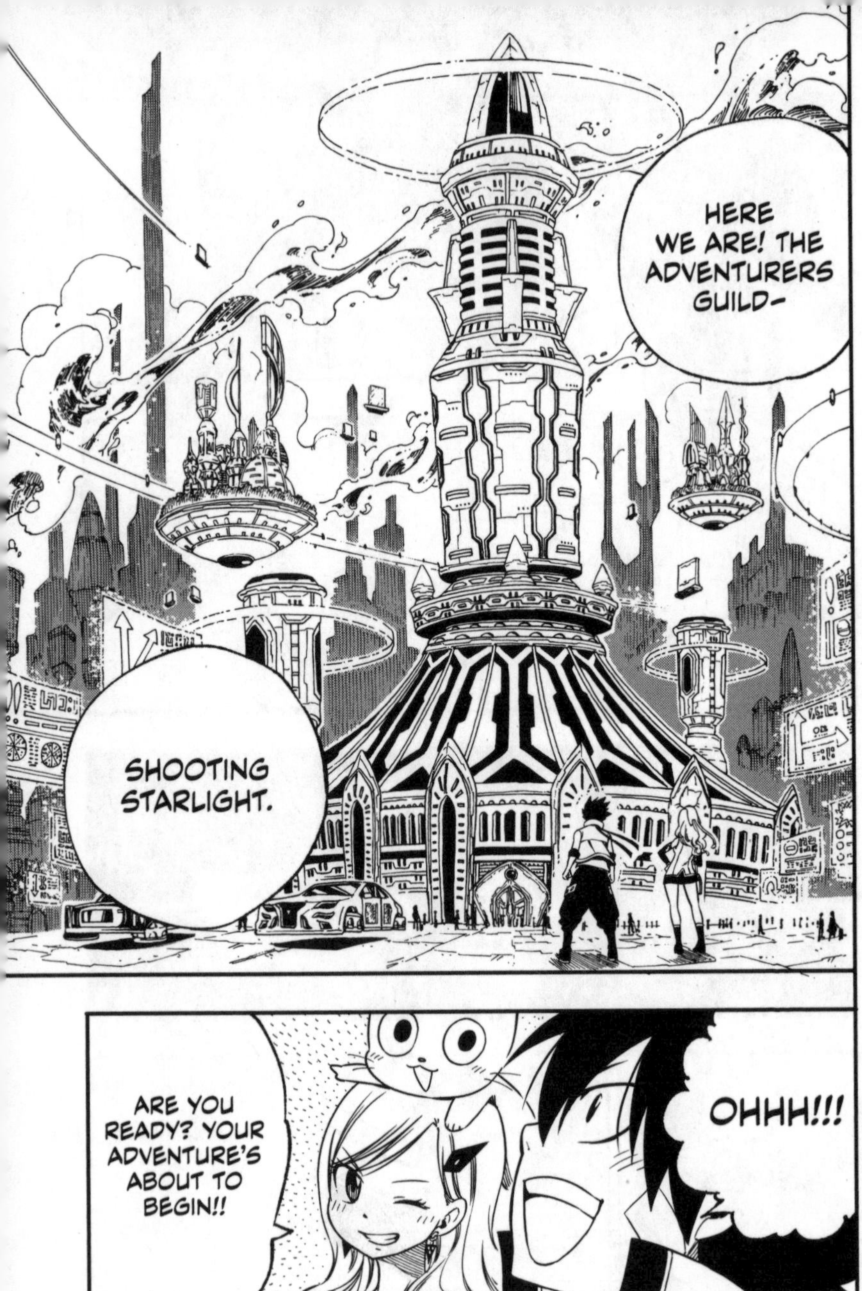
HERE WE ARE! THE ADVENTURERS GUILD–
SHOOTING STARLIGHT.
OHHH!!!
ARE YOU READY? YOUR ADVENTURE'S ABOUT TO BEGIN!!

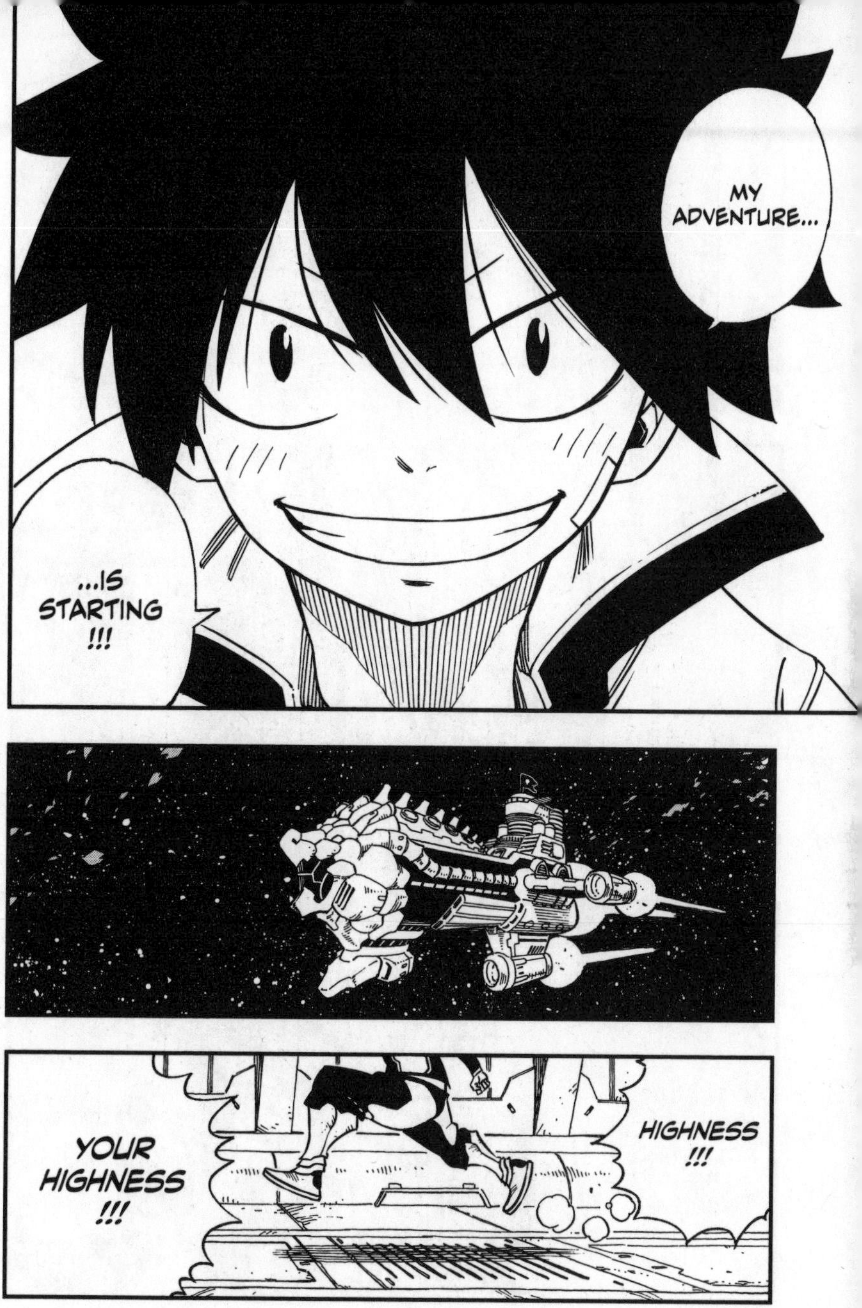
MY ADVENTURE...
...IS STARTING !!!
HIGHNESS !!!
YOUR HIGHNESS !!!

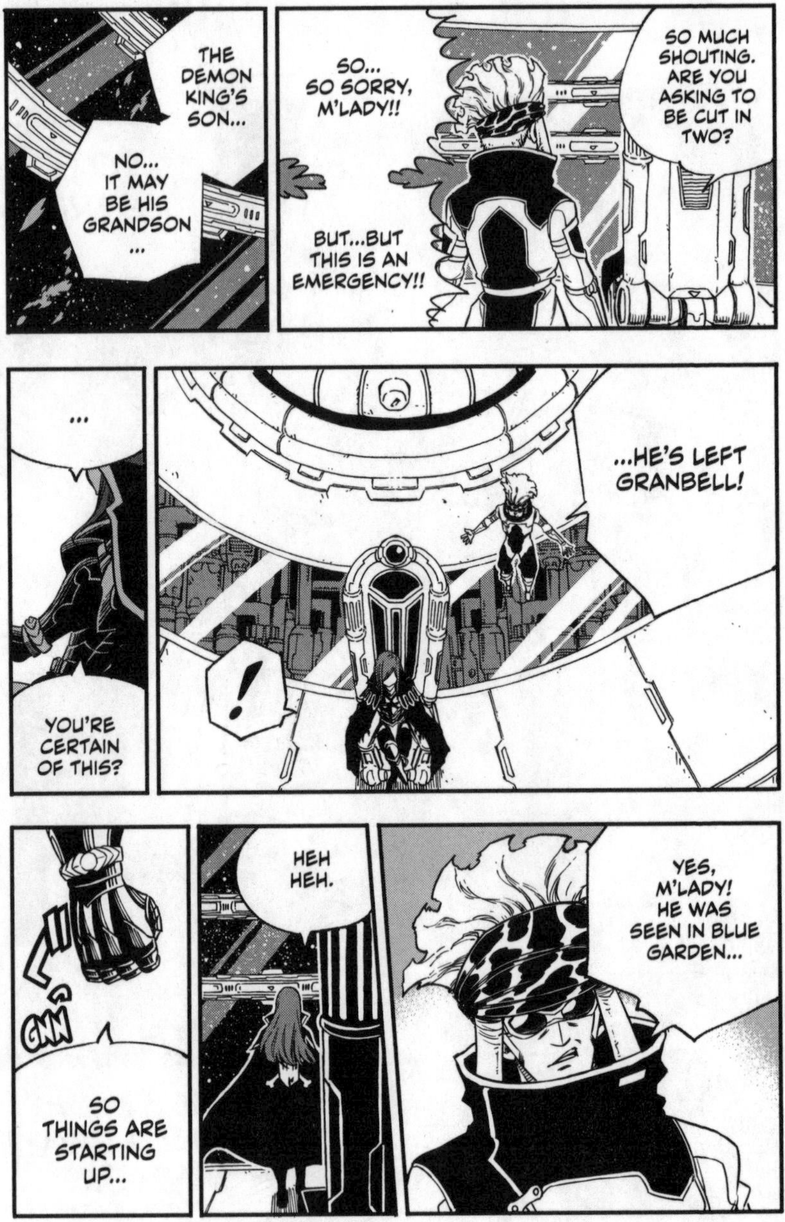
SO MUCH SHOUTING. ARE YOU ASKING TO BE CUT IN TWO?
SO... SO SORRY, M'LADY!!
BUT...BUT THIS IS AN EMERGENCY!!
THE DEMON KING'S SON...
NO... IT MAY BE HIS GRANDSON ...
...HE'S LEFT GRANBELL!
!
...
YOU'RE CERTAIN OF THIS?
YES, M'LADY! HE WAS SEEN IN BLUE GARDEN...
HEH HEH.
GNN
SO THINGS ARE STARTING UP...

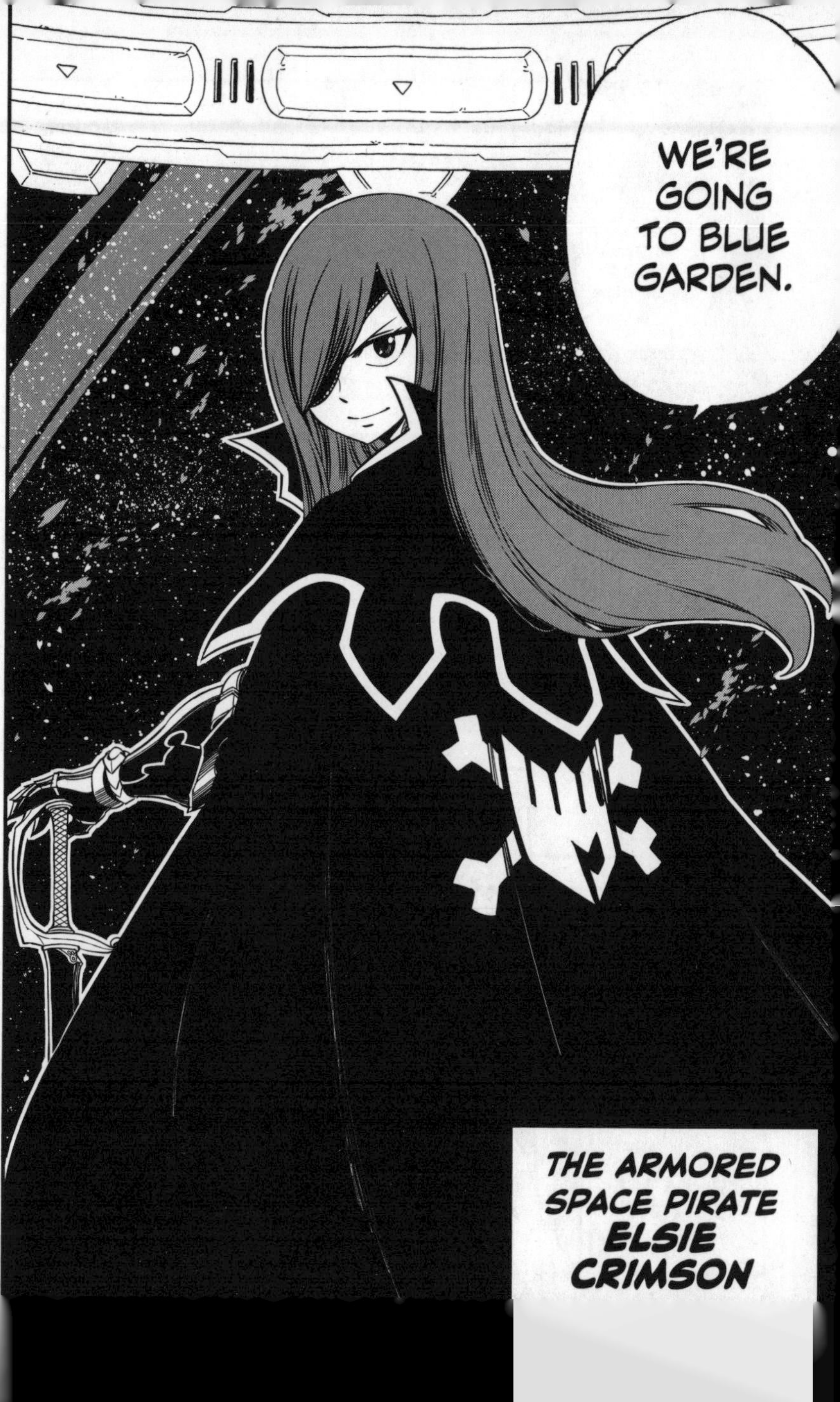
WE'RE GOING TO BLUE GARDEN.
THE ARMORED SPACE PIRATE ELSIE CRIMSON

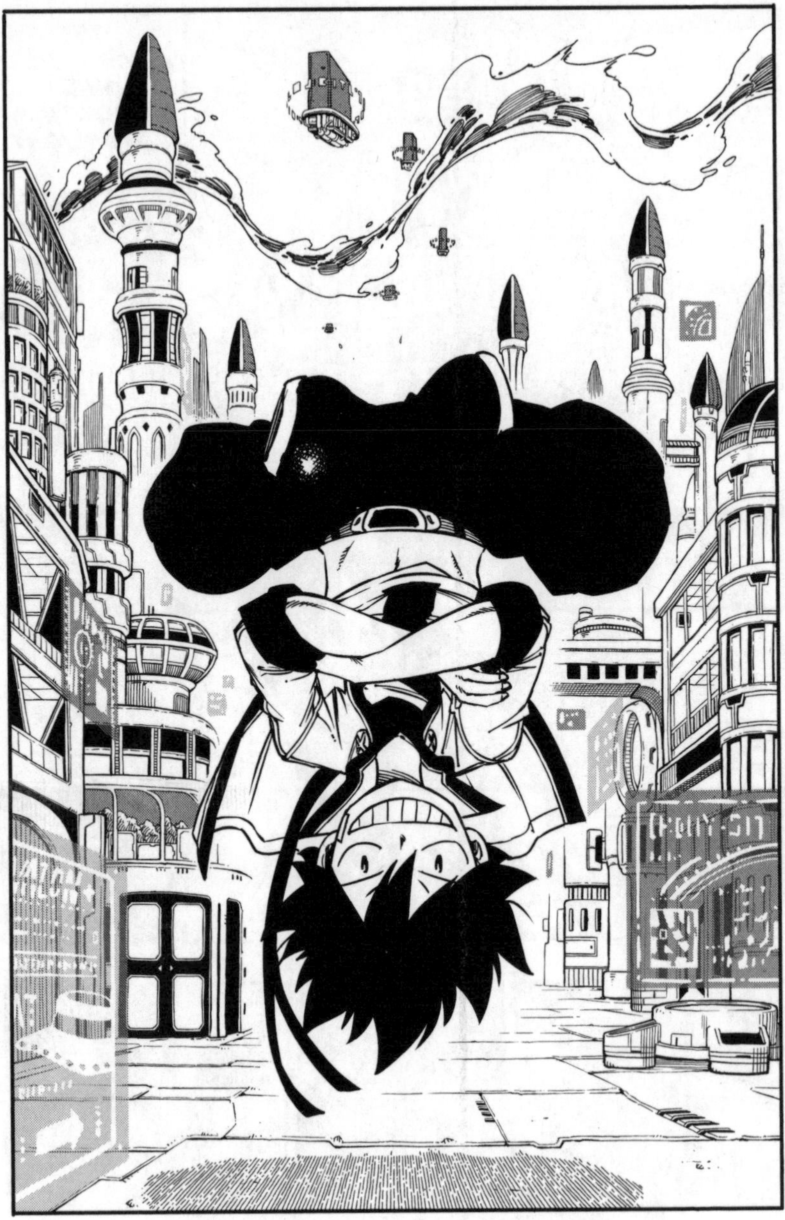

CHAPTER 3: ADVENTURERS

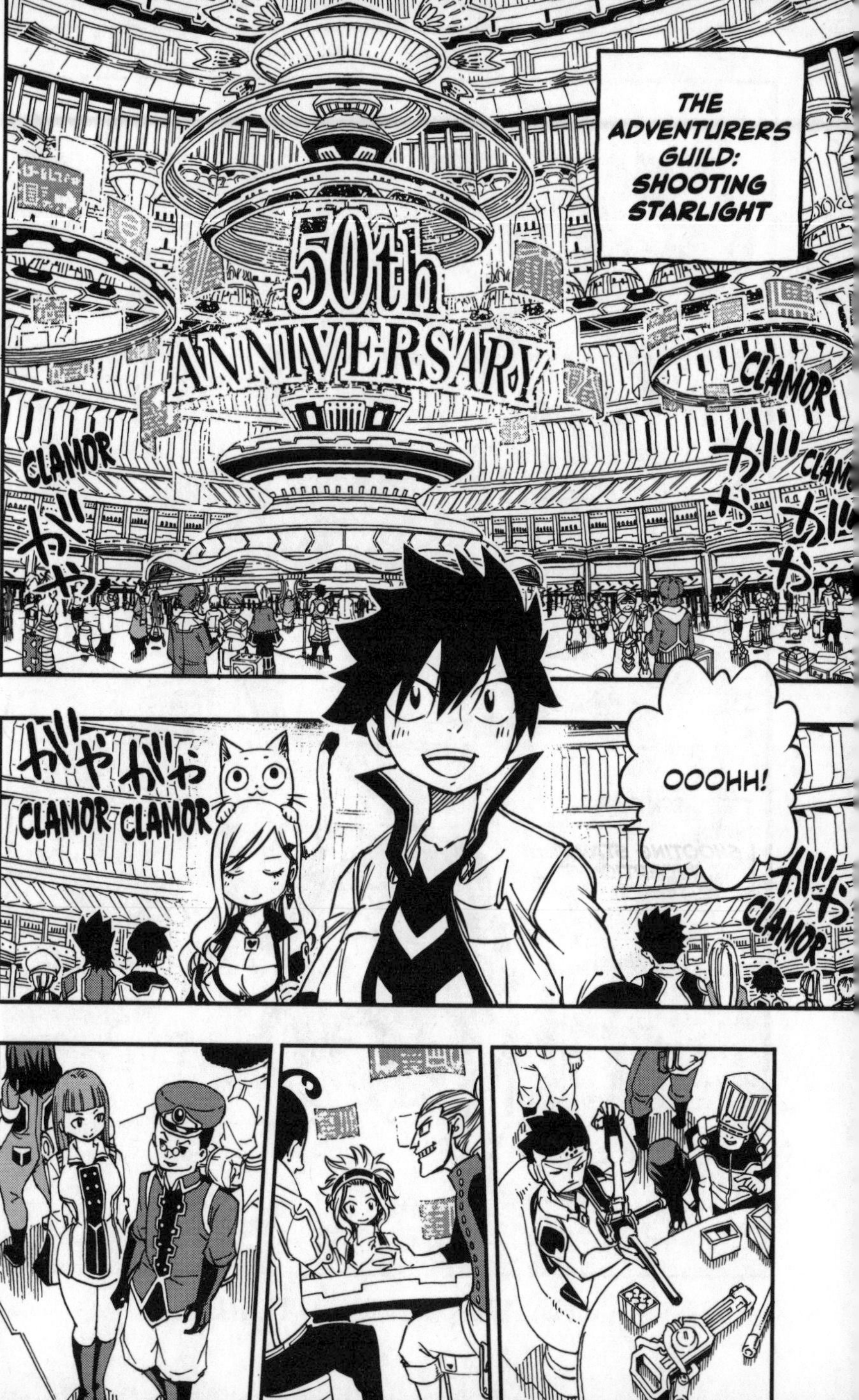
THE ADVENTURERS GUILD: SHOOTING STARLIGHT
CLAMOR
がや
CLAMOR
がや
50th ANNIVERSARY
CLAMOR
がや
OOOHH!
がや
CLAMOR
がやがや
CLAMOR CLAMOR

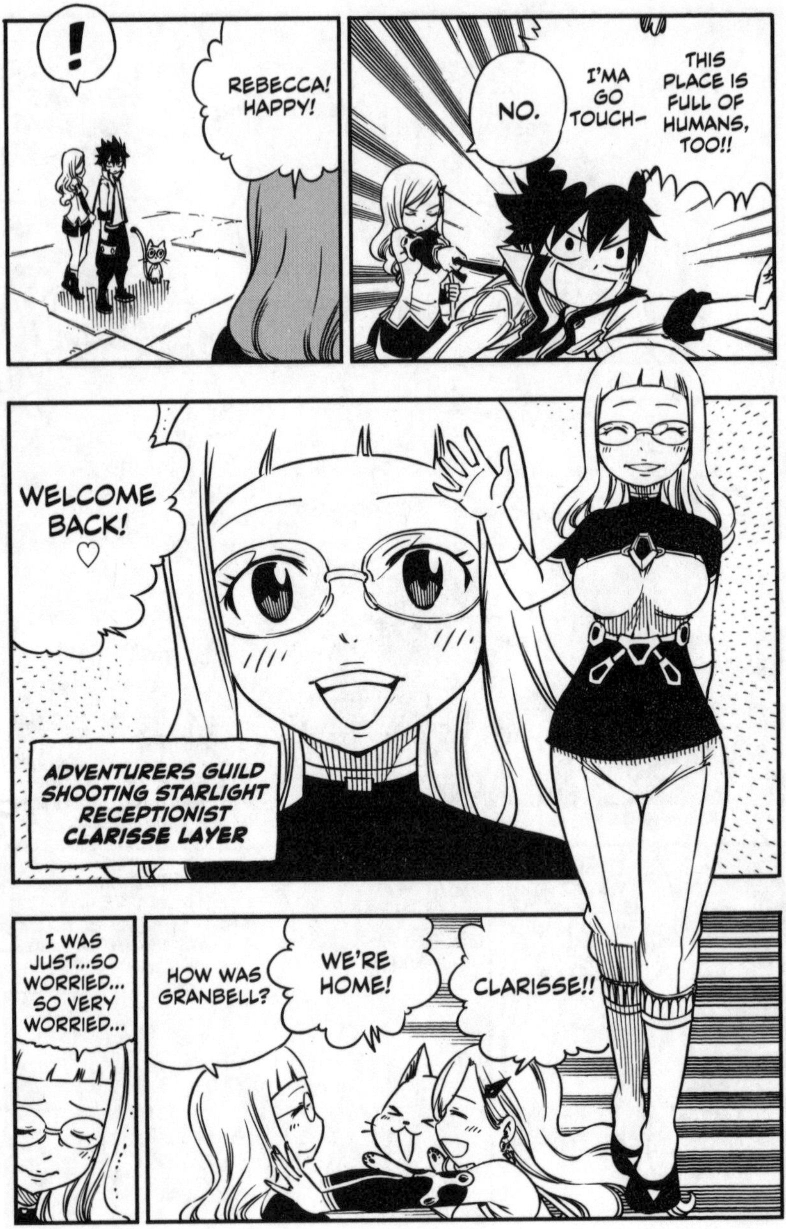
THIS PLACE IS FULL OF HUMANS, TOO!!
I'MA GO TOUCH-
NO.
REBECCA! HAPPY!
!
WELCOME BACK! ♡
ADVENTURERS GUILD SHOOTING STARLIGHT RECEPTIONIST CLARISSE LAYER
CLARISSE!!
WE'RE HOME!
HOW WAS GRANBELL?
I WAS JUST...SO WORRIED... SO VERY WORRIED...

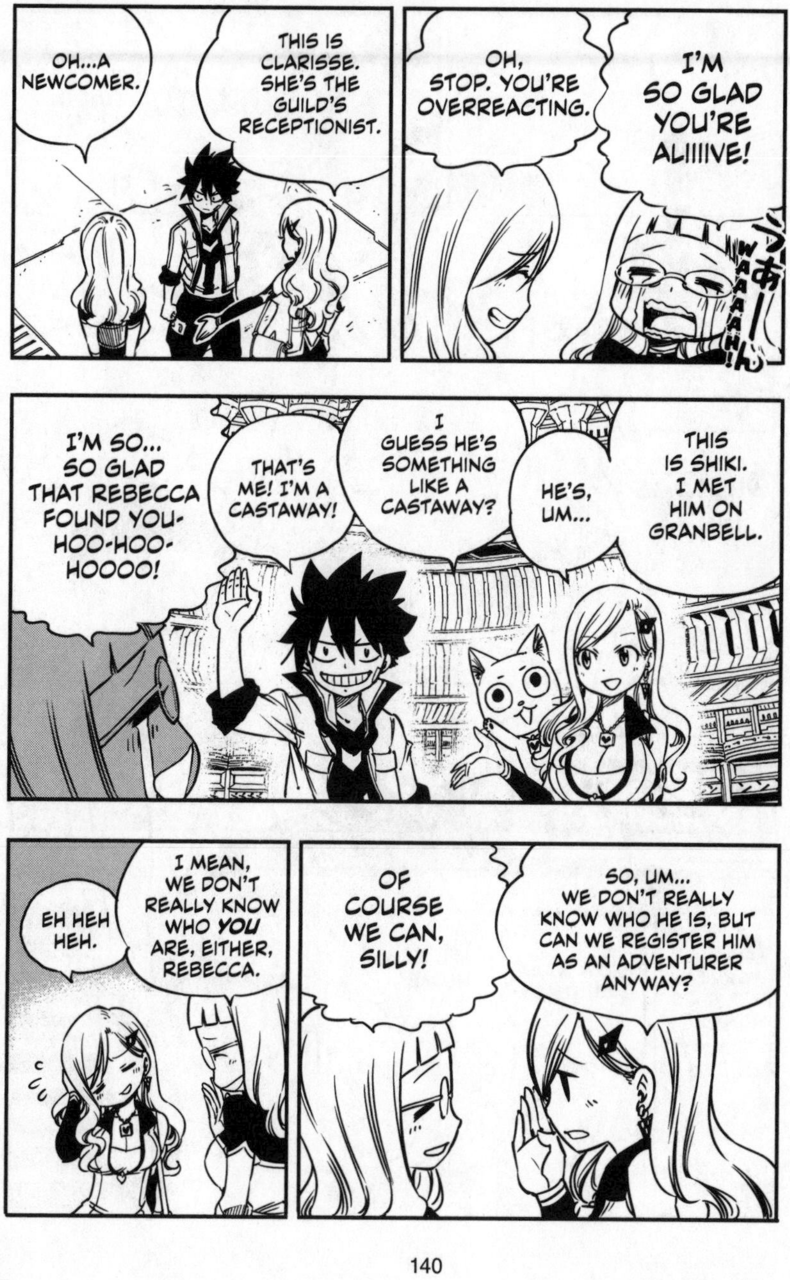
I'M SO GLAD YOU'RE ALIIIIVE!
OH, STOP. YOU'RE OVERREACTING.
うあ～ん
WAAAAAH!
THIS IS CLARISSE. SHE'S THE GUILD'S RECEPTIONIST.
OH...A NEWCOMER.
THIS IS SHIKI. I MET HIM ON GRANBELL.
HE'S, UM...
I GUESS HE'S SOMETHING LIKE A CASTAWAY?
THAT'S ME! I'M A CASTAWAY!
I'M SO... SO GLAD THAT REBECCA FOUND YOU-HOO-HOO-HOOOO!
SO, UM... WE DON'T REALLY KNOW WHO HE IS, BUT CAN WE REGISTER HIM AS AN ADVENTURER ANYWAY?
OF COURSE WE CAN, SILLY!
I MEAN, WE DON'T REALLY KNOW WHO *YOU* ARE, EITHER, REBECCA.
EH HEH HEH.

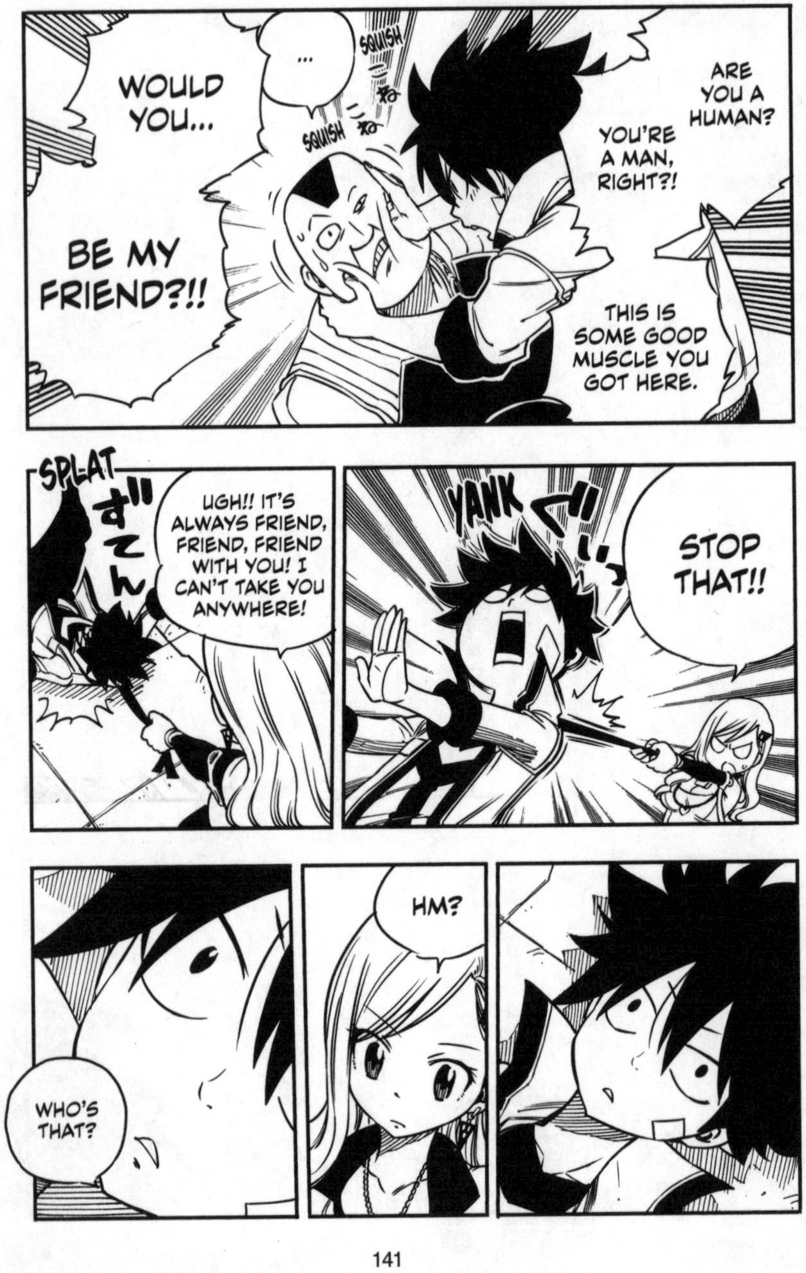
ARE YOU A HUMAN?
YOU'RE A MAN, RIGHT?!
SQUISH
...
WOULD YOU...
SQUISH
THIS IS SOME GOOD MUSCLE YOU GOT HERE.
BE MY FRIEND?!!
YANK
STOP THAT!!
UGH!! IT'S ALWAYS FRIEND, FRIEND, FRIEND WITH YOU! I CAN'T TAKE YOU ANYWHERE!
SPLAT
ずてん
HM?
WHO'S THAT?

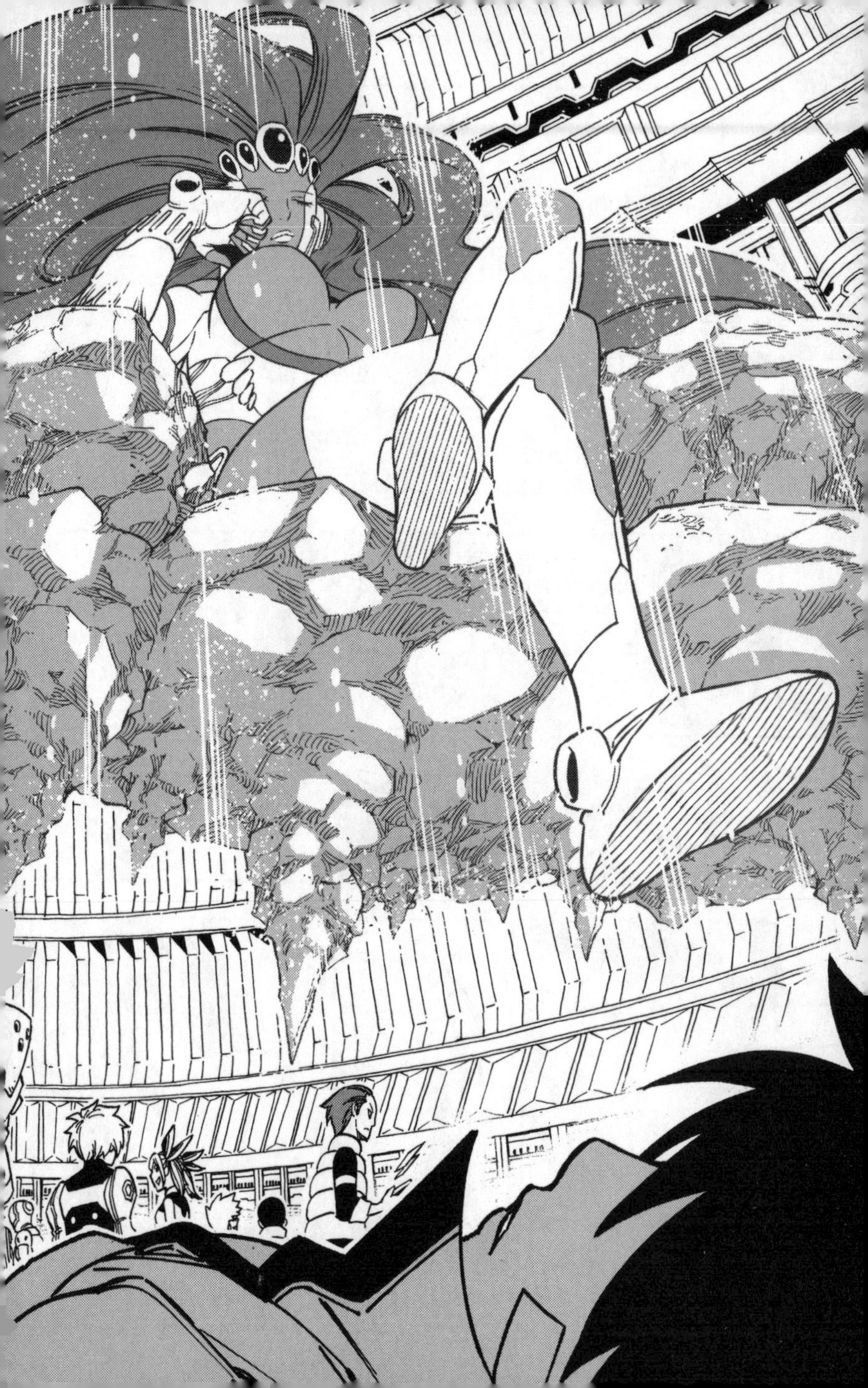

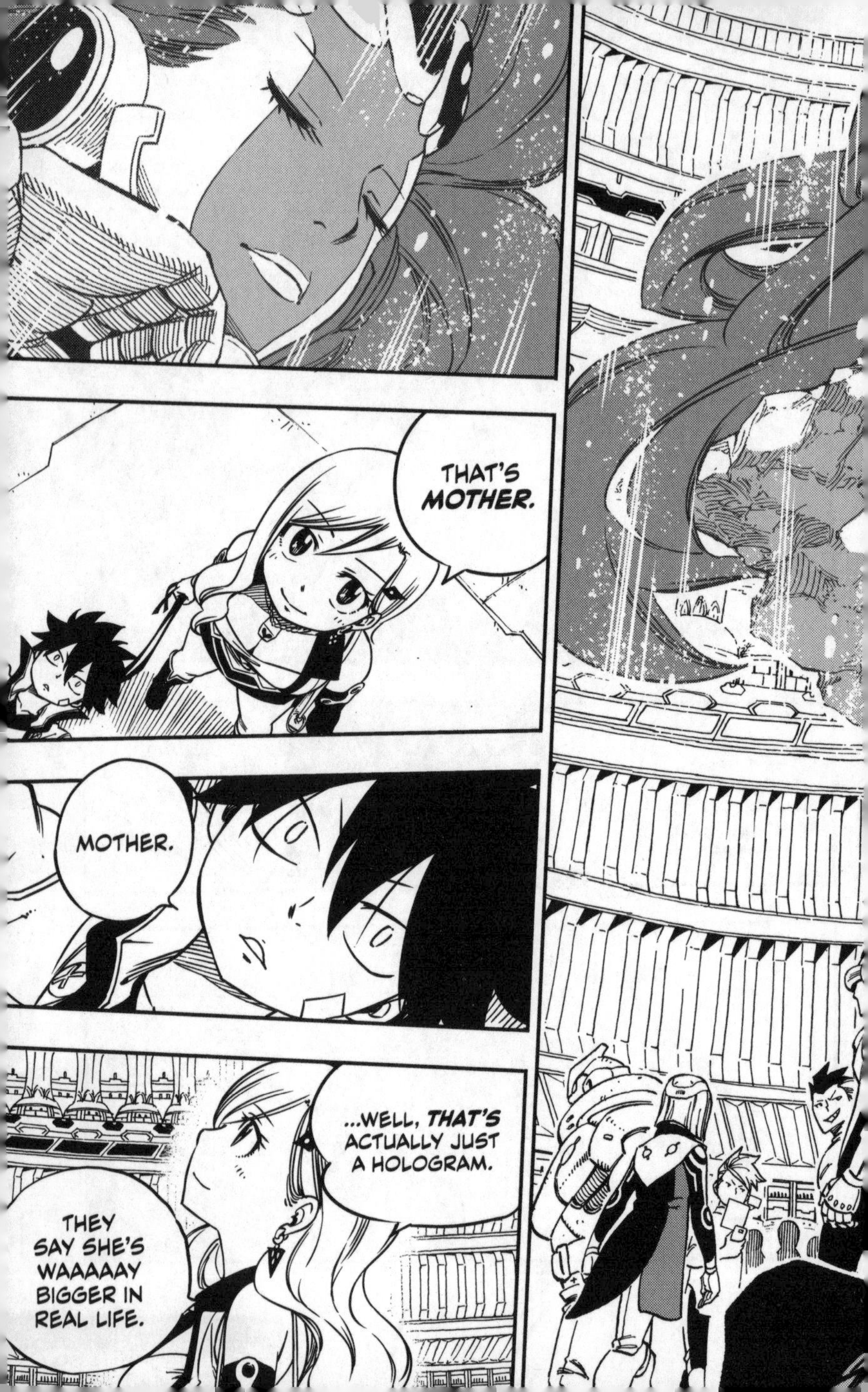
THAT'S MOTHER.
MOTHER.
...WELL, THAT'S ACTUALLY JUST A HOLOGRAM.
THEY SAY SHE'S WAAAAAY BIGGER IN REAL LIFE.

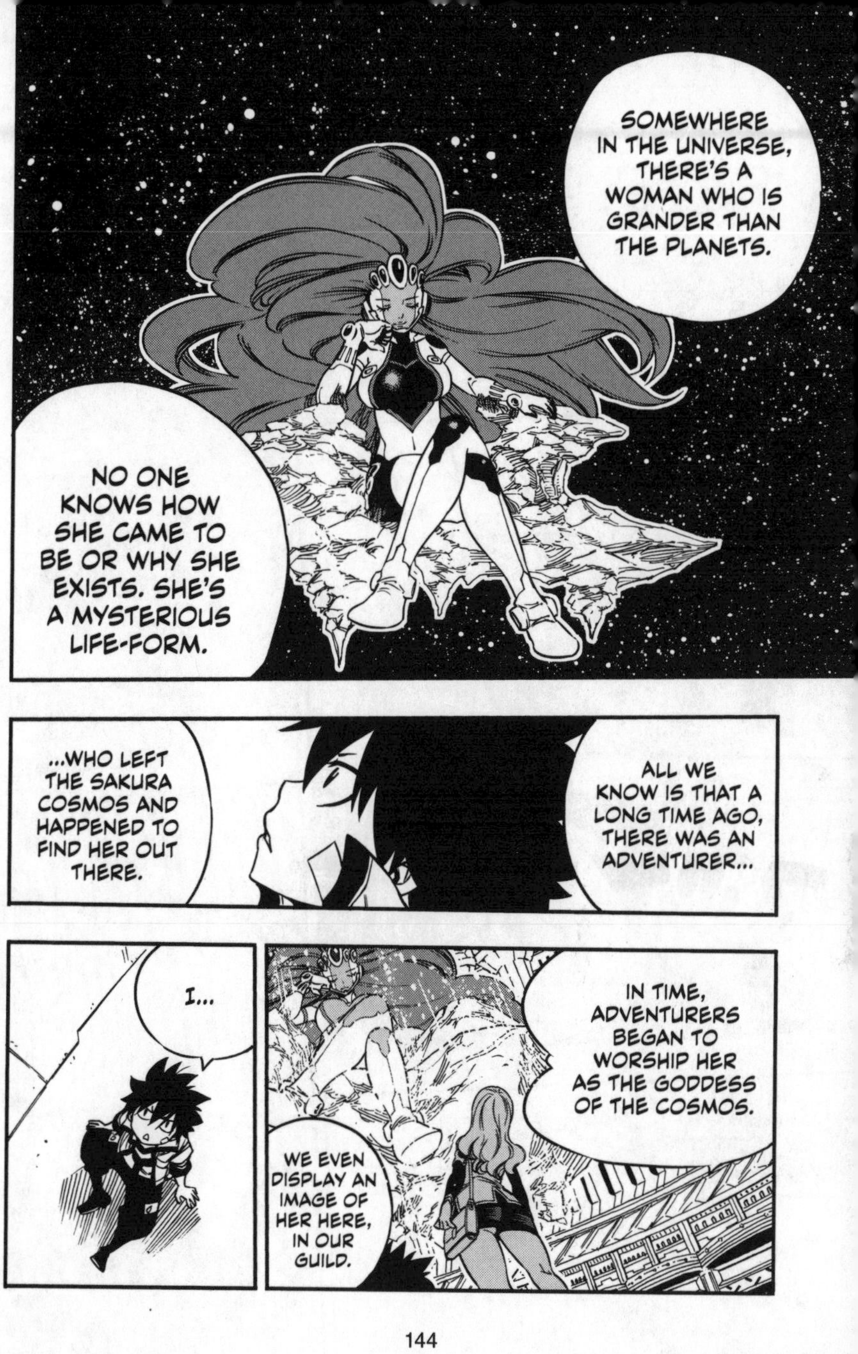
SOMEWHERE IN THE UNIVERSE, THERE'S A WOMAN WHO IS GRANDER THAN THE PLANETS.
NO ONE KNOWS HOW SHE CAME TO BE OR WHY SHE EXISTS. SHE'S A MYSTERIOUS LIFE-FORM.
ALL WE KNOW IS THAT A LONG TIME AGO, THERE WAS AN ADVENTURER...
...WHO LEFT THE SAKURA COSMOS AND HAPPENED TO FIND HER OUT THERE.
IN TIME, ADVENTURERS BEGAN TO WORSHIP HER AS THE GODDESS OF THE COSMOS.
WE EVEN DISPLAY AN IMAGE OF HER HERE, IN OUR GUILD.
I...

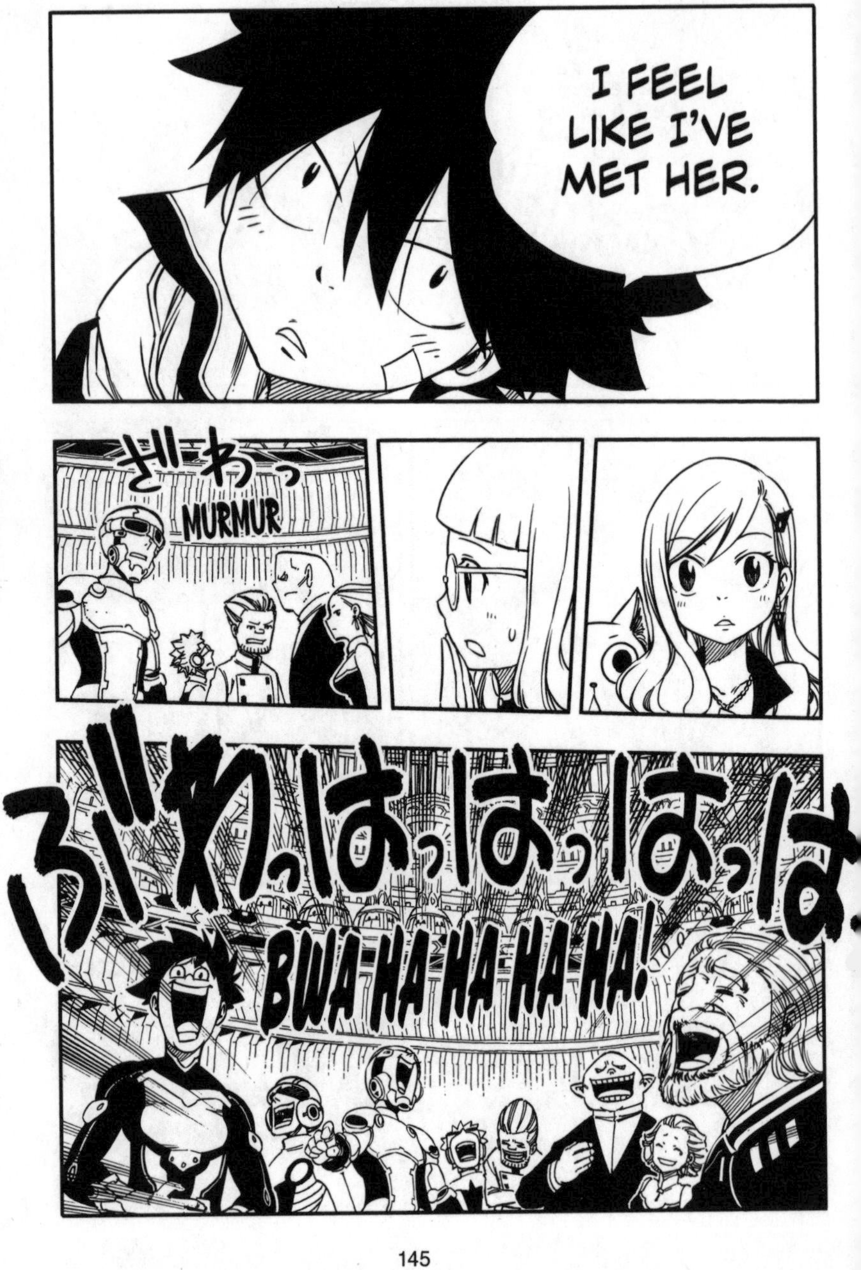
I FEEL LIKE I'VE MET HER.
ざわっ
MURMUR
ぶわっはっはっはっはっ
BWA HA HA HA HA!

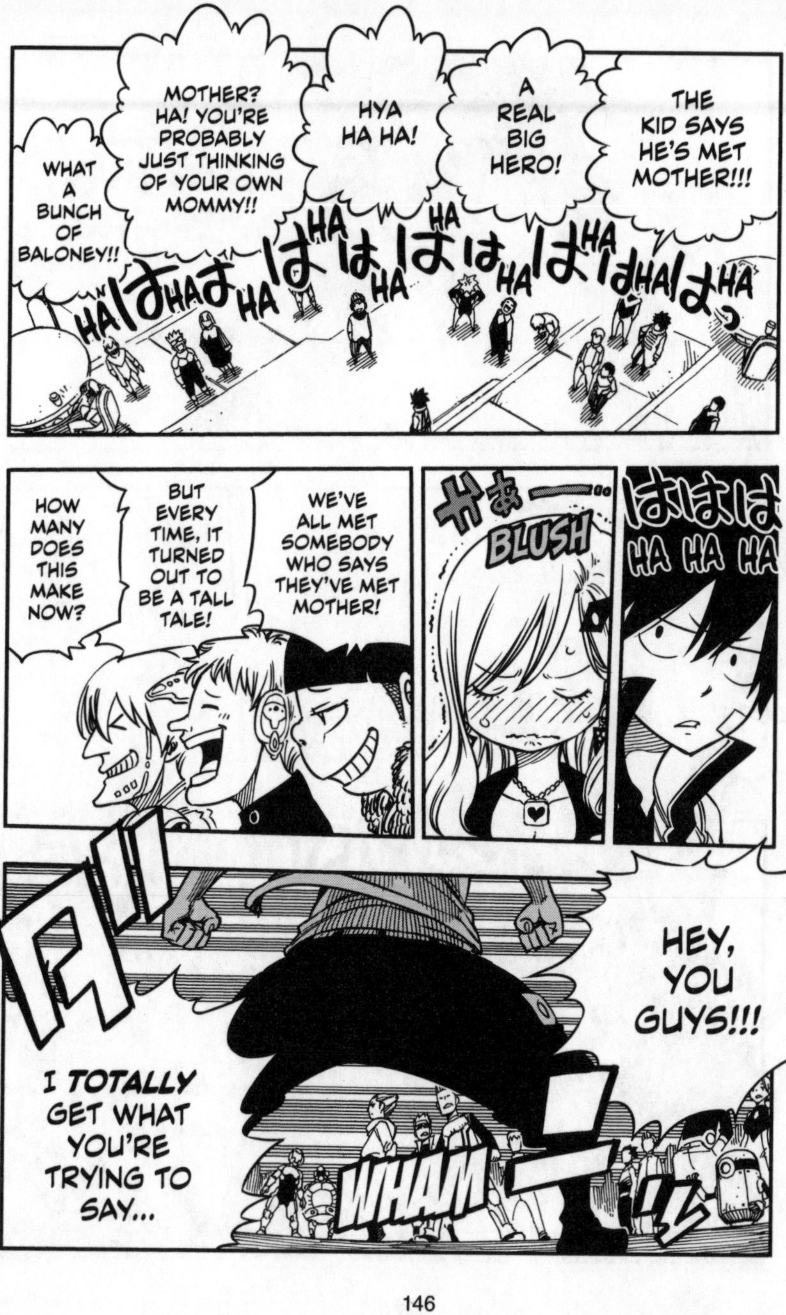
THE KID SAYS HE'S MET MOTHER!!!
A REAL BIG HERO!
HYA HA HA!
MOTHER? HA! YOU'RE PROBABLY JUST THINKING OF YOUR OWN MOMMY!!
WHAT A BUNCH OF BALONEY!!
HA HA HA HA HA HA HA HA HA HA HA HA
ははははHA HA HA HA
BLUSH
WE'VE ALL MET SOMEBODY WHO SAYS THEY'VE MET MOTHER!
BUT EVERY TIME, IT TURNED OUT TO BE A TALL TALE!
HOW MANY DOES THIS MAKE NOW?
HEY, YOU GUYS!!!
I *TOTALLY* GET WHAT YOU'RE TRYING TO SAY...
WHAM

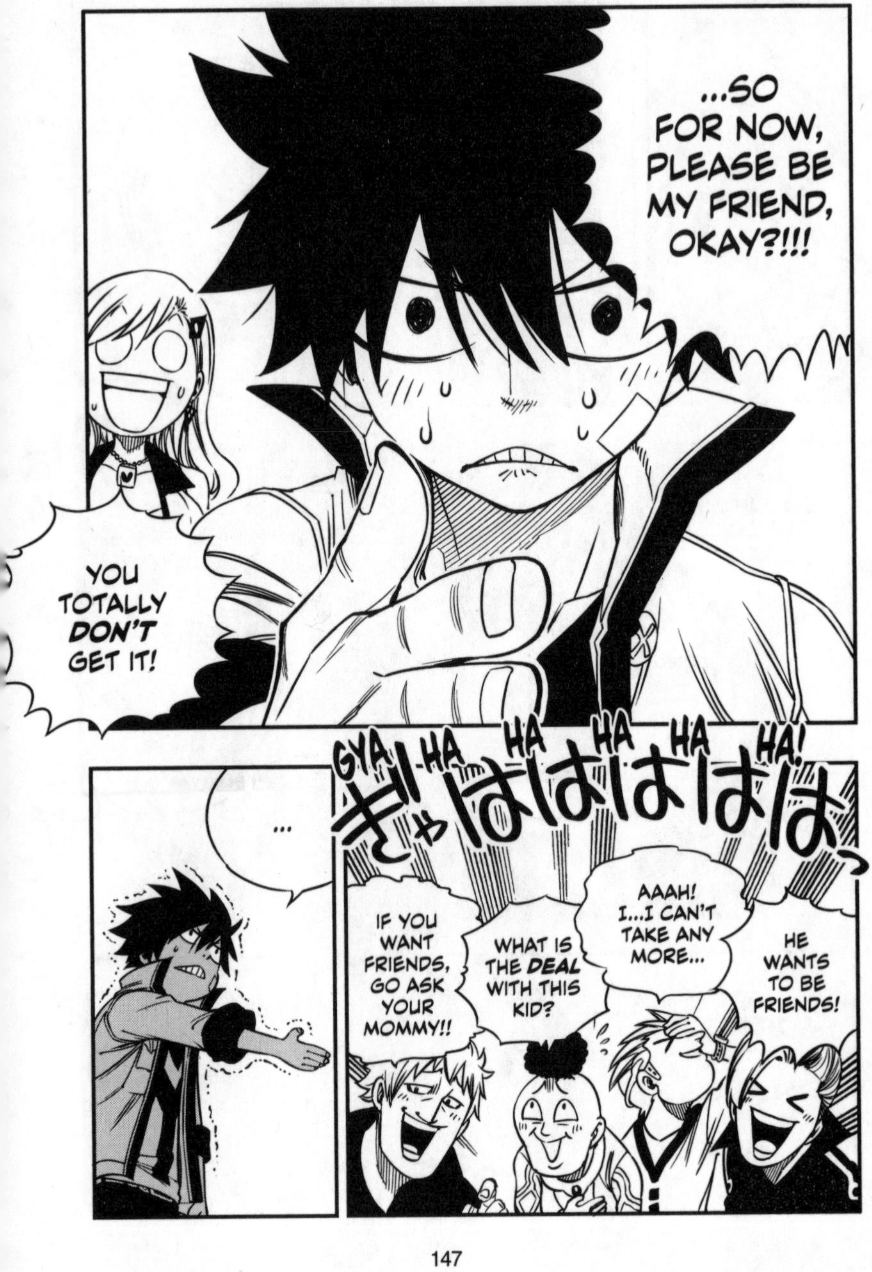
...SO FOR NOW, PLEASE BE MY FRIEND, OKAY?!!!
YOU TOTALLY *DON'T* GET IT!
GYA HA HA HA HA HA!
ぎゃはははははっ
HE WANTS TO BE FRIENDS!
AAAH! I...I CAN'T TAKE ANY MORE...
WHAT IS THE *DEAL* WITH THIS KID?
IF YOU WANT FRIENDS, GO ASK YOUR MOMMY!!
...

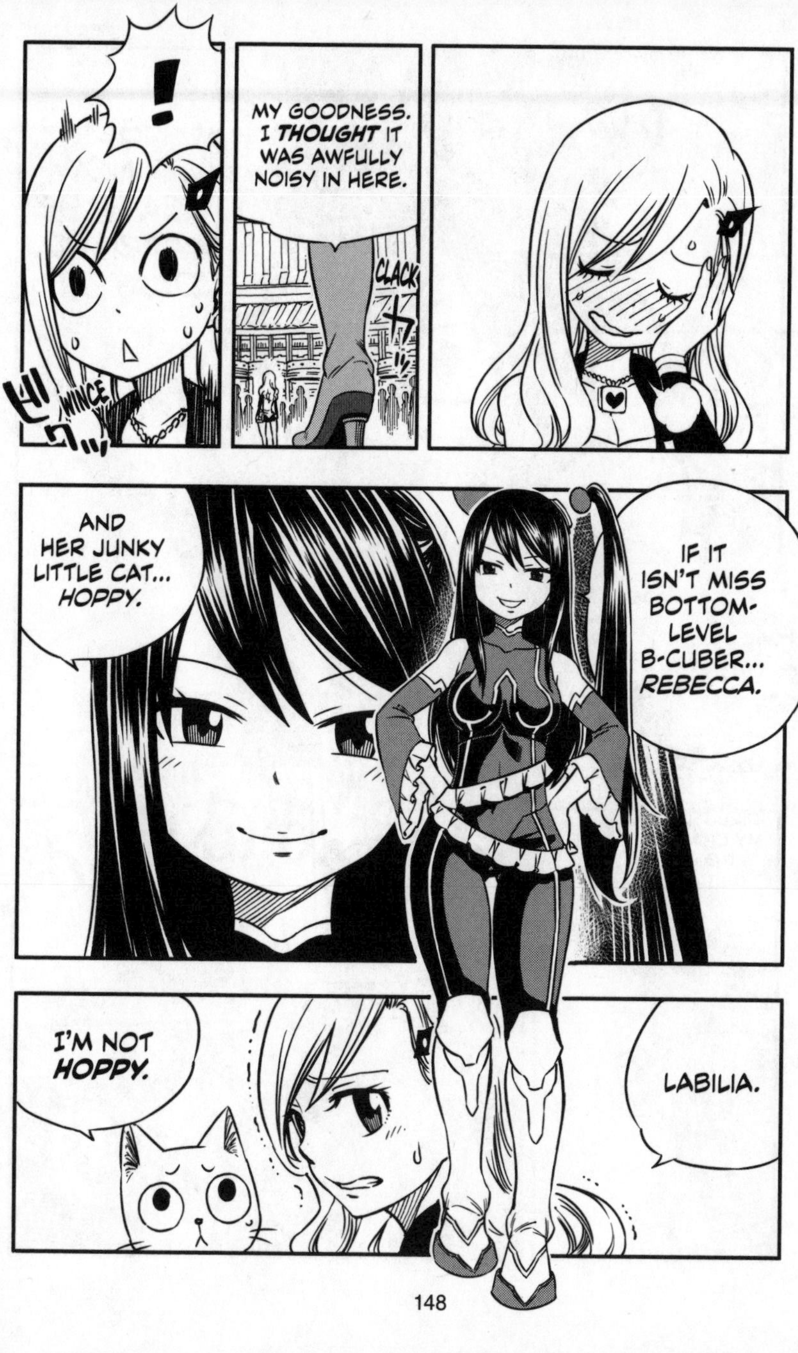
MY GOODNESS. I *THOUGHT* IT WAS AWFULLY NOISY IN HERE.
CLACK
!
WINCE
IF IT ISN'T MISS BOTTOM-LEVEL B-CUBER... *REBECCA.*
AND HER JUNKY LITTLE CAT... *HOPPY.*
LABILIA.
I'M NOT *HOPPY.*

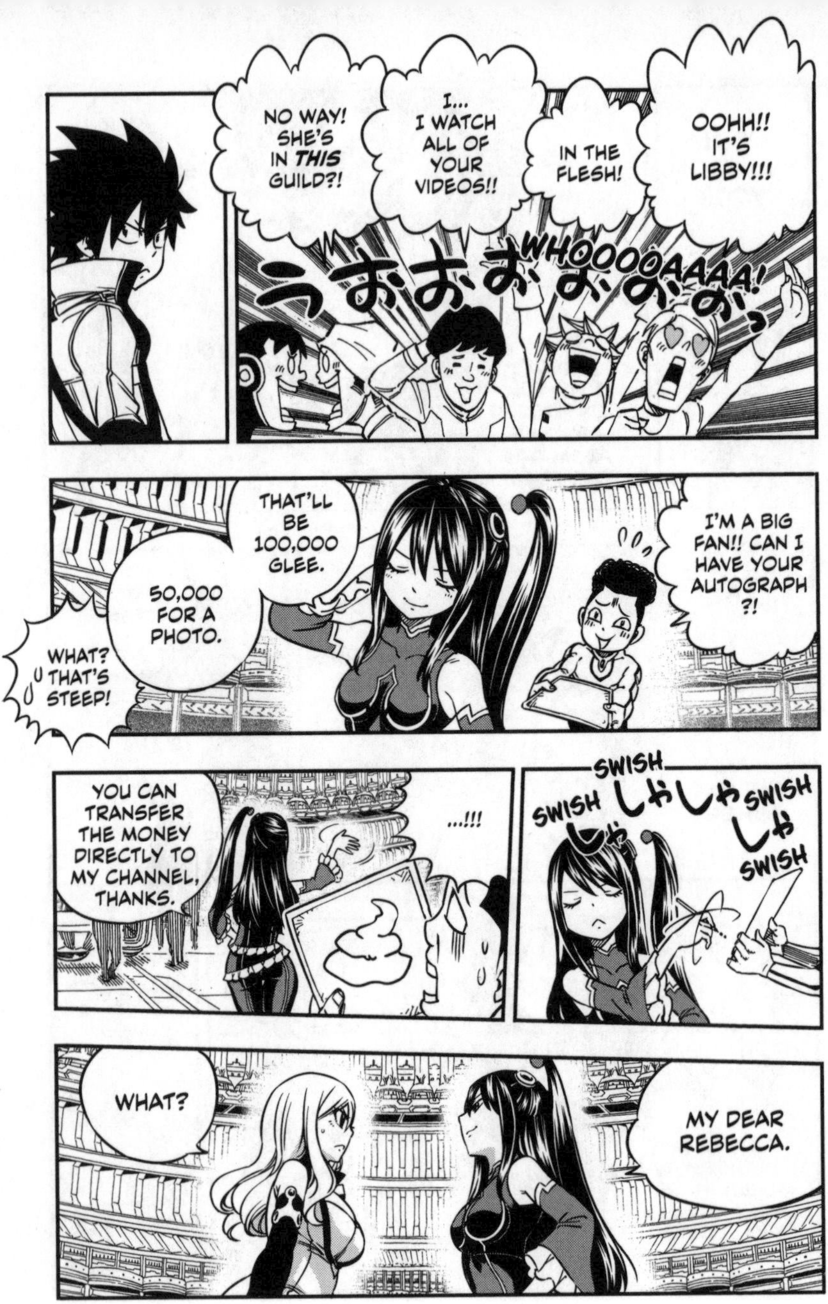
OOHH!! IT'S LIBBY!!!
IN THE FLESH!
I... I WATCH ALL OF YOUR VIDEOS!!
NO WAY! SHE'S IN *THIS* GUILD?!
WHOOOOAAAA!
I'M A BIG FAN!! CAN I HAVE YOUR AUTOGRAPH?!
THAT'LL BE 100,000 GLEE.
50,000 FOR A PHOTO.
WHAT? THAT'S STEEP!
SWISH
SWISH
SWISH
SWISH
...!!!
YOU CAN TRANSFER THE MONEY DIRECTLY TO MY CHANNEL, THANKS.
MY DEAR REBECCA.
WHAT?

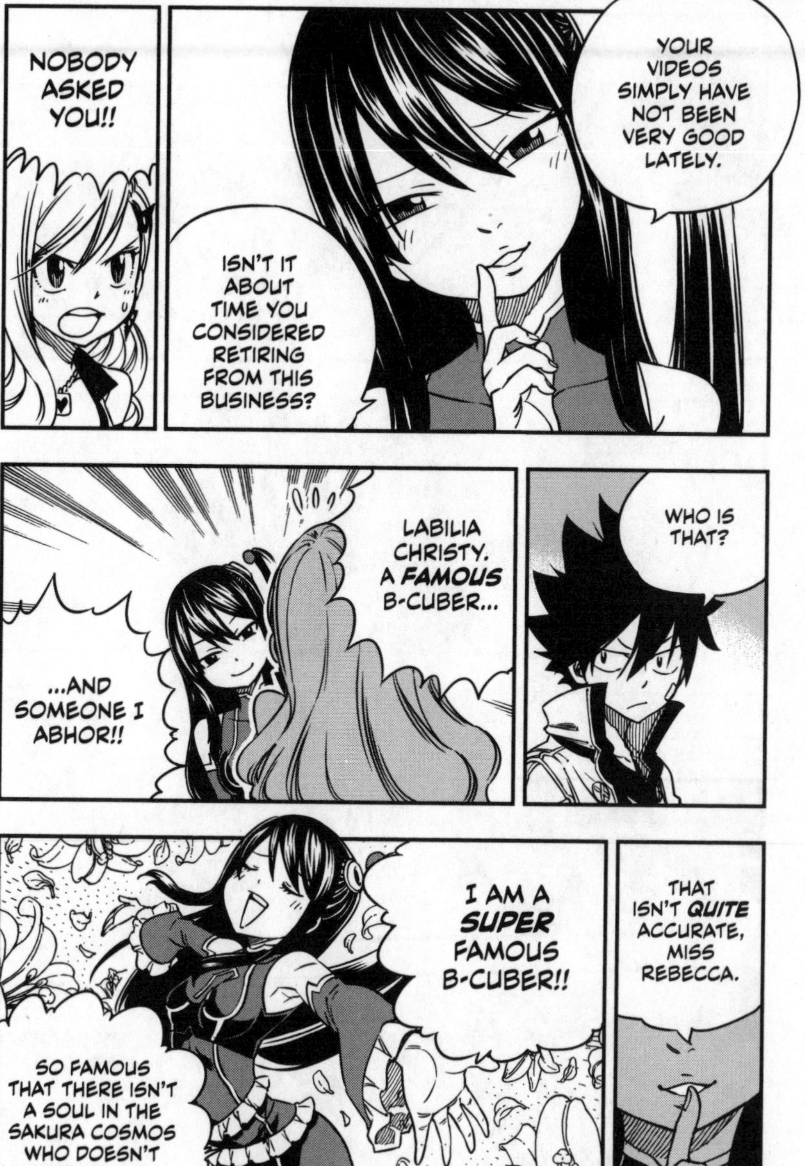
YOUR VIDEOS SIMPLY HAVE NOT BEEN VERY GOOD LATELY.
ISN'T IT ABOUT TIME YOU CONSIDERED RETIRING FROM THIS BUSINESS?
NOBODY ASKED YOU!!
WHO IS THAT?
LABILIA CHRISTY. A *FAMOUS* B-CUBER...
...AND SOMEONE I ABHOR!!
THAT ISN'T *QUITE* ACCURATE, MISS REBECCA.
I AM A **SUPER** FAMOUS B-CUBER!!
SO FAMOUS THAT THERE ISN'T A SOUL IN THE SAKURA COSMOS WHO DOESN'T KNOW ME!!!

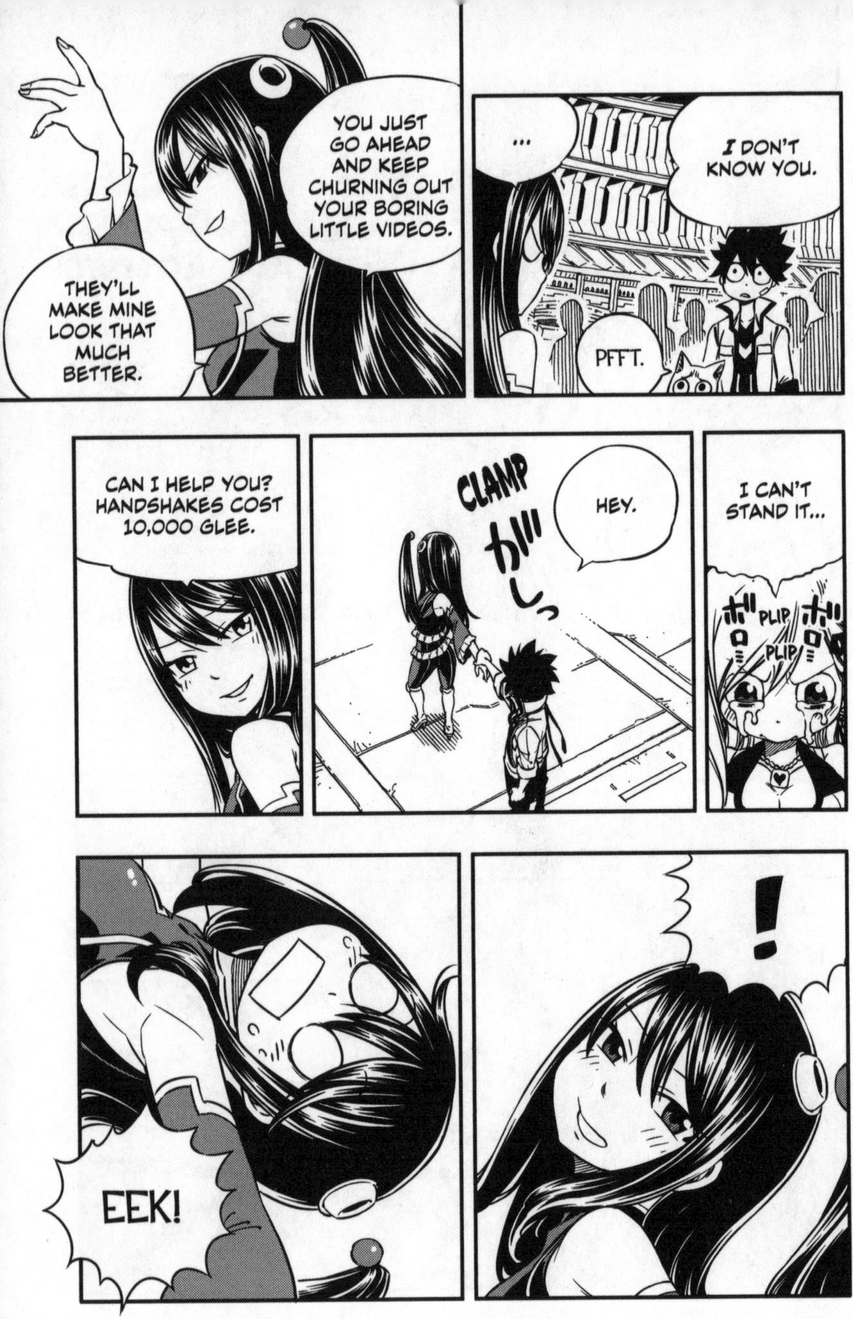
I DON'T KNOW YOU.
...
PFFT.
YOU JUST GO AHEAD AND KEEP CHURNING OUT YOUR BORING LITTLE VIDEOS.
THEY'LL MAKE MINE LOOK THAT MUCH BETTER.
I CAN'T STAND IT...
ボロ
PLIP
ボロ
PLIP
HEY.
CLAMP
がしっ
CAN I HELP YOU? HANDSHAKES COST 10,000 GLEE.
!
EEK!

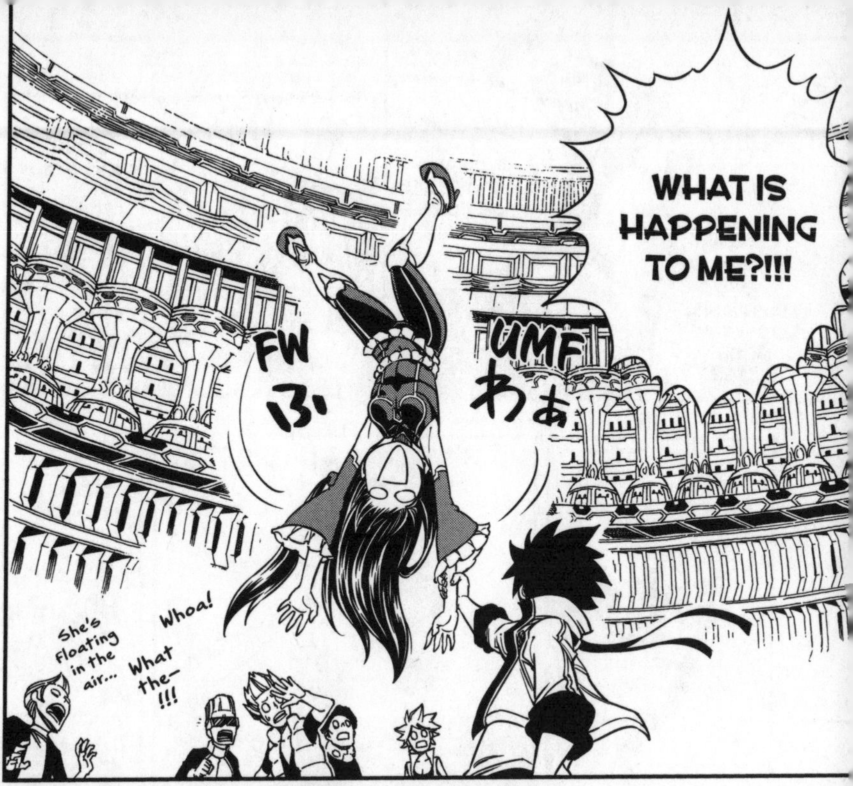
WHAT IS HAPPENING TO ME?!!!
FW ふ
UMF わぁ
Whoa!
She's floating in the air...
What the-!!!
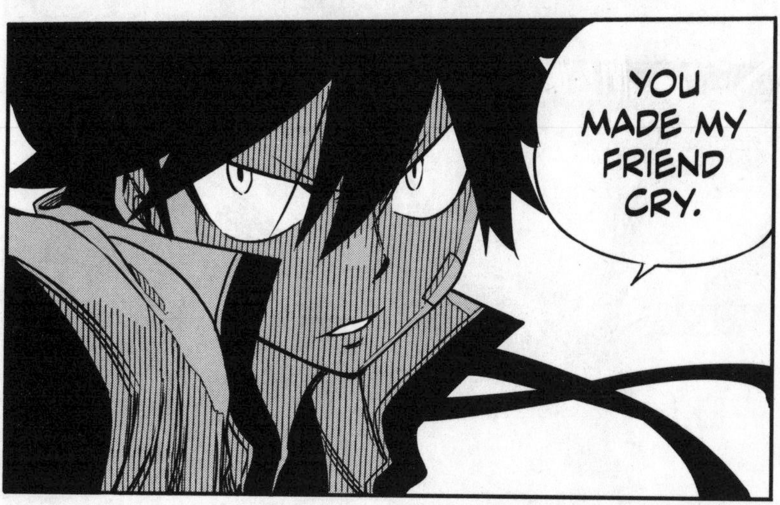
YOU MADE MY FRIEND CRY.

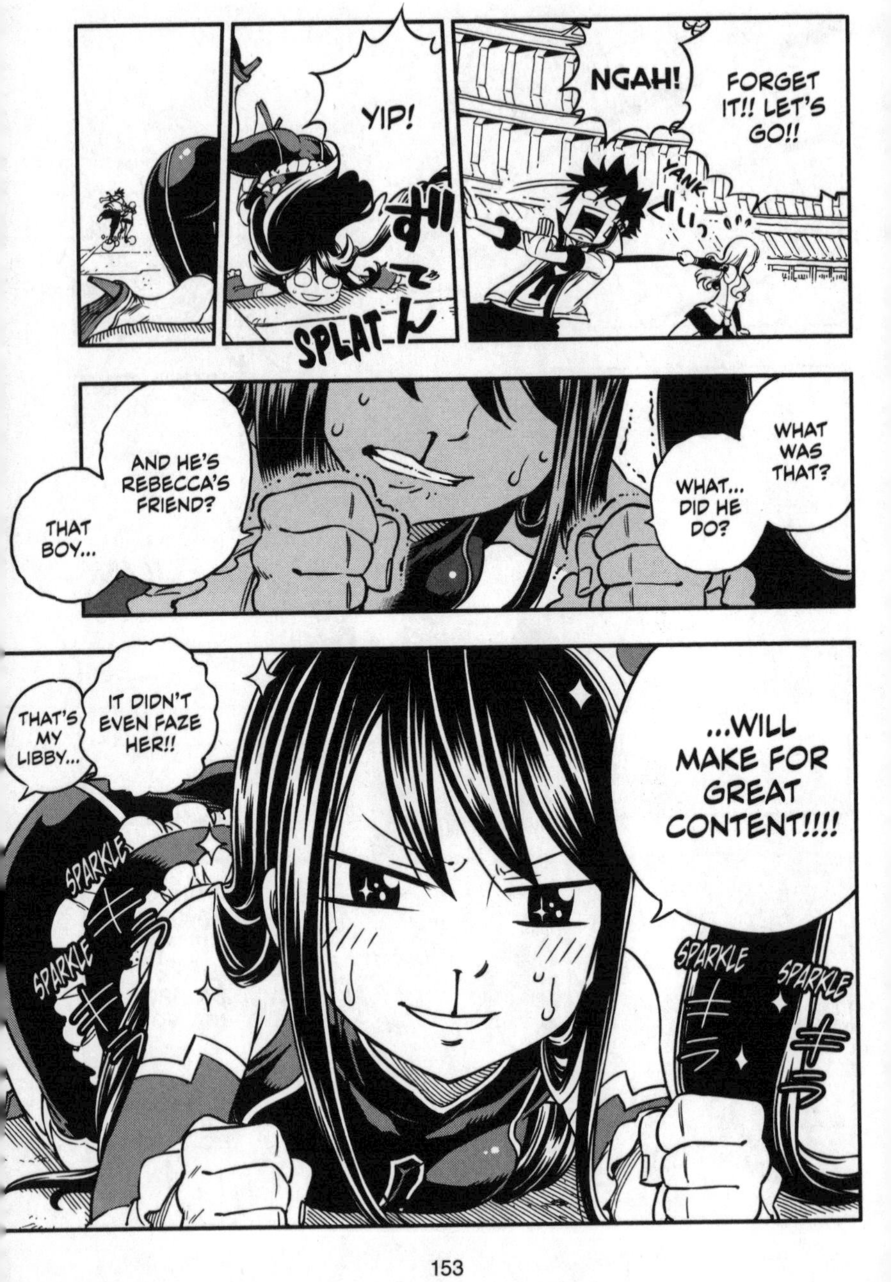
FORGET IT!! LET'S GO!!
NGAH!
YANK
YIP!
SPLAT
WHAT WAS THAT?
WHAT... DID HE DO?
AND HE'S REBECCA'S FRIEND?
THAT BOY...
...WILL MAKE FOR GREAT CONTENT!!!!
SPARKLE
SPARKLE
IT DIDN'T EVEN FAZE HER!!
THAT'S MY LIBBY...
SPARKLE
SPARKLE

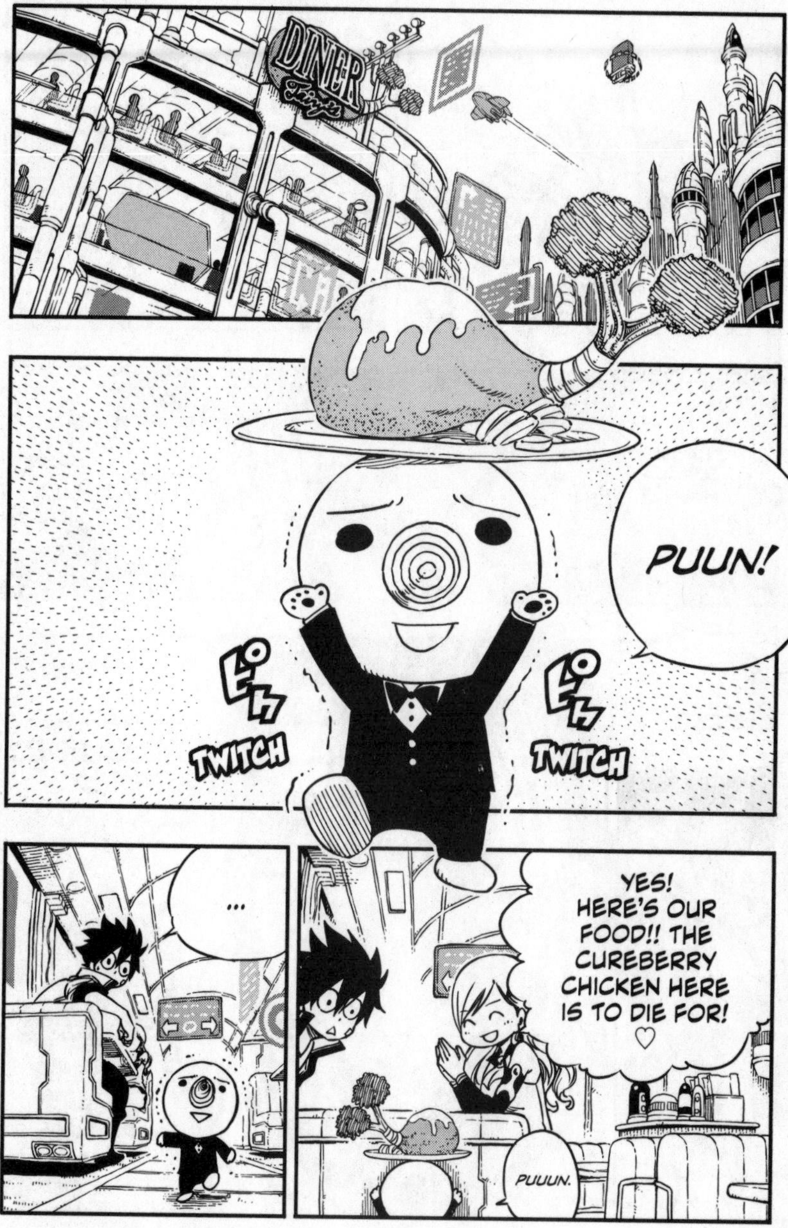
DINER
PUUN!
TWITCH
TWITCH
YES! HERE'S OUR FOOD!! THE CUREBERRY CHICKEN HERE IS TO DIE FOR! ♡
PUUN.
...

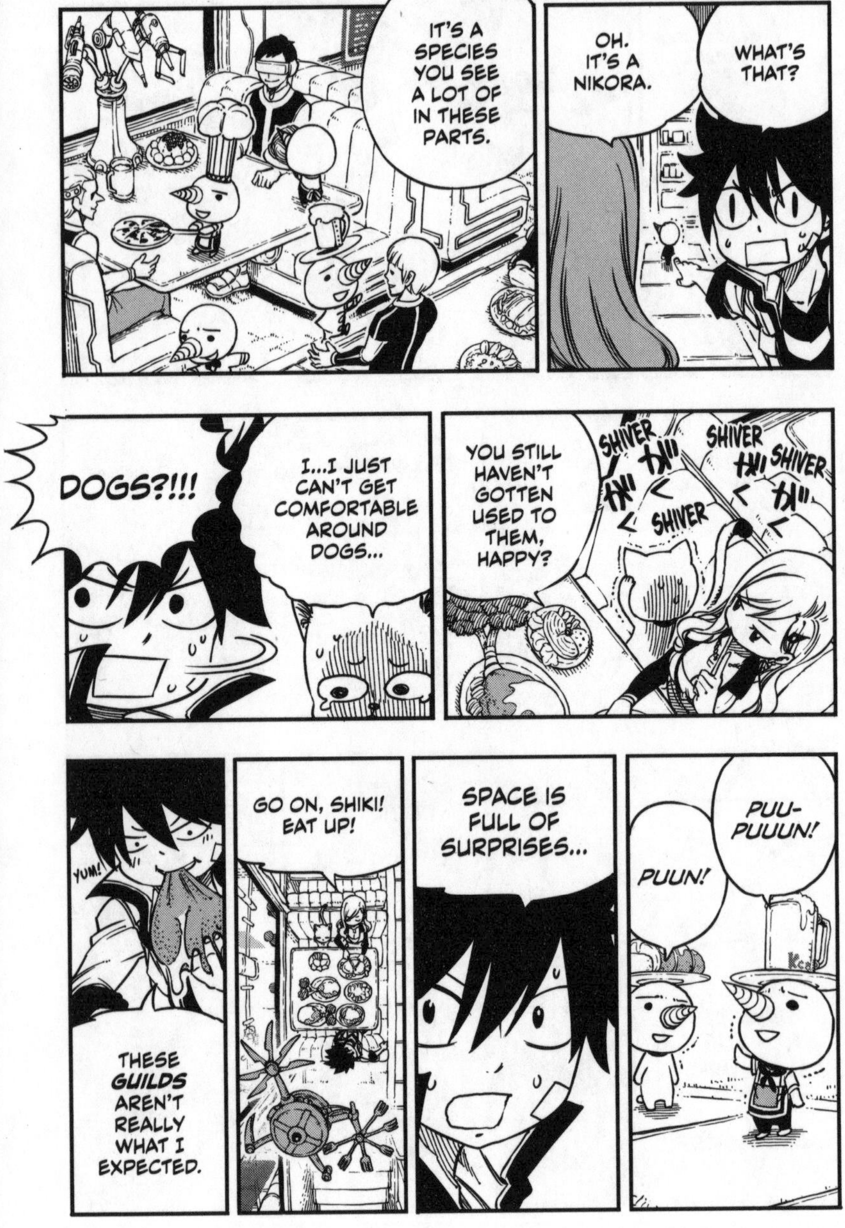
WHAT'S THAT?
OH. IT'S A NIKORA.
IT'S A SPECIES YOU SEE A LOT OF IN THESE PARTS.
YOU STILL HAVEN'T GOTTEN USED TO THEM, HAPPY?
SHIVER
SHIVER
SHIVER
SHIVER
I...I JUST CAN'T GET COMFORTABLE AROUND DOGS...
DOGS?!!!
PUU-PUUUN!
PUUN!
SPACE IS FULL OF SURPRISES...
GO ON, SHIKI! EAT UP!
YUM!
THESE GUILDS AREN'T REALLY WHAT I EXPECTED.

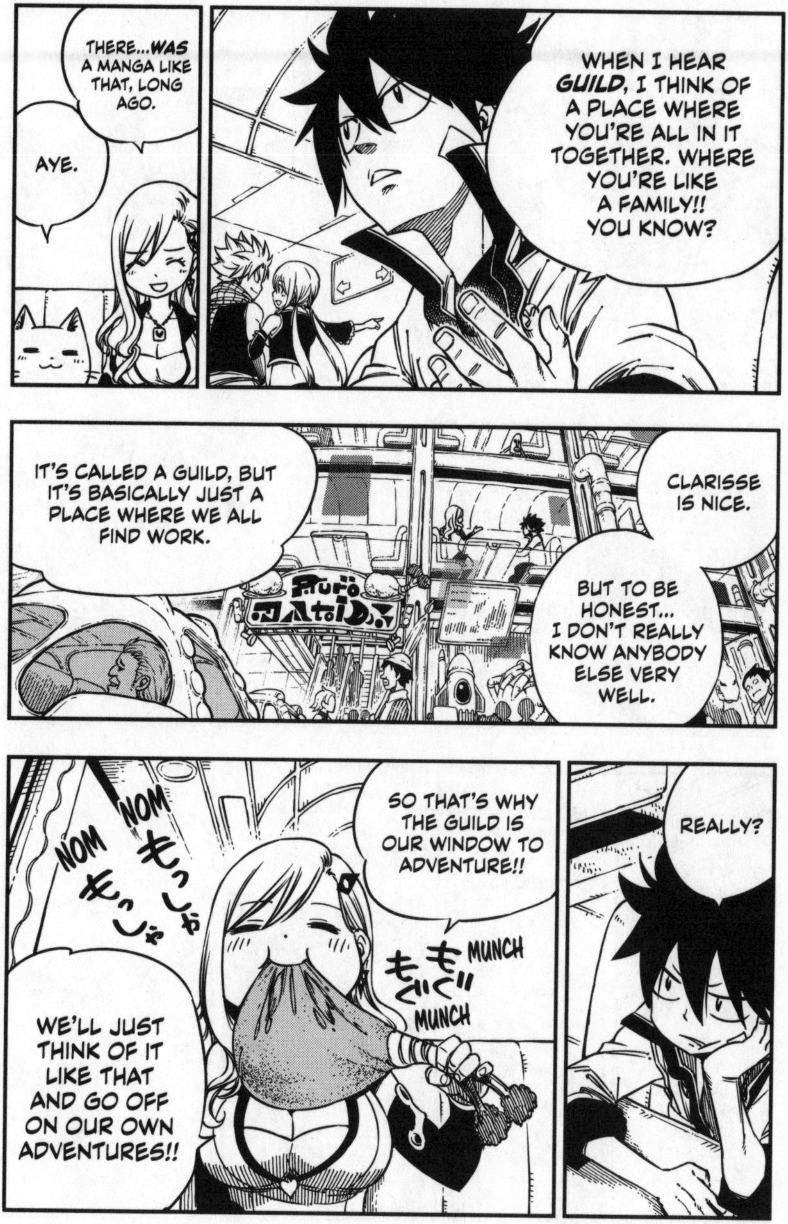

WHEN I HEAR **GUILD**, I THINK OF A PLACE WHERE YOU'RE ALL IN IT TOGETHER. WHERE YOU'RE LIKE A FAMILY!! YOU KNOW?
THERE...**WAS** A MANGA LIKE THAT, LONG AGO.
AYE.
CLARISSE IS NICE.
BUT TO BE HONEST... I DON'T REALLY KNOW ANYBODY ELSE VERY WELL.
IT'S CALLED A GUILD, BUT IT'S BASICALLY JUST A PLACE WHERE WE ALL FIND WORK.
REALLY?
SO THAT'S WHY THE GUILD IS OUR WINDOW TO ADVENTURE!!
MUNCH MUNCH
NOM NOM
WE'LL JUST THINK OF IT LIKE THAT AND GO OFF ON OUR OWN ADVENTURES!!

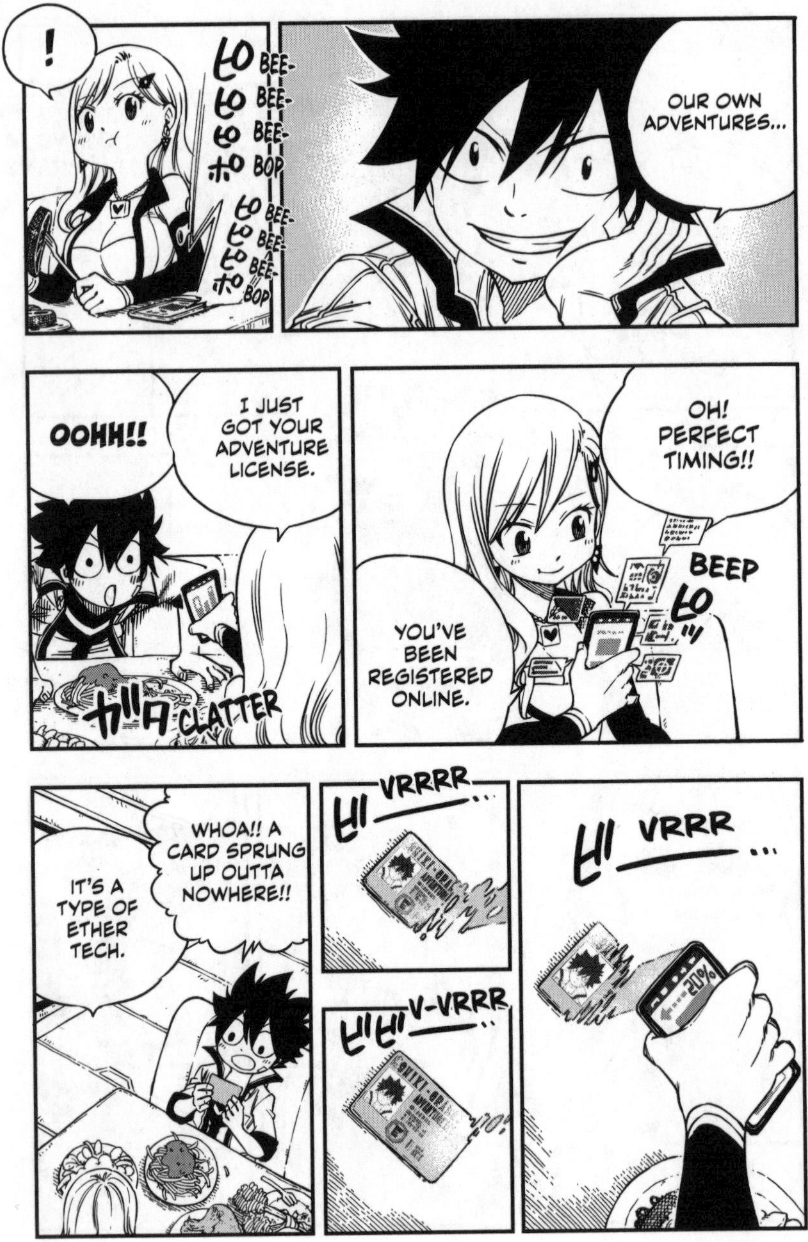
OUR OWN ADVENTURES...
!
BEE- BEE- BEE- BOP
BEE- BEE- BEE- BOP
OH! PERFECT TIMING!!
BEEP
YOU'VE BEEN REGISTERED ONLINE.
I JUST GOT YOUR ADVENTURE LICENSE.
OOHH!!
CLATTER
VRRR...
20%
VRRRR...
V-VRRR...
WHOA!! A CARD SPRUNG UP OUTTA NOWHERE!!
IT'S A TYPE OF ETHER TECH.

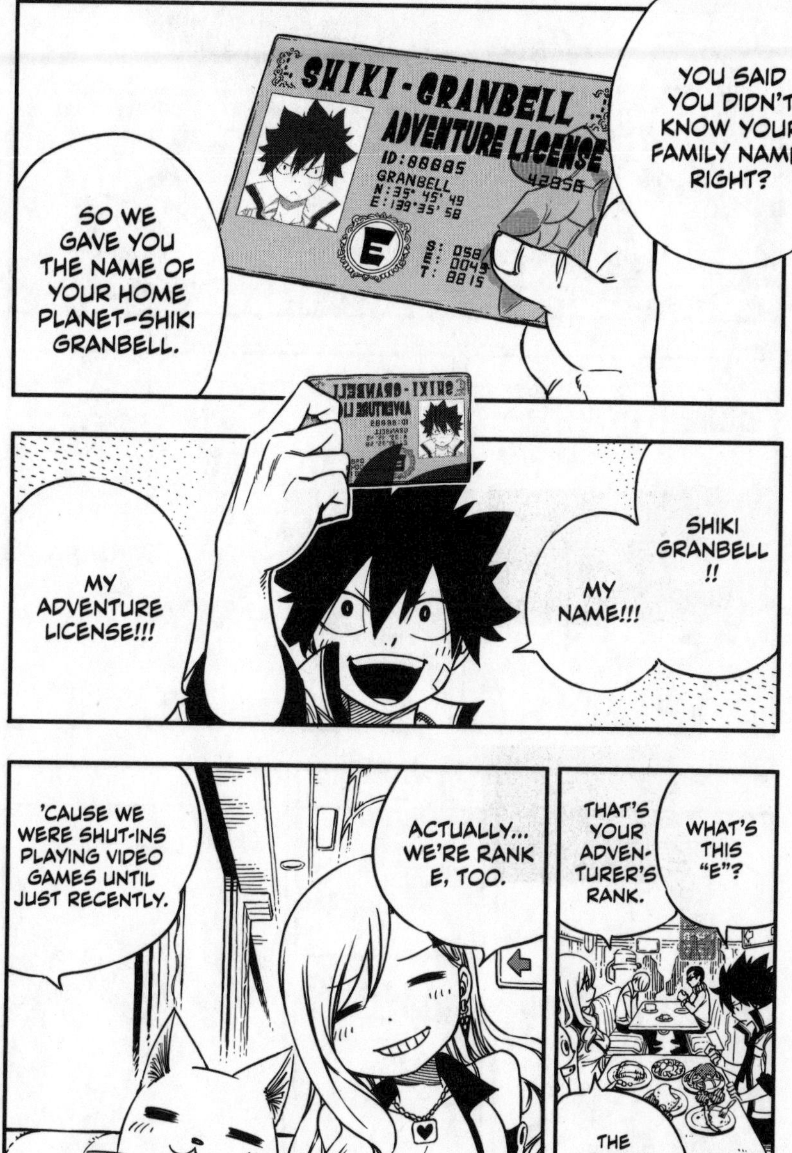
SHIKI - GRANBELL
ADVENTURE LICENSE
ID:88885
GRANBELL
N:35°45'49
E:139°35'58
42856
E
S: 058
E: 0043
T: 8815
YOU SAID YOU DIDN'T KNOW YOUR FAMILY NAME, RIGHT?
SO WE GAVE YOU THE NAME OF YOUR HOME PLANET—SHIKI GRANBELL.
SHIKI GRANBELL !!
MY NAME!!!
MY ADVENTURE LICENSE!!!
WHAT'S THIS "E"?
THAT'S YOUR ADVEN-TURER'S RANK.
THE LOWEST LEVEL.
ACTUALLY... WE'RE RANK E, TOO.
'CAUSE WE WERE SHUT-INS PLAYING VIDEO GAMES UNTIL JUST RECENTLY.

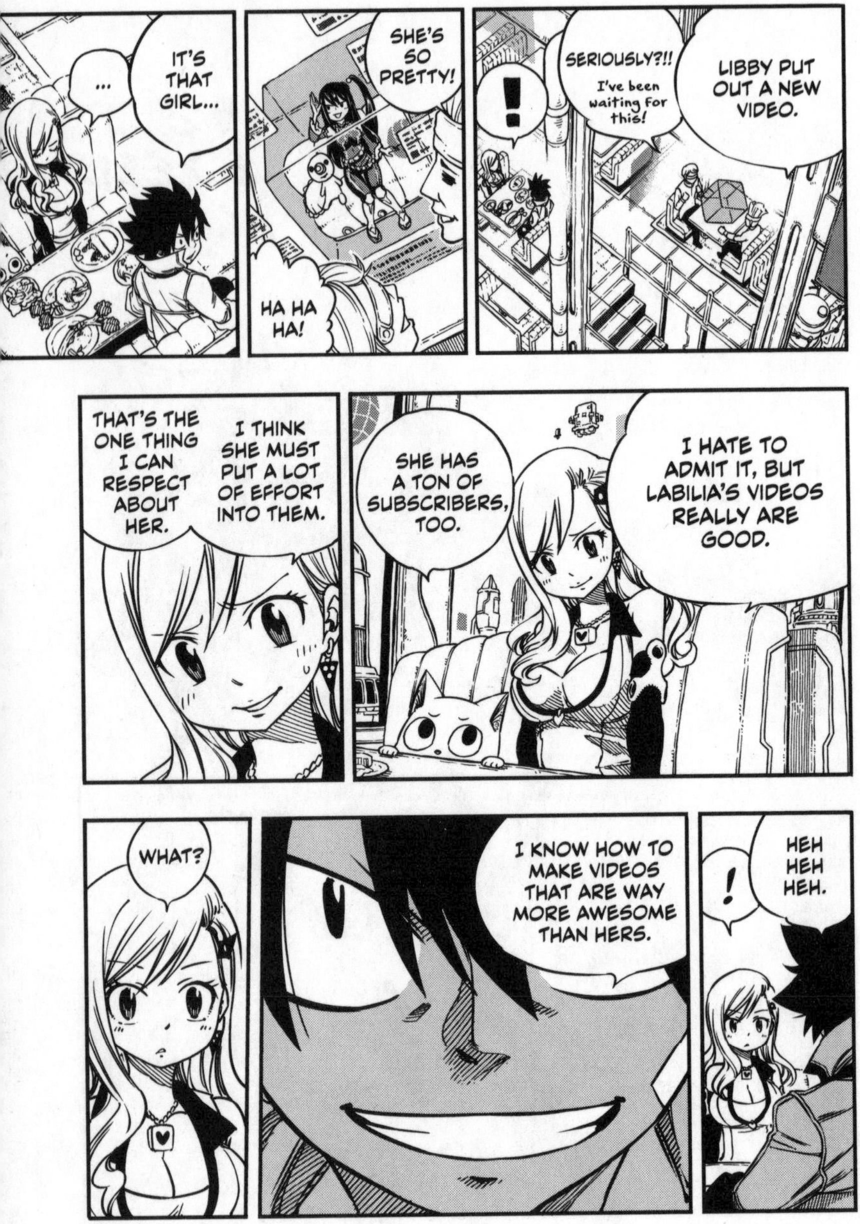
LIBBY PUT OUT A NEW VIDEO.
SERIOUSLY?!! I've been waiting for this!
!
SHE'S SO PRETTY!
HA HA HA!
IT'S THAT GIRL...
...
I HATE TO ADMIT IT, BUT LABILIA'S VIDEOS REALLY ARE GOOD.
SHE HAS A TON OF SUBSCRIBERS, TOO.
I THINK SHE MUST PUT A LOT OF EFFORT INTO THEM.
THAT'S THE ONE THING I CAN RESPECT ABOUT HER.
HEH HEH HEH.
!
I KNOW HOW TO MAKE VIDEOS THAT ARE WAY MORE AWESOME THAN HERS.
WHAT?

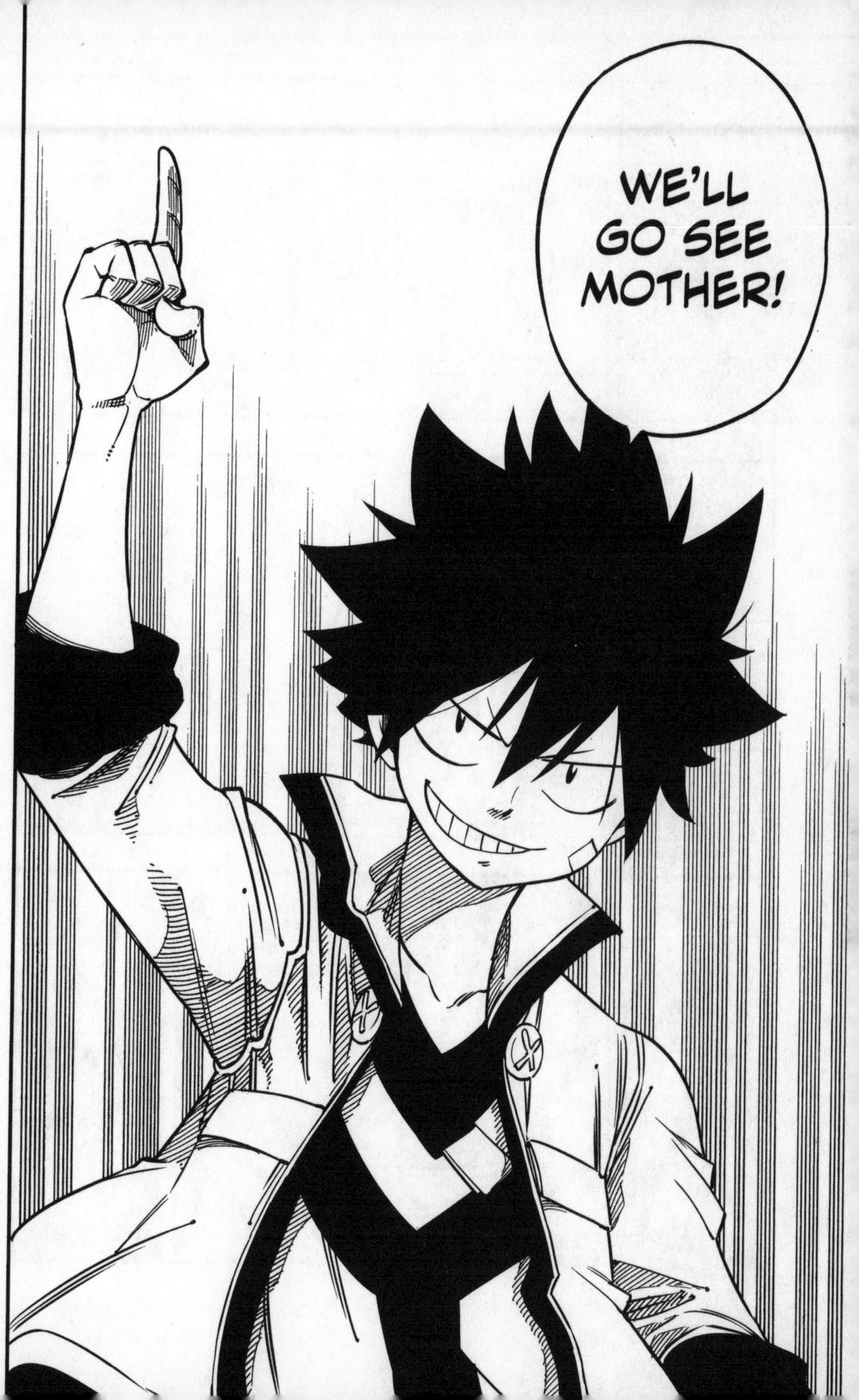
WE'LL GO SEE MOTHER!

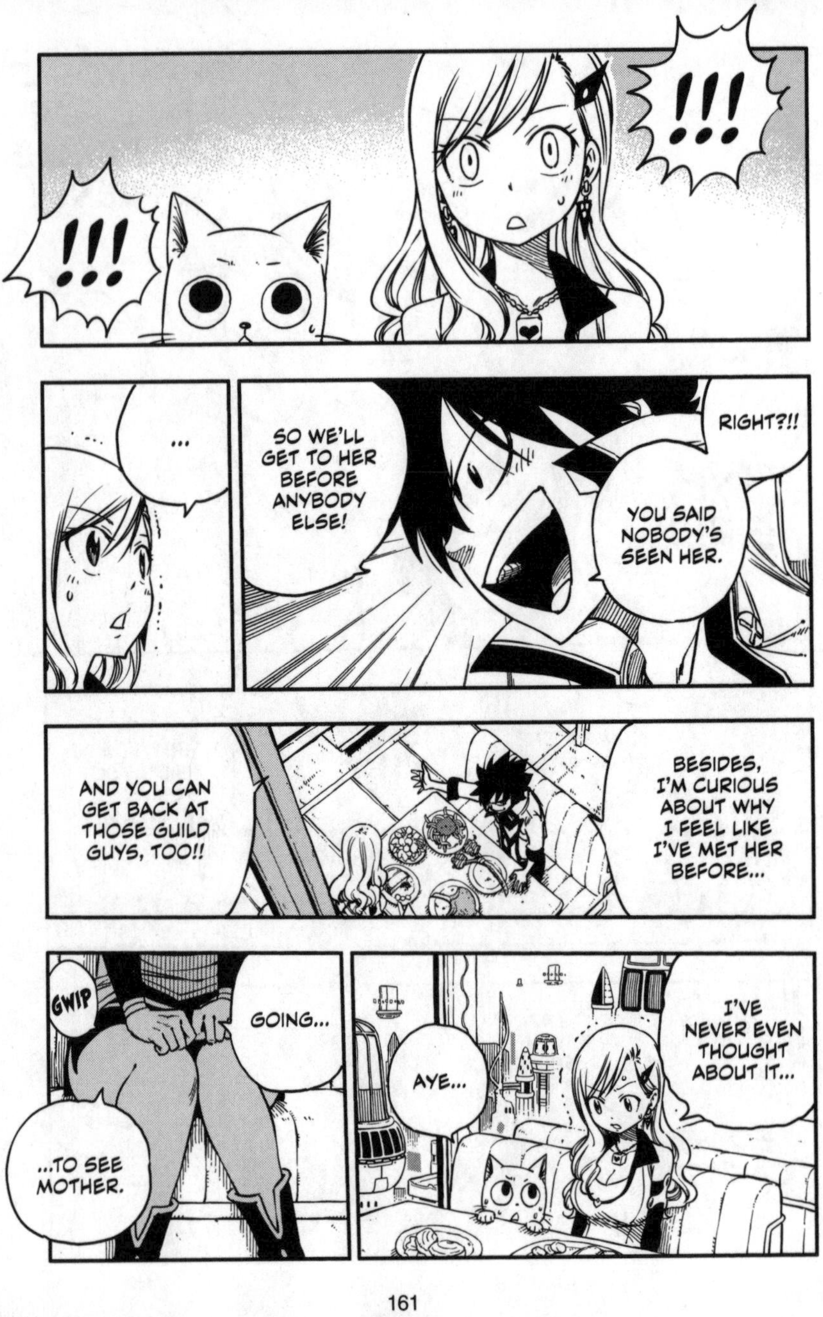
!!!
!!!
RIGHT?!!
YOU SAID NOBODY'S SEEN HER.
SO WE'LL GET TO HER BEFORE ANYBODY ELSE!
...
BESIDES, I'M CURIOUS ABOUT WHY I FEEL LIKE I'VE MET HER BEFORE...
AND YOU CAN GET BACK AT THOSE GUILD GUYS, TOO!!
I'VE NEVER EVEN THOUGHT ABOUT IT...
AYE...
GOING...
GWIP
...TO SEE MOTHER.

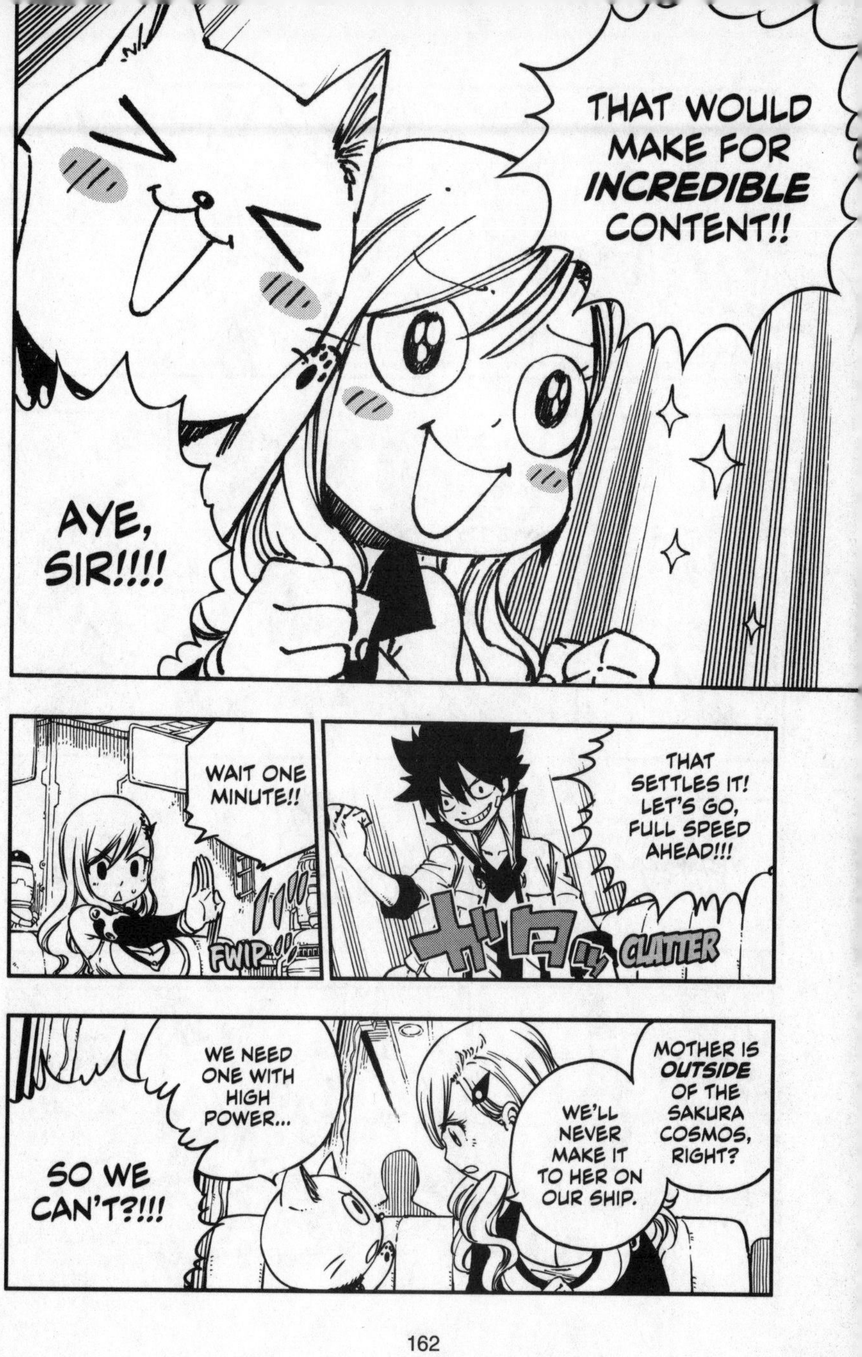
THAT WOULD MAKE FOR INCREDIBLE CONTENT!!
AYE, SIR!!!!
THAT SETTLES IT! LET'S GO, FULL SPEED AHEAD!!!
CLATTER
WAIT ONE MINUTE!!
FWIP
MOTHER IS OUTSIDE OF THE SAKURA COSMOS, RIGHT?
WE'LL NEVER MAKE IT TO HER ON OUR SHIP.
WE NEED ONE WITH HIGH POWER...
SO WE CAN'T?!!!

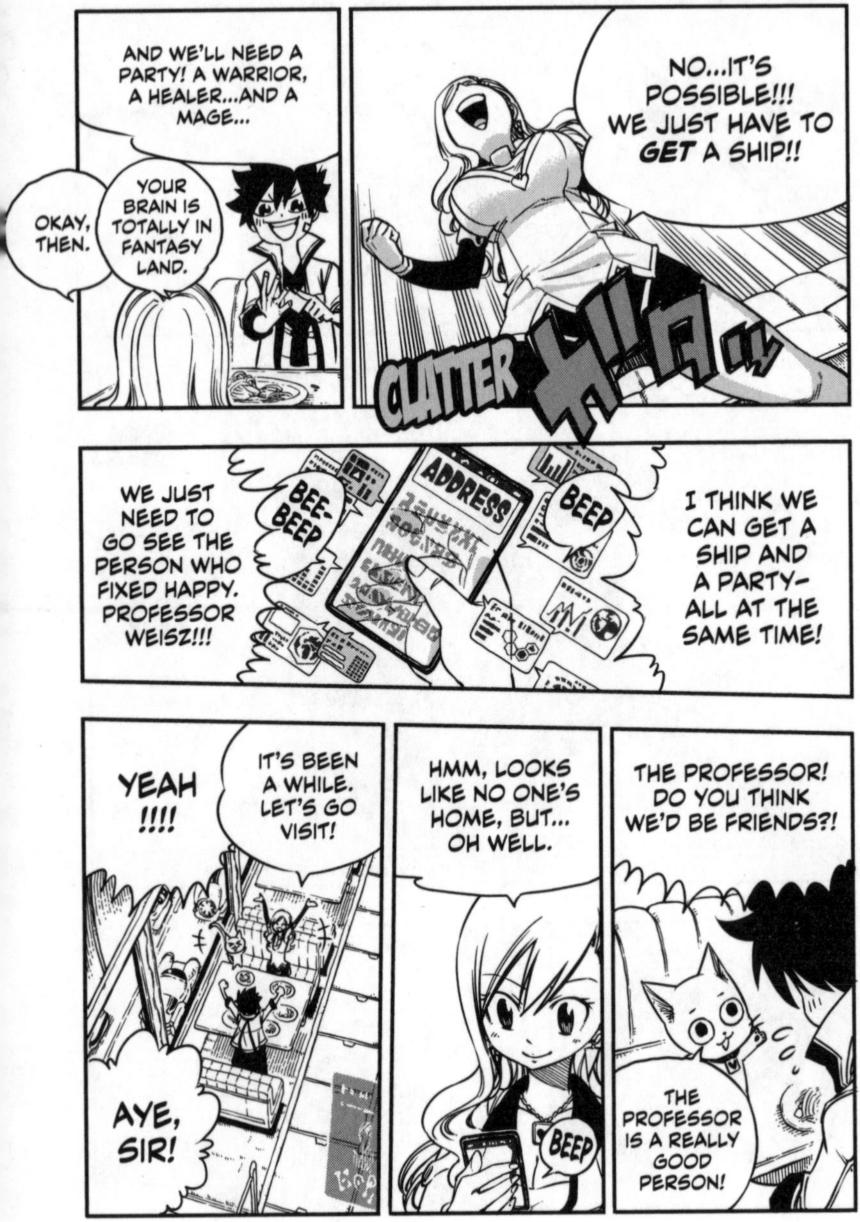
NO...IT'S POSSIBLE!!! WE JUST HAVE TO GET A SHIP!!
CLATTER
AND WE'LL NEED A PARTY! A WARRIOR, A HEALER...AND A MAGE...
YOUR BRAIN IS TOTALLY IN FANTASY LAND.
OKAY, THEN.
I THINK WE CAN GET A SHIP AND A PARTY-ALL AT THE SAME TIME!
BEEP
ADDRESS
BEE-BEEP
WE JUST NEED TO GO SEE THE PERSON WHO FIXED HAPPY. PROFESSOR WEISZ!!!
THE PROFESSOR! DO YOU THINK WE'D BE FRIENDS?!
THE PROFESSOR IS A REALLY GOOD PERSON!
HMM, LOOKS LIKE NO ONE'S HOME, BUT... OH WELL.
BEEP
IT'S BEEN A WHILE. LET'S GO VISIT!
YEAH !!!!
AYE, SIR!

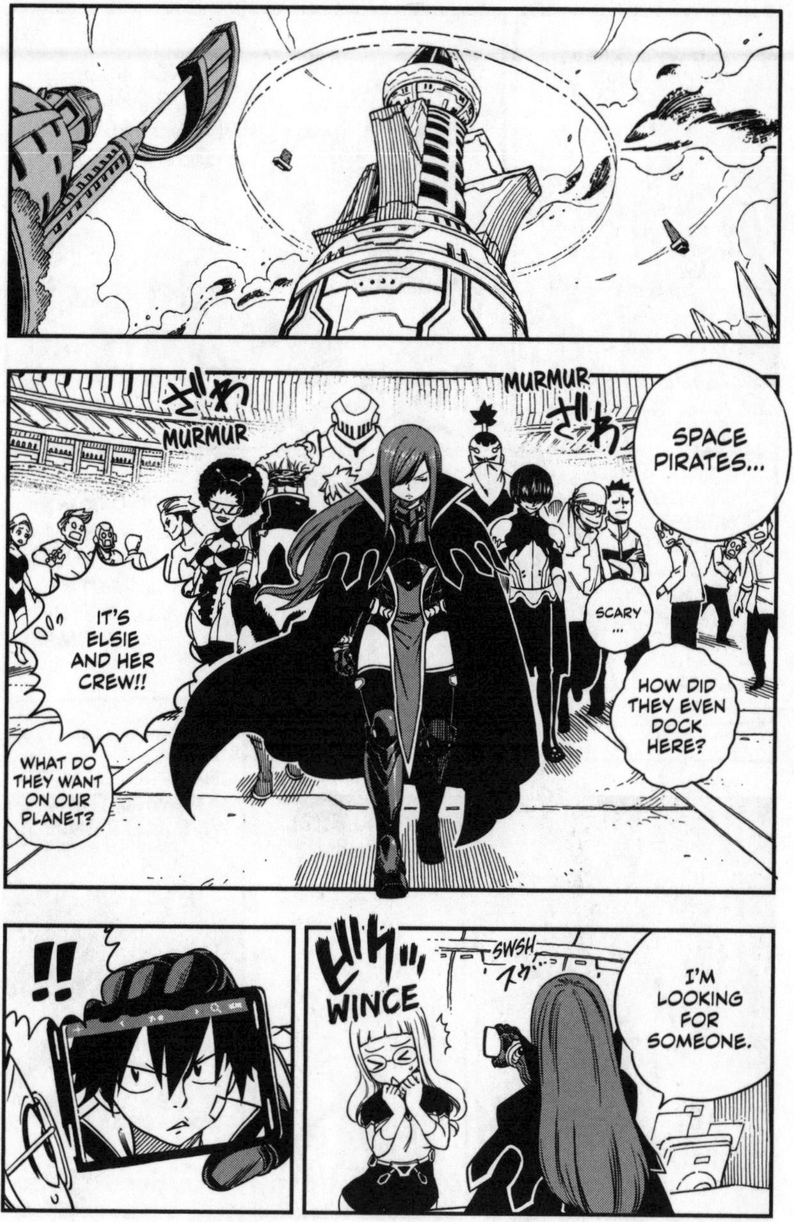
MURMUR
ざわ
SPACE PIRATES...
ざわ
MURMUR
SCARY ...
HOW DID THEY EVEN DOCK HERE?
IT'S ELSIE AND HER CREW!!
WHAT DO THEY WANT ON OUR PLANET?
I'M LOOKING FOR SOMEONE.
SWSH
WINCE
!!

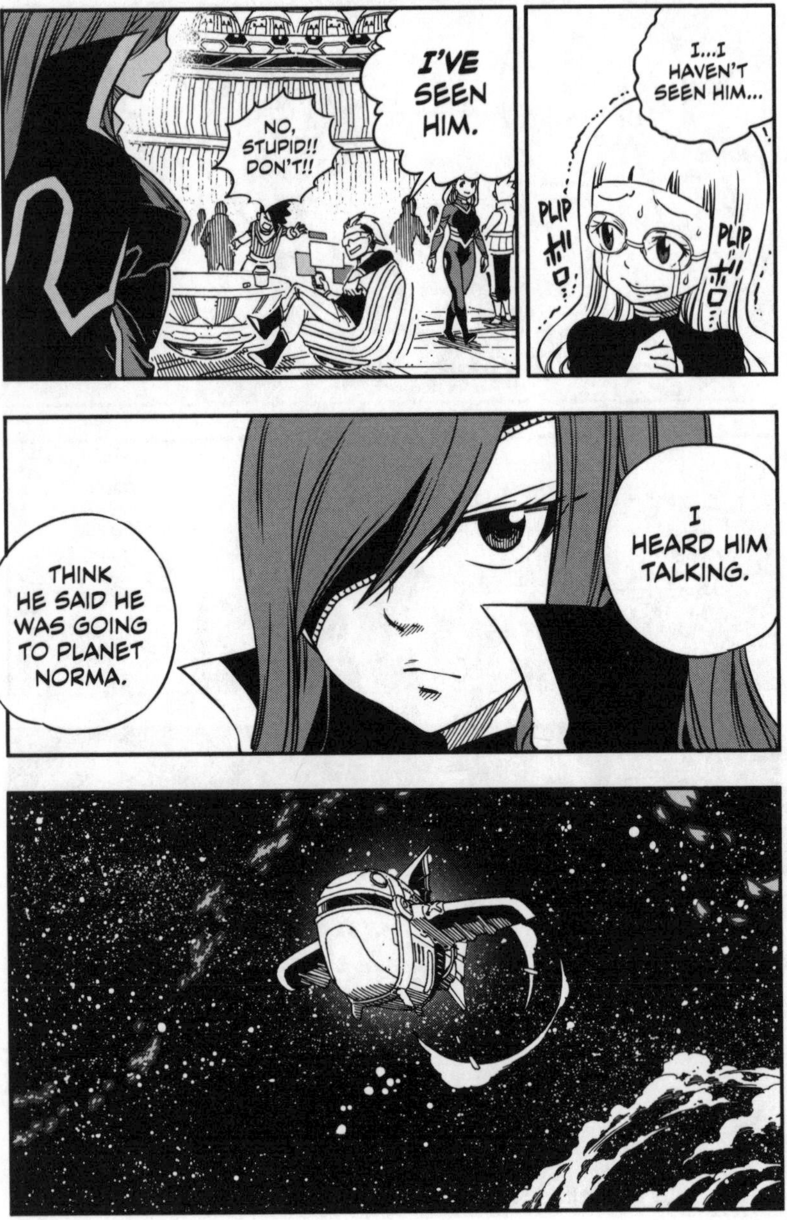
I...I HAVEN'T SEEN HIM...
PLIP
PLIP
I'VE SEEN HIM.
NO, STUPID!! DON'T!!
I HEARD HIM TALKING.
THINK HE SAID HE WAS GOING TO PLANET NORMA.

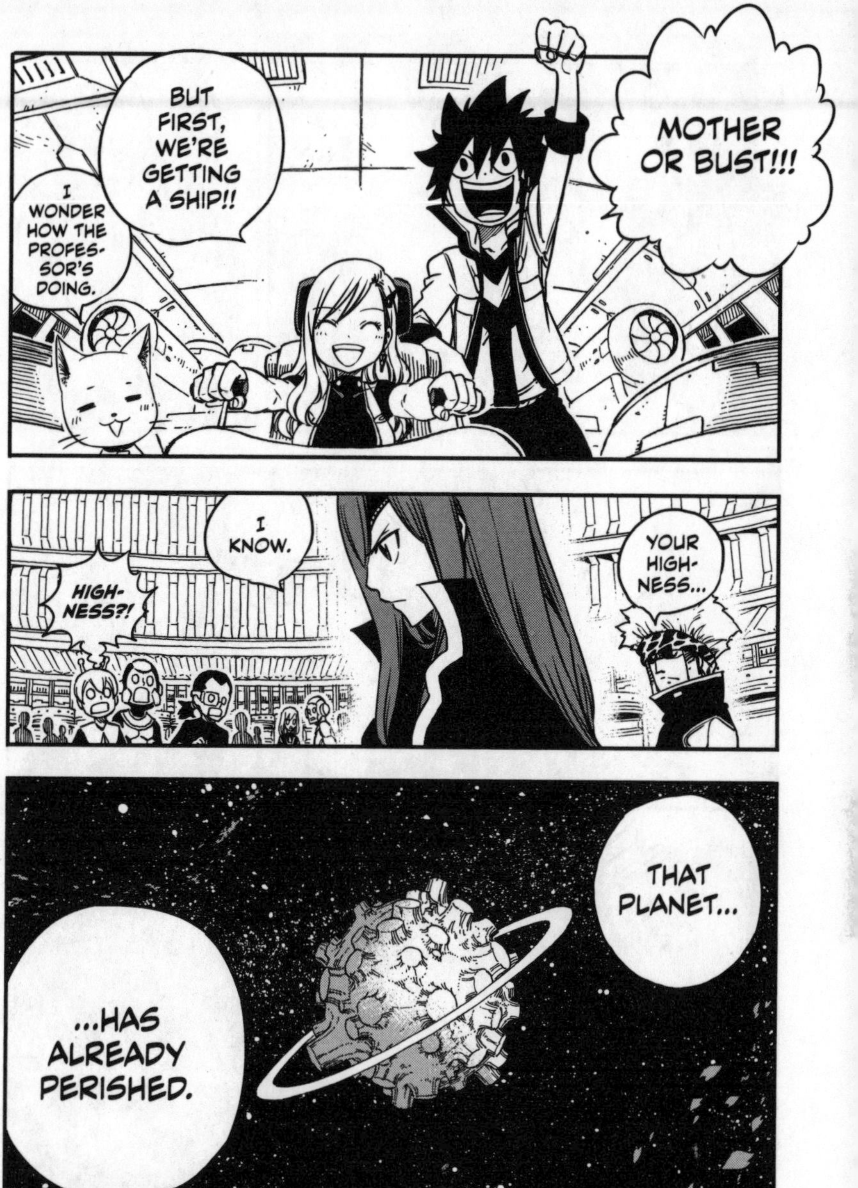
MOTHER OR BUST!!!
BUT FIRST, WE'RE GETTING A SHIP!!
I WONDER HOW THE PROFES-SOR'S DOING.
YOUR HIGH-NESS...
I KNOW.
HIGH-NESS?!
THAT PLANET...
...HAS ALREADY PERISHED.

EDENS ZERO

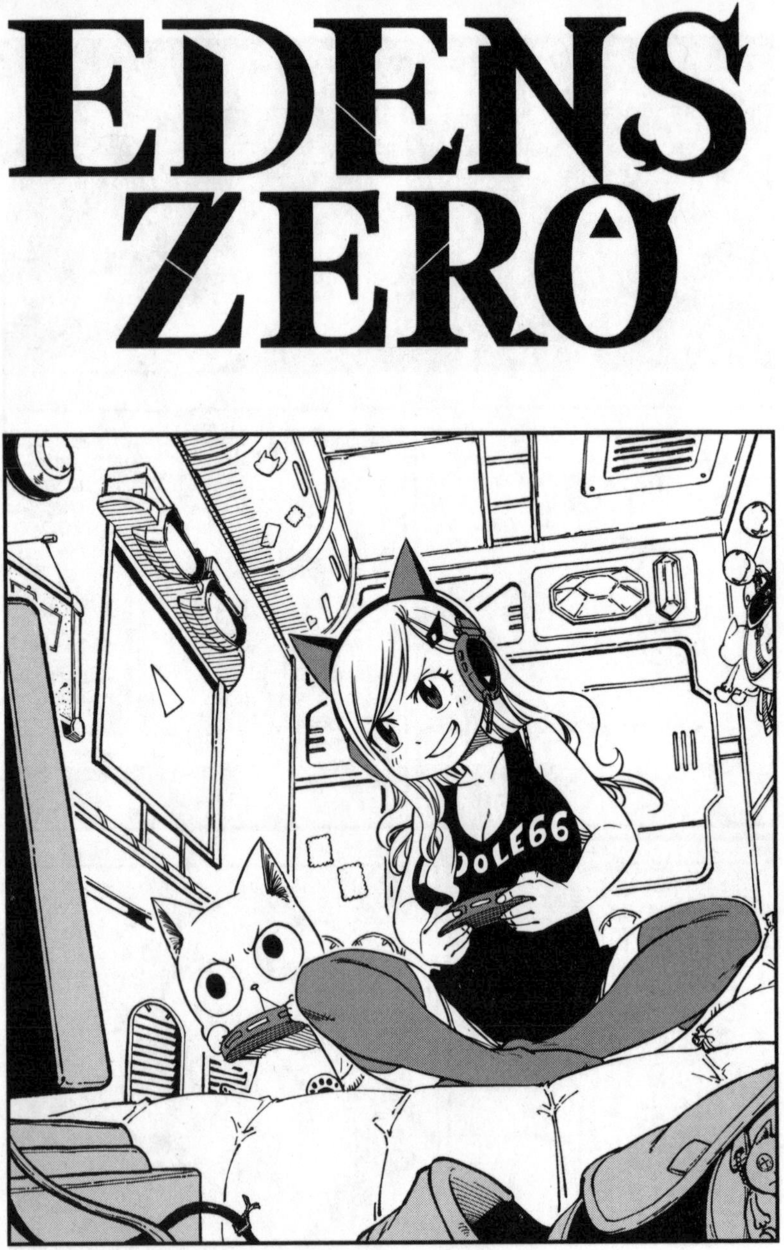

CHAPTER 4: NORMA

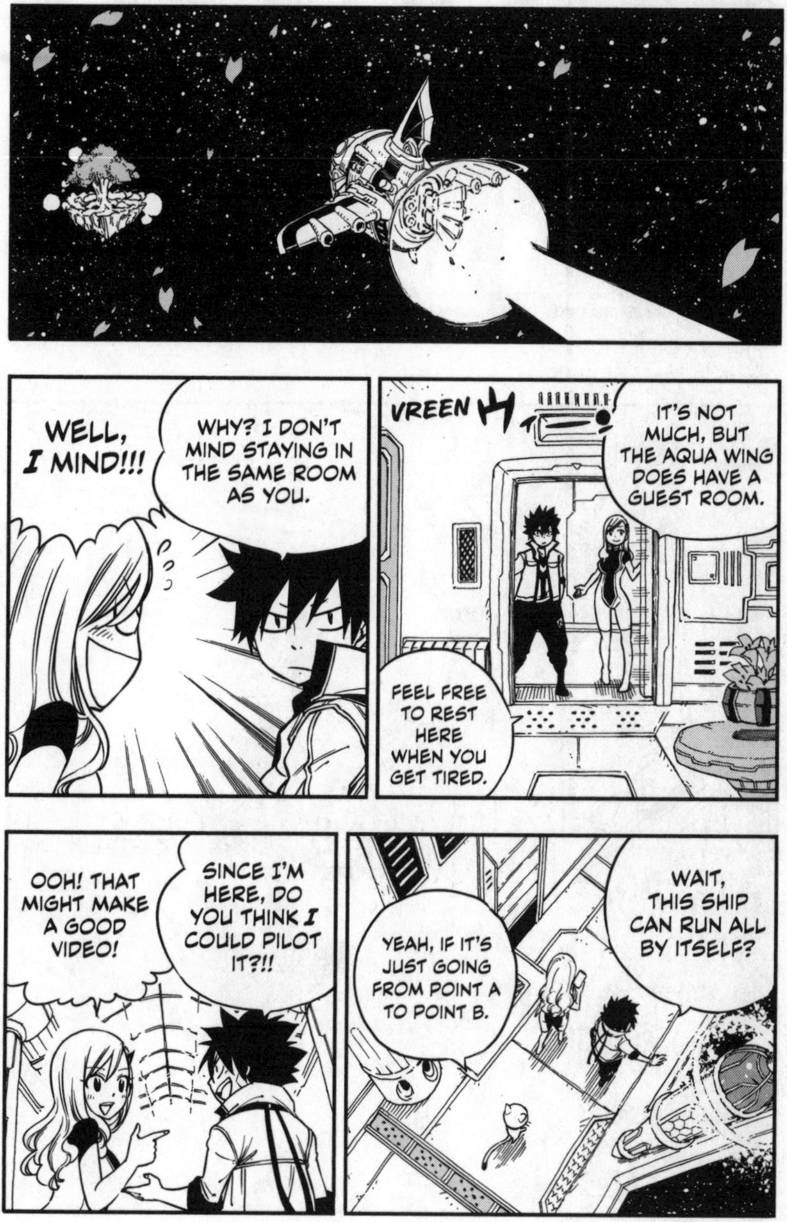
VREEN
IT'S NOT MUCH, BUT THE AQUA WING DOES HAVE A GUEST ROOM.
FEEL FREE TO REST HERE WHEN YOU GET TIRED.
WHY? I DON'T MIND STAYING IN THE SAME ROOM AS YOU.
WELL, I MIND!!!
WAIT, THIS SHIP CAN RUN ALL BY ITSELF?
YEAH, IF IT'S JUST GOING FROM POINT A TO POINT B.
SINCE I'M HERE, DO YOU THINK I COULD PILOT IT?!!
OOH! THAT MIGHT MAKE A GOOD VIDEO!

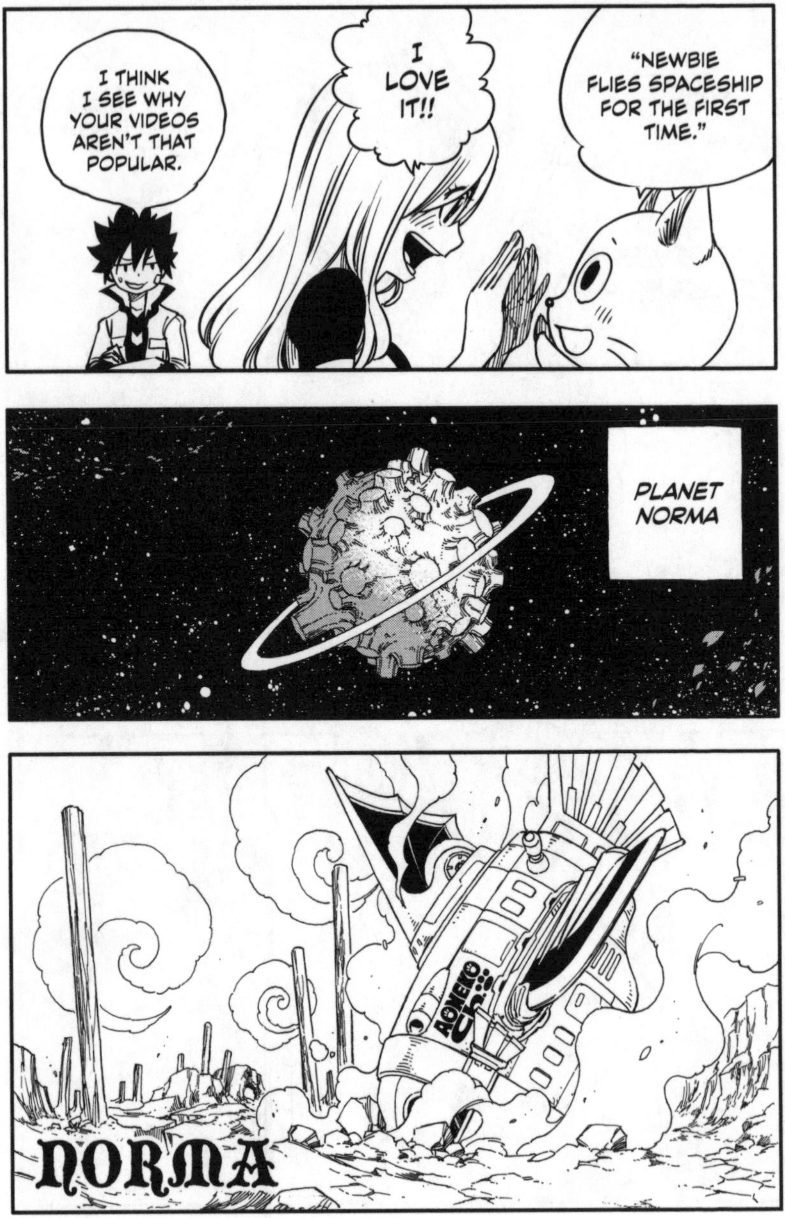
"NEWBIE FLIES SPACESHIP FOR THE FIRST TIME."
I LOVE IT!!
I THINK I SEE WHY YOUR VIDEOS AREN'T THAT POPULAR.
PLANET NORMA
NORMA

I CAN'T BELIEVE IT!!!
WHO CRASHES A SPACESHIP?
WHAT DO WE DO... ABOUT OUR SHIP?
HA HA HA! DIDJA GET A GOOD VIDEO?
YOU BET I DID!!
!!
ZHRG
RGH
RGH
RGH
HUP!

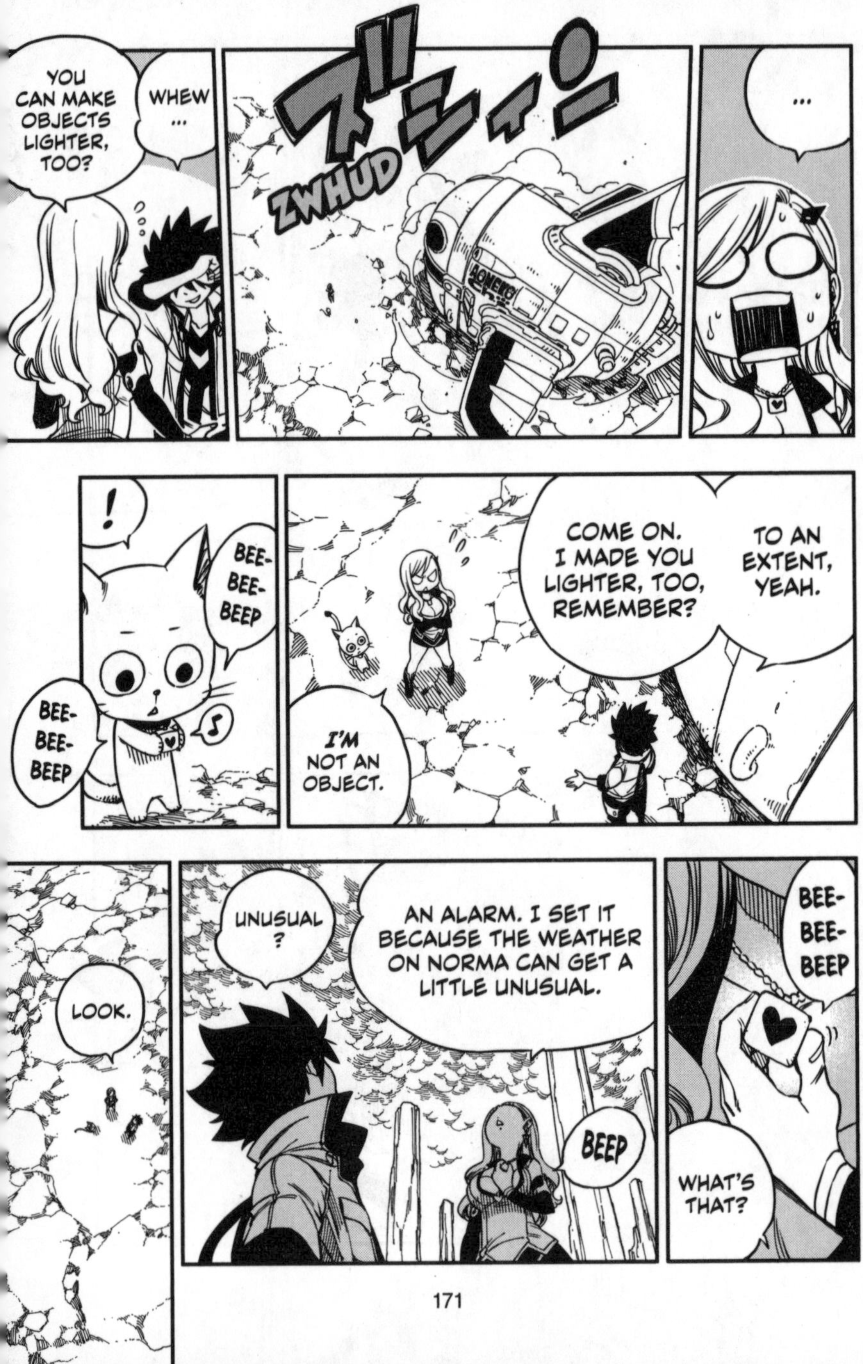
...
ZWHUD
WHEW ...
YOU CAN MAKE OBJECTS LIGHTER, TOO?
TO AN EXTENT, YEAH.
COME ON. I MADE YOU LIGHTER, TOO, REMEMBER?
I'M NOT AN OBJECT.
!
BEE-BEE-BEEP
BEE-BEE-BEEP
BEE-BEE-BEEP
WHAT'S THAT?
AN ALARM. I SET IT BECAUSE THE WEATHER ON NORMA CAN GET A LITTLE UNUSUAL.
UNUSUAL?
BEEP
LOOK.

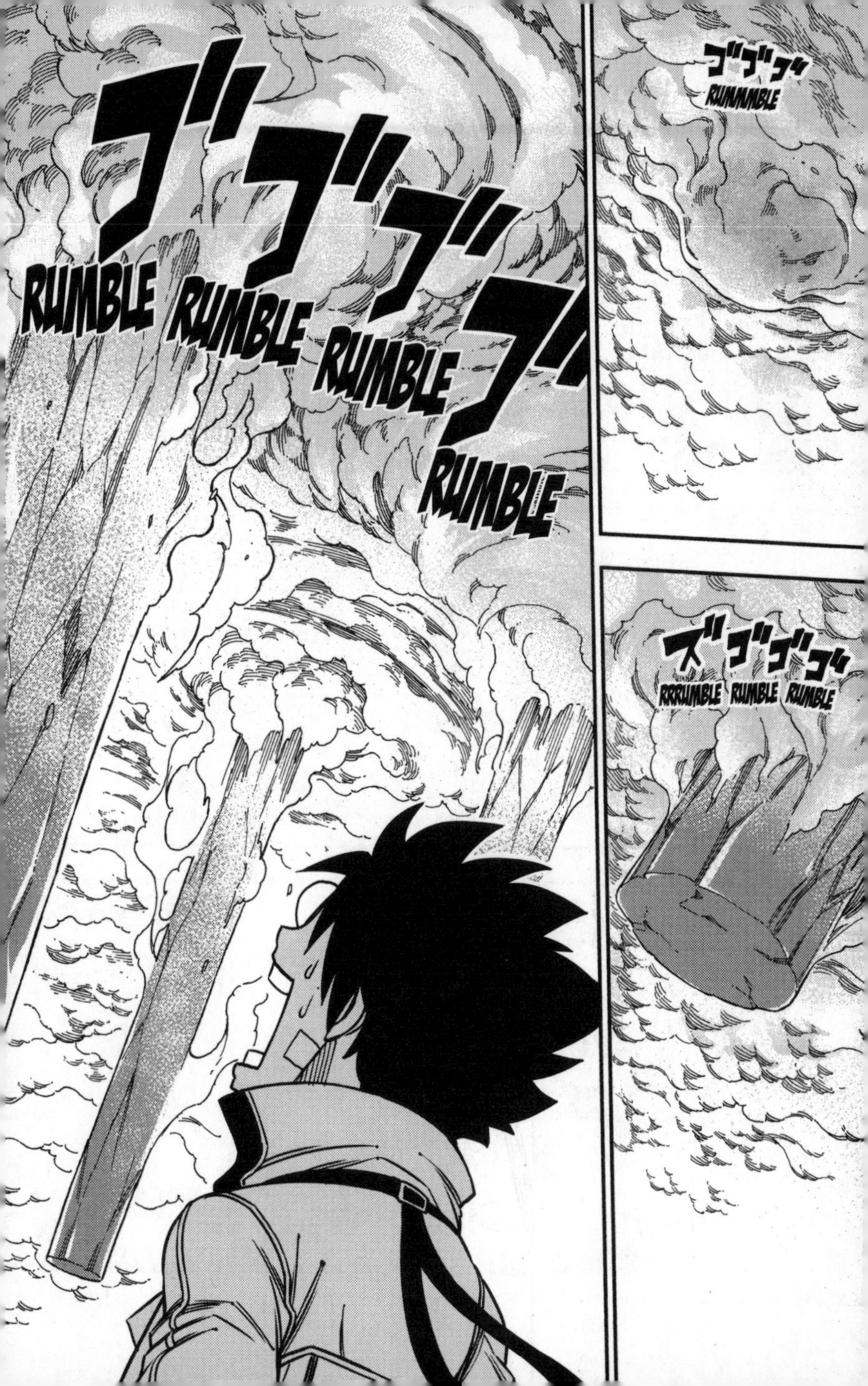
ゴゴゴ
RUMMMBLE
ズゴゴゴ
RRRUMBLE RUMBLE RUMBLE
ゴゴゴゴ
RUMBLE
RUMBLE
RUMBLE
RUMBLE

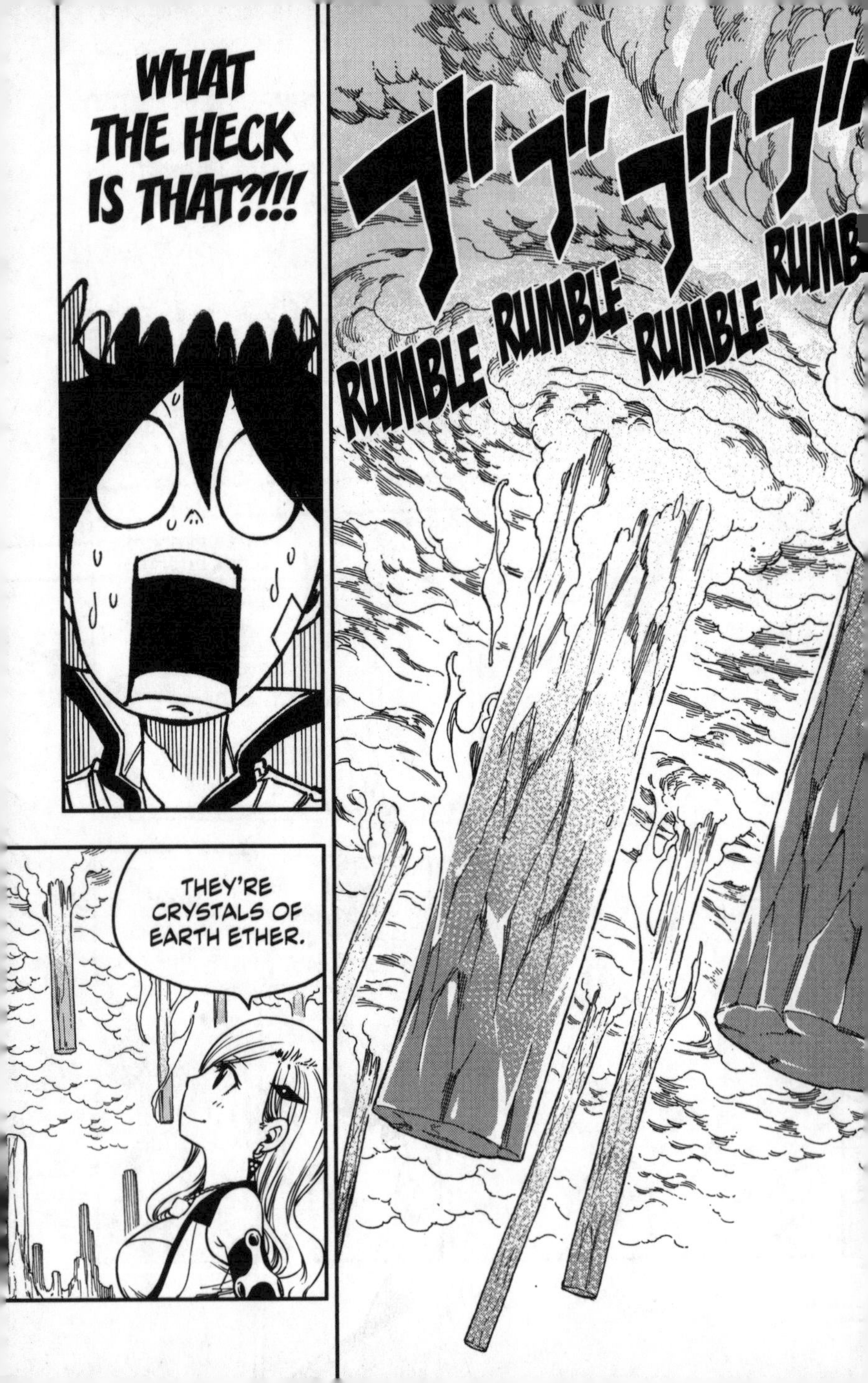
RUMBLE RUMBLE RUMBLE RUMB
WHAT THE HECK IS THAT?!!!
THEY'RE CRYSTALS OF EARTH ETHER.

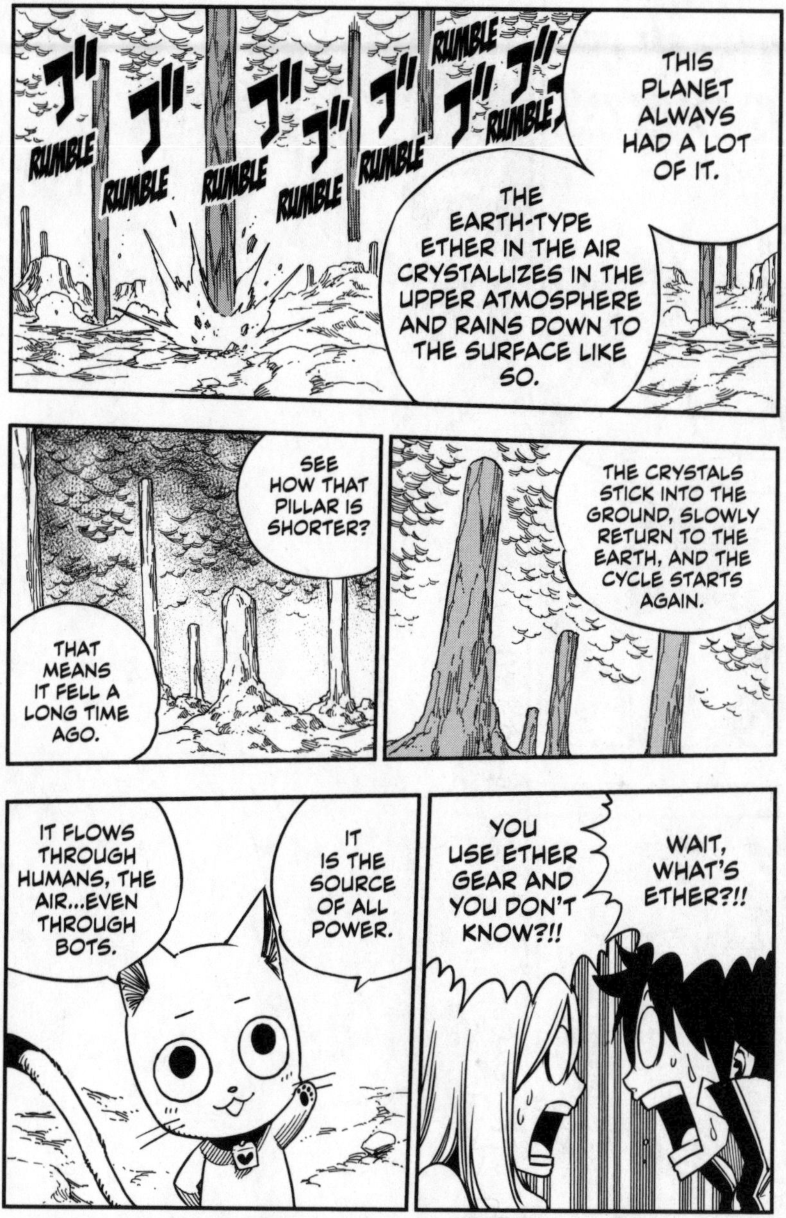
THIS PLANET ALWAYS HAD A LOT OF IT.
THE EARTH-TYPE ETHER IN THE AIR CRYSTALLIZES IN THE UPPER ATMOSPHERE AND RAINS DOWN TO THE SURFACE LIKE SO.
ゴゴ RUMBLE
ゴゴ RUMBLE
ゴゴ RUMBLE
ゴゴ RUMBLE
ゴゴ RUMBLE
ゴゴ RUMBLE
ゴゴ RUMBLE
ゴゴ RUMBLE
THE CRYSTALS STICK INTO THE GROUND, SLOWLY RETURN TO THE EARTH, AND THE CYCLE STARTS AGAIN.
SEE HOW THAT PILLAR IS SHORTER?
THAT MEANS IT FELL A LONG TIME AGO.
WAIT, WHAT'S ETHER?!!
YOU USE ETHER GEAR AND YOU DON'T KNOW?!!
IT IS THE SOURCE OF ALL POWER.
IT FLOWS THROUGH HUMANS, THE AIR...EVEN THROUGH BOTS.

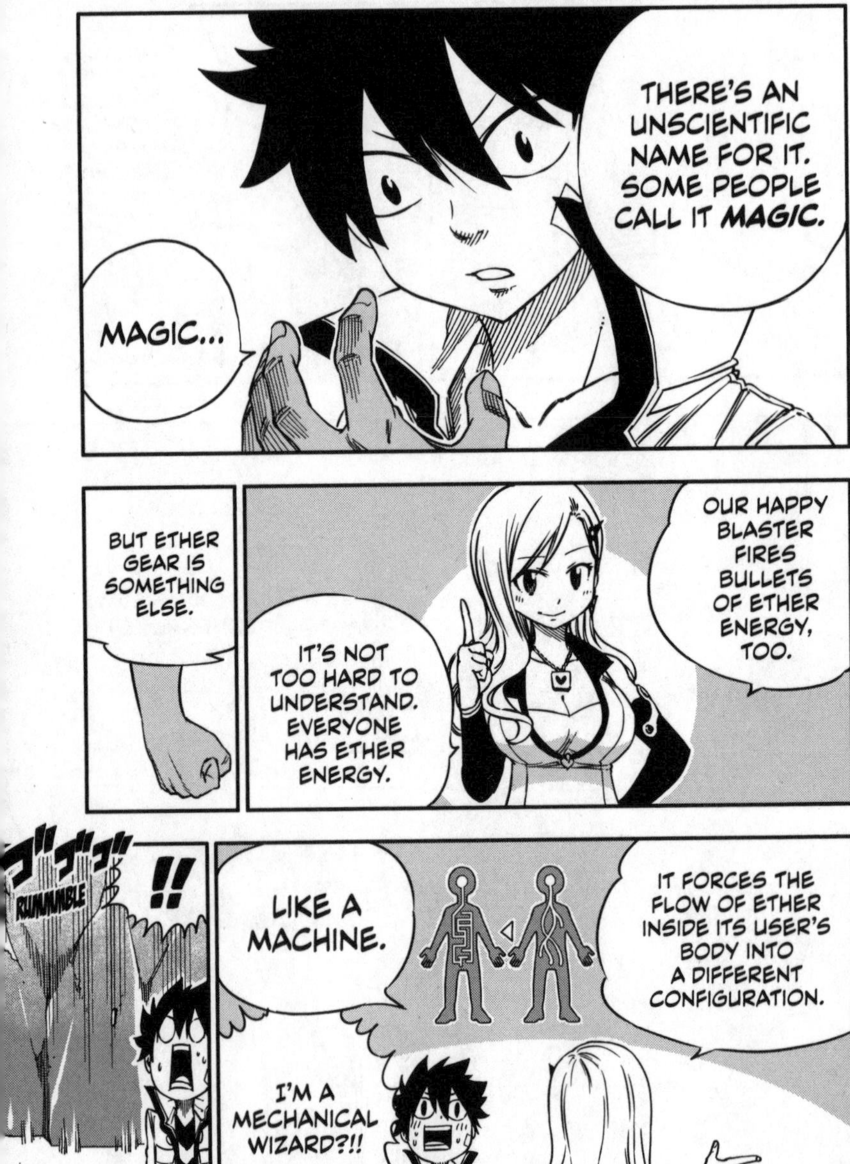
THERE'S AN UNSCIENTIFIC NAME FOR IT. SOME PEOPLE CALL IT **MAGIC.**
MAGIC...
OUR HAPPY BLASTER FIRES BULLETS OF ETHER ENERGY, TOO.
IT'S NOT TOO HARD TO UNDERSTAND. EVERYONE HAS ETHER ENERGY.
BUT ETHER GEAR IS SOMETHING ELSE.
IT FORCES THE FLOW OF ETHER INSIDE ITS USER'S BODY INTO A DIFFERENT CONFIGURATION.
LIKE A MACHINE.
I'M A MECHANICAL WIZARD?!!
ゴゴゴ
RUMMMBLE
!!

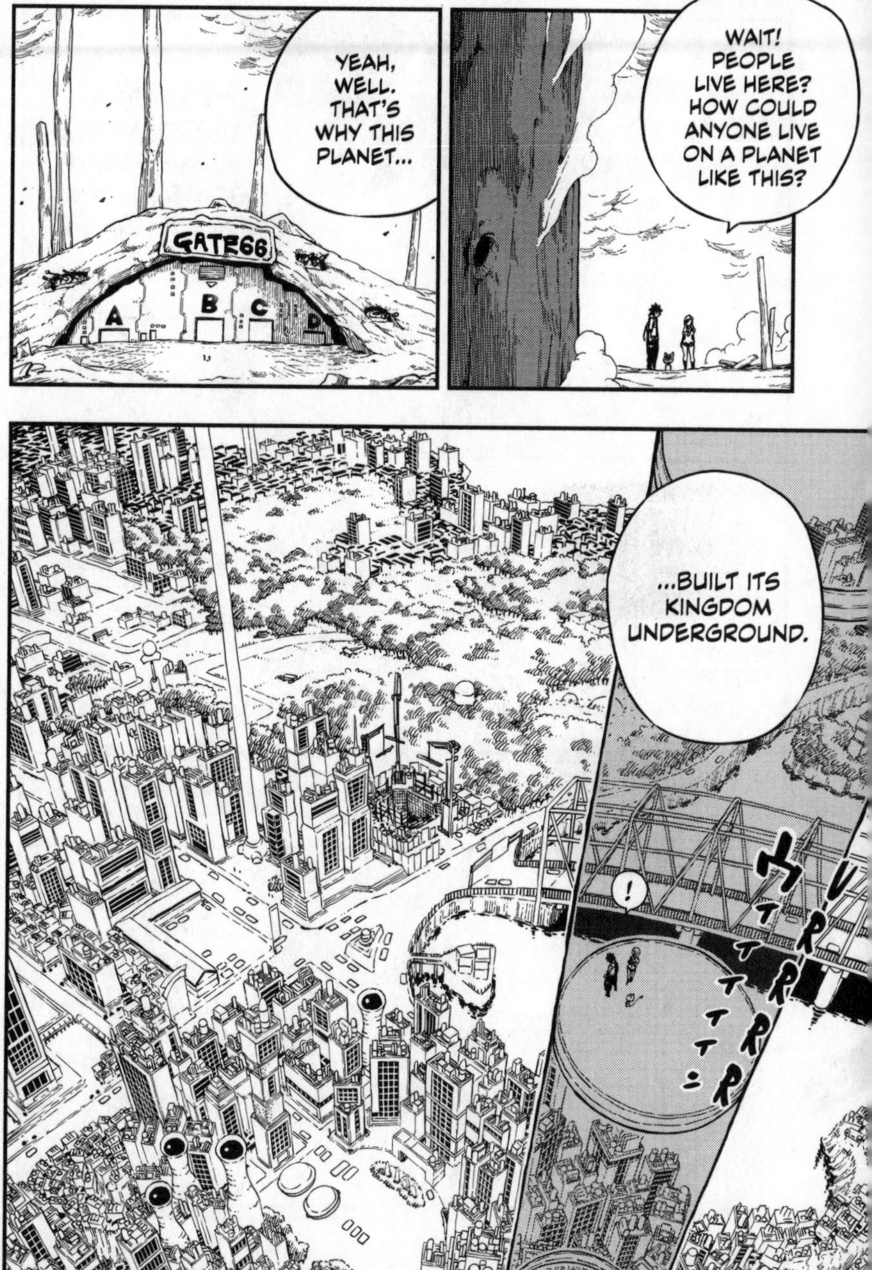
WAIT! PEOPLE LIVE HERE? HOW COULD ANYONE LIVE ON A PLANET LIKE THIS?
YEAH, WELL. THAT'S WHY THIS PLANET...
GATE66
A
B
C
D
...BUILT ITS KINGDOM UNDERGROUND.
!
VRRRR
TTTTT

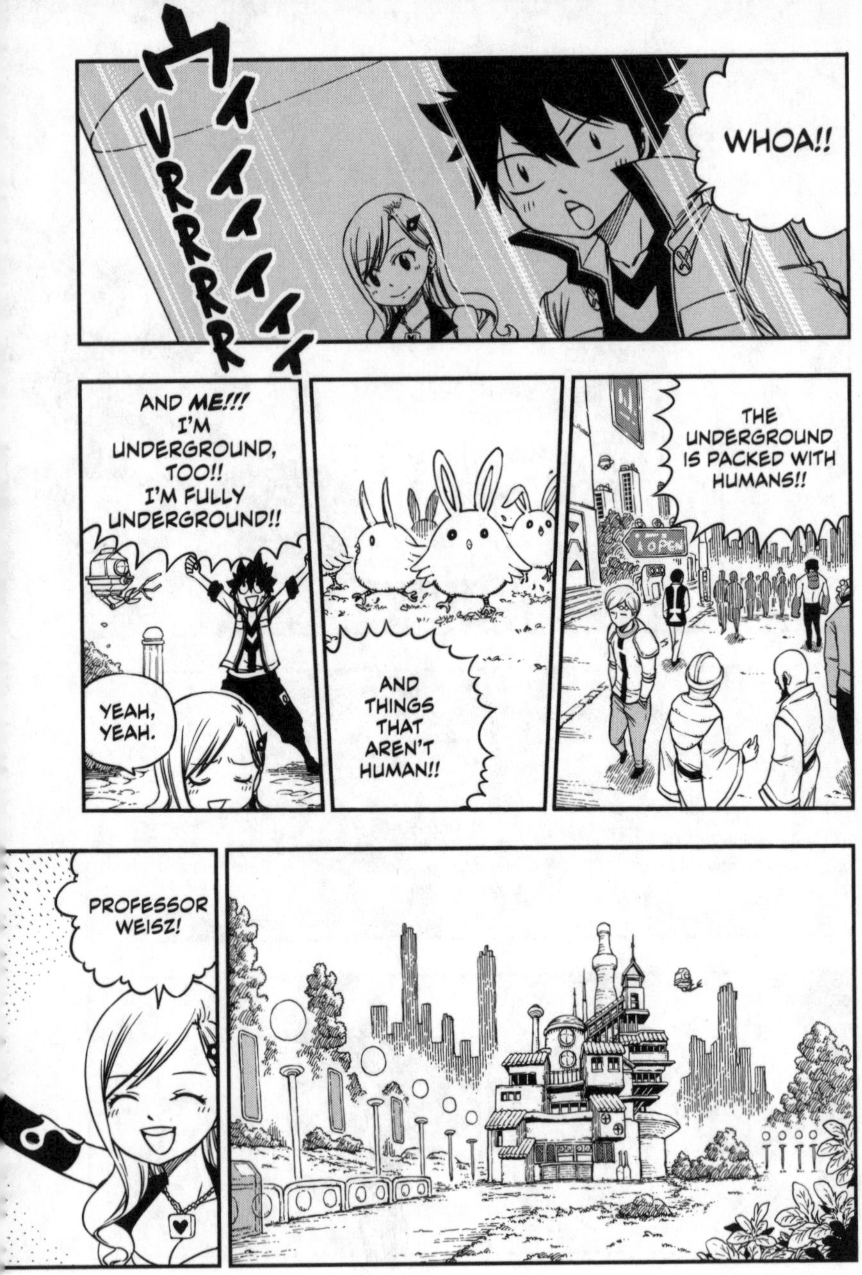
WHOA!!
VURRRRR
THE UNDERGROUND IS PACKED WITH HUMANS!!
AND THINGS THAT AREN'T HUMAN!!
AND ME!!! I'M UNDERGROUND, TOO!! I'M FULLY UNDERGROUND!!
YEAH, YEAH.
PROFESSOR WEISZ!

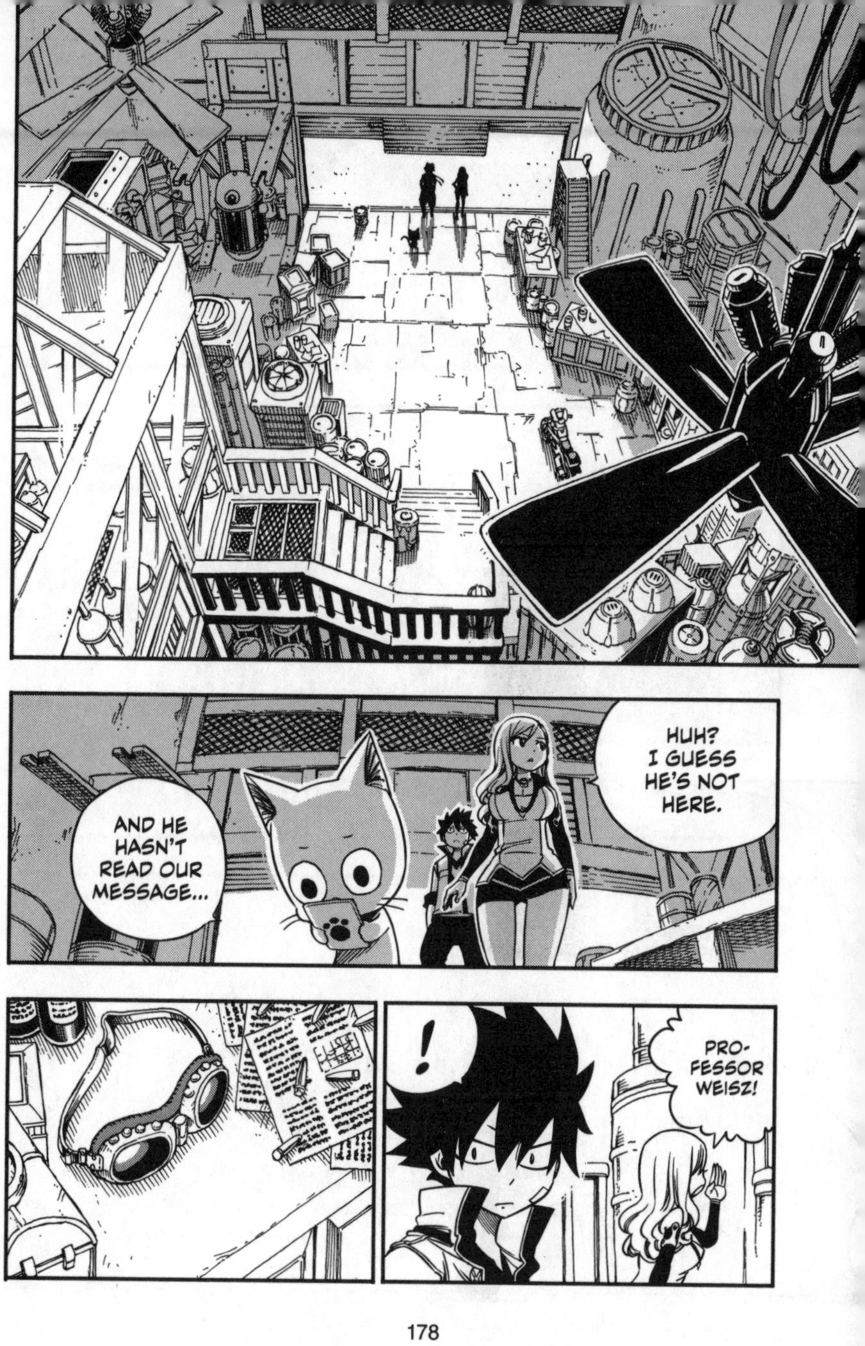
HUH? I GUESS HE'S NOT HERE.
AND HE HASN'T READ OUR MESSAGE...
PRO-FESSOR WEISZ!
!

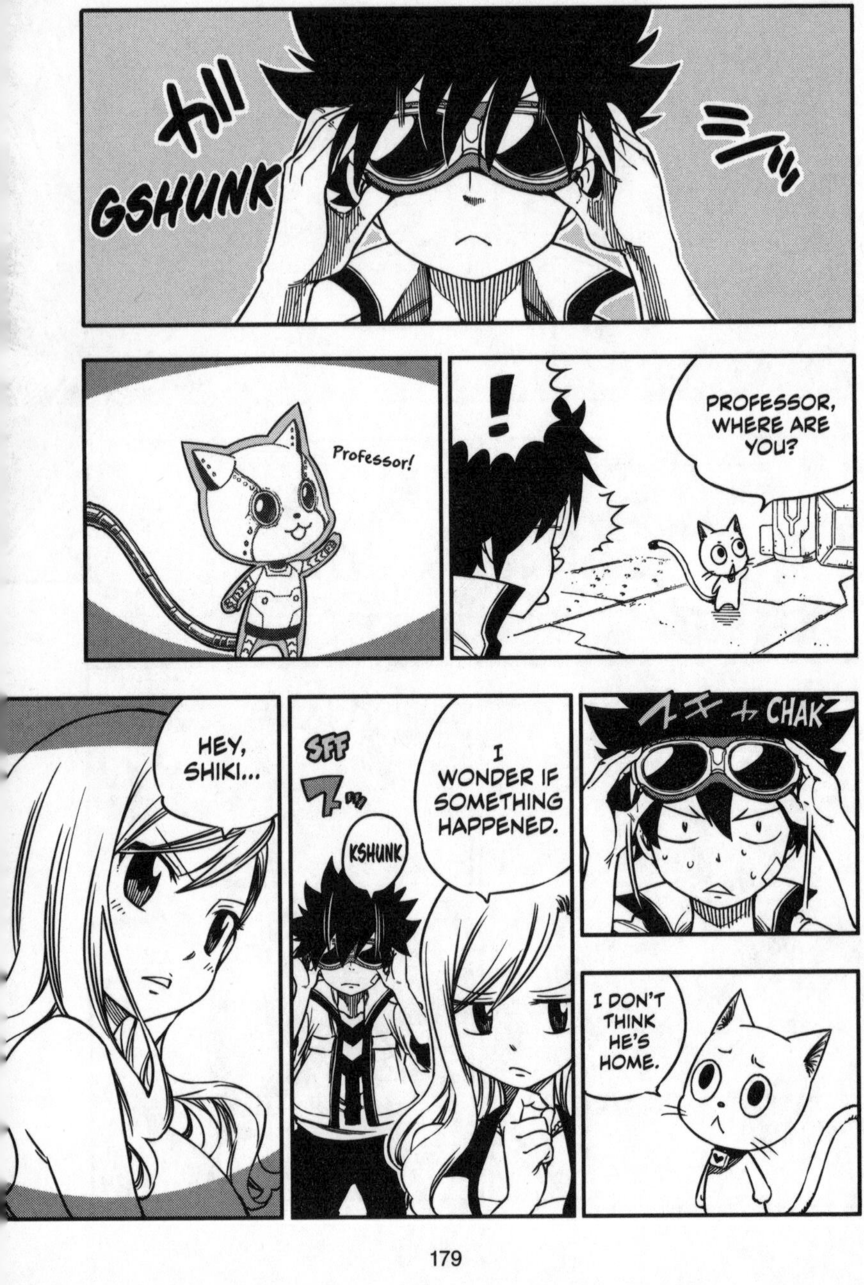
GSHUNK
!
PROFESSOR, WHERE ARE YOU?
Professor!
CHAK
I DON'T THINK HE'S HOME.
I WONDER IF SOMETHING HAPPENED.
SFF
KSHUNK
HEY, SHIKI...

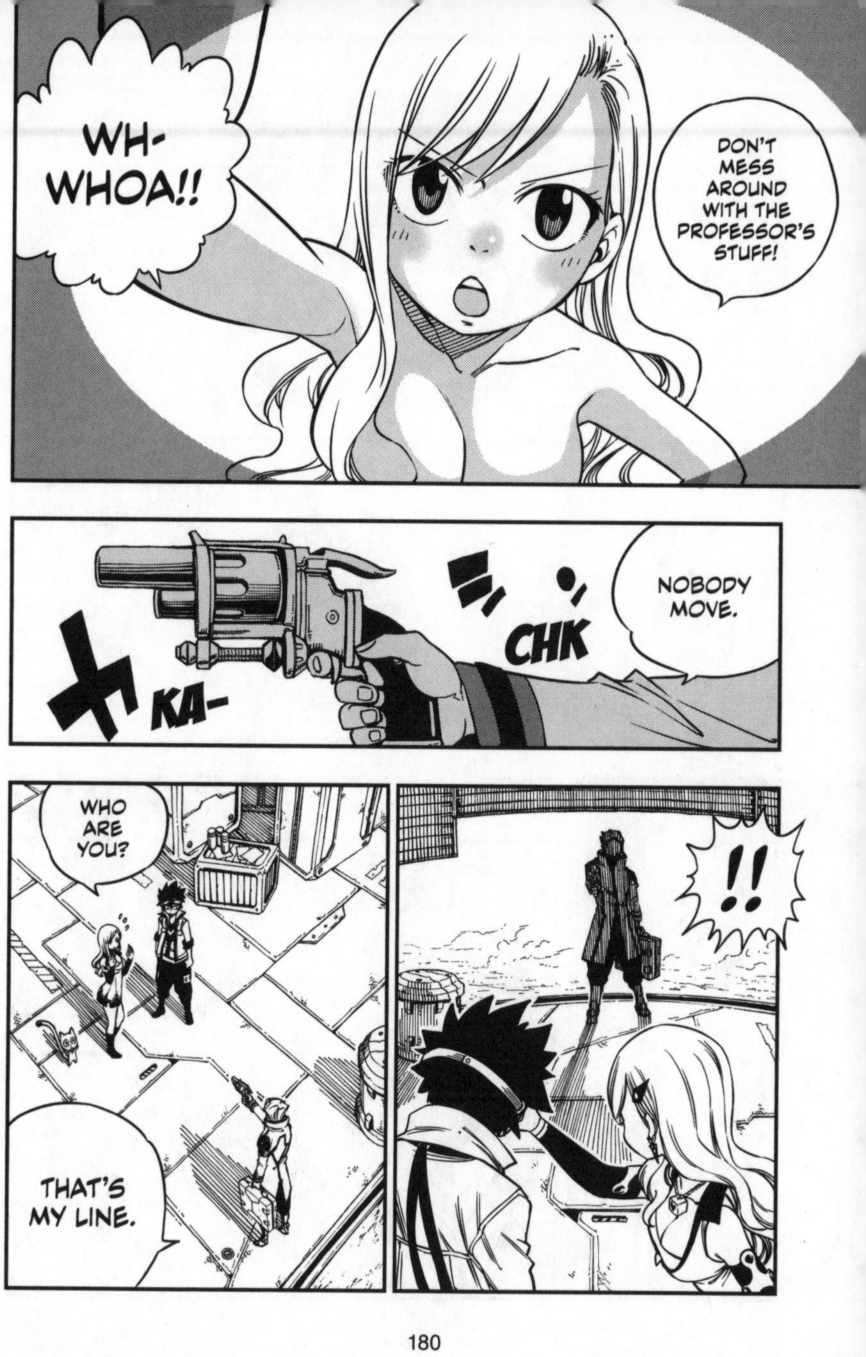
DON'T MESS AROUND WITH THE PROFESSOR'S STUFF!
WH- WHOA!!
NOBODY MOVE.
KA- CHK
!!
WHO ARE YOU?
THAT'S MY LINE.

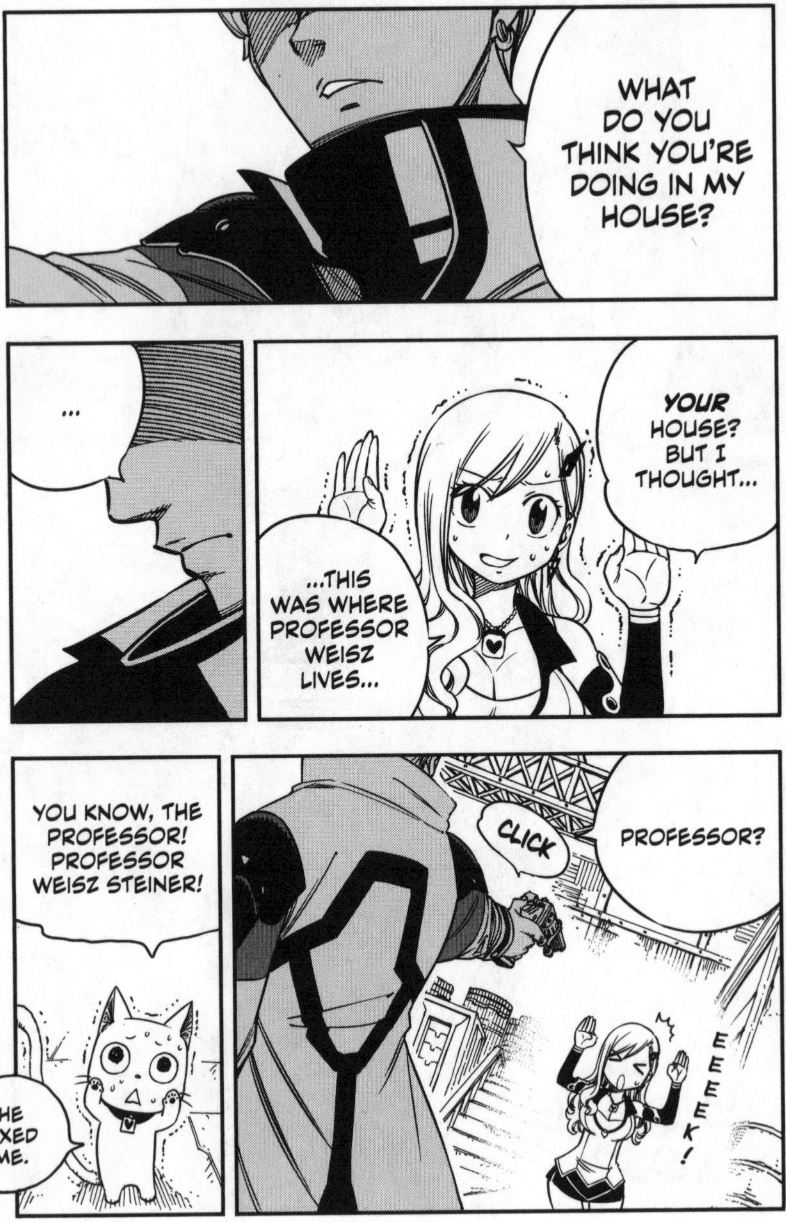
WHAT DO YOU THINK YOU'RE DOING IN MY HOUSE?
YOUR HOUSE? BUT I THOUGHT...
...THIS WAS WHERE PROFESSOR WEISZ LIVES...
...
PROFESSOR?
CLICK
EEEEEK!
YOU KNOW, THE PROFESSOR! PROFESSOR WEISZ STEINER!
HE FIXED ME.

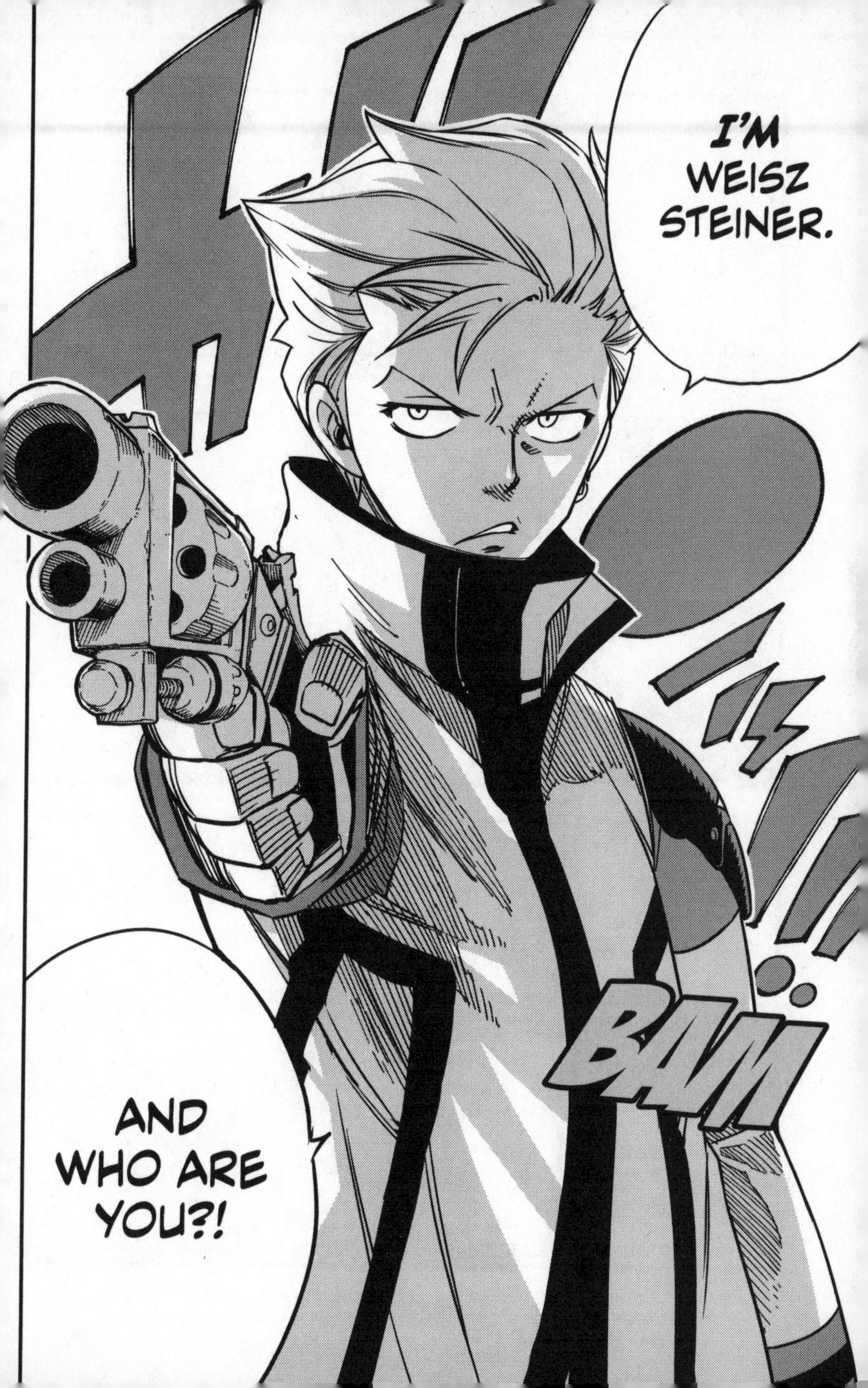
I'M WEISZ STEINER.
BAM
AND WHO ARE YOU?!

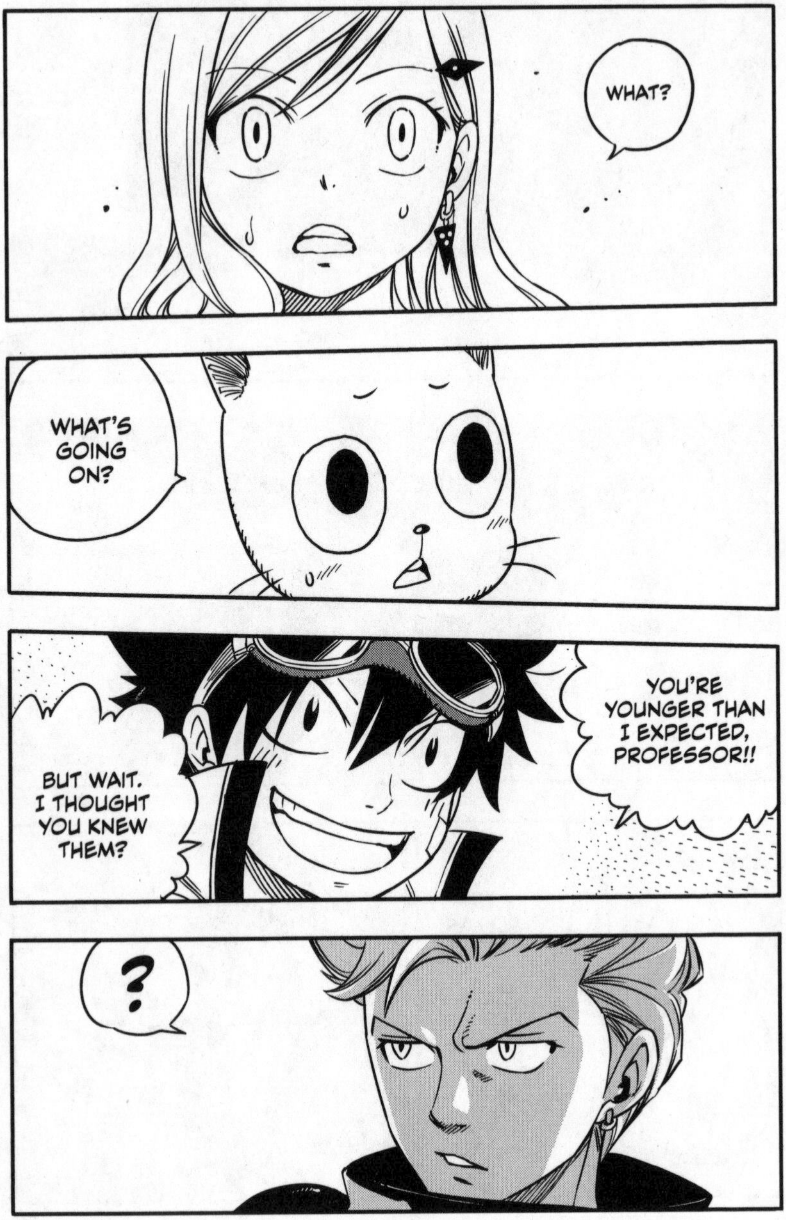
WHAT?
WHAT'S GOING ON?
YOU'RE YOUNGER THAN I EXPECTED, PROFESSOR!!
BUT WAIT. I THOUGHT YOU KNEW THEM?
?

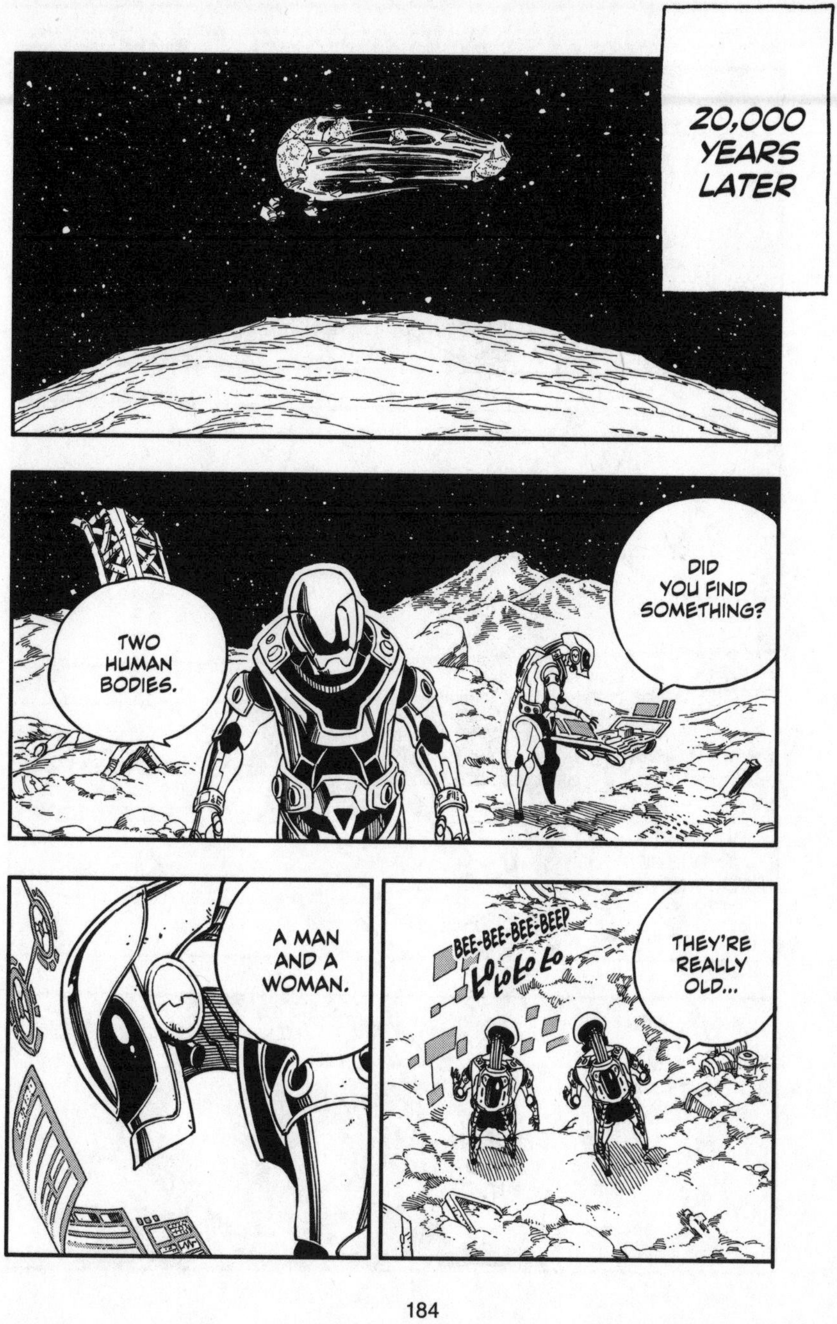
20,000 YEARS LATER
DID YOU FIND SOMETHING?
TWO HUMAN BODIES.
BEE-BEE-BEE-BEEP
THEY'RE REALLY OLD...
A MAN AND A WOMAN.

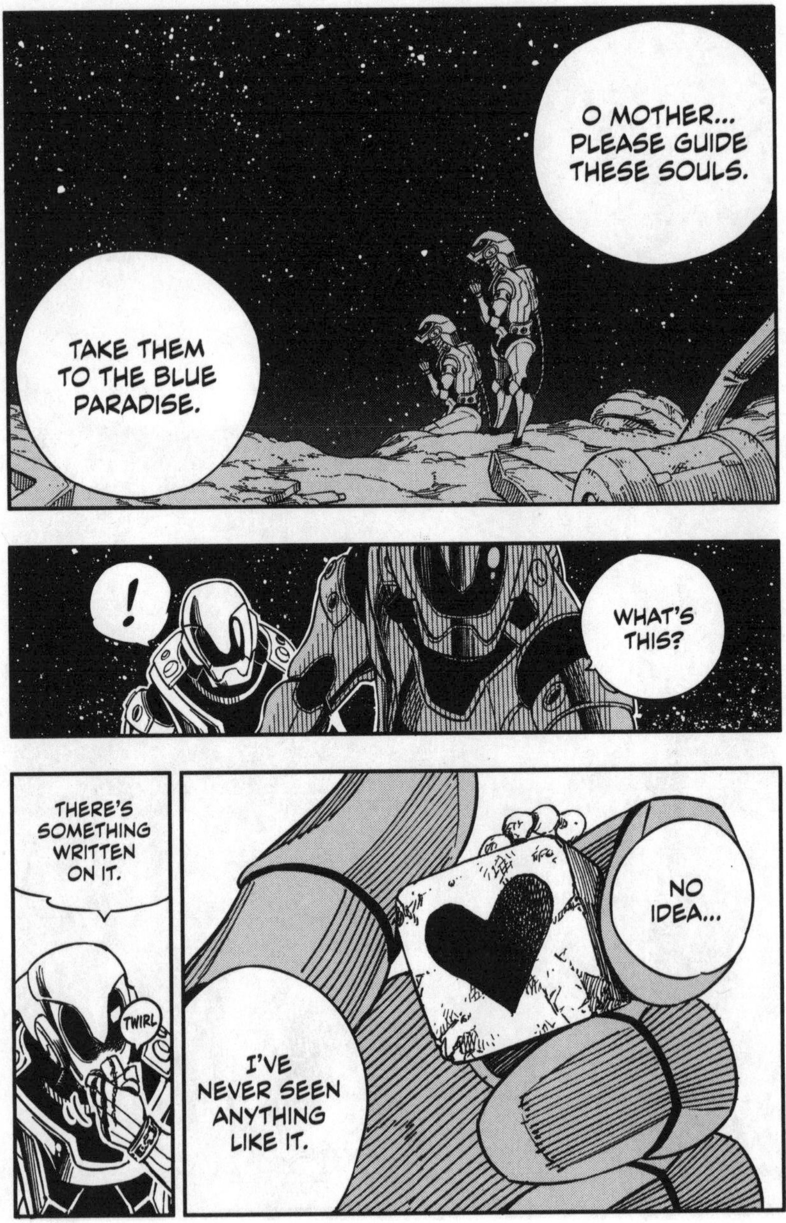
O MOTHER... PLEASE GUIDE THESE SOULS.
TAKE THEM TO THE BLUE PARADISE.
WHAT'S THIS?
!
NO IDEA...
I'VE NEVER SEEN ANYTHING LIKE IT.
THERE'S SOMETHING WRITTEN ON IT.
TWIRL

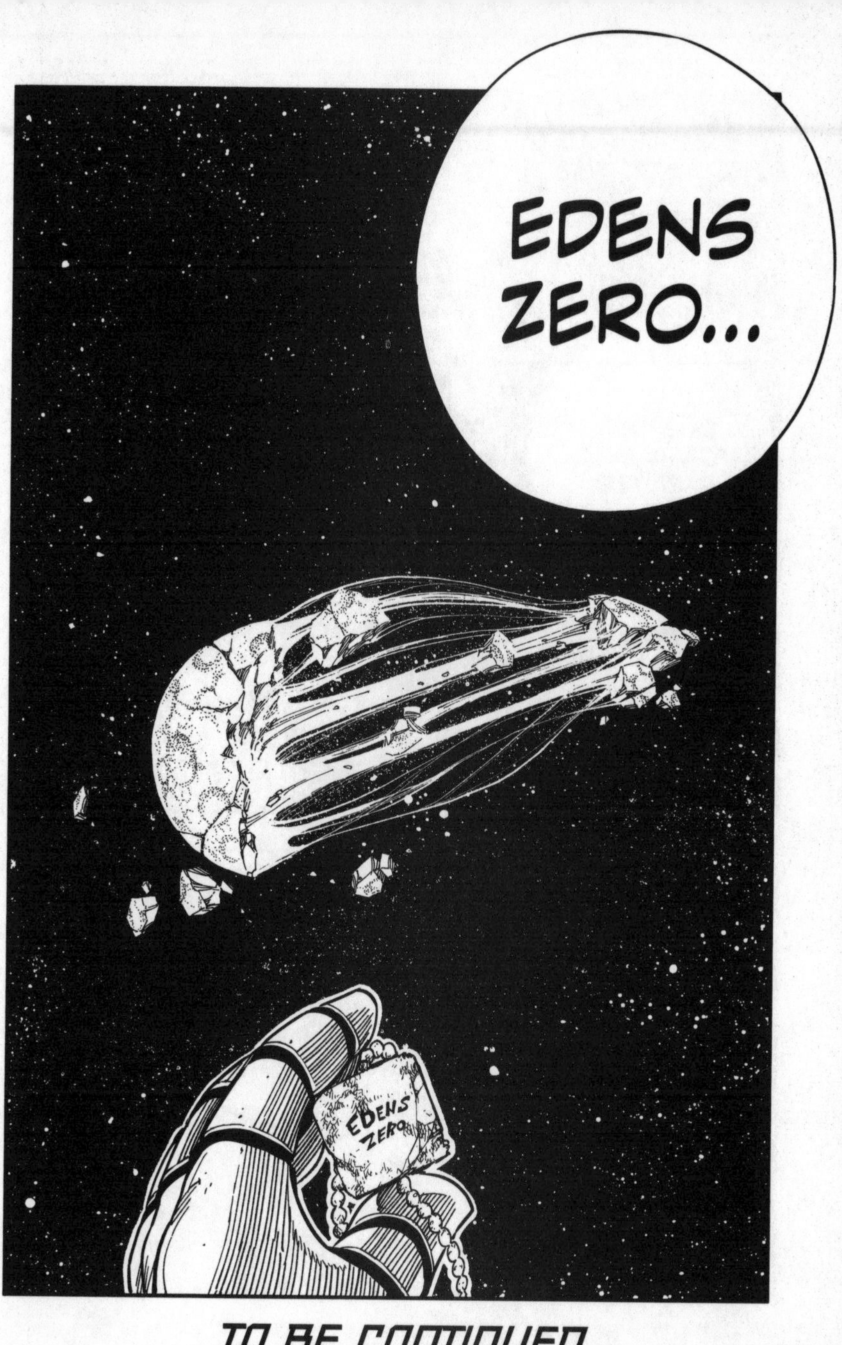
EDENS ZERO...
EDENS ZERO

TO BE CONTINUED...

BONUS QUEST: Find the Hidden Characters!

You can look for them when you read through again!

Rumor has it...familiar faces can be seen scattered throughout Planet Blue Garden...

EDENSZERO

AFTERWORD

After spending almost 20 years drawing "swords and magic" fantasy manga, even *I* thought my next series would be more of the same… But somehow, this sci-fi story began to unfold. I wonder why (*sweats*).

In Japan, we abbreviate "science fiction" to SF, so when I was a kid, I always assumed it stood for "space fantasy." So I made this manga a space fantasy SF. It's in space, but it's fantasy!

Now, as for the reason why I'm drawing an SF manga, it's because nobody else is doing it. I mean, technically speaking, someone is, and has done them—there were tons of them in the old days. But when you narrow it down to the keywords "shonen manga," "space," and "adventure," it's a type of manga you can't really find much of these days, right?! And that makes this a golden opportunity!! I *have* to do it!! ...Is kind of how the whole thought process went. So here I am, a manga artist who's not especially a sci-fi geek, drawing sci-fi manga as if I'm writing fantasy. The super sci-fi geeks might be all, "Well actually, in physics that's..." or "The relativity of..." but I'll just say, "I'm sorry... It's...it's fantasy, y'know." I will insist that all the wild technology works with the power of Ether. That's right—because this is a space fantasy!!

IT'S FULL SPEED AHEAD ON AN ADVENTURE TO THE UNKNOWN!!!

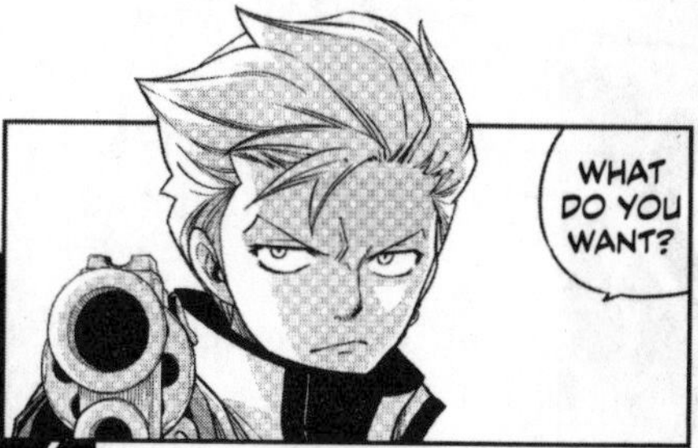
WHAT DO YOU WANT?

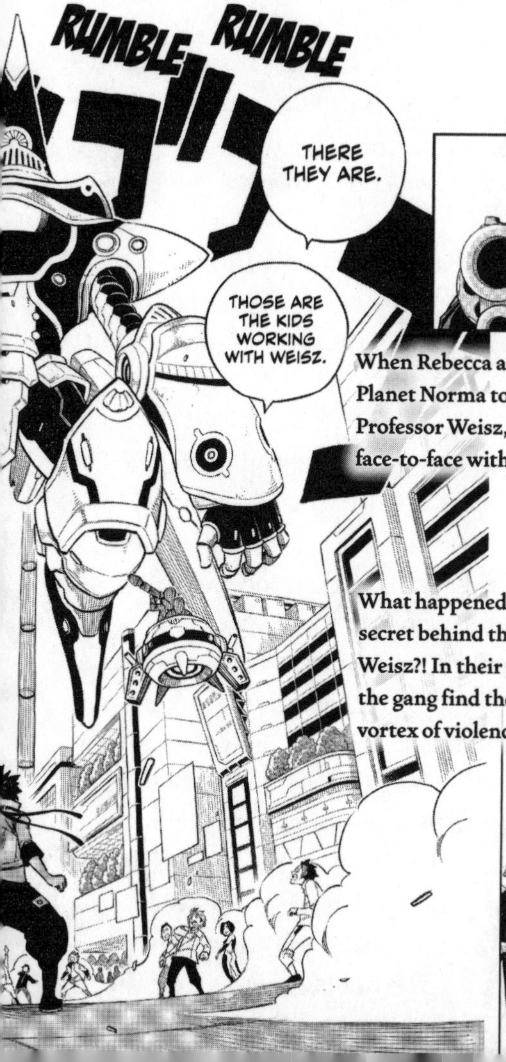
RUMBLE RUMBLE
THERE THEY ARE.
THOSE ARE THE KIDS WORKING WITH WEISZ.

When Rebecca and her friends go to Planet Norma to visit their old ally Professor Weisz, they find themselves face-to-face with the barrel of a gun....

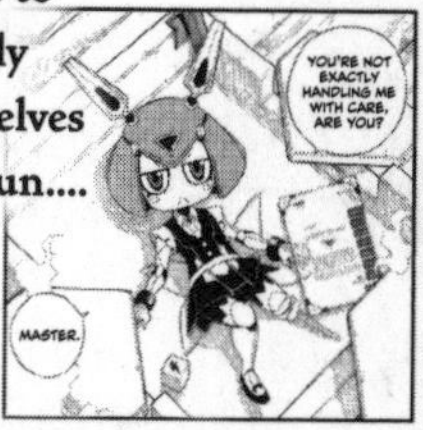
YOU'RE NOT EXACTLY HANDLING ME WITH CARE, ARE YOU?
MASTER.

What happened to the professor?! What is the secret behind the young man who calls himself Weisz?! In their search for the answers, Shiki and the gang find themselves in a vicious vortex of violence!

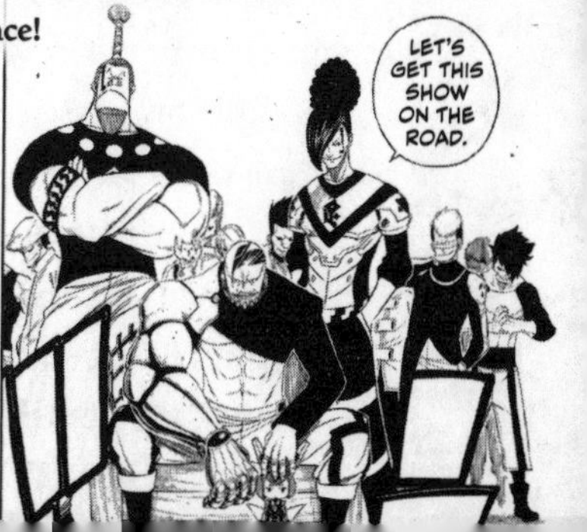
LET'S GET THIS SHOW ON THE ROAD.

Dreams, wonders, mysteries, and dangers of epic-proportions await Shiki and his friends!!

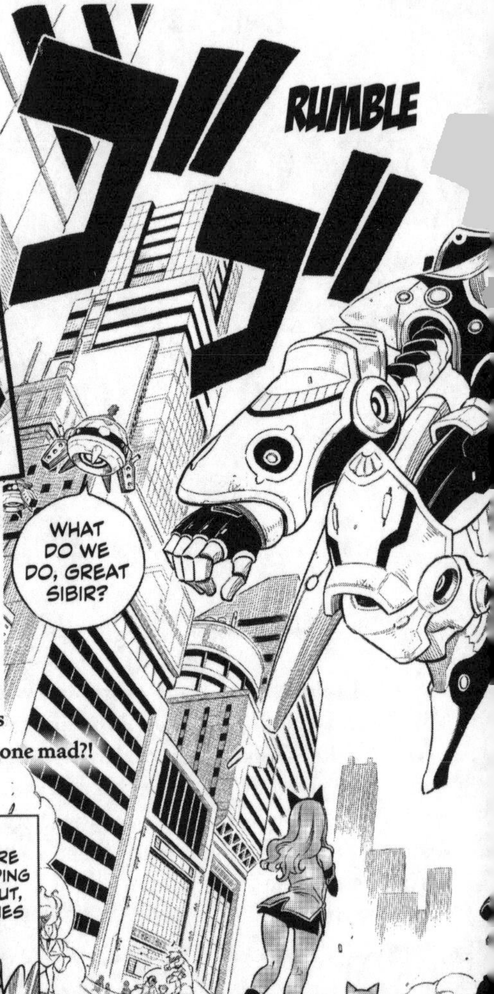
RUMBLE
WHAT DO WE DO, GREAT SIBIR?

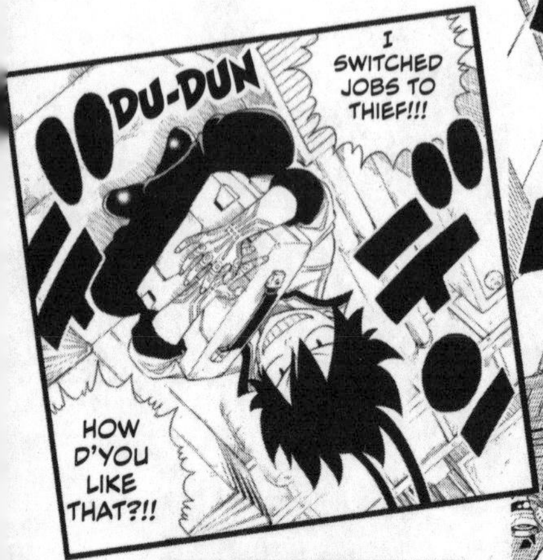
I SWITCHED JOBS TO THIEF!!!
DU-DUN
HOW D'YOU LIKE THAT?!!

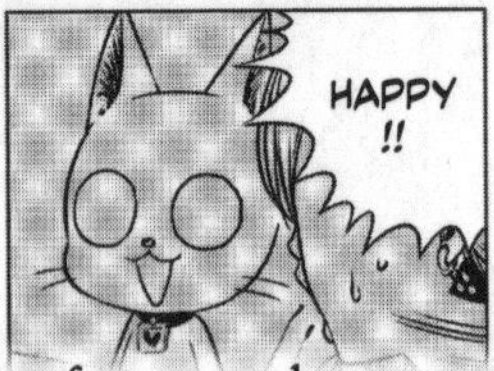
HAPPY !!

The series of unexpected events causes Happy to shut down?! And Rebecca's gone mad?! WHAT WILL BECOME OF OUR ADVENTURERS?!

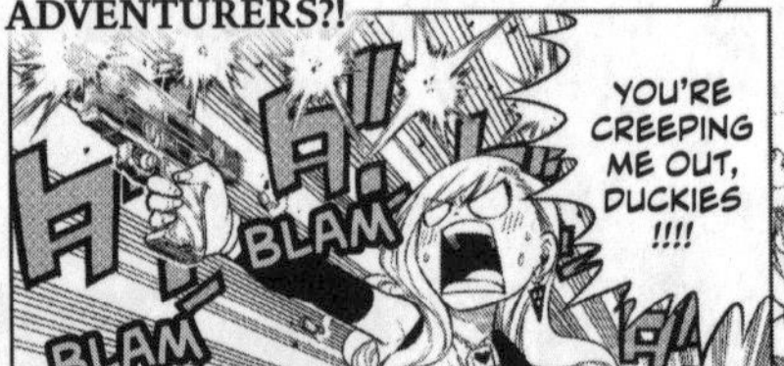
YOU'RE CREEPING ME OUT, DUCKIES !!!!
BLAM
BLAM
BLAM

EDENSZERO VOLUME 2

KC KODANSHA COMICS

Fairy Tail takes place in a world filled with magic. 17-year-old Lucy is a wizard-in-training who wants to join a magic guild so that she can become a full-fledged wizard. She dreams of joining the most famous guild, known as Fairy Tail. One day she meets Natsu, a boy raised by a dragon which vanished when he was young. Natsu has devoted his life to finding his dragon father. When Natsu helps Lucy out of a tricky situation, she discovers that he is a member of Fairy Tail, and our heroes' adventure together begins.

FAIRY TAIL

MASTER'S EDITION

FAIRY TAIL S

For the members of Fairy Tail, a guild member's work is never done. While they may not always be away on missions, that doesn't mean our magic-wielding heroes can rest easy at home. What happens when a copycat thief begins to soil the good name of Fairy Tail, or when a seemingly unstoppable virus threatens the citizens of Magnolia? And when a bet after the Grand Magic Games goes sour, can Natsu, Lucy, Gray, and Erza turn the tables in their favor? Come see what a "day in the life" of the strongest guild in Fiore is like in nine brand new short stories!

KC
KODANSHA COMICS

A collection of *Fairy Tail* short stories drawn by original creator Hiro Mashima!

THE SPACE OPERA MASTERPIECE FROM MANGA LEGEND LEIJI MATSUMOTO AVAILABLE FOR THE FIRST TIME IN ENGLISH!

LEIJI MATSUMOTO'S

Queen Emeraldas

KC
KODANSHA
COMICS

"If you like space cowboys and pirates or simply want to get lost in a strange dreamlike story, Kodansha's beautiful hardcover is worth checking out."
- Anime News Network

"It's not so much a manga as it is a song. But you'll want to listen to it again and again."
- A Case for Suitable Treatment

A new series from Yoshitoki Oima, creator of The New York Times bestselling manga and Eisner Award nominee *A Silent Voice*!

An intimate, emotional drama and an epic story spanning time and space...

TO YOUR ETERNITY

An orb was cast unto the earth. After metamorphosing into a wolf, It joins a boy on his bleak journey to find his tribe. Ever learning, It transcends death, even when those around It cannot...

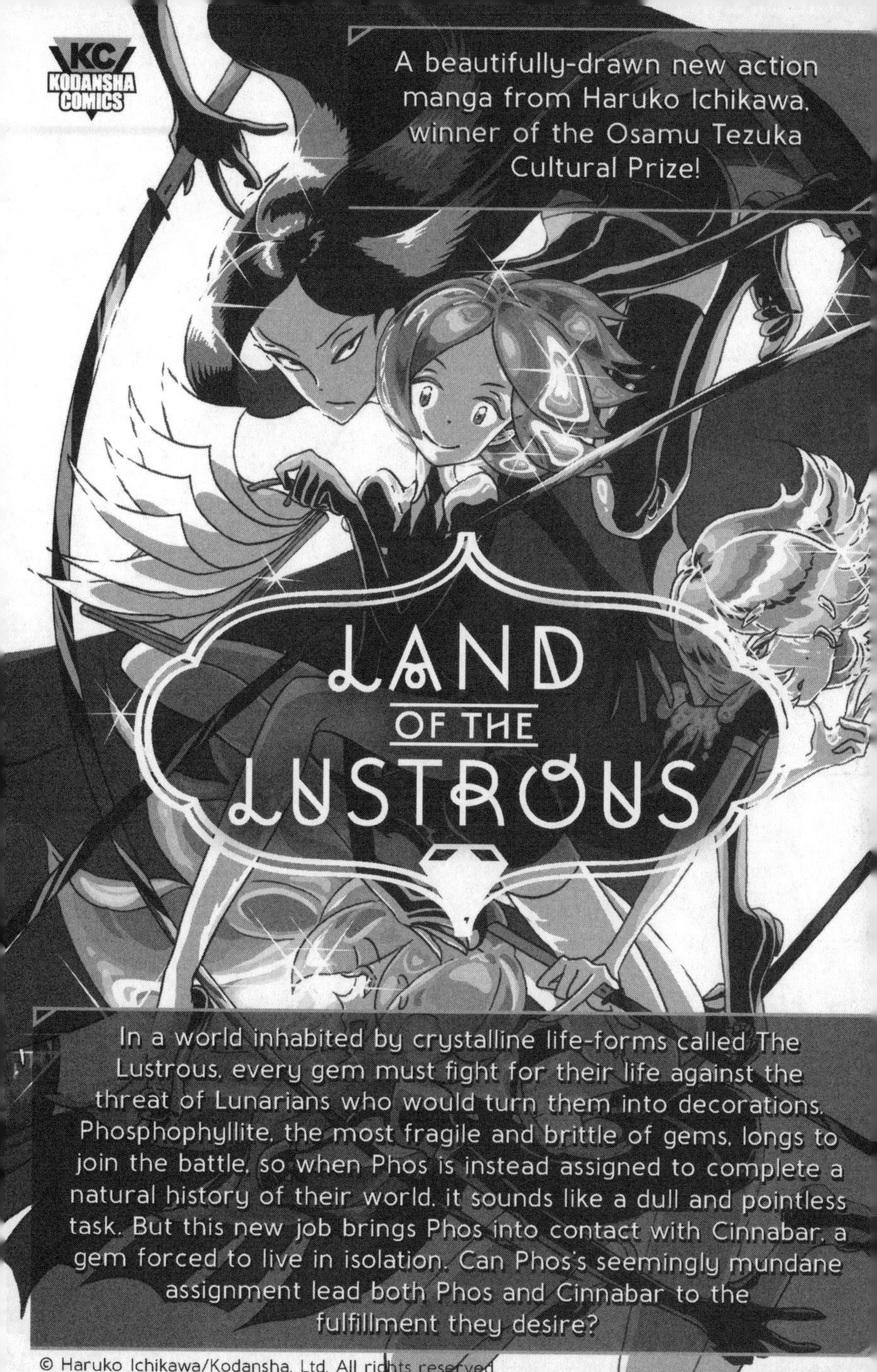
KC KODANSHA COMICS
A beautifully-drawn new action manga from Haruko Ichikawa, winner of the Osamu Tezuka Cultural Prize!
LAND OF THE LUSTROUS
In a world inhabited by crystalline life-forms called The Lustrous, every gem must fight for their life against the threat of Lunarians who would turn them into decorations. Phosphophyllite, the most fragile and brittle of gems, longs to join the battle, so when Phos is instead assigned to complete a natural history of their world, it sounds like a dull and pointless task. But this new job brings Phos into contact with Cinnabar, a gem forced to live in isolation. Can Phos's seemingly mundane assignment lead both Phos and Cinnabar to the fulfillment they desire?

ANIME COMING SUMMER 2018

The award-winning manga about what happens inside you!

"Far more entertaining than it ought to be... What kid doesn't want to think that every time they sneeze, a torpedo shoots out their nose?"

—Anime News Network

Strep throat! Hay fever! Influenza! The world is a dangerous place for a red blood cell just trying to get her deliveries finished. Fortunately, she's not alone. She's got a whole human body's worth of cells ready to help out! The mysterious white blood cell, the buff and brash killer T cell, the nerdy neuron, even the cute little platelets— everyone's got to come together if they want to keep you healthy!

Cells at Work!

By Akane Shimizu

KC
KODANSHA COMICS

New action series from Hiroyuki Takei, creator of the classic shonen franchise Shaman King!

In medieval Japan, a bell hanging on the collar is a sign that a cat has a master. Norachiyo's bell hangs from his katana sheath, but he is nonetheless a stray — a ronin. This one-eyed cat samurai travels across a dishonest world, cutting through pretense and deception with his blade.

By
Hiroyuki Takei

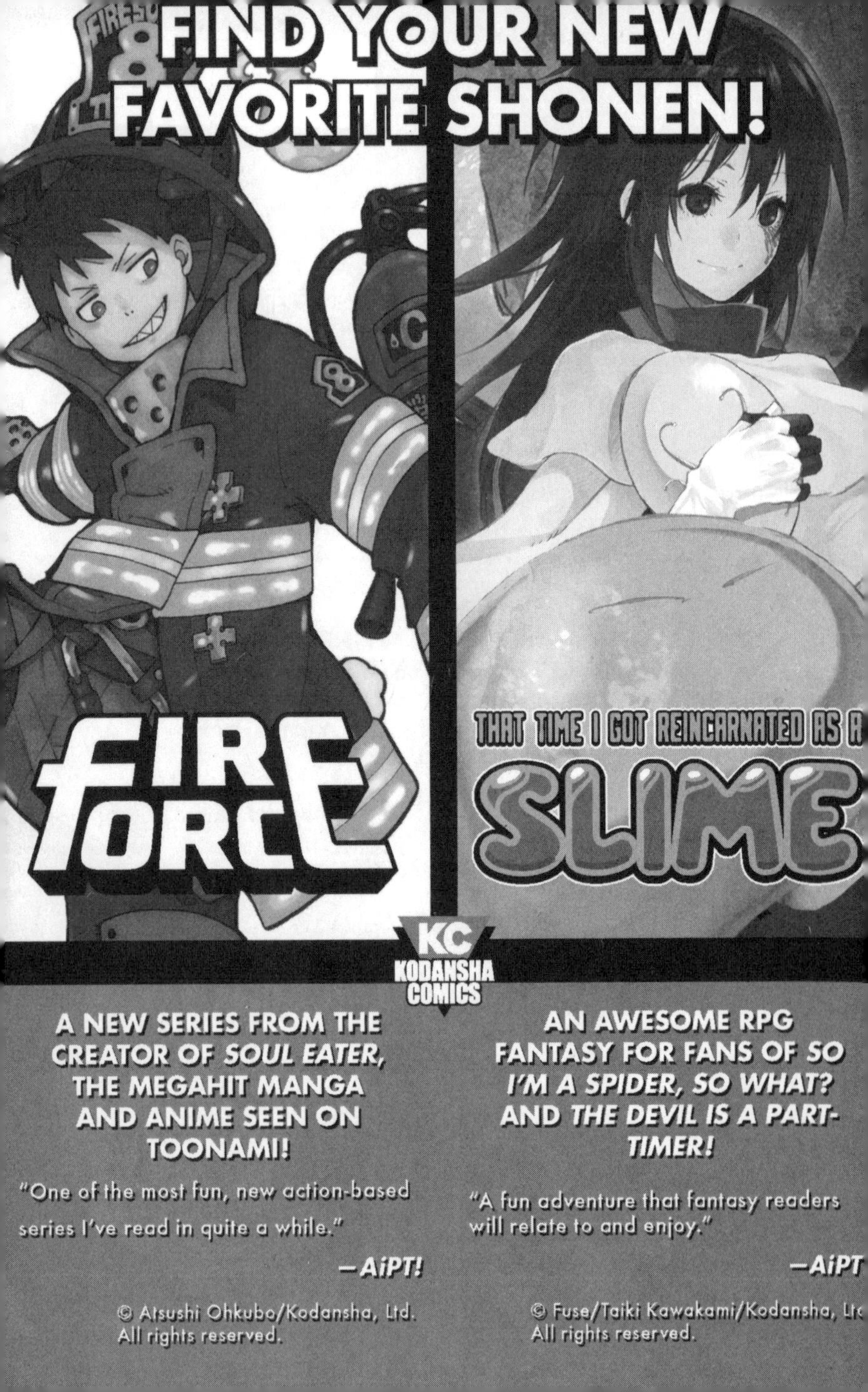
FIND YOUR NEW FAVORITE SHONEN!
FIRE FORCE
THAT TIME I GOT REINCARNATED AS A SLIME
KC KODANSHA COMICS

EDENS ZERO volume 1 is a work of fiction.
Names, characters, places, and incidents are the products of the author's imagination or are used fictitiously. Any resemblance to actual events, locales, or persons, living or dead, is entirely coincidental.

A Kodansha Comics Trade Paperback Original.

Published in the United States by Kodansha Comics, an imprint of Kodansha USA Publishing, LLC, New York.

Publication rights for this English edition arranged through Kodansha Ltd., Tokyo.

First published in Japan in 2018 by Kodansha Ltd., Tokyo.

ISBN 978-1-63236-756-3

Original cover design by
Atsushi Kudo, Erisa Maruyama (G x complex).

Printed in the United States of America.

www.kodanshacomics.com

9 8 7 6 5 4

Translation: Alethea and Athena Nibley
Lettering: AndWorld Design
Editing: Haruko Hashimoto
Kodansha Comics edition cover design by Phil Balsman